Forensic Mental Health Assessment in Criminal Contexts

This valuable compendium advances the understanding of mental health case law, making it highly accessible to practicing forensic professionals. Divided into two parts, the first section focuses on explaining important topics related to forensic psychological and forensic neuropsychological assessment, while the second section stands on its own as a collection of fascinating legal cases with high relevance to mental health and legal professionals interested in how mental health disorders impact criminal behavior among juveniles and adults.

The book begins with an accessible primer on abnormal behavior, exploring the links between criminal behavior and mental health disorders. It goes on to thoroughly describe what goes into forensic psychological and forensic neuropsychological evaluations, including discussion about the Federal Rules of Evidence, as they pertain to evidence-generation during the mental health evaluation process. The book also focuses on psychometric concepts, including reliability, validity, sensitivity, and specificity, as well as an exploration of 'science' and 'the law' which includes a discussion about the difference between science and pseudoscience, the different sources of law (constitutions, statutes, and case law), and how the intellectually competitive practice of law is similar to the enterprise of science. Ethical issues faced by the forensic mental health worker are also addressed. The second section of the book, Legal Cases for the Forensic Mental Health Professional, is an alphabetical summary of important and interesting legal cases with relevance for mental health professionals. These cases offer real-world significance while summarizing complex legal decisions through a neuropsychological sieve, to allow both legal and psychological communities to better understand each other's professions.

This book will be an invaluable resource for forensic psychologists, forensic neuropsychologists, forensic psychiatrists, and other mental health professionals whose work brings them into contact with the juvenile justice and adult criminal justice system. It will also be of interest to legal professionals, criminal justice departments, and law schools.

Noah K. Kaufman, PhD, ABN, ABPdN, ABPP, works primarily out of the Center for Neuropsychological Studies in Las Cruces, New Mexico, and is also a clinical assistant professor in the Department of Psychiatry at Texas Tech University Health Sciences Center. He is board certified in neuropsychology, pediatric neuropsychology, and forensic psychology, and has authored or co-authored multiple book chapters and peer-reviewed articles.

Shane S. Bush, PhD, ABPP, is Director of Long Island Neuropsychology, PC, an adjunct faculty member in the University of Alabama's Department of Psychology, and a neuropsychologist with the VA New York Harbor Healthcare System. He is board certified in clinical psychology, rehabilitation psychology, clinical neuropsychology, and geropsychology, and has more than 100 publications, including more than 20 books, many of which are related to forensic practice and ethical and professional issues.

Nicole R. Schneider, PhD, ABPP, is a forensic psychologist serving as a supervisor and clinic associate at the University of Denver and provides consultation in both criminal and civil legal proceedings around the world. She is board certified in forensic psychology.

Scotia J. Hicks, PhD, JD, is an appellate attorney at the law firm of Ehlert Hicks LLP, and a lecturer at the UC Berkeley School of Law.

Forensic Mental Health Assessment in Criminal Contexts

Key Concepts and Cases

Noah K. Kaufman, Shane S. Bush, Nicole R. Schneider, and Scotia J. Hicks

Routledge
Taylor & Francis Group
NEW YORK AND LONDON

First published 2022
by Routledge
605 Third Avenue, New York, NY 10158

and by Routledge
2 Park Square, Milton Park, Abingdon, Oxon, OX14 4RN

Routledge is an imprint of the Taylor & Francis Group, an informa business

Library of Congress Cataloging-in-Publication Data
Names: Kaufman, Noah K., author. | Bush, Shane S., 1965- author. | Schneider, Nicole R., author. | Hicks, Scotia J., author.
Title: Forensic mental health assessment in criminal contexts : key concepts and cases / Noah K. Kaufman, Shane S. Bush, Nicole R. Schneider and Scotia J. Hicks.
Description: Milton Park, Abingdon, Oxon ; New York, NY : Routledge, 2022. | Includes bibliographical references and index.
Identifiers: LCCN 2021041887 (print) | LCCN 2021041888 (ebook) | ISBN 9780367645083 (hardback) | ISBN 9780367644994 (hardback) | ISBN 9780367645090 (ebook)
Subjects: LCSH: Forensic neuropsychology.
Classification: LCC RA1147.5 .K38 2022 (print) | LCC RA1147.5 (ebook) | DDC 614/.15--dc23
LC record available at https://lccn.loc.gov/2021041887
LC ebook record available at https://lccn.loc.gov/2021041888

ISBN: 978-0-367-64508-3 (hbk)
ISBN: 978-0-367-64499-4 (pbk)
ISBN: 978-0-367-64509-0 (ebk)

DOI: 10.4324/9780367645090

Typeset in Bembo
by MPS Limited, Dehradun

Noah

To Cruz, for always inspiring me to become a better person and making me extremely proud with your courage and hard work. To Yesenia, for hanging with me all these years, going back to when we met by the pool tables, at Joe's Bar in Albuquerque. No way I would have been able to cobble any of this together without either of you in my life. Also, thanks to Cecil Reynolds, Ann Delpha, Sandro Galeo, Orion Cervio, and all the brilliant scholars I have learned from though long, lonely hours of reading and thinking.

Nicole

To the women, men, and children whose stories fill these pages and have helped to pave the way for more competent jurisprudence. Sometimes it's when the sky is darkest that the stars really shine. And to my family and friends who serve as my own personal Supreme Court and army of emotional support. A special nod to my amazing son Noah as well as to Valerie, Richard, and Delana for their consistent love and interest in all things me, and to my treasured mentors—particularly from my time at the University of Massachusetts Medical School's fellowship in Law and Psychiatry. If my attempts to express gratitude have ever fallen short, consider them published here for eternity.

Scotia

For J, A, C, and F, with love.

Shane

To Dana, Sarah, and Megan.

Contents

Section I

Foundational Topics in Forensic Psychological and Forensic Neuropsychological Assessment

Introduction

The first section of this book, Foundational Topics in Psychological and Forensic Neuropsychological Assessment, is about forensic psychology and forensic neuropsychology, but the ideas are nonetheless of relevance to mental health professionals from other disciplines (e.g., psychiatrists, social workers, and counselors). The material is also likely to be of interest to legal professionals (e.g., judges, defense attorneys, prosecutors, and probation officers) and educators. As defined in Chapter 2, the word *forensic* means "for law enforcement and courtroom purposes" (Clapp, 2007, p. 107). Hence, forensic psychology is the practice of psychology that is directed toward legal questions. Because this book focuses on adult criminal and juvenile justice law, the legal questions in both sections of the book typically take the following form:

- Was the defendant legally insane at the time he or she committed the offense?
- Is the defendant competent to stand trial?
- Will the defendant be a threat if released into the community?
- Did the defendant understand his or her Miranda warning and did he or she knowingly, intelligently, and voluntarily waive his or her Miranda rights?
- Did the defendant intend to cause very serious harm to another, or were his or her intentions less specific?
- Are there things we need to know about the defendant that might influence how he or she should be sentenced?
- Does the defendant have a diagnosis of intellectual disability?

In comparison to forensic psychology, forensic neuropsychology is the practice of neuropsychology that is directed toward legal questions. So the same legal questions posed to the forensic psychologist are also asked of the forensic neuropsychologist. However, neuropsychology—in contrast to psychology—involves the use of different methods, particularly including the use of more cognitive tests. In Chapter 1, "A Primer on Abnormal Behavior," we discuss mental health disorders that forensic psychologists and forensic neuropsychologists can assist legal professionals in understanding. In Chapter 2, "A Primer on

DOI: 10.4324/9780367645090-101

Forensic Psychological and Forensic Neuropsychological Evaluations," we provide more in-depth definitions of both forensic psychology and forensic neuropsychology, while also providing a framework for thinking about evidence generation with psychological and neuropsychological data. In Chapter 3, "Fundamental Measurement Concepts in Forensic Assessment," we flesh out the most important concepts that are specific to psychometric testing.

At various points in Section I, we use examples drawn from actual experiences we have had during the course of our professional work. We do this to bring the concepts and messages to life for the reader. Importantly, identifying case details have been replaced with non-identifying information, and some case details, culled from different cases, have been combined in some of our examples. These steps have been taken in order to bring the reader closer to actual issues encountered by forensic mental health evaluators, without coloring outside the lines of professional ethics or the law.

Section II of this book, Legal Cases for the Forensic Mental Health Professional, is about actual legal cases, known as *case law*, which we define in Chapter 4, "'Science' and 'the Law,'" as the collection of published legal decisions made by courts, either at the state or federal level. As explained in Chapter 4, not every legal case is published. Only those deemed to have significant precedential value are published, which is the vast minority of cases (Arnold, 1999). Similarly, published case law carries different weight for courts that are wrestling with a new decision. A prior ruling made by a higher court within the same jurisdiction is said to have *binding authority* over the lower court. This means that the lower court must follow the lead of the higher court, using the doctrine of *stare decisis*, which means "to stand by the things decided" (Clapp, 2007, p. 251). In comparison, courts may look to prior legal decisions within a different jurisdiction for guidance; however, these other-jurisdiction legal decisions do not have binding authority. Rather, they are said to have *persuasive authority*, which means the rationale used by the other-jurisdiction courts may include such persuasive reasoning that legal decision-making in other jurisdictions is influenced. Simply stated, prior legal cases frequently influence current legal cases, either directly (via binding authority) or indirectly (via persuasive authority). In Chapter 4, we explain these and related topics in much greater detail.

In Chapter 5, "Ethical Considerations in Forensic Mental Health Practice," we explore the role of professional ethics in the practice of forensic psychology and forensic neuropsychology. While this chapter focuses on ethics for forensic psychologists and forensic neuropsychologists, the messages nonetheless have direct bearing on the work of other mental health professionals operating in legal arenas. Similarly, legal professionals who rely on mental health experts will also find this content valuable.

This book is intended as a guide for both mental health and legal professionals, including psychologists, neuropsychologists, psychiatrists, forensic social workers, attorneys, judges, probation officers, and investigators. However, we also believe the material will be of interest to educators and their students at the undergraduate and post-undergraduate levels. The ideas and messages in the book reflect the professional experiences of the authors, as well as the available scholarship in the fields of forensic psychology, forensic neuropsychology, and adult criminal and juvenile justice law.

If there is a single epistemology (i.e., way of knowing) that cuts through both sections of this book, it is that of science. However, as we explain in Chapter 4, "science" is not a simple enterprise to define. If science is anything, it is characterized by ongoing intellectual discourse, which can become quite competitive at times. This is important because it means that our ideas in Section I are by no means set in stone or impervious to newer, better ideas. Rather, they should be viewed as part of a much larger scientific discussion that will continually change and evolve over time, which is what makes scientific thinking special. Goodstein (2011) explained this as follows:

> [Science] is one of the few areas of human endeavor that is genuinely progressive. There is no doubt that the quality of twentieth century science is better than nineteenth century science, and we can be absolutely confident that the quality of science in the twenty-first century will be better still. One cannot say the same about, say, art or literature. (p. 440)

Just as our ideas in Section I have a shelf life, by studying the mental health case law in Section II of this book, readers can see how ideas about just legal outcomes have also changed and evolved over the years. To illustrate, there was a time in the United States, not too long ago, when it was legal to execute those age 16 and older (see *Stanford v. Kentucky*, 1989). Similarly, rape was once punishable by execution in the United States (see *Coker v. Georgia*, 1977). Likewise, it was once okay for police in the United States to use physical violence to elicit confessions from suspects (see *Brown v. Mississippi*, 1936).

Although it is not realistic to look up and contextualize (i.e., "shepardize") and summarize every single important legal case with relevance to mental health, in Section II of this book, we have attempted to cast a wide net, in an effort to offer the reader a helpful sampling of some of the most important and interesting legal cases with relevance to defendants with mental health disorders and limitations.

Instead of attempting to organize the cases based on the issues addressed, we have organized them alphabetically. We chose to present the material this way to facilitate easy identification of the cases, but also because many cases address multiple issues, making it impossible to neatly organize them.

1 A Primer on Abnormal Behavior

Abnormal means "deviating from normal or average" and "unusual in an unwelcome or problematic way" (Merriam-Webster, n.d.). Criminal behavior (e.g., property crimes, rape, drug trafficking, assault, burglary, robbery, larceny, murder) fits within the broader category of abnormal behavior because it departs from the norm and is both unwelcome and problematic. There are other categories of abnormal behavior, called *mental health disorders*, with extremely high relevance to criminal behavior because sometimes the criminal behavior cannot be easily disentangled from the mental health disorder. Under these circumstances (i.e., when a mental health disorder is thought to be part of the driving force behind the criminal behavior), it becomes necessary to involve a forensic mental health professional to formally evaluate the defendant. Why? Because criminal justice systems have been established to seek justice. If an individual engages in criminal behavior because of a mental health disorder, culpability may shift off of the individual.

To illustrate, consider the following case details. A man calls 911 from the apartment where he stabbed his female roommate in the leg, just moments before. During the call, the man explains to the dispatcher that he had to stab his roommate because he realized she was helping the aliens that had him under surveillance. When the police arrive, the man puts up no resistance and makes no attempt to hide the attack weapon.

Now consider a different set of case circumstances. A 15-year-old male kidnaps a man at random. The teen is apprehended by police without any physical harm done to the kidnapping victim, but only after a high-speed car chase, during which the victim had a loaded gun pointed at him throughout the horrifying ordeal.

In the first case, the defendant is found to have a normal IQ, and toxicology reports indicate that he was not under the influence of any substances during the stabbing. However, the forensic psychological assessment leads to the finding that the man suffers from a delusional disorder. In the second case, the defendant was not found to have any mental illness, and no substances were involved during commission of the crime, but a forensic psychological evaluation reveals that the defendant's IQ is in the high-70s. Hence, in the first case, the criminal behavior was linked to mental illness, whereas in the second

DOI: 10.4324/9780367645090-1

case, the defendant was found to have borderline intellectual functioning (Ferrari, 2009), a neurodevelopmental disorder.

Notably, the childhoods of both defendants in these two cases were characterized by poverty and exposure to violent crime on a regular basis, including family violence. Additionally, both defendants were experiencing high levels of stress at the time the crimes were committed. Hence, the nurture side of the nature-nurture equation is important in these cases. In other words, explaining the criminal behavior using mental illness and a neurodevelopmental disorder, respectively, is only partially viable, given that most individuals with a delusional disorder do not stab their roommates and given that most people with borderline intellectual functioning do not kidnap and terrorize.

In this chapter, we discuss abnormal behavior, including overlap between mental health disorders and criminal behavior. We begin by considering early adverse family experiences in the development of maladaptive and criminal behavior patterns. Next, we explore the role of adolescent brain development in abnormal behavior, including criminal conduct. We then address the limitations of immature-brain explanations for criminal behavior. Finally, a big-picture view of scientifically supported mental health disorders and substance-use disorders is provided, using the *Diagnostic and Statistical Manual for Mental Disorders-Fifth Edition* (*DSM-5*; American Psychiatric Association, 2013).

Early Life Risk Factors for Abnormal Behavior

Using the Adverse Childhood Experiences (ACEs) questionnaire (see Table 1.1), Felitti et al. (1998) studied the relationships between adverse family experiences during childhood, subsequent risky health behavior, and the development of various forms of life-threatening diseases later in life. These researchers identified a strong causative connection between early negative family experiences and bad health outcomes.

The ACEs questionnaire has since been used in many other studies, resulting in the finding that maltreatment in childhood often predicts many other bad outcomes later in life. For example, scores on the ACEs questionnaire have been found to predict depression (Chapman et al., 2004), attempted suicide (Dube et al., 2001), intergenerational transmission of poor parenting (Murphy et al., 2014), illicit drug use (Dube et al., 2003); alcohol-use problems (Dube et al., 2002), risky sexual behavior (Meade et al., 2009), and criminality (Reavis et al., 2013).

The Reavis et al. (2013) study is particularly relevant here, because criminal behavior is often found to be anchored in toxic family dynamics early in life. For example, sexually abused boys in their study were up to 45 times more likely to direct violence toward dating partners in adolescence. Similarly, boys who were themselves physically or sexually abused, or who saw their mothers being abused, were much more likely to become aggressive with romantic partners in adulthood. These researchers concluded their discussion with the following:

Table 1.1 Adverse childhood experiences questionnaire.

Before the age of 18 years

1. Did a parent or other adult in the household often or very often swear at you, insult you, put you down, humiliate you, or act in a way that made you afraid that you might be physically harmed?
2. Did a parent or other adult in the household often or very often push, grab, slap, kick, hit, bite, throw something at you, or otherwise physically harm you?
3. Did an adult or person at least five years older than you ever touch or fondle you or have you touch their body in a sexual way?
4. Did you often or very often feel that no one in your family loved you or that your family didn't look out for each other or support each other?
5. Did you often or very often feel that you didn't have enough to eat, that you had to wear dirty clothes, that you had no one to protect you, that your parents were too drunk or high to take care of you, or that your parents were not taking you to the doctor when you needed medical treatment?
6. Was a biological parent ever lost to you through divorce, abandonment, or another reason?
7. Was your mother or stepmother sometimes, often, or very often pushed, grabbed, slapped, kicked, hit, bit, threatened with a weapon, or otherwise physically harmed?
8. Did you live with anyone who was a problem drinker or alcoholic or who regularly used street or addictive prescription drugs?
9. Was a household member depressed or mentally ill, or did a household member attempt suicide?
10. Did a household member go to prison?

Source: Adapted from Reavis et al. (2013) with permission.

> To us, these results suggest that in some boys, the intensively negative feelings stimulated by poor treatment from their attachment figures are associated with either an avoidance of intimacy, or a "bleeding out" of the feelings into their intimate relationships, in the form of violence. (p. 47)

The important message from the ACEs studies is that noxious family dynamics in childhood likely play a prominent role in abnormal—including criminal—behavior, both in adolescence and adulthood.

Adolescent Brain Development and Abnormal Behavior

Most adolescents do not engage in criminal behavior. However, of all the age groups, adolescents engage in criminal behavior more than children and adults (Steinberg, 2013). Although being a teenager does not exculpate those who commit crimes, it is increasingly accepted that there is something different about being a teenager.

For example, teens are more likely to be influenced by their peers (Gardner & Steinberg, 2005), including being more prone to engage in illegal behavior if with a group of deviant peers (Zimring, 2013). Teens are not as skilled as adults at thinking long-term (Green et al., 1999; Nurmi, 1991). Teens are more sensitive to immediate rewards than adults (Galvan et al., 2007). And teens can be more impulsive than adults (Defoe et al., 2015; Rosenbaum et al., 2018; Steinberg et al., 2009). In support of the view that adolescent brains are different from adult brains is the following from U.S. Supreme Court case, *Graham v. Florida* (2010): "developments in psychology and brain science continue to show fundamental differences between juvenile and adult minds. For example, parts of the brain involved in behavior control continue to mature through late adolescence" (p. 2027).

Most law-breaking adolescents mature out of their antisocial behavior by the time they become adults (Loeber, 1990; Loeber et al., 1993; Moffitt, 1993). Hence, many errant teens are eventually capable of functioning as responsible members of society. This is one reason why some argue that it may not be appropriate to sentence teens, using a sentencing framework or scheme that is appropriate for many adults, for crimes committed during adolescence.

Adolescent Versus Adult Brain Development

The normal teenage brain acquires the capacity to function like an adult brain by about age 16 years, but only in some areas of the brain. This cognitive parity between teens and adults is reflected in laws pertaining to consent for healthcare services. For example, NM Stat § 32A-6A-15 grants teens, age 14 and older—in the state of New Mexico—the right to consent to mental health treatment without the consent of their legal custodian. This cognitive parity also gives the impression that teenagers can be held to the same standard as adults with regard to normal, law-abiding behavior.

However, when adolescent brain development is considered more closely, it becomes apparent that teens lack important cognitive abilities, relative to adults, and that there might be a gap between teen cognitive and emotional functioning, which can lead to risky and illegal behavior for some teens. Relative to adults, teens also lack experience, which—not unlike practice or training—can improve cognitive functioning, thereby lowering the odds of criminal conduct.

A Dual-Systems Model for Adolescent Brain Development

Steinberg (2009) described a dual-systems model for understanding the neurobiology of risky behavior in adolescents. The first system is the *socioemotional system*, which is controlled by limbic and related regions of the brain. This brain system generates strong fight-or-flight emotions. The second system is the *cognitive control system*, which is primarily controlled by frontal regions of the brain. This brain system is believed to regulate and control the socioemotional system by putting on the brakes (Nelson & Trainor, 2007) or by providing "information on potential rewards and costs of future actions, so that optimal response choice can occur" (Blair, 2016, p. 6).

According to Steinberg's dual-systems model, puberty brings with it "a rapid and dramatic increase in dopaminergic activity" (p. 54), which makes teens more emotionally unstable. Meanwhile, the cognitive control system takes longer to develop, creating a temporal gap between emotionality and cognitive control of the emotions; teens are suddenly prone to experience new, stronger emotions not felt in childhood, but their teen brains are not yet capable of regulating the increased emotionality. This imbalance between the frontal cognitive control system and the subcortical socioemotional system of the brain is believed to increase risk-taking and illegal behavior during adolescence.

Two Types of Adolescent Brain Development

It is important to distinguish between two different types of adolescent brain development: (1) synaptic pruning; and (2) increased brain connectivity, facilitated by myelination that continues well past the teen years. The synaptic pruning is "more or less complete by age 16" (Steinberg, 2009, p. 55), whereas brain connectivity continues into early adulthood. Therefore, while some adolescent brain development is complete by about age 16, other brain development is not. One way to appreciate these two types of brain development is to consider average functioning using cognitive test norms.

For example, the California Verbal Learning Test-2nd Ed. (CVLT-II) (Delis et al., 2000) measures various dimensions of learning and memory, using a list of 16 words, read to the examinee five times. Using the female norms from the CVLT-II for the total number of words recalled across the five learning trials, the same raw score (i.e., total number of words correctly remembered across the five trials) translates into the same relative performance from age 16 years to age 44 years. In other words, a score at the 50th percentile at age 16 years corresponds with a score at the 50th percentile at age 44; there are no differences. This means that the brain of a 16-year-old female is, by and large, equally good at learning a list of words as a 44-year-old female. Age does not alter performance on this particular cognitive test from age 16 to age 44 years. This same pattern holds for males, although males score slightly lower than females.

In contrast, the ability to correctly define words, a subtest on many intelligence tests, *improves* beyond age 16. A score at the 50th percentile for someone age 16 years and 0 months, on the Vocabulary subtest from the Wechsler Abbreviated Scale of Intelligence (WASI) (Wechsler, 1999), would only be at the 21st percentile for 25- to 29-year-olds. This same pattern is evident on full-battery Wechsler intelligence tests and on tests of sustained visual and auditory attention. For example, on the Continuous Performance Test, 3rd Ed. (Conners, 2014), "All CPT 3 scores, with the exception of HRT Block Change, were significantly affected by age with medium to large effect sizes … as respondents got older, they were better able to selectively respond to target stimuli while ignoring non-target stimuli … older respondents were more consistent than younger respondents in their reaction times" (p. 56). An identical pattern holds for the Continuous Auditory Test of Attention (Conners, 2014).

Interestingly, peak performance is reached on some cognitive tests in the late-teen years. For example, on the Block Design subtest of the WASI, a timed visual-spatial problem-solving task, peak performance is reached at age 16 years and four months. After this age, performance stays the same until age 17 years 0 months, when a very slight drop occurs, which slowly continues with more aging. The same is true for the Matrix Reasoning subtest of the WASI, an untimed visual-spatial problem-solving task, and for subtests on the full-battery Wechsler intelligence tests.

Overall, some cognitive functions are fully developed by about age 16 years and remain stable into middle-adulthood. Other cognitive functions peak around age 16 years and then slowly decline. And other cognitive functions slowly improve with age and experience. Therefore, it is incorrect to think of brain development as a process that follows an identical developmental trajectory across the lifespan. Some brain abilities, perhaps due to synaptic pruning, are at their best around age 16 years. Meanwhile, other brain functions, owing to experience and increased brain connectivity that continues past the teen years, improve well into adulthood. Because of this heterogeneity in brain growth and functioning, immature-brain explanations for teenage criminal behavior have limitations, which we discuss next.

Limitations of Immature-Brain Explanations for Abnormal Behavior

If teenage brains are lagging behind adult brains in important ways, does this explain the finding that adolescents engage in criminal behavior more than adults? Is there a neurobiological, brain-immaturity explanation for teenage criminal behavior? Such a position is overly simplistic, from an empirical standpoint, because there are too many other viable explanatory variables. In other words, a *purely* neurodevelopmental explanation for teen criminality makes claims that are scientifically shaky. This position was explained by Morse (2005) as follows:

> Brains do not commit crimes; people commit crimes…in *Roper v. Simmons*, advocates for abolition of the death penalty for adolescents who committed murder when they were sixteen or seventeen years old argued that the demonstrated lack of complete myelination of the cortical neurons of the adolescent brain was reason to believe that sixteen and seventeen year old murderers were insufficiently responsible to deserve capital punishment. These types of responses, I claim, are the signs of a disorder that I have preliminarily entitled Brain Overclaim Syndrome [BOS]. (p. 397)

Although advances in neuroscience are certainly exciting and intuitively appealing to the public, as demonstrated by popular books in support of brain-based explanations of criminal behavior (Kiehl, 2014; Raine, 2013), a leap is frequently made from the available neuroscientific literature to an explanation for the abnormal, criminal behavior. In the case of teenagers, it is crucial to remember that most adolescents do not commit crimes. Hence, if brain immaturity is not leading to criminal behavior in the overwhelming majority of teenagers, something other than a *pure* brain-immaturity explanation is called for.

A Macro View of Abnormal Behavior Using *DSM-5*

As demonstrated through the ACEs literature, abnormal behavior arises for reasons other than brain immaturity. Early negative family experiences often play a determining role. And while having a mental disorder does not automatically mean someone will commit crimes, some of the most compelling explanations for criminal behavior are—to some extent—anchored in neurodevelopmental disorders, mental illness, brain damage, neurological disease, and substance use.

There are more people with mental illness in jails and prisons across the United States than in psychiatric facilities (Frank & McGuire, 2010). Similarly, over 60% of those in juvenile detention facilities have at least one mental health disorder (Teplin et al., 2002). Accordingly, the *DSM-5* (American Psychiatric Association, 2013) is quite valuable because it organizes and explains the most scientifically validated mental health disorders, which is particularly relevant in forensic assessment (see Scientific Versus Pseudoscientific Diagnosis in Chapter 4). Correspondingly, diagnoses included within the *DSM-5* are often viewed by courts as more scientifically supported than those not included in the *DSM-5* (e.g., see *State v. Alberico*, 1993, which is summarized in Section II).

This is not to say that the *DSM-5*, like its predecessors, is without limitations in general (Frances, 2009), or in forensic contexts (Frances, 2010). To illustrate, consider that a diagnosis of posttraumatic stress disorder (PTSD) can be made 636,120 different ways (Galatzer-Levy & Bryant, 2013), raising important questions about how homogeneous this diagnosis is. Similarly, Lareau (2012) articulated many limitations with earlier versions of the *DSM*; for example, homosexuality was considered to no longer be a mental illness based on votes from psychiatrists—hardly a scientific process—after originally being considered a mental illness in *DSM-2*. Finally, the *DSM-5* itself contains a Cautionary Statement for Forensic Use of *DSM-5*. With these caveats about the *DSM-5* noted, we describe *DSM*-5 disorders with high relevance to criminal behavior using three overarching categories: cognitive disorders, emotional disorders, and substance-use disorders.

Cognitive Disorders in DSM-5

Disorders that primarily affect the defendant's ability to think, problem-solve, pay attention, remember, communicate, and so forth are cognitive disorders. Cognitive disorders can arise in early development, result from brain damage or injury at any time in life, or emerge later in life, as a part of a progressive neurological disease like Alzheimer's disease. Table 1.2 contains neurodevelopmental and neurocognitive disorders with pertinence to understanding some criminal behavior.

Intellectual Disability

Intellectual disability is diagnosed when substantial deficits in both intellectual and adaptive functioning are measured before the age of approximately 18 years. The U.S. Supreme Court case of *Atkins v. Virginia* (2002) made it a violation of the Eighth Amendment to execute those with intellectual disability who are found guilty of capital murder, based on the following grounds: "Because of their disabilities in areas of reasoning, judgment, and control of their impulses … they do not act with the level of moral culpability that characterizes the most serious adult criminal conduct." This position taken by the court is in accord with the principle of *penal proportionality*, which dictates that sentences for crimes must be proportionate to the degree of culpability in the defendant. With the exception of the *Atkins* decision and related state-level hearings (e.g., NMSA 1978 § 31-9-1.6, 1999), a diagnosis of intellectual disability does not automatically translate into a specific legal outcome, like being incompetent to proceed or incompetent to make a plea deal. Nonetheless, it does function as an important red flag, indicating that the defendant needs to be handled differently by the courts.

Borderline intellectual functioning, listed in the *DSM-5* among "Other Conditions That May Be a Focus of Clinical Attention" rather than being a clinical diagnosis, has traditionally been defined in the *DSM* as an IQ in the 71–84 range. However, the definition of borderline intellectual functioning in *DSM-5* does not include an IQ score, making the determination more

Table 1.2 DSM-5 cognitive disorders relevant to understanding criminal behavior.

Intellectual Disability
Borderline Intellectual Functioning
Autism Spectrum Disorder
Tourette's Disorder (a type of tic disorder)
Other Specified Neurodevelopmental Disorder
Unspecified Neurodevelopmental Disorder
Attention-Deficit/Hyperactivity Disorder
Delirium
Major Neurocognitive Disorder due to Traumatic Brain Injury
Major Neurocognitive Disorder due to Neurological Disease
Mild Neurocognitive Disorder due to (complicated-mild, moderate, or severe) Traumatic Brain Injury
Mild Neurocognitive Disorder due to Neurological Disease
Unspecified Neurocognitive Disorder

subjective than it was in the past (Kaufman et al., 2020). Nevertheless, it remains important because it provides a way of describing those who fall short of a diagnosis of intellectual disability, but who nonetheless lack "ability to plan and structure [their] behavior with an end in view" (Das, 1973) (p. 27). Accordingly, full-battery IQ testing in forensic assessment has a valuable role, because it is the only way to objectively and comprehensively flesh out any intellectual deficits that fall in the borderline range.

Like intellectual disabilities, when a defendant is found to have borderline intellectual functioning, it does not automatically equate to a specific legal outcome. However, it does function as a clinical red flag, alerting concerned parties that the defendant's capacity to think, problem-solve, and skillfully navigate certain real-world challenges is qualitatively lower than most others. When this information is combined with other information about the defendant (e.g., a history of trauma, co-morbid mental illness, high levels of stress at the time of the offense, substance-use at the time of the offense), its relevance is easier to appreciate.

Autism Spectrum Disorder

Those with autism spectrum disorder may or may not have low IQs, although a very large percentage do (Pennington et al., 2019). Whether or not intellectual deficits are present, having autism impairs functioning in social settings by limiting the individual's social cognition, putting those with autism at a disadvantage. Hence, even someone with autism who does *not* have a lower IQ may be severely hindered by deficits in social cognition. Having autism is not currently thought to be a risk factor for criminal behavior (Lerner et al., 2012), but if someone with autism becomes a criminal defendant, it may be necessary to handle the case differently. In their discussion of Autism and the law, Kaufman and Bush (in press) wrote the following:

> Because autism is, by diagnostic definition, a mental disorder with "Symptoms [that] cause clinically significant impairment in social, occupational, or other important areas of current functioning" (APA, 2013, p. 50), those with autism may find themselves ensnared in imbroglios of a legal nature…When this occurs, a forensic assessment of autism can be extremely important because the assessment results, conveyed in a report, may be pivotal in the delivery of a fair, just legal outcome. (p. 15)

Tourette's Disorder

Tourette's disorder involves motor or vocal tics that persist for at least one year and have their onset before age 18. Motor tics typically involve the face or neck, but can sometimes affect the extremities; vocal tics usually involve grunting or coughing, but sometimes include cussing/swearing, which is termed *coprolalia* (Blumenfeld, 2014). In Tourette's disorder, there is dysregulation of the nigrostriatal dopamine pathway and part of the basal ganglia (i.e., the caudate). Additionally, it is believed that the frontal part of the brain, which plays a moderating role over the caudate, is unable to perform its job adequately.

Tourette's disorder is extremely uncommon, occurring in no more than eight per 1,000 school-aged children (American Psychiatric Association, 2013). Hence, it is less likely to come up in juvenile or adult criminal cases. But if it does arise, the symptoms may be misunderstood. For example, if coprolalia is encountered by the public, there is a risk that it will be mistaken for intentionally offensive behavior. Goldberg (2002) shared the following example of how this might play out:

> Many years ago I salvaged from a likely arrest a decently dressed young man who was walking up and down a line of passengers (myself among them) waiting to board an Amtrak train at the 30th Street Station in Philadelphia and cursing us out in the foulest conceivable language. He was also exhibiting characteristic motor tics, which I immediately recognized as Tourettic. As the cops were about to converge on him, I approached one of them and quickly explained what was going on. The officer listened and I was thankful to see him merely tell the man to get lost. (p. 183)

Delirium

Delirium is disturbance in cognitive functioning that develops within hours or days and represents a sudden and unexpected drop from pre-delirium functioning. It is caused by a medical condition, substance intoxication, withdrawal from a substance, toxin exposure, or a combination of the foregoing. Delirium is very rare in general, but because it occurs in 14–24% of those admitted into hospitals (American Psychiatric Association, 2013), it can become forensically relevant when confused, aggressive patients are charged with assaulting hospital staff or other patients.

Major Neurocognitive Disorder

A diagnosis of major neurocognitive disorder can be applied at any stage in life as the result of an *acquired* medical condition, such as a very serious traumatic brain injury (TBI). This *DSM-5* diagnosis would fit if the individual suffered a severe TBI (King et al., 2017; Sherer & Madison, 2005), followed by a significant drop in both cognitive functioning (attention, memory, language, etc.) and adaptive functioning (successful participation in school if a child or being able to pay bills if an adult). Other acquired causes of major neurocognitive disorder include strokes, exposure to neurotoxins, and infections (e.g., of the brain or meninges).

It is worth noting that if not using *DSM-5*, but instead relying on the International Classification of Diseases, Tenth Revision, Clinical Modification (ICD-10-CM; WHO, 2018), the diagnosis would be dementia, an important term to understand, given its long history in the neuropsychological and neurological literature. Indeed, *DSM-5* states, "Major [Neurocognitive Disorder] corresponds to the condition referred to in DSM-IV as *dementia*" (American Psychiatric Association, 2013, p. 607). In other words, major neurocognitive disorder and dementia can be viewed as synonyms, as evidenced by the fact that dementia ICD-10-CM diagnostic codes are interchangeable with the *DSM-5* major neurocognitive disorder diagnostic codes.

Similarly, use of the ICD-10-CM, instead of *DSM-5*, to diagnose cognitive and other mental health disorders is justified in forensic assessment because, like *DSM-5*, the ICD-10-CM is widely adopted by clinicians. A benefit, however, to using the *DSM-5*, instead of the ICD-10-CM, is that the *DSM-5* includes extensive descriptive information about the diagnoses, making it easier for all parties to understand what is meant when a given diagnosis is used.

Causes of major neurocognitive disorder most commonly have onset in adulthood and include the following: Alzheimer's disease; Parkinson's disease; Huntington's disease; frontotemporal degeneration; HIV infection; and vascular disease. With older adult defendants, it is particularly important to appreciate that major neurocognitive disorder might play a role in commission of the crime, as well as legal competence and culpability.

To illustrate, consider the following case details. A 75-year-old widow, who resides alone in her country home, accidentally hits a motorcyclist while driving her truck into town to get groceries. Tragically, the motorcyclist loses a limb, prompting the district attorney to file criminal charges. A subsequent forensic neuropsychological evaluation reveals that, at the time of the accident, the elderly defendant had major neurocognitive disorder thought to be caused by Alzheimer's disease. Not only does this change one's view of the alleged criminal behavior, but questions arise as to whether the defendant is even legally competent or in any way culpable.

Because the term "dementia" is generally thought of as only applying to older adults, it is perhaps counterintuitive that a diagnosis of major neurocognitive disorder could be applied to a minor, including a young child. Consider a six-year-old who developed normally, until contracting bacterial meningitis, an infection of the meninges, which is the protective covering of the brain. If not treated promptly with antibiotics, meningitis can cause very serious and permanent brain damage, which could justify a diagnosis of major neurocognitive disorder, if not also a diagnosis of intellectual disability (see p. 38 of *DSM-5*).

Mild Neurocognitive Disorder

It is normal for older adults to lose some cognitive functioning as a part of the aging process. This is not a disorder. However, loss of cognitive functioning due to aging falls on a continuum, with normal aging at one end of the spectrum and a major neurocognitive disorder (or dementia, if using ICD-10-CM) at the other end of the spectrum. If the older adult experiences "a modest cognitive decline from a previous level of performance in one or more cognitive domains (complex attention, executive function, learning and memory, language, perceptual motor, or social cognition)" (American Psychiatric Association, 2013, p. 605), a diagnosis of mild neurocognitive disorder might apply. Similarly, if a younger adult experiences "modest cognitive decline" due to an acquired medical condition (e.g., a TBI, a stroke, an infection, exposure to neurotoxins), mild neurocognitive disorder might apply.

Just as the term "dementia" is no longer used in the *DSM-5*, but is found in the ICD-10-CM, the term "mild cognitive impairment" is not used in the *DSM-5*, but is in the ICD-10-CM. Hence, the two terms—mild neurocognitive disorder and mild cognitive impairment—can be used interchangeably in most circumstances,[1] as evidenced by inclusion of the ICD-10-CM diagnostic code for mild cognitive impairment in *DSM-5*. This is worth noting to avoid confusion about terms, but also because there is an established scientific literature on mild cognitive impairment (Petersen, 2004; Smith & Bondi, 2013), which predates publication of the *DSM-5*. While there is some controversy about mild cognitive impairment (Dubois et al., 2007; Sardella, 2017), the fact that there is so much scientific literature on it makes it valuable to forensic evaluators.

To illustrate, one of us was hired to conduct a forensic neuropsychological adjudicative competence evaluation on a 77-year-old man. While—debatably—not found to have major neurocognitive disorder (i.e., no dementia), this defendant's auditory-verbal learning and memory skills were measured to be lower than 98% of his age-based comparison group (and even lower than what is normal for younger adults). Hence, his ability to effectively communicate with his attorney and mentally track legal proceedings—which play out through verbal discourse—was likely to be severely impacted by anterograde amnesia, which is the inability to make new memories. That is, this older adult could not adequately remember what others told him, particularly if not given multiple opportunities to encode or learn the new material. In contrast, some of his other cognitive functions were normal for his age and even in comparison to younger adults. Similarly, the history showed only mild problems with bill paying, grocery shopping, and food preparation, indicating that he could still function relatively independently, as long as new, more-complex tasks were not necessary. This was interpreted to justify ruling out a diagnosis of major neurocognitive disorder (or dementia). Nonetheless, because of the profound anterograde amnesia, a diagnosis to convey his cognitive deficits was justified. Because of the established neuropsychological literature on mild cognitive impairment (Smith & Bondi, 2013), that diagnosis was applied in the case to help convey the defendant's deficits with regard to the question of adjudicative competence. However, to support the opinion of adjudicative incompetence, more attention was drawn to the anterograde amnesia—based on the neuropsychological testing results—than the mild cognitive impairment diagnosis.

Notably, cases arise where it is difficult for the mental health clinician to differentiate between mild and major neurocognitive disorders. One clinician might characterize the deficits as mild (e.g., mild cognitive impairment or mild neurocognitive disorder), whereas another clinician might apply a diagnosis of dementia or major neurocognitive disorder. Under these circumstances, it is important for the forensic mental health evaluator to transparently provide the underlying basis for their opinion and to remember that the presence of a mental health diagnosis does *not* equate to a legal incompetence.

Emotional Disorders in DSM-5

Schizophrenia spectrum disorders are the most recognizable emotional disorders with relevance to the juvenile and adult criminal justice systems. It has been reported, for example, that those diagnosed with a schizophrenia spectrum disorder are eight times more likely to be found incompetent to stand trial (Pirelli et al., 2011). Accordingly, if a defendant is thought to be suffering from delusions, hallucinations, (extremely) disorganized thinking, abnormal motor behavior (e.g., remaining in a rigid posture), or negative symptoms (e.g., extreme emotional flatness, extreme lack of self-initiated behavior, extreme lack of speech), a schizophrenia spectrum disorder may need to be considered by a forensic mental health professional. While these disorders are rare, if found to be present, they can (a) form the basis for an insanity defense, (b) prevent some defendants from ever being legally competent, and (c) influence criminal sentences, if not having an entirely exculpatory effect.

Some schizophrenia spectrum disorders are not difficult to identify. If, for example, the defendant prefers to stand in a corner, in a rigid position, and mutter quietly to himself for hours in a row, even non-clinicians will likely appreciate the mental illness. In contrast, a pure delusional disorder may be extremely difficult to identify, particularly if the defendant does not want to be labeled as "crazy."

Recall the details from the case previously described involving the adult male who called 911 after stabbing his roommate. During the forensic neuropsychological evaluation, which focused on the defendant's mental state at the time of the offense, the IQ and the neuropsychological testing revealed no deficits. Similarly, the defendant scored well above recommended cutoff points on tests of both performance and symptom validity. And no clinical elevations were identified on the personality testing. It was not until about four hours into the assessment, during the latter portion of a second clinical interview, that it became apparent that a bizarre, persecutory delusion was under the surface, and had been for years. But because the defendant did not trust anyone, he was extremely guarded about telling the evaluator about how he was being spied on by aliens. This is why the symptoms were initially missed during the clinical interview and testing and why a second interview was conducted.

Table 1.3 DSM-5 emotional disorders relevant to criminal behavior

Schizophrenia Spectrum Disorders
Bipolar Disorders
Depressive Disorders
Posttraumatic Stress Disorder
Dissociative Disorders
Conversion Disorder with Attacks or Seizures
Non-Rapid Eye Movement Sleep Arousal Disorder Sleeping Walking Type
Cluster A Personality Disorders
Cluster C Personality Disorders

Table 1.3 contains other severe mental illnesses with potential relevance to criminal behavior. However, most of these disorders are extremely uncommon. For example, bipolar disorder is estimated to occur in less than 1% of the population during any given 12-month period, and dissociative identity disorder reportedly occurs just slightly more frequently, at 1.5% over a 12-month period (American Psychiatric Association, 2013). This is important because the diagnostic methods needed to correctly identify extremely rare disorders may not be adequate for legal proceedings under *Daubert v. Merrell Dow Pharmaceuticals* (1993), which emphasizes scientific methods with a known error rate. Kaufman et al. (2019) discussed this with regard to a diagnosis of postconcussive syndrome, sometimes applied to those who have experienced a concussion:

> Because current research indicates that the base rate for postconcussional syndrome is extremely low (McCrea, 2008), if not 0 (e.g., Boone, 2013; Rohling, Langhinrichsen-Rohling, & Axelrod, 2017), legal challenges can justifiably be raised when this questionable diagnosis is made with reasonable medical certainty because methods used to make the diagnosis are not likely to have demonstrated an accuracy rate that can overcome the low base rate…As explained by Faust and Ahern (2012), if a test achieves a predictive accuracy [rate] of 60% and playing the base rate [has an] accuracy [rate] of 80%, one uses the base rate over the test…a [method] cannot outperform the base rate unless it achieves an accuracy level that is greater than the frequency of the more common occurrence (or nonoccurrence). (p. 196)

Depression is the most common disorder in Table 1.3 and, as a result, it is more feasible to accurately diagnosis. For example, over a 12-month period, major depressive disorder occurs in approximately 7% of those in the United States, and this rate is much higher in those in the 18- to 29-year-old range (American Psychiatric Association, 2013). Additionally, it is not uncommon for depression to play a role in criminal behavior (Sher et al., 2015) or to impact a defendant's functioning during legal proceedings (Thomas, 2010; Warren et al., 2003), which could detract from a legal competence.

To illustrate, one middle-aged adult defendant independently confessed to shooting a stranger to death while driving down the freeway. The confession was made knowingly, intelligently, and voluntarily, but it likely would not have been given at all had the defendant not sunk into a state of severe depression. In a different case, a young adult defendant had an argument with his girlfriend via cell phone while walking down a sidewalk. After being hung up on, the defendant became despondent and randomly walked into a dwelling, stabbed the two female inhabitants to death, and then slit his own wrist with the same knife, in an unsuccessful attempt to kill himself. Although a depressive disorder is unlikely to have the exculpatory effect of a schizophrenia spectrum disorder, it is nonetheless relevant to understanding the behavior of those charged with crimes, it can affect legal competence, and it may become relevant at sentencing.

Substance Use Disorders in DSM-5

Substance use is a major driver of criminal behavior (Bagaric & Gopalan, 2016; Miller et al., 2006; Scribner et al., 1995). Those who commit crimes frequently do so while intoxicated. Others commit crimes to pay for their drug addiction. And others commit crimes after the substances are no longer detectible in their blood, but an indirect link is often hard to deny. When those with mental health disorders also develop substance-use problems, it is even *more* likely that criminal behavior will ensue (Lipsey et al., 2002; Parker & Auerhahn, 1998; Sher et al., 2000). Thus, sometimes criminal behavior cannot be easily disentangled from mental health disorders because the two go together (Beaver & Wright, 2011; Diamond et al., 2012; Fazel et al., 2009; Fridell et al., 2008; Kim et al., 2019). Stated differently, if it were possible to "control for" the effects of mental disorders on the expression of criminal behavior, there would be fewer criminals.

To illustrate this point, consider an individual suffering from persecutory delusions who commits arson, based on the belief that evil spirits live in the building and can only be stopped if burned. Clearly the motives of such an individual are different than the motive of one who commits arson with the intent to cause harm to those living inside the building. Of all the substances, methamphetamines and alcohol frequently play a role in aggressive criminal behavior, so they are described in more detail in this section, after discussion of adolescent substance use.

Adolescent Substance Use

Adolescent substance use is a problem for multiple reasons. First, having one's first alcoholic drink before the age of 14 years increases the likelihood of later developing an alcohol-use disorder by a factor of four (Grant & Dawson, 1997). A similar pattern involving marijuana use has also been reported (SAMSHA, 2019). Second, those who start using substances early in life are also at greater risk for accidental injuries (e.g., car accidents) and fighting (Hingson et al., 2009).

Adolescents drawn to substance use, particularly alcohol, may have different brain functioning from those who avoid substances (Lieb et al., 2002). For example, teens who gravitate toward using substances may have worse response inhibition than teens who do not start using substances (Nigg et al., 2006; Norman et al., 2011). This means that some teens may not be as capable of stopping themselves from engaging in substance use. In contrast, other research suggests that *all* adolescents—compared to adults—are less capable of controlling themselves (Hare et al., 2008). This latter view fits with the dual-system model for understanding adolescent brain development, described previously.

Like adults, there is a link between substance use and criminal behavior among adolescents (Sher et al., 2000). In support of this, a *DSM-5* diagnosis of conduct disorder is one of the most common comorbid diagnoses for teens with substance-use disorders (Wilens et al., 2003). In all likelihood, those with conduct disorder are predisposed to ignore the risks of trying substances. However, once a teen starts using substances, they may become more prone to engage in the behaviors needed to satisfy a diagnosis of conduct disorder. So there may be a bidirectional relationship between conduct disorder and substance use: having conduct disorder leads to substance use, but substance use can also lead to the development of conduct disorder.

Does adolescent substance use predict long-term problems? While research shows differences in neuropsychological functioning between substance-using teens, as compared to teens who do not use (Berk et al., 2014), the full extent of long-term deficits is not entirely clear. Moreover, as the previous discussion illustrated, teens who develop substance-use problems may have different brain functioning to begin with, making it challenging to know if any lasting problems are a result of pre-existing brain dysfunction, versus using substances during adolescence. In their coverage of this topic, Berk et al. (2014) concluded with the following: "Thus, alcohol and substance use during adolescence appear to be partially, but not completely irreversible. Further research is necessary to examine neurocognitive functioning separately for alcohol and substance use disorders" (p. 620). In other words, these authors reported that substance-use in adolescence may have some irreversible negative effects on neuropsychological functioning.

Methamphetamine Use

Methamphetamine use can substantially alter neuropsychological functioning during intoxication (Iudicello et al., 2014), including causing psychosis. Interestingly, the psychosis can persist after cessation of use (Barr et al., 2006):

> Studies conducted in Japan, where high levels of [methamphetamine] use have been prevalent for decades, report that between 36% and 64% of

> [methamphetamine] users who have experienced psychotic symptoms continue to present with these symptoms for more than ten days after cessation of the [methamphetamine] use, even though the [methamphetamine] is eliminated from the blood stream in less than five days. (p. 306)

Consistent with this idea, it is not uncommon for forensic mental health professionals to encounter defendants who have either committed crimes while under the intoxicating effect of methamphetamine, or within days after cessation of use. The latter case can present complexities because attributing the illegal behavior to the *direct* effects of the methamphetamine is difficult if the substance is already out of the defendant's system.

Some jurisdictions allow for a *mens rea*/diminished capacity defense when substance use is involved, whereas many other jurisdictions do not. In comparison, the insanity defense is available in most U.S. jurisdictions, but not if the *actus reus* (i.e., the bad act) was clearly caused by substance use (*Kane v. United States*, 1968). With methamphetamine, the user can sometimes be left in a compromised mental state after the substance is out of their body. This has been described by Packer (2009) as "settled" insanity.

To illustrate, consider the case of a psychologist hired to evaluate a young man who had a longstanding methamphetamine-use addiction, but who had ceased using all substances, except for nicotine, in the days leading up to the murder he committed. The toxicology report showed that, at the time the crime was committed, the defendant was not under the influence of drugs or alcohol. However, he was unequivocally psychotic at the time of the crime, as evidenced by multiple sources of information, including a video-recording of his bizarre behavior in the police station shortly after the murder. In this case, one expert opined that the man satisfied the definition of (settled) insanity in the state of New Mexico, whereas another expert opined that the murder was a result of substance use, therefore precluding an insanity defense.

Alcohol Use

Alcohol use is known to correspond with aggressive behavior (Lipsey et al., 2002; Parker & Auerhahn, 1998; Scribner et al., 1995), although the causative nexus is not straightforward and likely includes individual and social variables (Fagan, 1990). For example, a depressed person with a lower IQ who has grown up in a community where it is commonplace to use aggression to solve problems is more likely to become aggressive while under the influence of alcohol. In contrast, alcohol is much less likely to play a role in aggressive behavior if the user's expectations about the effect of alcohol do not support aggressive behavior (Lee et al., 2019).

The effects of alcohol intoxication on cognitive functioning have been compared to the effects of suffering brain damage (Peterson et al., 1990). Heavily intoxicated individuals temporarily lose their normal ability to exercise judgment and solve problems, not unlike the permanent status of someone who has suffered severe damage to certain areas of the brain. Similarly, those with serious alcohol-use problems may even lack the cognitive ability to correctly process facial expressions and speech tone in others when not intoxicated (Fama & Sullivan, 2014), setting the stage for an aggressive response in some social interactions. Importantly, however, cognitive dysfunction associated with alcohol use—whether during heavy intoxication or due to prolonged heavy use—does not lead to aggressive behavior in all.

With one major exception, to be discussed shortly, the effects of alcohol are temporary. Hence, alcohol consumption is typically only relevant to forensic assessment insofar as alcohol intoxication somehow played a role in the defendant's criminal behavior. In jurisdictions like the state of New Mexico, where a *mens rea*/diminished capacity defense can involve voluntary intoxication, it is important to ascertain the extent of the defendant's alcohol consumption around the time of the criminal act. In jurisdictions like the state of Montana, where voluntary-intoxication evidence can be blocked (*Montana v. Egelhoff*, 1996), the role of alcohol consumption at the time of the criminal act is negated. Alcohol intoxication, however, may still be relevant if a defendant is Mirandized and interrogated while still under the influence of alcohol. Likewise, alcohol intoxication at the time of the offense is likely to be relevant for the purposes of sentencing, because alcohol is known to affect judgment and intent.

WERNICKE-KORSAKOFF SYNDROME

Although not specifically included in *DSM-5*, a major neurocognitive disorder (dementia) can result from consistent, heavy alcohol use. Specifically, when an individual does not get adequate thiamine in their diet, which can happen with heavy drinkers, it can damage various areas of the brain: the mamillary bodies, thalamus, basal forebrain, and raphe nuclei. During the acute phase of this thiamine deficiency, the individual experiences a triad of symptoms: (1) confusion; (2) unsteady gait (gait ataxia); and (3) rapid, involuntary eye movement (nystagmus). If the damage is not reversed with prompt thiamine-replacement therapy, magnesium, and other nutritional supplementation, the brain damage can become permanent. Moreover, it can include severe memory impairment, characterized by the inability to make new memories (anterograde amnesia) and making up of false memories (confabulation).

If using the ICD-10-CM (WHO, 2020), *Wernicke's encephalopathy* is the neurological diagnosis used to describe the individual's functioning in the acute phase of the disease. *Wernicke-Korsakoff Syndrome*, also called alcohol dependence with alcohol-induced persisting amnestic disorder, is the ICD-10-CM diagnosis used to describe the condition of the individual who remains in a state of permanent brain damage. If using *DSM-5*, the diagnosis for Wernicke-Korsakoff Syndrome would be major neurocognitive disorder due to another medical condition (viz., thiamine deficiency or Wernicke-Korsakoff Syndrome).

THE "ALCOHOL BLACKOUT"

Those who consume enough alcohol to not remember what they have done are said to have experienced an "alcohol blackout" (Pressman & Caudill, 2013). Although there is little doubt that alcohol consumption negatively impacts memory while under the influence, there is considerable debate about whether an "alcohol blackout" can be used as justification for a *mens rea*/diminished capacity defense. Some assert that experiencing an "alcohol blackout" means the defendant was unable to form intent, while others assert that memory impairment during commission of the *actus reus* (the bad act) is not tantamount to being unable to form intent (Merikangas, 2004).

Pressman and Caudill (2013) argued that an "alcoholic blackout" is not a scientifically supported term, making it inadequate as a basis for a *mens rea*/diminished capacity defense in jurisdictions that use *Daubert* and Rule 702, or the state equivalents of these laws. These authors pointed out that an "alcoholic blackout" cannot be measured using biomarkers and that the condition is based only on the absence of memory for a distinct period of time, making it too subjective to satisfy *Daubert* or Rule 702.

However, Pressman and Caudill (2013) also drew a line between the level of intoxication required to have a blackout, versus more severe intoxication:

> The "alcoholic blackout" appears to be a distinct form of severe alcohol intoxication in which short-term memory is selectively impaired, while other cognitive and motor skills are unaffected or minimally affected. Blackout patients are not "fall down drunk." They do not appear to have obvious impairment in coordination, balance, social interaction, or speech. Rather, to all outward appearances, they are cognitively and physically intact. (p. 939)

Hence, these critics of the "alcoholic blackout" defense acknowledge that alcohol intoxication exists on a continuum, with the level of intoxication needed for a blackout at one end and more severe intoxication at the other end. So, according to the reasoning offered by Pressman and Caudill (2013), if the defendant's intoxication only affects memory at the time of the offense, there would be no grounds for a *mens rea*/diminished capacity defense. In contrast, if the level of intoxication included other signs of impairment (e.g., impaired judgment, slurred speech, lack of coordination, unsteady gait, impaired attention), then alcohol could be relied upon to help explain the defendant's criminal behavior.

Conclusion

In this chapter, we focused on understanding abnormal human behavior, including the overlap between criminal behavior—which is abnormal—and abnormal behavior resulting from abusive family relationships in childhood, immature brain development, cognitive disorders, emotional disorders, and substance-use disorders, all of which can contribute to the criminal behavior. When criminal behavior is committed by an individual who has a history of maltreatment in childhood, an immature brain, a cognitive disorder, an emotional disorder, or a substance-use disorder, a just legal outcome is more likely if the attorneys, judges, and juries are properly educated about the extent to which these factors impact the defendant. It is the job of the forensic mental health professional to provide this education.

As put forth in the Cautionary Statement for Forensic Use of *DSM-5* (APA, 2013), "a particular diagnosis does not imply a specific level of impairment or disability" (p. 25). Therefore, meeting *DSM-5* diagnostic criteria for a mental or substance-use disorder does not mean a crime can be explained away as a result of the disorder. Nor does it mean that neurodevelopmental, neurocognitive, or other psychiatric disorders can be used as the sole basis for concluding that a defendant is legally incompetent in one way or another. However, some *DSM-5* diagnoses are extremely relevant to legal questions that come before factfinders, making it important to have a more comprehensive understanding of this topic. Moreover, a review of mental health case law quickly leads to the realization that diagnoses contained within the *DSM* are recognized by courts as scientifically valid, whereas diagnoses *not* contained within the *DSM* are not (e.g., see *State v. Alberico*, 1993, summarized in Section II).

Given that many of those involved in the juvenile and adult criminal justice system have mental health disorders, it should not be surprising to learn that treatment for mental health disorders may reduce criminal behavior (Frank & McGuire, 2010). Likewise, given the causative role substance use plays in the commission of crimes, it should not be surprising to learn that treatment for substance-use disorders may reduce future criminal behavior (Gumpert et al., 2010). Criminal behavior is inextricably tied to mental health disorders and substance use, which may have roots in abusive upbringings. Similarly, brain immaturity can help explain some criminal behavior.

At one end of the continuum, we encounter very simplistic explanations for criminal acts ("He's pure evil" or "She's crazy"), but we can do much better than this. To do so, however, requires a more nuanced understanding of abnormal human behavior, as explained in this chapter.

Note

1 Mild cognitive impairment is used to characterize loss of cognitive functioning in older adults, whereas mild neurocognitive disorder can be applied to children, teens, younger adults, and older adults when there is cognitive decline due to brain injury, substance use, medication, or other medical conditions, including neurovascular disease, Alzheimer's disease, and other conditions that are more specific to older adults (e.g., frontotemporal degeneration, Parkinson's disease). Hence, mild neurocognitive disorder is a slightly larger umbrella term than mild cognitive impairment.

2 A Primer on Forensic Psychological and Forensic Neuropsychological Evaluations

Although it is not possible to explain everything about forensic psychological and forensic neuropsychological evaluations to legal professionals in a single chapter, we offer a primer on this topic, primarily directed at attorneys and judges. However, the material is also relevant to probation officers, investigators, students, educators, and certainly other forensic mental health professionals. It is our objective to advance the reader's understanding of what forensic psychological and neuropsychological evaluations involve. Additionally, we hope this new knowledge will facilitate more effective use of mental health experts by legal professionals.

The "Forensic" Evaluation

Forensic means "for law enforcement and courtroom purposes" (Clapp, 2007, p. 107). Therefore, a psychological evaluation that is forensic is one conducted for a *legal-oriented* reason (i.e., it aims to help answer a legal question). This is in contrast to a medical or psychological purpose, which is *treatment-oriented* (i.e., it aims to offer psychological treatment by supporting a patient's well-being). As one might expect, a neuropsychological evaluation that is forensic is a neuropsychological evaluation, done for a legal-oriented reason.

To illustrate, if a young man suffered a moderate to severe TBI (King et al., 2017) after being assaulted, his doctor might refer him for a treatment-oriented neuropsychological evaluation to obtain more information on the full extent of the TBI and how to help in his recovery. Or, if the young man showed symptoms of emotional trauma after being assaulted, his doctor might refer him for a treatment-oriented psychological evaluation, given concern about a possible diagnosis of PTSD and related treatment needs (e.g., psychotherapy). The young man may also have criminal or civil legal issues as a result of the assault, but addressing those problems is not the purpose of a treatment-oriented evaluation.

In contrast, if a criminal defense attorney experiences marked difficulty communicating with her client, the attorney might refer her client for a forensic psychological or a forensic neuropsychological evaluation, to generate evidence with relevance to the legal question of the defendant's adjudicative

DOI: 10.4324/9780367645090-2

Table 2.1 Definitions that clarify the difference between forensic psychology and forensic neuropsychology

"[Neuropsychology is the] Study of the relations between brain function and behavior." (Kolb & Whishaw, 2009, G-23)
"Clinical neuropsychology is a specialty in professional psychology that applies principles of assessment and intervention based upon the scientific study of human behavior as it relates to normal and abnormal functioning of the central nervous system. The specialty is dedicated to enhancing the understanding of the brain-behavior relationships and the application of such knowledge to human problems." (APA CRSPPP, 2010a, para. 1)
"Forensic psychology is defined broadly as the application of psychological research, theory, practice, and traditional and specialized methodology (e.g., interviewing, psychological testing, forensic assessment, and forensically relevant instruments) for the express purpose of providing assistance to the legal system." (Otto & Goldstein, 2013, p. 3)
"Forensic psychology is the professional practice by psychologists within the areas of clinical psychology, counseling psychology, school psychology or another specialty recognized by the American Psychological Association, when they are engaged as experts and represent themselves as such, in an activity primarily intended to provide professional psychological expertise in the judicial system." (APA CRSPPP, 2010b, para. 1)
"Forensic neuropsychology is defined as the application of neuropsychological evidence to inform legal questions … 'forensic neuropsychologist' (FN) simply means any neuropsychologist who provides opinions in a legal setting, irrespective of the frequency of this work." (Larrabee, 2012, p. 23)
"Forensic neuropsychology can be considered a subspecialty within neuropsychology whereby neuropsychological knowledge and services, including testimony and trial consultation, are provided to inform legal or administrative decisions." (Bush, 2017) (pp. xvii–xviii)

competence (i.e., competence to stand trial or proceed through the adjudicative process). Both of the young man's problems, a moderate to severe TBI and possible PTSD, are addressed with a treatment-oriented evaluation, either psychological or neuropsychological. But the female defendant's problem has a legal focus, which is why it is addressed with either a forensic psychological or forensic neuropsychological evaluation. Table 2.1 contains more formal definitions from the professional literature, which help clarify the difference between forensic psychology and forensic neuropsychology.

Psychological Versus Neuropsychological Evaluations

There are practical differences between a psychological and a neuropsychological evaluation, irrespective of whether the evaluation is legal- or treatment-oriented. Traditional psychological methods typically include a detailed clinical interview of the examinee, self-report questionnaires given to the examinee, rating scales given to those who know the examinee, and possibly other assessment methods like scientifically supported prediction formulas (i.e., actuarial models) or structured clinical interviews (First et al., 2016; Hoffmann, 2013; Hoffmann & Estroff, 2001). One important difference between a psychological and a neuropsychological evaluation pertains to the types of tests used.

A neuropsychological evaluation generally involves tests of memory, attention, executive functioning, sensory-motor functioning, and other brain-based functions that are not measured with traditional psychological methods. Notably, these neuropsychological tests are generally *in addition to* the methods used in traditional psychological assessment. In other words, the neuropsychological evaluation builds on the traditional psychological evaluation.

The administration of an intelligence test represents a point of overlap, meaning that both psychologists and neuropsychologists often give intelligence tests. Similarly, both psychologists and neuropsychologists place great importance on validity testing (Larrabee, 2012; Rogers & Bender, 2013), which is performed by both types of professionals to assess the accuracy and trustworthiness of the clinical data that has been collected. Hence, the distinction between a psychological evaluation and a neuropsychological evaluation is not always crisp; there can be gray area. Broadly speaking, however, a neuropsychologist will frequently rely on more cognitive testing than a psychologist. Likewise, a psychologist will often rely on less testing in general, or will use noncognitive tests such as self-report questionnaires that measure family dynamics (Robin et al., 2009) or checklists that measure psychopathy (Hare, 2003).

Neuropsychological testing leads to more accurate detection of brain damage and other cognitive deficits that are often missed by intelligence testing. Faust et al. (2012) explained this as follows: "A major rationale for neuropsychological testing is that it uncovers information that intellectual testing does not and is more sensitive than intellectual testing to neuropsychological deficit or brain damage" (p. 421). Therefore, neuropsychological testing can be particularly helpful in forensic assessment when a defendant's mental capacity or competence is in question. To further appreciate the incremental benefit from neuropsychological testing, the following case study described in Banich and Compton (2018) is illustrative:

> Dr. P. was a successful, middle-aged surgeon who used the financial rewards of his practice to pursue his passion for traveling and playing sports. Tragically, while he was undergoing minor facial surgery, the complications caused his brain to be deprived of oxygen for a short period. The ensuing brain damage had profoundly negative consequences for his mental functioning, compromising his ability to plan, to adapt to change, and to act independently. After the surgical mishap, standard IQ tests revealed Dr. P's intelligence to be, for the most part, in the superior range. Nonetheless, he could not handle many simple day-to-day activities and was unable to appreciate the nature of his deficits. His dysfunction was so severe that returning to work as a surgeon was impossible for him, and his brother had to be appointed Dr. P's legal guardian. (p. 333)

Simply stated, full-battery intelligence testing—as relevant and helpful as it can be in forensic assessment—does not measure certain aspects of cognitive functioning. Likewise, the clinical interview and traditional psychological testing cannot be relied upon to measure cognitive functioning. Hence, neuropsychological testing is often necessary, to generate a completer and more accurate picture of a defendant's cognitive functioning.

Another important distinction between a psychological and a neuropsychological evaluation relates not to the types of assessment methods used, but to the training and experience of the clinician doing the assessment. A forensic evaluator with extensive training and experience in neuropsychology will often view neuropsychological data differently than an evaluator who is not well-versed in neuropsychology. Likewise, an experienced, well-trained neuropsychologist may use different neuropsychological tests or calibrate the scores differently. This is important because different results can be generated depending on methods used, which can significantly affect legal decisions.

For example, a psychologist with a superficial understanding of neuropsychology might administer a battery of neuropsychological screening tests to a 78-year-old criminal defendant with a tenth-grade education, as a part of an adjudicative competence assessment. However, they may not consider that the tests in this screening battery have so much measurement error (discussed in Chapter 3), that the obtained scores cannot be relied upon for important legal decisions. Moreover, they may calibrate the *raw* scores based on both age and education, so that the *standard* scores tell us how the defendant performed compared to other 78-year-olds with limited schooling (Chapter 3 explains raw and standard scores).

Does this neuropsychological information map on to the legal criteria of adjudicative competence, which are loosely based on what is normal in the adult *general population*? No. One could argue that the scores, for this 78-year-old with a tenth-grade education, should be calibrated using a normative standard that is more similar to average adult functioning in the general population. This might call for the use of stratified population norms (Strauss et al., 2006), as are used with intelligence tests, or neuropsychological test norms that reflect a high school diploma *and* a level of cognitive functioning that is typical of most adults, rather than older adults.

By using the older-adult and less-educated norms, the 78-year-old defendant in this example obtains neuropsychological scores that, while beneficial for treatment-oriented purposes, do not convey the fact that, compared to the general population, he may have serious cognitive deficits. This, in turn, makes the defendant seem competent. But this information is very misleading, especially to factfinders (i.e., judges and juries), who cannot reasonably be expected to detect subtle sciolism of this type.

One other point is worth explaining. A neuropsychologist practicing in the United States, more often than not, starts out as a psychologist (Bowers et al., 2002), licensed as such in a given state, but adds to their knowledge base through the following: continuing education, accumulation of relevant experience, possibly completion of postdoctoral training in neuropsychology, and possibly board certification in neuropsychology. Hence, a neuropsychologist has the training and credentials of a psychologist, but has supplemented their skillset, to include extensive knowledge about the field of neuropsychology. This is important to appreciate because sometimes neuropsychologists are incorrectly characterized as having professional skills that are narrowly focused in an area that is tangential to adult criminal or juvenile justice law, when, in fact, neuropsychologists possess the same knowledge base and skills as clinical psychologists—but have gone further into understanding brain-behavior relationships by adding neuropsychological knowledge and tools to their clinical toolbox.

Board Certification

Attainment of board certification in a given mental health specialty indicates that the practitioner met certain foundational and functional competencies at the time that the certification was obtained. However, board certification does not guarantee that a given boarded specialist is better than a non-boarded specialist. Indeed, there are mental health professionals without board certification who are competent to practice, a reality that comports with Melton et al. (2017), who commented that degrees and credentials do not ensure quality work from forensic evaluators.

The pursuit of board certification, which is a national-level vetting process, involves multiple steps, typically including some combination of the following: credential review, relevant work experience, passing a written examination, passing a work sample review, and passing an oral examination. Although professionals completing such a rigorous peer review process are perhaps more likely to be competent to perform essential aspects of the specialty, the current scientific evidence for the superiority of board certification is inadequate. For example, of the scholarship that has been done (e.g., Faust et al., 2012; Lipner et al., 2013; Putnam et al., 1994; Rohling et al., 2003; Sharp et al., 2002; Torres et al., 2012), most of the work comprises opinion, as opposed to empirical investigation. This means that board-certification in a given specialty does not guarantee anything about the skills of the boarded practitioner.

With neuropsychology as an example, Faust et al. (2012) addressed this issue as follows: "… although the diplomate [i.e., board-certification] is sometimes described as an indicator of competence in neuropsychology, there is a lack of evidence to suggest a relation between attainment of the diplomate and diagnostic or predictive accuracy" (p. 368). Similarly, Rohling et al. (2003) concluded that the neuropsychological board-certification process was likely "only certifying between 16 and 52% of competent clinical neuropsychologists" (p. 331). In short, board-certification in neuropsychology should not be blindly accepted as evidence of professional competence, nor should a lack of board-certification be used as evidence of incompetence. This does not mean that future research will not uncover differences between boarded and non-boarded practitioners. Arguably, that line of research should become a priority.

Additionally, those with board certification may have followed different trajectories to obtain their certification. Hence, those with board certification are more heterogenous in their qualifications than one might think. Moreover, attorneys and judges are unlikely to care about how many feathers are in an expert's cap if that expert cannot consistently perform well in real-world settings, which is constantly being reevaluated with each new case. If an eminent forensic expert with an impressive curriculum vitae performs poorly in a given case, it could conceivably reduce the likelihood of ongoing forensic referrals. This is because legal proceedings include challenging cross-examination, not unlike the peer-review process in the scientific arena. In this regard, forensic assessment is more intellectually competitive and transparent than treatment-oriented assessment, which tends to involve much less scrutiny and corrective feedback. Although board certification is perhaps a sign of one's commitment to (a) a rigorous peer-review process, (b) demonstrating professional competence, and (c) continuing education, it is not a license for professional complacence or arrogance. Hence, cross-examining attorneys—whose courtroom performances are also under the microscope with each new case—should challenge experts with thoughtful cross-examination, designed to exclude low-quality evidence and to elicit all relevant facts. And experts should embrace this process.

"Evaluations," "Assessments," and "Examinations"

We are not aware of any meaningful distinctions between the terms "assessment" and "evaluation," so we use them interchangeably to mean a methodical process of collecting and interpreting psychological or neuropsychological data on defendants who are involved in the adult criminal, or juvenile justice systems. A more formal definition of "assessment" from the American Educational Research Association et al. (AERA, 2014) is helpful:

> Any systematic method of obtaining information, used to draw inferences about characteristics of people, objects, or programs; a systematic process to measure or evaluate the characteristics or performances of individuals, programs, or other entities, for purposes of drawing inferences; sometimes used synonymously with *test*. (p. 216)

The terms "assessment" and "evaluation" can be used interchangeably with a third term, "examination," which is encountered in the Federal Rules of Civil Procedure. As will be explained more later, this process, whether called evaluating, assessing, or examining, involves various combinations of the following: record review, interviewing of others (who know the defendant), interviewing of the defendant, observing the defendant, and psychological or neuropsychological testing of the defendant.

The Rules of Evidence, and Why They Matter for Forensic Assessment

Returning briefly to the two examples from earlier, the psychological and neuropsychological data collected on the young man with the moderate to severe TBI will be sized up differently than that collected on the female criminal defendant in one particularly important way: the female defendant's data, because it was collected for the explicit purpose of a legal question (i.e., adjudicative competence), will be filtered through that court system's evidentiary rules. By "evidentiary rules," we are referring to the Federal Rules of Evidence (FREs) at the federal level, or a given state's equivalent of those rules at the state level. In practical terms, this means that the criminal defendant's data must successfully pass multiple legal litmus tests before it can be relied upon as evidence in a court of law.

Because state governments and the federal government are "separate sovereigns," they each have their own rules limiting what facts lawyers may present to a factfinder (i.e., the judge or jury). Many states have modeled their rules in whole or in part on the FREs, though there are individual variations. The FREs were enacted in the United States in July of 1975 and are a collection of eleven articles, each of which contain different rules—Rule 101 through Rule 1103—concerning the specific circumstances under which evidence can be admitted into federal courts. Congress, with much input from the judiciary, created these rules to standardize how evidence is admitted and rejected throughout the federal system.

These rules, invoked by lawyers on both sides in courtrooms and interpreted by judges, dictate what information offered by one side or the other as proof of its claim will ultimately be considered by the factfinders as evidence in the case. The goal of these rules is a fair trial as guaranteed by the U.S. Constitution, with the role of the judge as gatekeeper (Faust et al., 2010). Hence, in order for psychological or neuropsychological data on a criminal defendant to be admitted into a court as evidence, that information must successfully pass through this legal sieve. The rules are designed so that proposed evidence is admitted unless opposing counsel objects to it, using one of the rules as a basis. The judge then rules on that objection, and the proposed evidence is either allowed to be presented to the factfinder (i.e., it is "admitted") or it is rejected (i.e., it is "excluded").

FREs with Particular Relevance to Forensic Evaluations

There are many FREs covering many different aspects of evidence—for example, relevance, prejudice, validity, and so forth. But some will have more pertinence to forensic psychological and neuropsychological assessment. Table 2.2 contains short summaries of the FREs that are most likely to be of interest to the forensic evaluator.

Of the short summaries in Table 2.2, some—more than others—should be fleshed out further. Rule 104(a) may be the first encounter that an expert has

Table 2.2 FREs with relevance to forensic psychology and forensic neuropsychology

Rule	*Significance*
104(a). Preliminary questions … in general.	"The court must decide any preliminary question about whether a witness is qualified … the court is not bound by evidence rules, except those on privilege." **Preliminary questioning of a potential expert, a form of "*voir dire*," can identify unqualified experts.**
104(c). Preliminary questions … a hearing without jury present.	"The court must conduct any hearing on a preliminary question so that the jury cannot hear it if: (1) the hearing involves the admissibility of a confession …" **If the referral question pertains to the validity of a confession and/or waiving of Miranda rights, a suppression hearing without the jury will take place first.**
106. … Recorded statements.	"If a party introduces all or part of a … recorded statement, an adverse party may require the introduction … of any other part—or any other … recorded statement—that in fairness out to be considered at the same time." **If one party shares part of an audio or video recording, the opposing party can obtain*all*recorded statements.**
201(b). Kinds of facts that may be judicially noticed.	"The court may judicially notice [i.e., automatically accept into evidence] a fact that is not subject to reasonable dispute [i.e., both parties in a dispute agree]." **If both sides of a dispute agree on admission of a fact, it will be admitted forthwith.**
401. Test for relevant evidence.	"Evidence is relevant if: (a) it has any tendency to make a fact more or less probable than it would be without the evidence; and (b) the fact is of consequence in determining the action." **Information will be deemed relevant—and admitted as evidence by the court—if that information satisfies certain requirements.**
402. General admissibility of relevant evidence.	"Relevant evidence is admissible unless [otherwise stated in the United States Constitution, a federal statute, the FREs, or the Supreme Court says so] … Irrelevant evidence is not admissible." **Any information deemed irrelevant is not admissible as evidence; *and* even relevant evidence will be blocked from admission if other rules (e.g., United States Constitution, a federal statute, the FREs, or the Supreme Court) say so.**
403. Excluding relevant evidence for prejudice, confusion, waste of time, or other reasons.	"The court may exclude relevant evidence if its probative value is substantially outweighed by a danger of one more of the following: unfair prejudice, confusing the issues, misleading the jury, undue delay, waste of time, or needlessly presenting cumulative evidence."

(*Continued*)

Table 2.2 (Continued)

Rule	*Significance*
	Even relevant evidence can be blocked from admission if its value is overridden by its liabilities (e.g., creating prejudice, confusing issues, misleading the jury, causing delay, wasting time, being overly cumulative).
501. Privilege in general.	"The common law—as interpreted by United States courts in the light of reason and experience—governs a claim of privilege unless any of the following provides otherwise: • the United States Constitution; • a federal statute; or • rules prescribed by the Supreme Court.But in a civil case, state law governs privilege regarding a claim or defense for which state law supplies the rule of decision." **Legal privilege (i.e., "a special right or exemption that the law allows to a person or class of persons" [Clapp, 2007, p. 206]) can be asserted under some circumstances, including psychotherapists and their patients. Hence, psychotherapist-patient communication is legally protected (see *Jaffee v. Redmond*, 1996).**
701. Opinion testimony by lay witnesses.	"If a witness is not testifying as an expert, testimony in the form of an opinion is limited to one that is: (a) rationally based on the witness's perception; (b) helpful to clearly understanding the witness's testimony or to determining a fact in issue; and (c) not based on scientific, technical, or other specialized knowledge within the scope or Rule 702." **Non-expert witnesses (i.e., fact/lay/sentient witnesses) can testify about their sensory perceptions (what they saw, heard, smelled, etc.) but are very limited about offering opinions.**
702. Testimony by experts.	"A witness who is qualified as an expert by knowledge, skill, experience, training, or education [Rule 104(a)] may testify in the form of an opinion or otherwise if: (a) the expert's scientific, technical, or other specialized knowledge [*Kumho v. Carmichael*, 1999] will help the trier of fact to understand the evidence or to determine a fact in issue; (b) the testimony is based on sufficient facts or data [*Daubert v. M.D.P.*, 1993; *G.E. v. Joiner*, 1997]; (c) the testimony is the product of reliable principles and methods [*Daubert v. M.D.P.*, 1993; *G.E. v. Joiner*, 1997]; and (d) the expert has reliably applied the principles and methods to the facts of the case [*G.E. v. Joiner*, 1997]." **Qualification as an expert in a case means the expert is believed to possess perspectives on issues**

(*Continued*)

Table 2.2 (Continued)

Rule	*Significance*
	that—if effectively shared with the factfinders in the form of an opinion—will increase the ability of the factfinders to make a just decision. Expert opinions must be solidly anchored in and logically flow from both (a) expert-related data and (b) trustworthy, expert-related ways of doing things. The expert must behave within the case (e.g., collect data, opine) in a way that meshes with the expert's area of expertise.
703. Bases of expert's opinion testimony.	"An expert may base an opinion on facts or data in the case that the expert has been made aware of or personally observed. If experts in the particular field would reasonably rely on those kinds of facts or data in forming an opinion on the subject, they need not be admissible for the opinion to be admitted. But if the facts or data would otherwise be inadmissible, the proponent of the opinion may disclose them to the jury only if their probative value in helping the jury evaluate the opinion substantially outweighs their prejudicial effect." **Expert opinion can be based on *any* information—but only if reliance on this information is reasonably typical of the expert's field. However, if this information—relied upon by the expert to form the opinion—would otherwise *not* be admitted as evidence, the judge may limit how much of this information is admitted, meshing with Rule 403.**
704(a) and (b). Opinion on Ultimate Issue.	(a) "An opinion is not objectionable just because it embraces an ultimate issue." (b) "In a criminal case, an expert witness must not state an opinion about whether the defendant did or did not have a mental state or condition that constitutes an element of the crime charged or of a defense. Those matters are for the trial of fact alone." **Experts*can*opine on the ultimate legal issue; however, experts in federal courts *cannot* opine about mental state at the time of the act(s) charged. (Notably, this limitation does not extend to all states. For example, in NM, experts *can* opine about a defendant's mental state at the time of the act[s] charged.)**
705. Disclosure of facts or data underlying expert opinion.	"Unless the court orders otherwise, an expert may state an opinion—and give the reasons for it—without first testifying to the underlying facts or data. But the expert may be required to disclose those facts or data on cross-examination." **Those having qualified as an expert in a particular case can opine about matters related to their**

(Continued)

Table 2.2 (Continued)

Rule	*Significance*
	expertise without establishing the foundation or basis for their opinion; however, and in accord with Rule 702, these experts must provide the foundation or basis for their opinions when asked to do so, which often occurs during cross-examination.
706. Court-appointed expert witnesses.	"On a party's motion or on its own, the court may order the parties to show cause why expert witnesses should not be appointed." "The court may appoint an expert that the parties agree on and any of its own choosing. But the court may only appoint someone who consents to act." "The court must inform the expert of the expert's duties." "The expert: (1) must advise the parties of any findings the expert makes; (2) may be deposed by any party; (3) may be called to testify by the court or any party; and (4) may be cross-examined by any party, including the party that called the expert." "The expert is entitled to reasonable compensation, as set by the court …" "The court may authorize disclosure to the jury that the court appointed the expert.""This rule does not limit a party in calling its own experts." **If willing, and if both sides agree, the court can appoint an expert, whom the court will then inform about their duties. Court-appointed experts must share their findings with both parties and be available for testimony, including cross-examination by both sides and the judge. Court-appointed experts receive financial payment for their services at a rate set by the court. The jury can know that the expert is court-appointed. A party in a dispute can still hire their own experts.**
803 (4) (A) and (B). Exceptions to the rule against hearsay … statement made for medical diagnosis or treatment.	(A) "is made for—and is reasonably pertinent to—medical diagnosis or treatment" (B) describes medical history; past or present symptoms or sensation; their inception; or their general cause." **Statements with reasonable pertinence to medical diagnosis, treatment, medical history, or symptoms/sensations are not excluded as hearsay.**
803 (18) (B). Statements in learned treatises, periodical, or pamphlets.	(A) "the statement [from a learned treatise] is called to the attention of an expert witness on cross-examination or relied on by the expert on direct examination" (B) "the publication is established as a reliable authority by the expert's admission or testimony, by another expert's testimony, or by judicial notice." **Statements in learned treatises (i.e., important, widely accepted writings) in the expert's field are not excluded as hearsay.**

(*Continued*)

Table 2.2 (Continued)

Rule	*Significance*
901 (a). Authenticating or identifying evidence in general.	"To satisfy the requirement of authenticating or identifying an item of evidence, the proponent must produce evidence sufficient to support a finding that the item is what the proponent claims it is." **For an item (e.g., a psychological test) to be admitted as evidence, the proponent of the item as evidence must first prove the item is what the proponent says it is.**
1101 (d) (1). Applicability of the rules … exceptions.	"These rules—except for those on privilege—do not apply to the following: (1) the court's determination, under Rule 104(a), on a preliminary question of fact governing admissibility." **The trial judge can override the FREs, excluding those pertaining to legal privilege, when making a decision about allowing testimony by an expert.**

with the application of the Rules of Evidence. If opposing counsel requests it, potential forensic experts must undergo a preliminary vetting process called *voir dire* ("to say truly"), which is an evaluation of the witness, to ensure that they in fact have expertise that would allow them to become an expert witness.

Rule 106 concerns audio or video recordings of events that are later submitted as evidence. In this context, it is sometimes invoked in situations where experts use a recording device during their assessment,[1] which can add to the quality and transparency of an assessment when used during a clinical interview (Otto & Krauss, 2009). However, if the expert relies on portions of that recorded information during their evaluation, *all* of what they have recorded becomes available to the opposing party—including information damaging to retaining party's case. Experts who want to use a recording device should consult with the retaining attorney, and must think through interview questions in advance. Otherwise, they may inadvertently elicit and memorialize information that violates a defendant's rights.

Rule 403 is important insofar as an expert generates evidence that, despite its relevance to the case, comes with so many problems that the relevant evidence is not worthwhile. To illustrate, consider the *Hare Psychopathy Checklist* (PCL; Hare, 2003), a well-researched instrument used to measure the construct of psychopathy. Although there is no doubt that this tool is extremely relevant to questions of future offending in the community, the name of the test could function as a liability, if it were to negatively bias factfinders against a defendant, by resulting in the labeling of the defendant as a "psychopath." This liability is particularly serious if the youth version of the PCL is used to label a teenager as a "psychopath," given that many wayward teens outgrow their antisocial behavior patterns by the time they reach adulthood (Loeber, 1990; Loeber et al., 1993) and given that the authors of the youth PCL include the following statement within the test manual (Forth et al., 2003): "It is inappropriate for clinicians or other professionals to label a youth as a 'psychopath'" (p. 17).

Rule 702 incorporates the holdings of three landmark U.S. Supreme Court cases, known as the "Daubert Trilogy": *Daubert v. Merrell Dow Pharmaceuticals, Inc.* (1993); *General Electric v. Joiner* (1997); and *Kumho Tire Company Ltd. v. Carmichael* (1999). Therefore, it is valuable for the expert to have a working knowledge of these three cases in order to fully understand Rule 702. The *Daubert* case, which applies to federal courts and states that have adopted *Daubert*, includes four tests flexibly used by judges to assess the admissibility of methods used by experts: (1) methods must be "scientifically valid," (2) methods must be "published or subjected to peer review," (3) methods must have a "known or potential rate of error," and (4) methods must have some "general acceptance" within the scientific community. The significance of the *Joiner* decision is that testimony by an expert can be excluded by the judge if an expert's opinion does not flow in a reasonably causal way from the expert's data ("Nothing in either *Daubert* or the Federal Rules of Evidence requires a district court judge to admit opinion evidence that is connected to existing data only by the *ipse dixit* [i.e., it-is-so-because-I-said-so logic] of the expert. A court may conclude that there is simply too great an analytical gap between the data and the opinion proffered."). *Kumho* is significant because it extended *Daubert* to experience-based methods, not only to science-based methods.

Rule 703 is relevant to forensic assessment because it effectively gives those qualified as an expert very wide latitude, and makes it possible for the expert to rely on information that would not be admissible if presented by a layperson. Rule 703 underscores the significant difference between expert witnesses (Rule 702) and fact/lay/sentient witnesses (Rule 701). Not unlike a queen in the game of chess, expert witnesses have much more latitude and potential to influence legal outcomes than do fact/lay/sentient witnesses. Because experts have such tremendous potential power, courts must effectively function as gatekeepers, as called for under Rule 702. Otherwise, experts may, accidentally or otherwise, abuse the power that comes from Rule 703, in effect masquerading as an expert on matters about which they lack expertise.

To illustrate, consider the expert who successfully gets through *voir dire* (Rule 104[a]), but then violates the tether range of Rule 702 with *ipse dixit* (i.e., it is so because I say it is so) reasoning that is divorced from scientific methodology. Such and individual, using the power that comes from Rule 703, could conceivably open the floodgates to unreliable information, using the pretext that "experts in the particular field would reasonably rely on those kinds of facts or data in forming an opinion on the subject."

Rule 1101(d) (1) states that expert testimony can be overridden entirely, if a judge decides to do so. This has never occurred in cases any of us have been involved in, so it is reasonable to conclude that it is uncommon.

Flowchart for Psychological and Neuropsychological Evidence Generation

Based on work by Marlowe (1995) and Heilbrun (1992), we have developed a flowchart for thinking about evidence of a psychological or neuropsychological nature (see Figure 2.1). The flowchart is intended to help forensic evaluators appreciate how their work is utilized by attorneys and judges, and to help attorneys and judges appreciate how forensic evaluators function within a legal framework. In this section, we explain this flow chart.

Voir Dire of the Prospective Expert Witness

As conveyed previously, the French translation of *voir dire* is "to say truly." Although this can mean questioning of prospective jurors from the venire (i.e., "jury pool"), it is a term that is also used to describe the vetting of prospective expert witnesses. It can be helpful if prospective experts generate questions for retaining counsel to use during *voir dire* of the expert, since attorneys may not know what stands out among the expert's qualifications as most impressive and relevant.

To illustrate, some experts may list membership with certain organizations as a credential, when all one has to do is pay the organization to be a member. Such a membership can be contrasted with board-certification, research publications, or

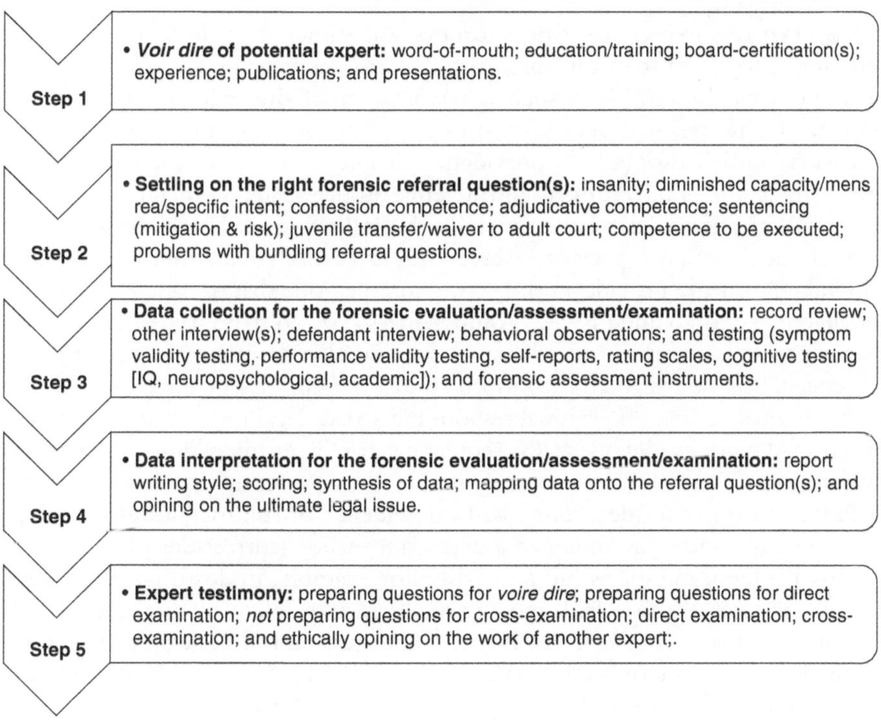

Figure 2.1 Flowchart for psychological and neuropsychological evidence generation.

Table 2.3 Potential questions to ask prospective psychological or neuropsychological experts during *voir dire*

"What degrees to you have?"
"Have you completed any postdoctoral training?"
"What board certifications do you have?"
"What exactly does board certification require?"
"What exactly do you do for a living?"
"How many years have you been practicing?"
"About how many peer-reviewed publications do you have?"
"What does 'peer-reviewed' mean and why is that important?"
"How many book chapters or books have you authored?"
"About how many psychological (or neuropsychological) evaluations have you conducted?"
"About how many times have you testified in court?"
"About how many times have you testified in a deposition?"

other relevant and more meaningful experiences, any of which require much more effort and peer review of the prospective expert. Table 2.3 contains potential questions to use during this early phase of evidence generation.

Settling on the Right Forensic Referral Question(s)

It has been our experience that attorneys sometimes struggle to know what question(s) to ask of their mental health expert. And yet this is a task that must be done well, because it is such a crucial part of the evidence-generation process. Therefore, it is necessary to explain this topic in more detail.

Packer and Grisso (2011) provided a helpful way of classifying referral questions in the adult criminal and juvenile justice systems. In their systems-based classification outline, they include the following six broad categories of referral questions: (1) capacity to waive Fifth and Sixth Amendment rights (i.e., Miranda rights) and provide a valid confession (i.e., one that is made knowingly, intelligently, and voluntarily); (2) competencies (viz., to stand trial, plead guilty, waive counsel, testify, proceed *pro se* [i.e., legally representing oneself], be sentenced, and be executed); (3) jurisdictional transfer of a juvenile (e.g., to an adult criminal court); (4) criminal responsibility (i.e., legal insanity and *mens rea*/diminished capacity defenses); (5) sentencing based on mitigating evidence or evidence of risk for future offending (either in the community or in a secure facility); and (6) other decisions based on evidence of risk for future offending (e.g., pretrial secure placement of a defendant or post-corrections placement).

Other referral questions can also arise. For example, in death penalty cases, forensic evaluators are relied upon to ascertain if a defendant has intellectual disability (*Atkins v. Virginia*, 2002) and, as a result, cannot be legally executed. Similarly, in the state of New Mexico, NMSA 1978 § 31-9-1.6, 1999, calls for an assessment of the defendant's IQ, although for a different reason (i.e., those found incompetent, dangerous, and "mentally retarded" in the state of New

Mexico are only subject to civil commitment, not criminal prosecution or criminal commitment; see *State v. Jacob F*, 2019, in Section II). But these six categories of questions from Packer and Grisso encapsulate the typical referral questions that are asked of the forensic evaluator in the adult criminal or juvenile justice setting.

Legal professionals sometimes do not realize that there is not one single, generic "psych eval" that is done to address forensic referral questions. For example, an assessment directed at adjudicative competence is not likely to include questions about the mental state of the defendant during the acts charged. In fact, an assessment of adjudicative competence should generally circumnavigate interview questions that begin to flirt with a violation of a defendant's Fifth Amendment right against self-incrimination. Similarly, an assessment of a defendant's capacity to waive Fifth and Sixth Amendment rights during the course of a police interrogation is not likely to involve interview questions about the acts charged. The landmark U.S. Supreme Court case of *Estelle v. Smith* (1981), involving a forensic psychiatrist who used information from a competency evaluation for the purposes of opining on future dangerousness without informing the defendant or their attorney, perhaps best captures how much damage an evaluating expert can do when they operate without discretion or respect for a defendant's constitutional rights.

In contrast, an assessment of criminal responsibility (also known as mental state at the time of the offense), which involves looking into legal insanity and/or *mens rea* (i.e., "guilty mind"), *demands* that the experts inquire—at length—about the details of the act(s) charged. Similarly, an assessment of future offending in the community requires that the expert seek out information on the defendant with a high likelihood of being inculpatory. To appreciate this last point, consider how probing and personal some of the items are on the Hare PCL, the Violence Risk Appraisal Guide-Revised (Rice et al., 2013), the Structured Assessment of Violence Risk in Youth (Borum et al., 2006), and the Youth Level of Service/Case Management Inventory 2.0 (Hoge & Andrews, 2011), four of the best instruments used to appraise the likelihood of future offending. For example, the Hare PCL seeks evidence that the defendant is a pathological liar, lacks remorse, and cannot form empathy—all information that could have an inculpatory, if not prejudicial effect. Therefore, legal professionals must understand that forensic evaluators develop and utilize different assessment protocols for each referral question and that it is very important to settle on the right referral question well in advance.

Relatedly, effective legal professionals appreciate that an ethical informed consent or notification process,[2] carried out by forensic evaluators before they start the formal assessment process, requires that the evaluator explain the purpose of the assessment to the defendant. This includes informing the defendant what the referral question is. If the retaining attorney has not clearly settled on a referral question in advance, the forensic evaluator will not be able to obtain a truly informed consent from the defendant; at best, they will obtain an *uninformed* consent, which is insufficient because the defendant has not been given fair warning about how the information elicited from them will be used in their case.

Problems can arise when attorneys ask multiple referral questions at once. These so-called "bundled" evaluations can increase the likelihood that the evaluator will generate evidence that is harmful to a defendant's case by violating their rights (e.g., their Fifth Amendment right to *not* self-incriminate). To illustrate, one of us was once hired by a defense lawyer to assess adjudicative competence, but also risk for future offending in the community, on the same defendant at the same time. The defendant was found to be incompetent, which retaining counsel was pleased to learn. But the defendant was also found to be at an extremely elevated risk for re-offending, if released into the community.

Had the retaining attorney only asked the single question of adjudicative competence, nothing would have been learned about all the proverbial skeletons in this defendant's closet—skeletons that significantly upped the odds that he would return to his wayward habits if released. Additionally, no inculpatory evidence would have been generated by the defendant's defense counsel. Hence, when multiple referral questions are asked of the forensic evaluator, evidence may be generated that does not mesh with the goals of retaining counsel—particularly if the nature of the bundled referral questions differs.

For example, two questions pertaining to two different legal competencies or capacities may yield very similar findings, because the evaluative processes are similar; a defendant found *incompetent* to proceed may also be found *incapable* of intelligently waiving Miranda rights. In contrast, if the evaluator is asked to look into both a legal competence *and* risk for future offending, the likelihood of inculpatory findings not germane to the question of competence may increase. Moreover, addressing two referral questions requires more time and effort from the evaluator, which is more expensive. If the evaluator can effectively address a single referral question, thereby helping the factfinder(s) to make a more just decision about a particular matter (e.g., a legal competence), there may be no need to ask other referral questions.

It is best for attorneys to think through the different forensic referral questions before committing to one. Part of this process will often include discussion with the expert. Attorneys who do this are more likely to get answers to their questions that help their case; such attorneys are also considerably less likely to find themselves blindsided by the outcome of the evaluation.

In contrast, attorneys who give little prior thought to the importance of a well-formulated referral question and who rush into the assessment process with their evaluators may get answers to questions that they do not want. Asking the right referral question, at the right time, with the right defendant, can make all the difference. Similarly, asking the wrong referral question, at the wrong time, with the wrong defendant, can generate evidence that is unhelpful to the defendant's legal goals, or outright harmful. Moreover, it can be an expensive waste of time and resources.

Data Collection for the Forensic Evaluation

Lally (2003) used the word "tripod" to describe three essential sources of information for the evaluating forensic expert: record review, interview of the defendant, and test data. To these we add the following: *interview of other(s)* and *appearance and behavioral observations* of the defendant during the interview and testing process. All five of these data-collection topics are explained next, beginning with record review.

Record Review

Forensic evaluators are expected to seek out relevant records for review as a part of a comprehensive forensic assessment (American Psychological Association, 2013; Lally, 2003). However, we are not aware of any widely adopted standards or even guidelines for forensic evaluators with regard to *precisely* what records to seek out and what records to avoid. But this does not mean that experts have carte blanche when it comes to obtaining collateral records to review. To illustrate, it is conceivable that a medical record would contain information of a highly personal nature (e.g., documentation of a sexually transmitted disease) that has nothing to do with the referral question. Similarly, it is within the realm of possibility that a defendant's psychotherapist might document statements made by the defendant that were elicited on the grounds that the statements would be legally protected under therapist-patient privilege (e.g., *Jaffee v. Redmond*, 1996; FRE 501).

If one zooms out to view this issue from afar, it seems reasonable to conclude that some sort of gatekeeping needs to happen with regard to what records can *legally* and *ethically* be reviewed by the forensic expert. One possible strategy is that the expert could defer to the attorneys with regard to legal violations to be avoided, including therapist-patient privilege, protections related to the Fifth Amendment right against self-incrimination, and other laws. Meanwhile, the expert could assume responsibility for ethical professional behavior related to record review, which includes avoiding harm, not going beyond what is stated during the informed consent process, minimizing intrusions on privacy, and so forth. If one were to adopt this strategy, the expert might craft a statement for the legal party retaining their services (i.e., retaining legal counsel or the court), to be included in a service agreement. Possible examples of such statements are contained in Table 2.4.

Although a gatekeeping responsibility is needed to exclude certain records (e.g., medical records with sensitive and irrelevant information or records protected by therapist-patient privilege), other records are less likely to require gatekeeping. Moreover, these other records may be very germane to the referral question. It would always, for instance, be relevant to obtain medical records documenting *current* medications. Similarly, school records would seem to be relevant to criminal referral questions pertaining to a legal competence. Likewise, prior mental health assessments directed toward mental

Table 2.4 Possible statements for retaining parties regarding collateral records

Please provide me with any available records on the defendant that have relevance to the referral question(s), but which do not violate legal privileges (e.g., therapist-patient privilege), constitutional rights (e.g., the Fifth Amendment right against self-incrimination), or any laws. I am not an attorney, so I am relying on you to function as a gatekeeper, to ensure that I do not unintentionally or unknowingly break any laws or otherwise violate the legal rights of the defendant.
In order to fulfill my professional responsibility as an evaluating expert, my field requires that I make reasonable efforts to obtain collateral records that are relevant to the referral question(s). Therefore, please provide me with all discoverable records with relevance to the referral question(s).
Please provide me with all *discoverable* records with relevance to the referral question(s). Please do not exclude a *discoverable* record only because it contains information that you believe might affect my opinion. Please do exclude records that are clearly irrelevant to the referral question(s) and/or that violate the defendant's legal privileges, constitutional rights, or any laws.
Because the referral question pertains to mental state at the time of the offense, I am specifically requesting the following records: police reports that document the alleged criminal behavior that supports the criminal charges; audio or video records of the arrest; medical records documenting medication taken by the defendant *at the time of the acts charged*; toxicology reports at the time of the arrest; and the full statutory definition of each criminal charge, including wording that conveys any specific intent. Other records that are of potential relevance include these: medical records documenting *current* medications; school records; and mental health assessment records that document a mental diagnosis, cognitive functioning, and/or validity of assessment data.
Because the referral question pertains to risk for offending in the community, I am requesting *all* available school, mental health, medical, and legal records on the defendant.

health diagnosis, cognitive functioning, or validity of assessment data would also seem highly relevant to criminal referral questions of legal competence.

If the referral question pertains to mental state at the time of the offense (i.e., insanity or *mens rea*/diminished capacity), police reports, witness statements and relevant audio or video recordings (e.g., at the time of the arrest), documentation of prescribed medication at the time of the acts charged, post-arrest toxicology reports, and a full definition of the criminal charges—containing all of the elements of each charge—should be requested by the evaluator. With regard to a full definition of the criminal charges, this is necessary if the referral question pertains to *mens rea*/diminished capacity. That is, in order to opine that the defendant did, or did not, have the requisite *mens rea* ("guilty mind" or specific intent), one must know what elements of each charge contain this higher level of *mens rea.* A defendant might be charged with several crimes, only some of which may have elements of specific intent, and this is very important for the evaluator to know.

Overall, we cannot see any obvious legal or ethical reason why a forensic mental health expert, addressing a criminal or juvenile justice referral question, would *not* want to obtain medical records documenting *current* medications, school records, or mental health assessment records that document mental diagnosis, cognitive functioning, or the validity of assessment data. At the same time, ethical reasons to exclude specific details from these collateral records may arise, requiring of the expert some calibration of their professional conduct (e.g., redaction of certain information). If the referral question centers around mental state at the time of the offense, other records (e.g., police reports, audio or video recordings of the arrest, post-arrest toxicology reports) also become relevant and should be requested. Similarly, if the forensic evaluator is asked to render an opinion on potential for future offending in the community, safeguards on the extent of collateral records become less relevant, because this referral question demands access to the most inculpatory information in a defendant's past.

Finally, it is worth noting that defense attorneys have to make strategic decisions about what information can make its way into discovery. As a result, there may be times where a forensic evaluator wants collateral information from retaining defense counsel, in order to properly address a referral question, but defense counsel opts to *not* provide the information. Under these circumstances, it would be necessary for the forensic evaluator to describe any limitations imposed on their assessment as a result of not being granted access to requested records.

Interview of Other(s)

It can be extremely valuable to obtain the perspectives of others who know the defendant. In death penalty cases, this is essentially a requirement (e.g., Cunningham, 2010; DeMatteo et al., 2011; *Rompilla v. Beard*, 2005). However, some family members may minimize or overstate deficits and problems when describing a defendant, or they may themselves have the same limitations as the defendant (e.g., a lower IQ), which can result in information that is less helpful than one might think (e.g., consider the Dilution Effect, discussed later; Nisbett et al., 1981). But sometimes information generated from interviewing others can make or break a case.

For example, one of us was involved in an assessment pertaining to risk for future offending in the community. The defendant, through the clinical interview and testing, provided no information to suggest he would be at risk for offending if released into the community. In fact, he was quite intelligent (Full Scale IQ = 118), very reasonable, and generally likeable. But when his adult children, ex-wife, and siblings were interviewed, it quickly became evident that he was a very high risk.

Because the pregnancy is so important for healthy brain development (Bakker et al., 2011; Cokkinides et al., 1999; DiPietro, 2004; Hackshaw et al., 2011; Little, 1998; Milberger et al., 1997; Polanska et al., 2015), interviewing the mothers of criminal defendants about pregnancy health and meeting of important developmental milestones can pay dividends. To illustrate, if an evaluator learns that the pregnancy was not planned, that the mother consumed alcohol during the first trimester before realizing she was pregnant, and that the defendant suffered anoxia (i.e., lack of oxygen to the brain) during a complicated delivery, the evaluator can be on the lookout for the sort of cognitive deficits that might translate into legal incompetence, or support a diagnosis of intellectual disability in a death penalty case. Notably, this is the sort of information that can be extremely valuable when the referral question centers around mitigation for the purposes of sentencing. It is also information that a criminal defense attorney can obtain, as a part of deciding whether their client might benefit from an in-depth mental health assessment.

When eliciting background information like this from someone who knows the defendant, it is essential to apprise the informant about the purpose of the assessment, before ambushing them with invasive interview questions. Similarly, it can be very helpful to think through, and list the exact questions to be asked. At the same time, the evaluator does not want to be so rigid and inflexible with their questions that they fail to elicit important information.

Interview of Defendant

Rogers and Shuman (2006) wrote, "We maintain that standardization is the bedrock of empirically based knowledge. Without standardization, diagnoses and forensic conclusions are vulnerable to imprecision and error" (p. 368). These same authors include structured clinical interviews as an example of a standardized, empirically based methodology. We agree. Therefore, some sort of structured interview like the Structured Clinical Interview for DSM-5 (SCID-5) (First et al., 2016), the Practical Adolescent Dual Diagnosis Interview (PADDI) (Hoffmann & Estroff, 2001), or the Comprehensive Addictions and Psychological Evaluation-5 (CAPE-5) (Hoffmann, 2013) is recommended with defendants. That said, when clinicians become overly rigid about eliciting information from those they evaluate, they might miss something valuable, a message well articulated by Meyer et al. (2001):

> When interviews are highly structured, clinicians can lose the forest for the trees and make precise but errant judgments (Hammond, 1996; Tucker, 1998). Such mistakes may occur when the clinician focuses on responses to specific interview questions (e.g., diagnostic criteria) without fully considering the salience of these responses in the patient's broader life context or without adequately recognizing how the individual responses fit together into a symptomatically coherent pattern. (p. 144)

One of us conducted a forensic assessment of a young woman that illustrates the importance of flexibility in interviewing. The young woman arrived to the appointment with her father, but she was so paranoid that she could not bring herself to get out of the car. To accommodate her, the evaluator came out of the office and engaged the defendant, and her father, in a highly unstructured conversation, characterized not by planned and sequential interview questions, but by a very soft tone of voice and down-to-Earth conversation—all carefully chosen to get past the defendant's paranoia. It took about 30 minutes, but it worked. Once the defendant was comfortably in the office, the evaluator was then able to proceed by using a structured-interview approach.

Appearance and Behavioral Observations

It is one thing to observe that a defendant is wearing unfashionable clothing or that they are losing their hair. It is another thing altogether to observe, through careful measurement and use of appropriate norms (Nellhaus, 1968), that the defendant has *microcephaly*, an uncommonly small head circumference known to correspond with cognitive and intellectual deficits (Maria, 2009; Ropper, 2009). Similarly, a defendant with a resting tremor may be suffering from a disease of the basal ganglia on the contralateral (i.e., opposite) side of their brain from the tremor; alternatively, a defendant with an intention tremor, detected using the finger-to-nose test, may have disease of the cerebellum on the ipsilateral (i.e., same) side of their brain as the tremor (Banich & Compton, 2018).

Observations like these are relevant to forensic assessments because tremors, categorized under the larger umbrella term of hyperkinetic movements, can point toward neurological disorders that can subtly or severely affect cognitive functioning. If, for example, it is determined that a defendant has Parkinson's disease, it is known that about 40% of these individuals will develop dementia (American Psychiatric Association, 2013). If, for example, it is learned that the defendant has Huntington's disease, it is known that those afflicted will die within about 15 years after motor symptoms first appear (American Psychiatric Association, 2013).

Forensic evaluators spend considerable amounts of time sitting across the table from defendants, perhaps more than the attorneys, judges, and members of the jury. It follows, therefore, that this time should be used wisely by the evaluator, which means being on the lookout for soft and hard neurological signs, which may prove to be clinical bread crumbs that get the forensic evaluator closer to a scientific answer to a legal question. Table 2.5 contains common soft and hard neurological signs to consider when observing a criminal defendant during a forensic assessment. Larner (2016) provides a more in-depth look at neurological signs.

Testing

A psychological or neuropsychological test is "an evaluative device or procedure in which a systematic sample of a test taker's behavior in a specified domain is obtained and scored using a standardized process" (AERA et al., 2014, p. 224). Testing is not new. It has been used for centuries, going back at least to about 2200 B.C., when Chinese law required the use of tests to ensure that public officials were competent (Bush & Kaufman, in press). Table 2.6 contains landmark historical events in the history of psychological and neuropsychological testing.

Table 2.5 Common soft and hard neurological signs with potential relevance to forensic assessment

Soft Neurological Signs	*Hard Neurological Signs*
Motor overflow (i.e., when intentional motor activity sparks unintentional motor activity; *posturing* is contralateral motor stiffening and *mirroring* is contralateral motor activity that is identical on both sides)	Visual field defects (i.e., partial blind spots [scotomas] or entire blind areas with a brain-based cause; CN II)
Truncal ataxia (i.e., imbalance; often involves cerebellum dysfunction; measured with Romberg test; enlarged ventricles [hydrocephalus] can affect pathways projecting from the rear of the brain to the frontal lobes, causing truncal ataxia)	Cerebral palsy (i.e., motor dysfunction with a brain-based cause, originating very early development, usually in utero or during a complicated delivery)
Appendicular ataxia (i.e., difficulty with smooth and precise manual-motor timing and coordination; measured with finger-to-nose test or heel-to-shin test; also called *dysmetria;* possible cerebellum dysfunction)	Hemiplegia (i.e., paralysis on one side of the body caused by brain damage/ dysfunction; often a result of stroke, infections, TBI, multiple sclerosis)
Dysdiadochokinesis (i.e., difficulty generating rapid, alternating motor movements; measured with the hand-to-thigh test; possible cerebellum dysfunction).	Seizures (i.e., electrical disturbance in the brain caused by imbalance between inhibitory and excitatory neurotransmitters; affects motor behavior, emotions, cognitive functioning; often a result of stroke, infections, and TBI)
Transitional or primitive pencil grasp (i.e., any pencil grasp that markedly deviates from a tripod grasp)	Witzelsucht (i.e., "excessive and inappropriate facetiousness or jocularity … observed following frontal [especially orbitofrontal] lobe injury" [Larner, 2016, p. 373])
Clumsiness	Ptosis (i.e., a droopy eyelid; often a result of stroke, myasthenia gravis [neuromuscular disorder], TBI, myopathy [muscle tissue disease]; CN III)
Dysarthria (i.e., brain-based difficulty correctly producing the sounds of speech)	Asymmetrical mydriasis or anisocoria (i.e., pupil dilation in one eye, but not the other; often caused by stroke, TBI, and inflammation; CN III)
Suppression effects on double-simultaneous stimulation testing (i.e., incoming sensory information [visual, auditory, tactile] is suppressed because the magnitude of the sensory input, passing through the thalamocortical connections, is reduced as a result of	Diplopia (i.e., double vision; often caused by stroke, TBI, tumors, multiple sclerosis, inflammation, and infection; CN III, IV, and VI)

(*Continued*)

Table 2.5 (Continued)

Soft Neurological Signs	*Hard Neurological Signs*
presenting sensory input to both sides of the brain at once)	
Hyperkinesis (excessive motor output, including tics, tremors, *chorea* [dance-like motor movement], *akathisia* [continual leg movement], etc.)	Dysconjugate gaze (i.e., inability to move the eyes at the same time; CN III, VI)
Hypokinesis (lack of motor output, including *bradykinesia* [slowness], *dystonia* [sustained, rigid motor positions], *akinesia* [less initiation], etc.)	Nystagmus (i.e., involuntary movement of eyeballs; CN III, VI)
Gait irregularities (i.e., difficulty walking)	Anosmia (i.e., partial or total inability to smell for a brain-based reason; frequently caused by infection, TBI, tumor, and degenerative disorders; CN I)
Dysfluent speech (i.e., difficulty translating ideas into spoken language)	Facial palsy (i.e., facial paralysis; frequently caused by stroke, tumors, multiple sclerosis, neuropathies [nerve damage], TBI, infection, inflammation, myasthenia gravis; CN VII)
Astereognosis (i.e., difficulty identifying an object by touch only)	Central vertigo (i.e., a spinning sensation with a more serious neurological cause [e.g., brainstem demyelination, TBI, tumor, multiple sclerosis, infection]; CN VIII)
Peripheral vertigo (i.e., a spinning sensation with a less serious cause [e.g., drug-induced, migraine-related])	Dysphagia (i.e., difficulty swallowing or chewing; CN V, VIII, IX, X, XII, or corticobulbar tract)

Soft neurological signs are "nonspecific signs suggestive of neurologic impairment that occur frequently in the normal population, although they do occur with greater frequency in clinical populations" (Loring, 1999, p. 148); hard neurological signs are strongly indicative of brain dysfunction or disease, in contrast to soft neurological signs. CN = cranial nerve.

Reynolds and Livingston (2012) posed an important question, one which legal professionals likely ask as well: "Why do psychologists use tests so often in their professional practice?" (p. 21). These authors go on to state the following, about the benefits of testing:

> The answer is simple: People are not very good at judging other people objectively, and most "non-test" assessment procedures involve subjective judgment. If you are like most people, on more than one occasion your first impression of someone later proved to be totally wrong. Someone who initially seemed aloof and uncaring turns out to be kind and considerate. Someone who initially appeared conscientious and trustworthy ends up letting you down. The undeniable truth is that people are not very good at judging other people in the absence of months and

Table 2.6 Landmark historical events in the history of psychological and neuropsychological testing

2200 B.C.	Competence of Public Officials Tested by Chinese
1600s	Swinburne developed a test for criminal defendants involving their ability to measure a yard of cloth or correctly state the days of the week.
1809	Carl Frederich Gauss, a German mathematician, recognized that some variables in nature distribute in a bell-shaped curve (i.e., the "normal curve" or the "Gaussian curve"), which he used to address scientific questions.
1835	Lambert Adolphe Jacques Quetelet of Ghent, France (now Ghent, Belgium), used the bell-shaped/normal/Gaussian curve to study human characteristics. Some view Quetelet to be the founder of the field of statistics.
1869	Sir Francis Galton, an English scientist, published *Classification of Men According to Their Natural Gifts*. Some view Galton as one of the founders of the field of psychology.
1905	Alfred Binet and Theodore Simon, French psychologists, developed an intelligence test to identify educatable children.
1917	Robert Mearns Yerkes, an American psychologist, published two group-administered IQ tests (Army Alpha [a verbal test] and Army Beta [a nonverbal test]), for use with military recruits during World War I.
1939	David Wechsler, a Romanian-American psychologist, published the Wechsler-Bellevue Intelligence Scale, which has since developed into the currently used Wechsler Adult Intelligence Scale-Fourth Edition (WAIS-IV).
1949	The first edition of Wechsler Intelligence Scale for Children was first published. This test has since been developed into the currently used Wechsler Intelligence Scale for Children-Fifth Edition (WISC-V).
1940s	Minnesota Multiphasic Personality Inventory first published. This self-report questionnaire has since become one of the most widely used and well-researched objective test of personality.
1930	Karl Spencer Lashley, an American psychologist, published *Basic Neural Mechanisms of Behavior*, and went on to develop ideas that would lead to the field of neuropsychology.
1949	Donald Olding Hebb, a Canadian psychologist, published *The Organization of Behavior: A Neuropsychological Theory*. He is considered by some to be the founder of the field of neuropsychology.

Source: Adapted, in part, from Sattler (2001) and Reynolds and Livingston (2012).

> perhaps even years of consistent exposure to them. The reason is that all of us are susceptible to a host of biases and prejudices that undermine our judgment. (p. 21)

A valuable contribution to the psychological testing literature came from Meyer et al. (2001), who outlined and explained the many ways that psychological testing can lead to better decision-making. Table 2.7 contains a summary of benefits associated with using psychological and neuropsychological testing.

Table 2.7 Benefits of psychological and neuropsychological testing from Meyer et al. (2001, p. 144)

"Clinicians may overlook certain areas of functioning and focus more exclusively on presenting complaints."
"[Examinees] … are often poor historians and/or biased presenters of information."
"Psychological assessments generally measure a large number of personality, cognitive, or neuropsychological characteristics simultaneously. As a result, they are inclusive and often cover a range of functional domains, many of which might be overlooked during less formal evaluation procedures."
"Psychological tests provide empirically quantified information, allowing for more precise measurement of [examinee] characteristics than is usually obtained from interviews."
"Psychological tests have standardized administration and scoring procedures … Standardization also can reduce legal and ethical problems because it minimizes the prospect that unintended bias may adversely affect the [examinee]."
"Psychological tests are normed, permitting each patient to be compared with a relevant group of peers, which in turn allows the clinician to formulate refined inferences about strengths and limitations."
"Research on the reliability and validity of individual test scales sets formal assessment apart from other sources of clinical information … Without this, practitioners have little ability to gauge the accuracy of the data they process when making judgments."
"By incorporating multiple methods, the assessment psychologist is able to efficiently gather a wide range of information to facilitate understanding the [examinee]."

Performance validity tests (PVTs) and *symptom validity tests (SVTs)* (Larrabee, 2012) are some of the more valuable tests a forensic evaluator can use, because these tests can uncover invalid data (i.e., data that cannot be relied upon by factfinders). Specifically, PVTs are used to identify invalid performances on performance-based tests (e.g., IQ, memory, or reading comprehension tests), whereas SVTs are used to identify invalid answers on self-report questionnaires, whether those answers are due to anything from inadequate attention to test questions or due to intentional impression management (e.g., malingering).

Because these tests have limitations, it is important for the forensic evaluator to openly discuss these limitations so that factfinders are not misled. In making this point, Kaufman and Bush (2020) emphasized that the same validity test cutoff scores cannot be applied to all litigation populations; for example, those with lower IQs may "fail" validity tests using cutoffs that work well for higher-functioning defendants, but which establish too high a bar for lower-functioning defendants. Similarly, a recent systematic review of PVTs in non-forensic/treatment-oriented populations from McWhirter et al., (2020) concluded that "PVT failure was common in all clinical groups described, with failure rates for some groups and tests exceeding 25%" (p. 945). Despite these limitations, it is still important for the forensic evaluator to use these tests as a part of a comprehensive forensic assessment. Evaluators who do not test for validity are coloring outside the lines of generally accepted practice (Bush et al., 2014; Bush et al., 2005; Heilbronner et al., 2009).

Self-report tests of relevance to forensic assessment include objective personality tests. These are questionnaires that involve true-false answers or

Likert-scale answers (e.g., 0 = not true, 1 = somewhat true, 2 = very true), and they are objectively scored. Self-report tests typically include SVTs that are embedded within the instrument, to accompany the clinical scores that are generated. Common self-report tests used in forensic assessment include the Personality Assessment Inventory (PAI) (Morey, 2007) and the Minnesota Multiphasic Personality Inventory-2, Restructured Form (MMPI-2-RF) (Ben-Porath, 2012). It is important to ensure that the defendant has the requisite reading skills before using a self-report test (AERA et al., 2014).

Rating scales are questionnaires filled out by a person who know the examinee. For example, it can be very helpful for a parent to provide their perspective on their child's functioning. Likewise, teachers can fill out rating scales, thereby providing helpful and relevant information on a child's functioning in school. Like objective personality tests, rating scales often include SVTs, embedded within the instrument. This can be extremely helpful in forensic assessments, where interested parties may generate information on a defendant that is not accurate. The Behavioral Assessment System for Children-Third Edition (BASC-3) (Reynolds & Kamphaus, 2015) is a commonly used rating scale to measure mental health functioning. The Adaptive Behavior Assessment System-Third Edition (ABAS-III) (Harrison & Oakland, 2015) is a commonly used rating scale to measure adaptive functioning, which must be measured when diagnosing intellectual disability.

Cognitive testing is a broad category that includes IQ tests, neuropsychological tests, and academic achievement tests (e.g., tests of reading comprehension or math knowledge). These tests are particularly useful to forensic referral questions of legal capacity (e.g., to waive Miranda rights) and competence (e.g., adjudicative competence), given that legal capacity and competence require a minimal ability to think and problem-solve. To appreciate this point, consider the following definitions of intelligence:

> The aggregate or global capacity of the individual to act purposely, to think rationally, and to deal effectively with his [or her] environment. (Wechsler, 1944, p. 3)
>
> What we measure with [intelligence] tests is not what the tests measure—not information, not spatial perception, not reasoning ability. These are only a means to an end. What intelligence tests measure is something much more important: the capacity of the individual to understand the world about him and his resourcefulness to cope with its challenges. (Wechsler, 1975, p. 139)
>
> "[Intelligence is] mental activity involved in purposive adaptation to, shaping of, and selection of real-world environments relevant to one's life" (Spearman, 1923, p. 300)
>
> "Intelligence is not an entity within the organism but a quality of behavior. Intelligent behavior is essentially adaptive, insofar as it represents effective ways of meeting the demands of changing environment. Such

> behavior varies with the species and with the context in which the individual lives." (Anastasi, 1986, pp. 19–20)
>
> [Intelligence is] the ability to plan and structure one's behavior with an end in view (Das, 1973, p. 27)

Simply stated, juvenile and adult criminal defendants very frequently end up in the justice system because their capacity to skillfully think through life challenges is substantially limited compared to others. Likewise, these same individuals, once arrested, often struggle navigating their way through legal proceedings. It follows that adequately measuring the cognitive functioning of some defendants can help factfinders better understand these individuals.

Forensic assessment instruments (FAIs) are tests that are specifically developed to address forensic referral questions. As explained by Grisso (2003), "FAIs may improve our ability to conceptualize the relations between legal definitions of abilities and the psychological constructs associated with human capacities" (p. 43). The MacArthur Competence Assessment Tool-Criminal Adjudication (MacCAT-CA) (Poythress et al., 1999) is an FAI developed to address the question of adjudicative competence or competence to stand trial. Similarly, the aforementioned Violence Risk Appraisal Guide-Revised (VRAG-R) and Structured Assessment of Violence Risk in Youth (SAVRY) are FAIs developed to address questions of future offending. FAIs can be helpful in forensic assessments, making it worthwhile to consider their use.

That said, the automatic adoption of an FAI—without consideration of reliability and validity evidence—can be problematic. For example, the Miranda Rights Comprehension Instruments (MRCI) (Goldstein et al., 2014), an FAI for use when the referral question centers around a defendant's capacity to understand a Miranda warning, includes adult norms established with lower-IQ adults. This is problematic because it is not particularly helpful to know if a criminal defendant scored as low as other lower-IQ adults, given that a valid waiver of Miranda rights hinges, in part, on an *intelligent* waiver of those rights. This FAI, arguably, would be much more valuable if the norms were established with normal-IQ adults.

Some FAIs are structured interviews that cannot be quantitatively scored, which means it is not possible to know how reliable the FAI is, a topic discussed more in Chapter 3. A test with low reliability is not unlike standing on a scale and finding that you weigh 150lbs, 197lbs, and then 112lbs. Notably, this is not a limitation for *all* structured interviews, and it is important to appreciate the difference between FAIs with a structured-interview format that is quantitative, versus those that are not. Why? Because not knowing an FAI's reliability means one cannot know the error rate for the FAI, an important topic taken up in Chapter 3 because of its emphasis in the *Daubert* decision and FRE 702.

This distinction becomes concrete by comparing two FAIs used to collect data on defendants whose adjudicative competence is being assessed: the Juvenile

Adjudicative Competence Interview (JACI) (Grisso, 2005) and the Fitness Interview Test-Revised (FIT-R) (Roesch et al., 2006). The JACI is a structured interview for collecting data on juveniles whose adjudicative competence needs to be evaluated. However, there is no way to quantify how the youth performed on the JACI, so an error rate cannot be known. In contrast, the FIT-R is also a structured interview for collecting data on defendants, age 11+, but it is one that *can* be quantitatively scored and studied. As a result, researchers can study the FIT-R and generate reliability coefficients, which can then be used to establish an error rate for the FAI, thereby being more likely to comport with *Daubert* and Rule 702, or the state equivalent of these laws. Hence, not all FAIs using a structured-interview format are the same, when viewed through the lens of *Daubert* and Rule 702, or the state equivalent of these laws.

Similarly, some tools used in forensic assessment may not in fact be FAIs, despite having that appearance. For example, the Competence to Stand Trial Assessment Instrument (CAI), and its revised version (the CAI-R or R-CAI), have been challenged by forensic scholars. Grisso (2003) wrote that "the CAI does not really have the status of an 'instrument'" (p. 129). Likewise, Rogers and Shuman (2006) said the following about the CAI:

> The CAI continues to be used by a surprising number of forensic clinicians. We have seen a "revised version," referred to as the "CAI-R," used occasionally in forensic practice. Importantly, this so-called revision has not been validated and is not recognized in recent scholarly reviews (Grisso, 2003; Stafford, 2003). Attorneys should observe that the CAI was not intended as a formal psychological measure and that its research has largely been limited to early studies … If the CAI (or CAI-R) is misrepresented as a formal measure, the forensic clinicians are vulnerable to vigorous cross-examination on both *Daubert* and ethical grounds. (p. 173)

Finally, it should be clearly stated that *exclusive* reliance on an FAI as a part of a forensic assessment is almost never advisable, because FAIs do not adequately chart important clinical territory (e.g., validity, cognitive functioning), which are important reasons why forensic mental health experts are deemed expert in the first place. Recall the definition of Rule 702 from Table 2.2: Expert opinions must be solidly anchored in and logically flow from both (a) expert-related data and (b) trustworthy, expert-related ways of doing things. Insofar as a mental health expert can generate more relevant expert-related data on a defendant using multiple expert-related methods, factfinders will be in a better position to engage in just legal decision-making. To further appreciate this point, consider the following from Roesch et al. (2006):

> It is important to note that competency assessment instruments such as the FIT-R comprise only one part of adolescent competency evaluations. While the FIT-R may be useful in assessing a youth's functional legal capacities, evaluators should also assess for cognitive limitations,

psychopathology, and developmental immaturity, since these factors could lead to legal impairments. (p. 31)

Going beyond the FAI by seeking neurodevelopmental information (e.g., the quality of the pregnancy) and measuring cognitive limitations (e.g., a low IQ and neuropsychological deficits), is precisely why forensic neuropsychological assessment, as opposed to forensic psychological assessment, can be so valuable to judges and juries, who are trying to make more informed decisions about important legal matters.

To convey the importance of going beyond the FAI and generating other expert-related data, consider the following illustrative sketch: 15-year-old criminal defendant facing a life sentence for first-degree murder charges; history of epilepsy since childhood; history of placement in special education; history at age 13 of a *moderate* TBI (i.e., loss of consciousness of approximately five hours and posttraumatic amnesia of approximately three days); family report of massive head bruising and edema (i.e., swelling of the head) while hospitalized for the brain injury; occipitofrontal circumference (i.e., head size) measured to be two standard deviations above average two years post brain injury; history of having to re-learn how to speak and walk following brain injury; a full-scale IQ in the low-70s; auditory-verbal story memory lower than 98% of age-based comparison group; reading comprehension found to be lower than 94% of high school graduates; and validity testing passed by defendant. Exclusive use of an FAI with no known error rate in a serious case like this would clearly be problematic, mainly because the FAI would not measure most of the defendant's most relevant deficits, but also because use of methods without a known error rates is not in step with *Daubert* or Rule 702 (and yet this is exactly the approach one evaluating expert used). Moreover, not only would a case like this demand extensive cognitive testing, but also expert-related knowledge about epilepsy and head injury severity in youths (see Kaufman & Bush, 2020 for a recent review). So while FAIs can sometimes add valuable information to the decision-making process, many forensic cases demand much more.

Data Interpretation for the Forensic Evaluation

Even if the forensic evaluator manages to collect pristine, unbiased data on a defendant, problems with *interpretation* of the data can arise, leading to expert testimony that is flawed and unhelpful to factfinders. Decisions about report-writing style can affect interpretation of data, if for no other reason, because these style choices effectively weight information differentially. Difficulties with combining and synthesizing large amounts of information on a defendant can increase the likelihood of bias when interpreting data. And once data are organized reasonably well, it is necessary to map the data onto the referral question(s), to support opinions, including opinions about the ultimate legal issue. These important topics are explained next.

Report Writing Style and Content

At one end of the writing-style continuum is use of tables, graphs, figures, and so forth, whereas a simple narrative approach is at the other end of this spectrum. Report headings and subheadings are commonly used to organize the presentation of the information, although to varying extents. Some authorities assert that forensic reports *must* be written in a narrative style, but this does not mesh with what is known about the effectiveness of presenting certain types of information in other formats (Evergreen, 2017; Tufte, 2001). That being said, opining about an ultimate legal issue, for example, requires explanation, which undoubtedly lends itself to a narrative style. Given that there are many ways to present information in a forensic report, it follows that there is perhaps no single best way. This outlook was expressed by Meharg (2017), who also emphasized the importance of writing forensic reports that satisfy the needs of legal professionals:

> Because creativity is characterized by divergence, originality, and expressiveness, variation in the basic structure and format of neuropsychological reports is both expected and valued. There is also a need to remain mindful that the forensic report must function effectively within the justice system and thus requires balancing creative expression with the demand for precision, clarity, and comprehensiveness. (p. 398)

There is other valuable reading in this area (Grisso, 2010; Otto et al., 2014; Witt, 2010) that goes beyond report-writing style, to also address report content. Highlights from this literature include the following: clearly stating the purpose of the report; logically sequencing the presentation of different types of information within the report; clearly separating descriptive, foundational information (e.g., observations or history) from the expert's opinion on the referral question; excluding irrelevant information; relying upon, where feasible, all relevant types of information (relevant records, statements elicited from knowledgeable others, relevant in-session observations, test scores, etc.); adequately weighting data when forming opinions; avoiding language that might be confusing to legal professionals (or juries) or otherwise convey a lack of professionalism; making inappropriate use of tests to address the referral question; providing thorough explanations for opinions; relying on descriptive, foundational information presented earlier in the report; and including discussion on competing explanations for the data, even those that run contrary to the expert's opinion on the referral question.

To this list, we add *discussion of limitations*, which meshes with the Specialty Guidelines for Forensic Psychology (SGFP) (American Psychological Association [APA], 2013) and the Ethical Principles of Psychologists and Code of Conduct (EPPCC) (APA, 2010). In other words, forensic reports should include some discussion of any limitations encountered during the data-collection and data-interpretation process. More will be said about this, under the heading of *synthesis of the data.*

Scoring

By "scoring," we are generally talking about assigning a numerical value to a test-taker's performance, either on a test item or question, or on the entire test. Because numbers and calculations are often involved when scoring a test, errors can be made. Therefore, it is important to double-check one's work, especially if a factfinder's decision about an important matter might hinge on test scores. Sometimes it is even valuable to double-check the work of another expert, particularly if there are reasons to suspect mistakes.

However, rescoring of another expert's testing can devolve into a petty, unprofessional activity for experts, which plays into the adversarial gamesmanship that is the special province of litigating attorneys, at which point the following from Greiffenstein and Kaufmann (2012) becomes particularly relevant: "Legitimate courtroom practices and ethical attorney behavior would be considered unethical if practiced by a neuropsychologist" (p. 26). Simply put, it is one thing to make a flagrant scoring error that drastically alters the quality of the evidence, and another to make a small error, about which courtroom attention may have more of a prejudicial effect than anything else.

When data on a test-taker are "scored," we are effectively making a statement about the performance of the individual test-taker. It follows, therefore, that we need to be thoughtful about this. Scoring problems can arise when we compare the defendant's performance to the wrong standard, resulting in a norm-referenced score that is actually not helpful (see Chapter 3). Consider Standard 9.02(b) from the EPPCC (APA, 2010): "Psychologists use assessment instruments whose validity and reliability have been established for use with members of the population tested" (p. 12). Also consider Guideline 10.02 from the SGFP (APA, 2013): "Forensic practitioners use assessment instruments whose validity and reliability have been established for use with members of the population assessed" (p. 15). If, for example, the referral question pertains to a legal competence (or capacity) that boils down to a minimum level of cognitive functioning, the threshold or requirement for competence represents a boundary between reasonably normal functioning (i.e., being competent) and abnormal functioning (i.e., being incompetent). Hence, it makes sense with this sort of referral question to compare the defendant to what is considered normal in the population at large, making an IQ test—or other cognitive tests yielding scores based on stratified population norms (Strauss et al., 2006)—very appropriate. Stratified population norms are well-suited to forensic referral questions of competence and capacity for most defendants.

Therefore, if one were to develop new norms involving criminal defendants, in an attempt to comport with Standard 9.02(b) or Guideline 10.02, the scores based on this new comparison group might well generate evidence of little value. It is less helpful to learn, for example, that an incompetent individual scored similarly to other incompetent individuals, which is more likely if the comparison group consists only of criminal defendants. When the referral question is anchored in what is normal in the general population, stratified population norms are quite helpful, because they tell us how far from normal the defendant scored.

However, this does not mean that norms established for criminal defendants are *never* valuable. If, for example, the question shifts from adjudicative competence, which is closely connected to normal functioning within the population, to adequate effort output on a validity test, the point of comparison must also shift. To illustrate, consider a case involving an adult person of color defendant with a history of placement in special education, only a sixth-grade education, a history of severe abuse and trauma, severe mental illness, but also veritable cognitive deficits. What is the appropriate threshold on a validity test for this individual?

Arguably, the only way to establish such a threshold or cutoff score would be to develop norms for a validity test, using a sample of individuals that are matched to the defendant in as many ways as possible. *And*, of paramount importance, this normative sample would also have to be made up of participants who fully engaged/tried on the validity test, during the development of the test norms. If the defendant described previously did not score in a reasonably similar way to this appropriate comparison group, legitimate concerns could be posed as to the validity of the test data.

There is an important takeaway message here. When we "score" data on a test-taker, we are making a statement about their performance, in reference to some standard (e.g., a percentage or number correct or a group average). But that statement has to make sense. If the support for the statement gets lost in complicated details about the comparison point for computing the score, the score may become extremely misleading to factfinders. Similarly, if the score is derived by comparing the test-taker to the wrong comparison group, the score may be of no value. An example is helpful.

In the foregoing case involving a defendant with a sixth-grade education, he obtained the following Test of Memory Malingering (TOMM; Tombaugh, 1996) scores: 38, 43, and 42. This led one expert involved in the case to diagnose the defendant as a "malingerer," on the basis that he did not score above the recommended cutoff score in the TOMM manual: "Any score lower than [X] on Trial 2 or the Retention Trial indicates the possibility of malingering" (p. 19). The problem with this conclusion is that it is far from scientifically clear that the recommended cutoff score in the TOMM manual leads to the accurate identification of malingering in criminal defendants who *also* have a history of placement in special education, only have a sixth-grade education, have a history of severe abuse and trauma, have severe mental illness, and have veritable cognitive deficits. Moreover, a quick read of Appendix A in the TOMM manual reveals that almost 20 of those in the clinical sample generated scores below the recommended cutoff score. Therefore, in a case like this, it would be very important for the forensic evaluator to draw attention to the limitations of the methods being used to generate the test scores, which not only comports with both the EPPCC and SGFP but is also in step with common sense.

In other words, was this defendant malingering to qualify for special education as a child? Similarly, did this defendant malinger not being able to get past the sixth grade?[3] The point here is straightforward: experts using validity tests need to acknowledge the limitations of these methods, rather than making over-confident conclusions about malingering that, when viewed through the lens of common sense, are vulnerable to attack for good reason.

Neuropsychologists frequently use demographic variables to correct, adjust, or calibrate scores. This is typically done with age, sex, ethnicity, and years of schooling, since all of these variables are known to correlate with neuropsychological scores to varying extents. However, years of schooling should generally not be used as a control variable when the referral question pertains to a legal competence or capacity. The reason why is that years of schooling and cognitive functioning, unlike the other demographic variables, have a *bidirectional* relationship. This means that how much schooling one gets is influenced by one's cognitive functioning and one's cognitive functioning is influenced by how much schooling they receive (Boone, 2013). Accordingly, when the referral question pertains to a legal competence or capacity, which reflects a standard that is expected of normal-functioning members of a population, *not* controlling for schooling makes sense, as does using 12 years of schooling, since this is how much schooling an average person would be expected to receive.

This is not a perfect solution, but it is much better than calibrating for years of schooling and generating a score that makes no sense with regard to the legal referral question. For example, knowing if a criminal defendant's auditory-verbal memory is normal compared to other adults with only a third-grade education is less helpful than knowing that this criminal defendant's auditory-verbal memory is lower than 95% of other adults with a high school diploma. Likewise, it would make no sense to compute a defendant's IQ in comparison to those who have a third-grade education; the bar would be so low that their IQ would seem normal, if not high. Such information would be less likely to lead to improved decision-making by factfinders, who are asking the expert for helpful information that they would not otherwise have.

Synthesis of the Data

Much can go awry when forensic evaluators synthesize all the data they have collected, making this topic of particular importance. It is perhaps at this point during this course of data-interpretation that bias can most affect the evidence generated by the forensic expert. This is because the bias can work its way into the expert's combining of information, often without the expert realizing it. For this reason, we agree with others who have already written about this topic (Faust & Ahern, 2012; Gowensmith & McCallum, 2019; Zappala et al., 2018) and believe that debiasing techniques are justified.

An article on debiasing by forensic evaluators, written by Borum et al. (1993), provides an excellent summary of biasing influences and corrective measures the clinician can take to debias. Sources of bias in this paper include the following: inaccuracy from overreliance on memory; limitations in complex configural analysis; underutilization of base rates; confirmatory bias; misestimation of covariation; hindsight bias; overconfidence; overreliance on unique data; and confusing fact with statistical artifact. In their conclusory comments, these authors stated that "the literature suggests that knowledge or awareness of these limitations alone is insufficient" (p. 64), meaning that clinicians might read about bias and debiasing techniques, only to forget about or neglect them when actually conducting a forensic evaluation and writing up the report. Therefore, more concrete strategies to debias are worth discussion.

One way to limit the impact of bias during data synthesis is to use a checklist when writing a report. Airline pilots and surgeons routinely use checklists in their work to ensure completeness and accuracy (Gawande, 2011). Use of a checklist during forensic report writing can be accomplished different ways, one of which is to simply include a table within the forensic report that lists major sources of bias. Using this table as a checklist, the forensic evaluator might then describe in narrative fashion the extent to which various sources of bias have been considered and addressed. Table 2.8 contains a non-exhaustive list of sources of bias that may occur during data interpretation, along with examples.

In addition to considering bias during data interpretation, it can be helpful to generate a list of other limitations, which can be discussed at some point in the forensic report. For example, a forensic evaluator might use a test with a defendant that has norms or a recommended criterion (e.g., a cutoff score) that is not entirely appropriate for the defendant. Assuming the potential benefits of the test outweigh the liabilities, it would be essential for the evaluator to explain the limitations of the test in the report. Another limitation to discuss might pertain to restricted access to collateral information, despite attempts by the evaluator to obtain this information. To illustrate, it is recommended that forensic evaluators use the Attorney CST Questionnaire (Zapf & Roesch, 2009) with defense counsel during the course of an adjudicative competence evaluation. In reality, even well-intentioned attorneys may not have time to fill out this questionnaire, which should be noted in the report as a limitation.

Overall, effective synthesis of data on defendants requires dispassionate and objective consideration of factors, influences, and limitations, all of which may add complexity to the evaluator's opinions. This is, however, much easier said than done. Moreover, retaining attorneys may not always appreciate it, especially those who are used to "marionette experts"—that is, experts who allow attorneys to function as their puppeteer. Nonetheless, this approach seems to be congruent with how science is properly conducted, which—under FREs 702 and 703—is precisely the reason why forensic evaluators are allowed to opine so freely during legal proceedings.

Mapping Data Onto Referral Question(s)

Psychologists and neuropsychologists, by virtue of their training in test selection and use, can generate considerable amounts of data during a forensic

Table 2.8 Sources of bias for forensic evaluators during data interpretation and examples

Sources of Bias During Data Interpretation	*Examples of Bias with Forensic Evaluators*
Overreliance on memory by the evaluator	Evaluator fails to take notes during the clinical interview.
Limits of in-the-head data integration	Evaluator does not use an actuarial model, wherever available.
Base rate neglect	Evaluator ignores (a) how often individuals from a specific population score below a cutoff score on a validity test, (b) how often individuals with healthy brains score low on a large battery of neuropsychological tests, or (b) how uncommon a certain mental health diagnosis is in the population.
Confirmation bias	Evaluator only looks for data that support their hypothesis.
Illusory correlation	Evaluator incorrectly concludes that two variables (e.g., symptoms and a disorder) are causatively linked because they do not consider alternative explanations for the symptoms.
Hindsight bias	Evaluator's opinion about an important topic (e.g., a diagnosis or an ultimate issue) is influenced by pre-existing information on that topic (e.g., the prior opinion of another evaluator).
Clinician overconfidence	Evaluator forms an opinion with unsupported overconfidence.
The allure of unique, exotic, or "sexy" data	Evaluator is influenced by information that draws a lot of attention, even though that information may not incrementally add new, valuable information (see Dilution Effects).
Regression to the mean	Evaluator does not consider the possibility that data of an extreme nature (e.g., an unusually high or low test score) might not replicate upon future assessment due to measurement error.
Dilution effects	Evaluator overweights clinically tangential information, thereby diluting the weighting of other clinical information that is highly relevant.
Diagnosis momentum	Evaluator automatically re-applies a diagnosis already made, without any critical thought about whether the diagnosis is accurate.
Financial pressure	Evaluator opines about an ultimate issue in a way that increases the likelihood that the retaining counsel will hire them again in the future, in order to obtain financial security.
Institutional pressure	Evaluator working at a state psychiatric facility succumbs to hospital pressure to find a defendant competent, thereby freeing up hospital beds and pleasing their supervisor.
Adversarial allegiance	Evaluator aligns themselves with the goals of retaining counsel, thereby losing objectivity.
Attractiveness/halo effects	Evaluator (a) incorrectly concludes that a defendant has normal cognitive functioning, based on positive

(*Continued*)

Table 2.8 (Continued)

Sources of Bias During Data Interpretation	*Examples of Bias with Forensic Evaluators*
	superficial characteristics or (b) opines favorably about the defendant because the defendant is extremely likeable or good-looking.
Unattractiveness/horn effects	Evaluator (a) incorrectly concludes that a defendant has cognitive deficits, based on negative superficial characteristics or (b) opines unfavorably about the defendant because the defendant is not likeable or is otherwise unattractive.
Direct data neglect	Evaluator (a) relies on a low self-report score from a personality questionnaire, and ignores interview or other data that unequivocally proves the self-report score wrong (e.g., PAI-A *ANT* is normal, but teen admits to putting animals into microwaves until they explode) or (b) rigidly relies on the results of an actuarial tool, even though the prediction generated from the actuarial tools has been proven wrong in the particular case (e.g., VRAG-R predicts very low recidivism, but defendant stabs another inmate while in jail).
Anchoring effects	Evaluator's opinion is made in reaction to the opinion already made by another evaluator, who typically generates subpar work, rather than considering the possibility that the first evaluator—despite often generating subpar work—might be correct.
Framing effects	Evaluator's opinion about a defendant having autism is influenced by the diagnostic opinion contained in a report that is thorough, well-written, and generated by a team of evaluators at a university.
Representative heuristic	Evaluator makes a diagnosis of PTSD due to sexual abuse because the evaluator has seen this pattern in most of those they evaluate.
Availability heuristic	Evaluator makes an important clinical decision about a defendant, based on new information they just read about or learned about during a continuing education seminar.
Stereotyping effects	Evaluator (a) opines negatively about a female defendant because he has come to believe that "all women are dramatic" or (b) opines negatively about a police officer defendant because she, without realizing it, harbors subtle stereotypes about "all cops abusing power."
Self-referencing effect	Evaluator went to the same high school as the defendant, which skews the evaluator's view of the defendant.
Fundamental attribution error	Evaluator overly attributes antisocial behavior to the defendant, rather than to their environment.

assessment. But it is crucial that these data be relevant to the referral question. It is also necessary for the evaluator to organize the data around the referral question, so that a logical connection between the data and the referral question can be made by legal professionals and factfinders.

To illustrate, consider one part of the legal definition of adjudicative competence in the state of NM, as delineated under NMRA 6-507.1: "sufficient present ability to consult with the defendant's lawyer with a reasonable degree of rational understanding." Using this prong as a heading within the report, the evaluator could present information from the Attorney CST Questionnaire, the aforementioned test that measures the attorney-defendant relationship (Zapf & Roesch, 2009). Likewise, the evaluator could report the defendant's verbal IQ and scores from relevant neuropsychological tests (e.g., tests of auditory-verbal attention, working memory, and delayed memory). Similarly, the evaluator could present other relevant information (e.g., difficulties they had effectively communicating with the defendant during the evaluation) under this heading.

Opining on the Ultimate Issue(s)

Among forensic psychology scholars (Melton et al., 2017; Rogers & Ewing, 1989, 2003), there is no consensus as to whether forensic evaluators should offer opinions on the ultimate legal issue (legal insanity, *mens rea*/diminished capacity, adjudicative competence, risk for future dangerousness, etc.). Moreover, there is a traditional expectation in some jurisdictions that the evaluator *will* opine on the ultimate issue. Our position is that opining on the ultimate issue, assuming it is allowed in one's jurisdiction, is acceptable professional conduct. However, we also believe it necessary to opine with an awareness that the ultimate decision resides with factfinders and that it is the expert's responsibility to help factfinders make more informed decisions. Accordingly, it is essential to provide a thorough explanation of the foundation supporting the expert's ultimate opinion. Rushing directly to the ultimate opinion typically is inappropriate and discordant with the purpose of seeking expert opinions in the first place (i.e., to educate factfinders so *they* make more just legal decisions; see FRE 702).

Expert Testimony

The fifth stage in our flowchart is expert testimony, which is when the expert discusses their findings. This includes direct examination and cross-examination. In the following sections, we explore relevant issues pertaining to this final stage in the evidence-generation process.

Preparing Questions for Direct Examination

Attorneys are busy and frequently do not know what information in the report is most relevant to the ultimate issue. Accordingly, it can be very helpful for the expert to prepare questions for *direct examination*, so the attorney knows what to ask about. As is explained more later, this preparation can include questions about the work of other experts (e.g., an expert retained by the opposing side) because it is reasonable for the factfinders to understand why one expert approached the evaluation process differently from another expert. This can be fleshed out in a pre-testimony meeting between the attorney and the expert.

Not Preparing Questions for Cross-Examination

It might seem logical that a retained expert would prepare questions for retaining counsel for the purposes of cross-examination of the opposing expert. In accord with what has already been written about this (Drogin, 2001; Drogin et al., 2007), this is *not* appropriate. The role of the testifying expert witness is to educate legal professionals and factfinders, so a more just legal decision is reached, not to try to help any one side win their case. If an expert's findings happen to align with retaining counsel's legal objectives, that expert is more likely to testify, and their findings may well help retaining counsel win their case. But winning the case is never the objective of the testifying expert witness, which is why it is not advisable to prepare cross-examination questions for retaining counsel.

This under-appreciated, but very important, message comes into focus when considered in the context of professional roles, of which there are five: (1) evaluating expert (witness); (2) record-reviewing expert (witness); (3) expert consultant (not a witness); (4) fact/lay/sentient witness; and (5) treating clinician witness. As explained by Kaufman and Bush (2021), "Roles (1) and (2) have "witness" in parentheses because the expert may not ultimately testify as a witness. Experts can ethically switch from the role of evaluating or record-reviewing expert to that of consultant within the same case, but not the reverse; they cannot ethically switch from consultant to evaluating or record-reviewing expert" (p. 12). For more on this important matter, see the following: Drogin (2001), Drogin et al. (2007), and Kaufman and Bush (2021).

Direct Examination

Direct examination is questioning of a witness by retaining counsel, for the purposes of making a particular case. Direct examination is not unlike a dance. When it goes well, one can *feel* it. And vice versa: poorly executed direct examination does not feel good. Perhaps more than anything else, it is crucial for both parties to carefully attend to what the other is saying, and respond accordingly. In our experience, some of the best direct examination is characterized by an attorney who is genuinely interested in what the expert has to say, which is different from monotonously running through a list of questions that are always used by the attorney. Similarly, experts who communicate their findings with conviction, which is not the same as unsupported overconfidence, are more likely to engage and persuade (Cramer et al., 2009).

Considerable preparation by the expert and the attorney is also important, which is why it is recommended that experts prepare some questions for retaining counsel. However, if the attorney-expert communication appears scripted, it is less likely to seem—or be—genuine. Therefore, attorneys should allow their honest curiosity about the expert's findings to influence what they inquire about. Additionally, direct examination is an opportunity for retaining counsel to ask questions of their expert that may not always support the attorney's argument, because doing so is preferable to letting the expert walk into a buzzsaw on cross-examination.

Unfortunately, some attorneys ask questions during direct examination that not only convey a lack of preparation but also generate information that may detract from what the expert has to say. To illustrate, one of us was once asked by retaining counsel about our status as being board-certified in forensic psychology, incorrectly thinking we had this particular qualification. For more on the topic of direct examination, we recommend Otto et al. (2014).

Cross-Examination

Cross-examination of the expert witness is questioning of the witness by opposing counsel for the purposes of exposing errors, inconsistencies, and other problems with the expert's findings. Otto et al. (2014) described the answering of direct-examination questions "as hitting slow-pitch softballs, whereas responding to questions presented by the [cross-examining attorney] is akin to facing curveballs, sliders, and change-ups in a game of hardball" (p. 171). We agree. That being said, how one is cross-examined varies widely.

One of us, while testifying electronically during the COVID-19 pandemic, had the experience of a very limp cross-examination, presumably because the attorney was understandably affected by the stress of the pandemic—if not also the added responsibility of having to provide childcare *during* the hearing. This example can be contrasted with another experience involving an in-person, nine-hour deposition, by as many (heavily caffeinated) attorneys, all of whom worked from scripts prepared by a consulting expert who had identified vulnerabilities in the testifying expert's report.

Perhaps more than anything else, it is important for the expert to simply remain an advocate for their opinions when being cross-examined. Similarly, it is important for experts to remember that both science and the law are enterprises characterized by intellectual competition (discussed more in Chapter 4). In other words, the testifying expert's opinions *should* be challenged, as this functions as yet another safeguard against unscientific opinions. In contrast, when attorneys resort to ad hominem (i.e., personal) attacks of the expert, or use aggressive communication (e.g., yelling and handwaving) to intimidate, attention is diverted away from what really matters—namely, introduction of relevant scientific information that "will help the trier of fact to understand the evidence or to determine a fact in issue" (FREs, 2017, p. 15). For more on the topic of cross-examination, we recommend Otto et al. (2014) and Brodsky (2004).

Ethically Commenting on the Work of Another Expert

It is worth noting that commenting on the work of another expert who is also involved in the same case is not unethical or unprofessional, nor is it the same as operating as a consultant for retaining counsel. But it is important that the expert not slip into the role of advocate for anything other than their own opinions, while remaining respectful of the other expert. Kaufman and Bush (2021, p. 172) recently addressed this topic by posing and answering the following ethical question:

> *Question.* What should a forensic neuropsychologist do if they have concerns about a colleague's selection, use, or interpretation of symptom or performance validity tests in a given case?
>
> *Answer.* Guideline 11.05 from the SGFP states, "When evaluating or commenting upon the work or qualifications of other professionals involved in legal proceedings, forensic practitioners seek to represent their disagreements in a professional and respectful tone, and base them on a fair examination of the data, theories, standards, and opinions of the other expert or party." Because experts will understandably vary in their understanding of the research on validity testing, Guideline 11.05 is extremely relevant and helpful on this ethical question. In contrast, if it becomes evident that the colleague's interpretation of the validity data is *flagrantly* discordant with the research, then Standard 1.04 (Informal Resolution of Ethical Violations) from the EPPCC, which parallels Guideline 7.03, becomes relevant: "When psychologists believe that there may have been an ethical violation by another psychologist, they attempt to resolve the issue by bringing it to the attention of that individual, if an informal resolution appears appropriate and the intervention does not violate any confidentiality rights that may be involved." Finally, the American Academy of Clinical Neuropsychology (Sweet, 2003) has a position paper that addresses ethical complaints made during the course of legal proceedings, which emphasizes the value in postponing formal investigations "until the end of any adversarial proceeding that could benefit the complainant" (p. 444). In short, the best course of action would likely be to follow Guideline 11.05 from the SGFP.

To better understand what professionally commenting on another's work might look like in a real situation, an example is helpful. One of us was once involved in a case where the expert for the opposing counsel had given test materials to the attorney, who was using the test materials during his cross-examination. Attorneys are not supposed to have access to many psychological and neuropsychological tests, and yet the expert for the opposing counsel had shared the testing materials with his retaining counsel, to assist with cross-examination. The problems with this expert's work (i.e., sharing test materials with retaining counsel) was calmly and respectfully explained to the expert being cross-examined.

As an aside, rather than report this other expert to the licensing board, the colleague was approached after the case in a respectful manner with information that included supporting details from the state administrative code, which forbid psychologists from sharing testing materials with non-psychologists. The misguided expert apologized for his actions, promised to not do it in the future, and was thankful for the collegial way of addressing the issue.

Video Recording and Virtual Evaluations

Based in large part on a body of empirical evidence, professional organizations in the field of neuropsychology consistently discourage a third-party presence during forensic neuropsychological evaluations (Axelrod et al., 2000; Axelrod, et al., 2000b; Hamsher et al., 2001; Lewandowski et al., 2016). Meanwhile, leaders in the field of forensic psychology take a much different stance (Otto & Krauss, 2009). This discrepancy puts forensic neuropsychologists in a difficult position, particularly those whose board-certification was granted by a professional organization that has taken the time to publish a policy statement articulating why neuropsychologists should *not* allow third-parties, including a recording device, in the room during evaluations.

Although there are many opinion pieces arguing for third-party involvement during forensic assessments (Siegel & Kinscherff, 2018), actual *studies* are hard to identify in the literature. In contrast, there are multiple studies showing that having a third-party, including a recording device, in the room during testing can negatively impact how the examinee performs (Constantinou et al., 2002, 2005; Gavett et al., 2005).

Perhaps part of the issue is that many forensic psychologists do not do much, if any cognitive testing. Some do not do any testing, relying only on the interview and review of records. Meanwhile, neuropsychologists conduct extensive testing. It would follow, therefore, that forensic psychologists who do not routinely administer multiple neuropsychological tests, and are unfamiliar with the scientific literature on this matter, would not have a full appreciation for how disruptive a third-party might be. Similarly, forensic psychologists are not likely to have the way they practice impacted, because their methods are frequently limited to "a combination of clinical interview, structured interviews and self-report measures" (Gallagher et al., 2020) (p. 15). Hence, if we are to be guided by the scientific research in this area, inclusion of third-parties during neuropsychological evaluations remains a concern.

Due to the COVID-19 pandemic, some mental health professionals have moved in the direction of videoconferencing (VC) to conduct forensic assessments (Mulay et al., 2021), on the basis that it is safer for examinees and examiners. Now that there are multiple effective vaccines for COVID-19, however, this stance is less relevant than it was before vaccines had been introduced. Hence, any scholarly contributions about how to safely practice forensic psychological or forensic neuropsychological assessment written *before* the dissemination of COVID-19 vaccines are not clearly applicable to the current circumstances.

Notably, even among some of those who wrote about how to modify one's practice during the COVID-19 pandemic, concerns remained about the limitations of VC assessments. For instance, consider the following from Chenneville and Schwartz-Mette (2020): "Autism evaluations rely heavily on behavioral observations of the child. In some cases, creative thinking may facilitate good enough solutions; in other cases, standard assessment protocols may not be possible to carry out as planned [in a VC environment]." (p. 6). Similarly, Marra et al. (2020) concluded that teleneuropsychology has "good support" (p. 1) with older adults; however, these authors went on to say that many neuropsychological measures "lack sufficient support at this time" (p. 1) for use in a VC or teleneuropsychology environment.

Despite enthusiastic opinions about virtual forensic assessment (Luxton & Lexcen, 2018), it is not difficult to appreciate that virtual testing has major limitations, including very few actual studies on the equivalence of virtual and face-to-face assessment. And, of the studies that have been conducted (Lexcen et al. 2006), the literature does not include replication of findings. More importantly, there is good reason to question how generalizable findings are from a single study on a structured clinical interview to intelligence and neuropsychological tests. In other words, the virtual platform may prove to be acceptable for some methods (e.g., structured clinical interview), but not others (viz., full-battery intelligence and neuropsychological testing). This could mean that the proper practice of forensic neuropsychology—as opposed to only forensic psychology—could effectively be negated by the adoption of virtual assessment methods. While this is a concern for the field of forensic neuropsychology, it is also—and more importantly—a concern for criminal defendants who are likely to benefit from the more scientifically objective neuropsychological methods.

To appreciate this point about the importance of forensic neuropsychological assessment, as opposed to forensic assessment characterized primarily by interview and self-report questionnaires administered through a virtual platform, we go back to the question posed earlier by Reynolds and Livingston (2012): "Why do psychologists use tests so often in their professional practice?" (p. 21). And now reconsider the answer given by these authors: "The answer is simple: People are not very good at judging other people objectively, and most 'non-test' assessment procedures involve subjective judgment" (p. 21).

Insofar as forensic assessment moves further and further away from actual testing, it becomes increasingly reasonable to ask ourselves if criminal defendants are truly receiving the due process they are afforded under the U.S. Constitution. If a non-criminal older adult suspected of having dementia is afforded a neuropsychological assessment as a part of routine *treatment-oriented* care, it stands to reason that teens, young adults, and older adults in the juvenile and adult criminal justice systems should also be given the opportunity to have their cognitive deficits measured and characterized in *legal-oriented* settings, so that just legal decisions can be made about them.

Conclusion

Legal professionals seek the opinions of psychologists and neuropsychologists because of their expertise in abnormal human behavior. These opinions are sought by legal professionals in order to develop a more nuanced understanding of juvenile and adult criminal defendants, and in order to answer the legal questions. For example, sometimes it is necessary to put *past* abnormal behavior under the microscope, as is the case when a defendant makes a confession of questionable validity or when a defendant commits a bad act due to a mental disorder. At other times, legal professionals want to know if mental limitations are preventing a defendant from functioning up to par *now*, resulting in a legal incompetence of some sort (e.g., incompetence to stand trial, make a plea deal, legally represent themselves, or be executed). Irrespective of whether the referral question is past-, now-, or future-oriented, the work is not carried out for treatment-oriented reasons. Rather, it is done for legal purposes, making the work *forensic*.

Psychologists and neuropsychologists have similar skillsets, but there are also important differences that legal professionals should understand—especially including the stronger emphasis on cognitive testing by neuropsychologists. This distinction has particular relevance to forensic assessment, given the emphasis on "scientifically valid" methods with a "known or potential rate of error" (see *Daubert v. Merrell Dow Pharmaceuticals, Inc.,* 1993), because cognitive tests frequently live up to this requirement, whereas other data-collection methods do not.

Certain rules of evidence, either at the federal or state level, are essential for forensic evaluators to know, because these rules establish a tether range that limits what the expert can do within a given case. For example, a prospective expert could be blocked from testifying if they are unable to make it through the preliminary vetting process known as *voire dire*. And if the expert does survive *voire dire*, their opinions could again be muffled or negated entirely if the methods underlying their opinions are deemed unscientific or if the nexus between the scientific methodology and the opinion is lacking.

Evidence-generation by the forensic expert takes place sequentially, beginning with selection of a given expert based on their professional background (e.g., degrees, experience, board-certifications, scholarly contributions). The next step is to settle on the right referral question, which is followed by data collection and then data interpretation—two steps characterized by various forms of bias that must be considered. Finally, the forensic expert testifies about their findings during direct and cross-examination, which demands a high level of professionalism and acceptance for the adversarial, intellectually competitive nature of legal proceedings.

Forensic neuropsychologists differ from many forensic psychologists with regard to third-party involvement during forensic assessment. While forensic neuropsychologists are discouraged by their professional organizations to allow third-party presences during cognitive testing (Axelrod, Barth, et al., 2000; Axelrod, Heilbronner, et al., 2000; Hamsher et al., 2001; Lewandowski et al., 2016), this expectation is not present for forensic psychologists, which creates conflict between the two related specialties. This difference likely reflects the fact that neuropsychologists (and those they evaluate) will be affected by a third-party presence during testing, whereas forensic psychologists and other mental health professionals (and those they evaluate) will not be affected, given that they often do not use many, or any, tests.

Despite differences between forensic psychology and forensic neuropsychology, the two specialties are supported by large bodies of scholarship that can help factfinders (i.e., judges and juries) make better decisions. Moreover, there is so much valuable scholarship within each specialty area that it is impossible for any single forensic evaluator, a forensic psychologist or a forensic neuropsychologist, to have a firm handle on *all* of this scholarship. This matters because a particular forensic psychologist might know so much about forensic psychology that their opinions end up being more valuable to the factfinder(s) than those proffered by the forensic neuropsychologist. Alternatively, a forensic neuropsychologist might uncover a single piece of neuropsychological evidence that "make[s] a fact more or less probable than it would be without the evidence" (FRE 401). Simply stated, forensic psychological and forensic neuropsychological evaluations both have the potential to tremendously improve legal decision-making, thereby leading to more just legal outcomes.

Notes

1 A distinction should be made between use of a recording device during a clinical interview, versus neuropsychological testing. The liabilities with using recording devices during neuropsychological testing are discussed later in this chapter.

2 Some defendants (e.g., those who are incompetent to stand trial) are incapable of providing consent, in which case notification is all that is required.

3 We want to credit attorney, Mr. John McCall, for posing these excellent "common sense" questions while cross-examining a forensic psychologist, during the course of case.

3 Fundamental Measurement Concepts in Forensic Assessment

The fields of psychology and neuropsychology are set apart from the other mental health fields in one particularly important way: psychologists and neuropsychologists have extensive training in the selection and use of psychological and neuropsychological tests. Testing is particularly valuable and relevant to forensic assessment because—of the five data-collection sources explained in Chapter 2—tests are frequently more grounded in science, thereby meshing with *Daubert v. Merrell Dow Pharmaceuticals* (1993) and FRE Rule 702, and the state-level versions of these laws. However, in order to develop a more explicit understanding about why tests are scientific, one needs a fundamental understanding of psychometric concepts, which is the topic of this chapter.

Criterion-Referenced Scores

As explained in Chapter 2, "scoring" means assigning a numerical value to a test-taker's performance, either on a single test item or question, or on the entire test. A criterion-referenced approach to scoring is a way of interpreting data on a test-taker, based not on a comparison to others, but to a specific level of performance, standard, or criterion. On this topic, Reynolds et al. (2009) offered the following:

> Probably the most common example of a criterion-referenced score is percent correct. For example, when a teacher reports that a student correctly answered 85% of the problems on a classroom test assessing the student's ability to multiply double digits, this is a criterion-referenced interpretation. Although there are a variety of criterion-referenced scoring systems, they all involve an *absolute* [italics added] evaluation of examinees' performances as opposed to a *relative* [italics added] evaluation. That is, instead of comparing their performances to the performances of others (a relative interpretation), a criterion-referenced interpretation attempts to describe what they know or are capable of doing—the *absolute* [italics added] level of performance. (p. 80)

DOI: 10.4324/9780367645090-3

In the foregoing, the term *absolute* means the test-taker's behavior is evaluated based on whether the test-taker knows or can do a specific thing, whereas the term *relative* means the test-taker's behavior is evaluated through a comparison to the behavior of others. The distinction between these two terms is important.

For example, in order to obtain board certification in forensic psychology, candidates must successfully obtain correct answers on a certain percentage of approximately 200 test questions within eight different domains (e.g., *Criminal Competence; Criminal Responsibility; Law, Precedents, Court Rules, and Civil and Criminal Procedure*). Board certification in neuropsychology requires a similar standard. Because the threshold for success on these tests is not made in reference to how others do on the test, these tests are criterion-referenced.

Similarly, satisfying the requirements of adjudicative competence, set forth in *Dusky v. United States* (1960), is another example of a criterion-referenced standard. A criminal defendant's adjudicative competence is not assessed with regard to how many others are competent; rather, the threshold for competence is based on whether or not the defendant can surmount the hurdles set forth by *Dusky v. United States* (1960): "[the] test must be whether he has sufficient present ability to consult with his lawyer with a reasonable degree of rational understanding—and whether he has a rational as well as factual understanding of the proceedings against him." Notably, however, there is no quantitative criterion in the *Dusky* standard, which makes the final assessment of competence more open to subjective interpretation of data. Nonetheless, adjudicative competence—and other ultimate issues addressed in forensic assessments—is an example of a criterion-referenced interpretation of data on a defendant.

Norm-Referenced Scores

A norm-referenced approach is a way of interpreting data on a test-taker, based on a comparison to others. Norm-referenced scores are computed by transforming a *raw score* into a *derived score*, which communicates how well the test-taker did in comparison to a specified group. *Developmental scores* (e.g., age- and grade-equivalents) and *scores of relative standing* (e.g., percentile ranks, *z*-scores, *T*-scores, IQ scores, scaled scores) make up the two categories of derived scores.

Developmental Scores

Two developmental scores are typically encountered in a forensic assessment: an *age-equivalent* score and a *grade-equivalent* score. Both of these developmental scores are based on how the test-taker performed in comparison to the average of a given age group or grade. To illustrate, a test of reading comprehension may be given to a criminal defendant, resulting in a grade-equivalent score, telling us that the criminal defendant obtained as many correct answers as the average third-grader. While ostensibly relevant and helpful, developmental equivalents can be very misleading and, as a result, have been heavily criticized in the scientific literature. Of the many criticisms, the following explanation from Salvia et al. (2010) is worth sharing here:

> A second grader and a ninth grader might both earn grade equivalents of 4.0, but they probably have not performed identically. We have known for more than 30 years that younger children perform lower level work with greater accuracy (for instance, successfully answered 38 of the 45 problems attempted), whereas older children attempt more problems with less accuracy (for instance, successfully answered 38 of the 78 problems attempted). (Thorndike & Hagen, 1978, p. 41)

Hence, saying that a particular adult criminal defendant scored at the ninth-grade level on a test of reading comprehension has limitations because the adult defendant may have approached the test differently than the average ninth-grade student. Arguably, a better way of measuring the reading comprehension skills of a criminal defendant would be to compare their raw score (i.e., how many correct answers they obtained) to other adults who are known to read reasonably well, thereby generating a score of relative standing. What adults are likely to read reasonably well? One comparison point would be adults who have completed high school, or those who have about a 12th-grade education.

Scores of Relative Standing

Scores that quantitatively show how a test-taker performed in relation to a specific group are scores of relative standing. A *percentile rank* (PR) tells us the percentage of others in the comparison group above which the test-taker scored. If an individual has a PR of, say, 34, we know that they scored better than about 34% of others in the comparison group.

Within the broader category of *scores of relative standing*, we find what are termed *standard scores*, which are scores with an established *mean* (*M*; i.e., average) and *standard deviation* (*SD*), defined by Pagano (1994) as "the average deviation of the raw scores about their mean" (p. 77). By establishing or scaling a group of scores so they have a known *M* and *SD*, it becomes possible to identify the PR. Typically encountered standard scores include the following: *z*-scores ($M = 0$, $SD = 1$); *T*-scores ($M = 50$, $SD = 10$); IQ scores ($M = 100$, $SD = 15$); and scaled scores ($M = 10$, $SD = 3$). We agree with Salvia et al. (2010) who said, "We favor the use of percentiles. These unpretentious scores require the fewest assumptions for accurate interpretation … Professionals, parents, and students readily understand them" (p. 45). This view, in favor of percentiles, simplifies the issue of descriptive labels, about which attempts have recently been made to establish uniformity (Guilmette et al., 2020). In other words, if a clinician reports a percentile and clearly explains what it is in a report or during testimony, we believe this approach is just as understandable—if not more understandable—than using a descriptive label such as "average," "within normal limits," "impaired," "superior," and so forth.

Test Reliability

According to Reynolds and Livingston (2012), who provide an extremely clear and thorough discussion of reliability and related topics, "reliability refers to constancy or stability of assessment results" (p. 110). The magnitude of this constancy or stability is expressed as a reliability coefficient, r_{xx}, defined by the American Educational Research Association et al. (AERA, 2014, p. 222) as "a unit-free indicator that reflects the degree to which scores are free of random measurement error." Reynolds and Livingston (2012) include a table that summarizes the major types of reliability, which we have adopted (see Table 3.1).

All of the reliabilities contained in Table 3.1 are quantified using a reliability coefficient, defined by Reynolds and Livingston as "the proportion or percentage of test score variance attributable to true score variance" (p. 116). Variance is a number that measures the average of the squared differences between scores and the average (or mean) of the scores, thereby giving a quantitative sense of how much scores vary from each other. So if a particular

Table 3.1 Major types of reliability

Type of Reliability Estimate	*Number of Test Forms*	*Number of Testing Sessions*	*Summary*
Test–retest	One form	Two sessions	Administer the same test to the same group at two different sessions.
Alternative forms: • Simultaneous administration	Two forms	One session	Administer two forms of the test to the same group in the same session.
• Delayed administration	Two forms	Two sessions	Administer two forms of the test to the same group at two different sessions.
Split-half	One form	One session	Administer the test to a group one time. Split the test into two equivalent halves.
Coefficient alpha or KR-20	One form	One session	Administer the test to a group one time. Apply appropriate procedures.
Inter-rater	One form	One session	Administer the test to a group one time. Two or more rates score the test independently.

Source: Adapted from Reynolds and Livingston (2012).

test has a reliability coefficient of, say, 0.83, then 83% of the test score variance (i.e., how much a group of scores vary from their mean) is said to be due to true score variance. This means that 17% of the variance is due to measurement error (error = 1.0 minus r_{xx}).

To understand the foregoing statements, which are admittedly esoteric, it is necessary to briefly touch on classical test theory (CTT), which was developed in the early- to mid-1900s. The idea with CCT is that a test-taker's observed score is equal to their true score, plus some degree of random measurement error, which is represented with a formula: $X_i = T + E$. In this formula, X_i is the examinee's observed score (i.e., the score they get on the test); T is the examinee's true score, a hypothetical score since we can never know the true score; and E is the random measurement error. In short, CCT says the test-taker's observed score is part true score and part random measurement error.

The foregoing formula, $X_i = T + E$, can be rewritten using the variance, defined earlier as a number that measures the average of the squared differences between scores and the mean of the scores. As explained earlier, computing the variance gives us a quantitative sense of how much scores vary from each other. A high variance value means the scores vary a lot and a low variance score means the scores are more similar to each other. Variance is depicted as σ^2.

When the formula, $X_i = T + E$, is rewritten using the variance of the test ($\sigma^2{}_X$), the variance of the true score ($\sigma^2{}_T$), and the variance associated with random measurement error ($\sigma^2{}_E$), it is as follows: $\sigma^2{}_X = \sigma^2{}_T + \sigma^2{}_E$. Using this rewritten formula, the reliability of a test can be mathematically represented as follows: $r_{xx} = \sigma^2{}_T/\sigma^2{}_X$. In other words, we can think about a reliability coefficient as a ratio of two types of variance: true score variance divided by the variance of the entire test.

Returning to the example from earlier, if a particular test has a reliability coefficient of 0.83, 83% of the variance in test scores is due to true score variance. If the test were perfectly constant or stable—that is, perfect psychometric reliability—100% of the test score variance would be due to true score variance. Such a test would have no measurement error. In reality, tests are characterized by some degree of measurement error, which can be quantified if we know the reliability coefficient of the test: error = 1.0 minus r_{xx}. In very simple language, knowing a test's reliability coefficient allows us to quickly calculate how much measurement error is associated with the test, which maps directly on to *Daubert v. Merrell Dow Pharmaceuticals* (1993) and FRE Rule 702, and the state-level equivalents of these laws.

Returning to Table 3.1, each of the major types of reliability are quantified using a different reliability coefficient. For example, measuring test–retest reliability involves checking to see how much scores on the same test correlate with each other at two different points in time. A group of examinees would take the test at Time 1 and then again at Time 2, say two weeks later or three months later. Each test-taker would have two scores, one for each time, making it possible to calculate a correlation.

It is important to appreciate that each type of reliability is affected by different sources of measurement error. For example, test–retest reliability is affected by time sampling. This means the timing of test administration, which can vary across the two time points, can change scores. If, for example, a student has a cold when she takes the test at Time 2 (an internal source of measurement error), being sick might cause her to score lower. Similarly, if a different student gets distracted by his teacher's ringing phone at Time 1 (an external source of measurement error), that could cause him to score lower.

In contrast, split-half reliability is affected by content sampling. This means the correlation between test items is affected by poor or imbalanced selection of test content across the two halves of the test. With split-half reliability, a test is divided in half and test-takers' scores on test items, for each half, are correlated with each other. If the test items from one half of the test are much more difficult than the test items from the other half of the test, the correlation will attenuate.

In short, reliability coefficients quantify the relationship between test items, but under varying circumstances. The same test items may be correlated with each other across two points in time (test–retest reliability). Different test items may be correlated with each other at one point in time (split-half, coefficient alpha, or KR-20). Two different tests may be correlated with each other at one point in time (alternate forms). Or, the same test may be given by two different subjective raters at one point in time (inter-rater reliability).

How reliable must a test be? This depends on the nature of the question being addressed. Reynolds and Livingston (2012) recommend a reliability coefficient of 0.90 or higher if the results will be used to make extremely important decisions that are not easily reversed. For example, assessing a legal competency is an important decision that may not be easily reversed, meaning that tests with reliability below 0.90 may inject unacceptable levels of measurement error into the decision-making process. This makes forensic assessment instruments (FAIs) with no known error rate potentially problematic.

For example, the JACI, an FAI described in Chapter 2, has no known error rate because it cannot be scored. Instead, one subjectively gleans information from examinee responses to interview questions, a process that could conceivably result in markedly different conclusions about adjudicative competence, depending upon what information the evaluator chooses to emphasize and weight. In contrast to the JACI, other FAIs *can* be quantitatively scored, making it possible to compute a reliability coefficient and measure the test's error rate.

Reynolds and Livingston (2012) recommend 0.70 as an acceptable reliability coefficient if the test is being used for screening purposes, which means the decision being made based on the test results *can* be easily reversed. Hence, if a screening test incorrectly identifies someone as having a problem, and the test has an error rate of 30%, that is not a problem if the incorrect identification can be easily reversed once more reliable testing has been done.

So, for example, if a forensic evaluator were using a screening test for adjudicative competence with a 30% error rate, and the test incorrectly identified certain defendants as incompetent, that error may be unacceptable. Therefore, in situations where it is extremely important to get it right—which is often the case in forensic assessment—it makes sense to use highly reliable tests from the outset. Unfortunately, it is not uncommon to encounter forensic psychologists using screening tests with low reliability and to *not* follow up their results with tests that have less measurement error.

Standard Error of Measurement

As defined earlier, the SD is "the average deviation of the raw scores about their mean" (Pagano, 1994, p. 77), which gives us a sense of how much a group of scores differ or vary from each other. The SD is calculated by taking the square root of the variance, which was also explained earlier. Large SDs reflect wide variability among a group of scores, while small SDs reflect little variability among a group of scores. It is easy to compute the SD in an actual sample of scores, if one knows all the scores. Because the SD cannot actually be calculated on a *theoretical* distribution of scores, it is sometimes estimated. The standard error of measurement (SEM)—defined by Reynolds and Livingston (2012) as "the standard deviation of the distribution of scores that would be obtained by one person if he or she were tested on an infinite number of parallel forms of a test comprised of items randomly sampled from the same content domain" (pp. 135–136)—is an example of an *estimated* SD. The AERA (2014) offer a slightly different, but nonetheless helpful, definition of the SEM:

> The standard deviation of an individual's observed scores from repeated administrations of a test (or parallel forms of a test) under identical conditions. Because such data generally cannot be collected, the standard error of measurement is usually estimated from group data. (pp. 223–224)

The main value of the SEM is that it allows us to generate confidence intervals, which are bands around an examinee's obtained score or, more precisely, around their estimated true score. This is important because it speaks to the degree of measurement error associated with the test, as emphasized in the *Daubert* decision (methods must have a "known or potential rate of error") and FRE 702 ("the testimony is the product of reliable principles and methods."). The SEM is easily calculated using a test's SD and the test's reliability coefficient (r_{xx}). The formula is as follows: $SEM = SD\sqrt{1 - rxx}$.

The amount of measurement error associated with a test score increases as a function of the test's SEM, which is a function of the test's reliability. The less reliable the test, the larger the SEM is going to be, which will lead to wider confidence intervals around the examinee's test score. Briefer tests generally have lower reliability coefficients, which translates into more measurement error. This is why longer assessments, involving tests with larger reliability coefficients, can generate evidence of much higher quality.

In their discussion of the problems with abbreviated-battery intelligence tests, versus full-battery intelligence tests, Kaufman et al. (2015) said the following:

> The standard error of measurements (SEMs) for abbreviated-battery IQ tests are *considerably larger* than is the case for full-battery IQ tests, which is important because we use SEMs to create confidence intervals around our IQ scores. The larger the SEM, the wider the confidence intervals around the IQ score, which puts the examiner in the undesirable position of having less confidence in their findings. Accordingly, an estimate of one's IQ, accompanied by roomy confidence intervals—say, from 74 to 92—is like being 95% confident that you will have a pleasant day or get hit by a truck while crossing the street. (p. 85)

When tests have a lot of measurement error, which increases as a function of the size of the SEM, they become less and less helpful to the decision-making process. In contrast, when tests have very little measurement error, they can generate highly reliable information, which is more helpful to decision-makers and comports with the requirements of *Daubert v. Merrell Dow Pharmaceuticals* (1993) and FRE 702 and related state-level cases (e.g., *State v. Alberico*, 1993).

Test Validity

Reliability increases as a function of the number of test items, as just noted. Therefore, tests with more test questions are more reliable. This makes sense because the examiner has, in effect, sampled more of the examinee's behavior. This only holds, however, if the sample of behavior is relevant. For example, if one were interested in measuring intelligence and the IQ test included test questions about food and beverage preferences, the IQ test *content* would be inappropriate, since food and beverage preferences have no relationship to intelligence. Stated another way, the evidence for test validity based on test content would be lacking.

Test validity, according to AERA (2014), is "the degree to which accumulated evidence and theory support a specific interpretation of test scores for a given use of a test. If multiple interpretations of a test score for different uses are intended, validity evidence for each interpretation is needed" (p. 225). In other words, use of a test is said to be valid if that particular use of the test is supported by scientific evidence. Reynolds and Livingston (2012) defined validity as "the appropriateness or accuracy of the interpretation of test scores" (p. 155). These authors also noted that "it is not technically correct to refer to the validity of a test [because] … Validity is a characteristic of the interpretations given to test scores" (p. 155). Whereas validity has historically been conceptualized as something that, not unlike reliability, can be quantified and measured, contemporary definitions of test validity emphasize how the test is used and interpreted.

It has long been accepted that tests cannot be valid if they lack reliability. This is important because a test's value to a forensic referral question can be ruled out based only on an appraisal of a test's reliability; if it lacks adequate reliability, it cannot be used in a valid manner. So while the definition of test validity has evolved away from saying a test is valid or invalid, nothing has changed about reliability being a necessary condition for validity; that is, a test cannot be used and interpreted validly if reliability has not first been established.

How does one *validly* use and interpret a test? This is, perhaps, less straightforward than appraising a test's reliability because, "validation is a process, one that involves an ongoing, dynamic effort to accumulate evidence for a sound scientific basis for proposed test interpretations" (Reynolds & Livingston, p. 155). Whereas a psychologist can look for tests with high reliability coefficients, it is not as easy to know if a test can be validly used with certain populations or under certain circumstances. A test user can turn to a test manual for evidence of validity; however, this is not enough, since evidence against the validity of a test may not be present in the manual. Such evidence is often more likely to be encountered in the scientific literature, which is always evolving. That said, validity evidence for tests comes from multiple sources, three categories of which will be explored next.

Content Validity Evidence

First, tests that appropriately sample from the larger domain of interest are said to have *content validity evidence*. For example, if a test purports to measure the construct of depression, it would be expected to have items that are a reflection of this construct: feels hopeless; thinks about suicide; cannot enjoy oneself; wants to sleep all day (or cannot fall asleep); and so forth. So-called face validity evidence is easily confused with content validity evidence; the former is superficial evidence of validity, whereas the latter "is acquired through a systematic and technical analysis of the test content" (Reynolds & Livingston, 2012, p. 164). Interestingly, some test items with high content validity may not have face validity, meaning that the test item truly samples from the domain of interest, even though it does not appear to do so. Also of interest, tests lacking in face validity might not perform as well and might not be accepted by the general public, who are looking for easy-to-spot reasons to see the test as valid. Therefore, face validity is perhaps more important than one might realize.

Criterion-Related Validity Evidence

Second, *criterion-related validity evidence* is based on establishing relationships between tests that purport to measure the same thing. This can be accomplished, for example, by seeing if intelligence test A correlates with intelligence tests B, C, and D. Alternatively, the criterion can be something other than a test, like real-world functioning (e.g., school grades) or number of future arrests, in which case a correlation between the test and the real-world variable is statistically examined. As another example, criterion-related validity evidence would be present if a test measuring risk for future violent behavior correlated strongly with future violent acts.

Criterion-related validity evidence is typically generated by establishing relationships between the test and other relevant variables at the same point in time, or at some future point in time. For example, concurrent evidence for a test of anger might come from number of arguments one has had in the week prior to taking the anger test. Predictive evidence for a test of anger could be based on a correlation between the anger test score and future number of physical fights.

Whatever the criterion variable (e.g., another test or real-world functioning), it is important that the criterion also be reliable and valid. Ideally, the criterion should be something considered to be the best example of the construct of interest, although this may not always be possible. And under no circumstances should there be *criterion contamination*, which is when the test score and the criterion variable are not independent. Criterion contamination was part of the basis for Kaufman's (2020) critique of the Autism Diagnostic Inventory-Revised (ADI-R; Lord et al., 1994) and the Autism Diagnostic Observation Scale-Second Edition (ADOS; Lord et al., 2012), which employed a research design where "clinicians used clinical judgment to form an opinion about which participants had autism, but these clinicians knew whether or not the ADI-R and ADOS pointed toward, or away from, an autism diagnosis, setting the stage for a hindsight bias scenario" (p. 7).

In other words, scores on the ADI-R and ADOS—two tests used to assess autism—were correlated with the clinical judgments of clinicians as to the presence of autism; however, the clinicians knew the ADI-R and ADOS scores *before they formed their clinical judgements* about whether or not the study participants had autism. Hence, the clinical judgements were influenced, or contaminated, by knowledge of the ADI-R and ADOS scores. This would not have been a problem if the clinicians formed their opinions about the presence or absence of autism *without* knowing what the ADI-R and ADOS tests said before they rendered their clinical opinions.

Another type of criterion-related validity evidence is discriminant evidence. This is when a test does not correlate with things (e.g., other tests or real-world functioning) that it should not correlate with. For example, scores on a psychopathy test should not positively correlate with real-world generosity or compassionate parenting, demonstrated over many years. In comparison, convergent evidence comes from correlations between the test and other criteria for which one would expect to see a relationship. For example, scores on a psychopathy test might positively correlate with scores on a substance-use test or with number of alcoholic beverages consumed each weekend.

Consequential Validity Evidence

Third, *consequential validity evidence* is based on the consequences of using a test to improve decision-making, but also the consequences of *not* using a test for decision-making. For example, if an intelligence test is used to make a diagnosis of borderline intellectual functioning (Ferrari, 2009), the diagnosis could cause an examinee, or their family members, to feel bad. What parent wants their child to be given a diagnosis based on having a lower IQ? What adult wants to receive a diagnosis based on having a lower IQ? But what if this diagnosis is then relied upon, as a mitigating factor, to help inform a judge during a sentencing hearing? One could argue that use of the test has led to a more just legal outcome, insofar as the judge views the diagnosis as justification for a more therapeutic, rather than punitive, sentence.

The Validity Argument

Reynolds and Livingston (2012) present the idea of a *validity argument*, which "involves the integration of numerous lines of evidence into a coherent commentary" (p. 179). We interpret this to mean that the test user is responsible for justifying their use of the test. Notably, this does not automatically mean that a particular test can only be used if it has norms based on a sample of individuals who are similar to the test-taker, although that is sometimes desirable (recall the discussion from Chapter 2 on "scoring"). In the context of forensic assessment, a validity argument would mean the evaluator is ready to be cross-examined about why they used a certain test to address a particular question, or why they opted to *not* use a test to improve decision-making.

Sensitivity and Specificity

Tests are used to improve accuracy in decision-making, which is why they have been developed and widely embraced (Dahlstrom, 1993). We can operationalize *accuracy* by comparing a test's results to what is actually known. The more the test results mesh with what is actually known, the more accurate the test. This relationship between test results and a known outcome—for example, disorder truly present or disorder truly absent—is depicted in a contingency table (see Table 3.2).

If we only consider those truly known to have a disorder and cross-tabulate this information with the results of the test (i.e., test is positive or test is negative), we can compute the test's sensitivity: (TP/(TP + FN)). In simple language, "sensitivity is the percentage of those correctly identified by the test as having the [disorder]" (Kaufman, 2020, p. 7). If we only consider those truly known to *not* have a disorder and cross-tabulate this information with

Table 3.2 Contingency table

	Disorder Truly Present	*Disorder Truly Absent*
Test Positive	A (True Positives)	B (False Positives)
Test Negative	C (False Negatives)	D (True Negatives)

the results of the test (i.e., test is positive or test is negative), we can compute the test's specificity: (TN/(TN + FP)). In simple language, "specificity is the percentage of those correctly identified by the test as *not* having the [disorder]" (Kaufman, 2020, p. 7).

The problem with sensitivity and specificity is that they are both backward-looking (Grimes & Shulz, 2002). So while sensitivity and specificity have descriptive value with regard to how a test performed in the past, on a particular sample, and under certain circumstances, clinicians and factfinders are often more interested in what will happen in the future. This is where positive and negative predictive values come into play, the next topic of discussion.

Statements about a test's sensitivity and specificity cannot always be generalized to other settings. That is, the validity evidence of a test with a particular sample, including sensitivity and specificity, may not generalize to other test-takers. Assuming it does, the test-user will still have to make decisions about using a test with high sensitivity versus one with high specificity, because it is rare for tests to have both high sensitivity and high specificity. For example, if failure to identify a disorder carries potentially severe consequences (e.g., death due to undetected illness), it is important to use a test with high sensitivity. If failure to identify a disorder does not carry severe consequences (e.g., almost no likelihood of a bad health outcome), it is important to use a test with high specificity.

To illustrate using a forensic example, it makes sense to use a test with very high sensitivity for detecting sexually violent recidivism. In contrast, it makes more sense to use a test with high specificity for detecting future truancy among youthful offenders. We do not want to miss preventing future sexual violence, whereas missing the detection of future truancy is not going to have severe consequences.

Positive and Negative Predictive Accuracy

As stated earlier, clinicians and factfinders are often more interested in what will happen in the future, which is where positive and negative predictive values can be more helpful than sensitivity and specificity. If we only consider those with positive test results, and cross-tabulate this with what is truly known (i.e., truly has the disorder and truly does not have the disorder), we can compute the positive predictive value: (TP/(TP + FP)). Stated plainly, this is the probability of truly having the disorder if the test is positive. In contrast, if we only consider those with negative test results, and cross-tabulate this with what is truly known (i.e., truly has the disorder and truly does not have the disorder), we can compute the negative predictive value: (TN/(TN + FN)). Stated plainly, this is the probability of truly *not* having the disorder if the test is negative.

Positive and negative predictive values are influenced by the base rate of the disorder in the study sample. Therefore, if the sample includes many individuals who truly have the disorder, the base rate will be high. Likewise, if the sample only has a small number of individuals who truly have the disorder, the base rate will be low. This is very important because the positive and negative predictive values in one setting may not generalize to other settings, where the base rate is different. This was cogently explained by Grimes and Shulz (2002) as follows:

> Clinicians must know the approximate prevalence of the condition of interest in the population being tested; if not, reasonable interpretation is impossible. Consider a new PCR test for chlamydia, with a sensitivity of 0.98 and specificity of 0.97 (a superb test) … a doctor uses the test in a municipal sexually transmitted disease clinic, where the prevalence of Chlamydia trachomatis is 30%. In this high-prevalence setting … 93% of those with a positive test actually have the infection. Impressed with the new test, the doctor now takes it to her private practice in the suburbs, which has a clientele that is mostly older than age 35 years … Here, the prevalence of chlamydial infection is only 3%. Now the same excellent test has a predictive positive value of only 0.50 … Here, flipping a coin has the same predictive positive value (and is considerably cheaper and simpler than searching for bits of DNA). This message is important, yet not widely understood: when used in low prevalence settings, even excellent tests have poor predictive positive value. (p. 883)

Hence, evidence of a test's validity (e.g., a high positive predictive value) in a study where the base rate for the condition of interest is high cannot be generalized to other settings—if the base rate for the condition of interest is much lower in the other setting. This ties into the discussion from Chapter 2 on "scoring" and has relevance to forensic assessment whenever the forensic evaluator is trying to generate reliable information that will improve decision-making in scenarios where the base rate for the condition of interest deviates from the base rate in the study. To illustrate, performance and symptom validity tests have not been studied in many forensic samples, which can translate into overestimates of malingering, as explained in Chapter 2 (see "Scoring.").

Youden's J Index, Hit Rate, and Diagnostic Odds Ratio

It can be valuable to combine sensitivity and specificity information into a single score, that describes the *overall* accuracy of a test. One available statistic is Youden's J Index (Youden, 1950). It is computed as follows: (sensitivity + specificity − 1.0). Youden's J Index is valuable because, unlike the positive and negative predictive values, it is *independent* of the sample base rate. In practice, Youden's index will fall somewhere between 0 and 1, not unlike a positive correlation coefficient, making it easy to interpret. However, some have criticized this statistic for being difficult to interpret (Glas et al., 2003).

An alternative to Youden's J index is the Hit Rate, another index of a test's overall accuracy. Hit Rate is computed as follows: (TP + TN)/(TP + TN +

FP + FN). It is "the percentage of those correctly identified by the test, both in terms of true positives and true negatives" (Kaufman, 2020, p. 6). Unfortunately, the Hit Rate *is* influenced by the sample base rate, which means the higher the sample base rate, the higher the hit rate; likewise, if the base rate of the condition is low in the sample, the Hit Rate will also be low.

For this reason, generalizations about a test's Hit Rate from a sample to a real-world situation cannot be made if the base rate of the condition of interest differs across settings. To illustrate, a study could be done on the Hit Rate of a malingering test, using a sample with a large number of malingerers. The test might demonstrate a good Hit Rate in the study. But the test will not perform as well in real-world settings where the base rate of malingerers is lower, or not known to be high.

Another way of combining all the information in Table 3.2 to get an overall test accuracy score is to compute a diagnostic odds ratio: odds ratio = (A/B)/(C/D); or (sensitivity × specificity)/((1 – sensitivity) × (1 – specificity)). Scores on the diagnostic odds ratio can be as low as zero or as high as infinity. Tests that do not outperform chance have an odds ratio of 1.0, meaning the test is not helping in the identification of the condition of interest. This is analogous to having a "50/50" chance (i.e., 50/50 = 1.0). Therefore, it is important that the odds ratio be greater than 1.0; ideally, this value will be considerably higher than 1.0. As the name states, the diagnostic odds ratio is a *ratio*, meaning one value divided by another value. More specifically, it is a ratio divided by another ratio. Using Table 3.2, it is the true positives (A) divided by the false positives (B), which is then divided by the false negatives (C) divided by the true negatives (D). Stated more plainly, assuming the diagnostic odds ratio on a validity test comes out to be 12, one could say, "If you failed the validity test, you are 12 times more likely to have generated invalid information than if you did not fail the validity test," which combines the good and the bad qualities of the test into a single, understandable statement about how effective the test was at correctly identifying those who generate invalid information in the original group of participants.

Conclusion

Forensic mental health professionals collect data on defendants to better understand their abnormal behavior, which is then relied upon by legal professionals for the purposes of just decision-making. If legal professionals and factfinders (i.e., judges and juries) knew as much about abnormal human behavior as mental health professionals, there would be no need for expertise in this particular area. But that is not the case. Of the five sources of information relied upon by forensic experts, described in Chapter 2, testing data is frequently the least subjective. The flip side to this coin is that it is more objective, and therefore more scientific.

But it is not adequate to say, "testing is more scientific," as will be explained in Chapter 4. What does such a statement *really* mean? Perhaps more than anything else, it means that we can actually measure, in a quantitative way, the extent to which a method is prone to error, which comports with the *Daubert* decision, FRE Rule 702, and the state equivalent of these laws. Moreover, the process of doing this is a result of years of critical scientific thinking, which has culminated in generally accepted practices that are based largely on CCT, described in this chapter. To illustrate, when a psychological or neuropsychological test is published, the manual must include extensive information on the test's psychometric reliability, as well as validity evidence (AERA et al., 2014).

When forensic experts review records, it is highly subjective. When forensic experts interview a defendant without a structured clinical interview that can be scored, the information generated can be also highly subjective. The same holds for interviewing of others and observations made about a defendant's appearance and behavior during testing. However, because the opining of experts in legal settings is frequently controlled by the *Daubert* decision and FRE Rule 702, or the state equivalents of these laws, it is valuable to use methods that have known error rates, whenever possible. This is precisely why psychological and neuropsychological tests deserve special attention in the forensic setting. And it is why we have devoted an entire chapter of this book to fundamental measurement concepts in forensic assessment.

4 "Science" and "the Law"

Forensic mental health professionals rely on scientific findings to support their opinions. But what is a scientific finding? Forensic mental health professionals must also have an understanding of the law. But what is "the law"? In this chapter, we will consider these questions in greater detail, beginning with discussion of science.

"Science"

What is science? This important question was posed by O'Donohue et al. (2007), who wrote, "Surprisingly, there has not been a clear, consistent answer to this question." (p. 9). These authors offered various ways of conceptualizing science, three of which we have summarized in Table 4.1, and will explore next.

Science as Error Correction

First, *science as error correction* comes from Sir Karl Popper, a philosopher who said that science is a way of solving important problems. Popper noted that humans stand out from animals by their ability to think critically and test hypotheses. It is this testing of hypotheses, in an ongoing attempt to falsify them, that is at the core of the Popperian scientific process. And it is the explanatory power of an overall theory that dictates whether or not that theory will endure. Perhaps counterintuitively, Popperian proponents of a theory are not defensive about their ideas. Rather, they constantly welcome new ideas that challenge their thinking. There are no sacred cows under the model of science as error correction.

To illustrate, consider that it is currently accepted that one of the upper limits for a mild traumatic brain injury (mTBI) is loss of consciousness of no more than 30 minutes. In other words, if one loses consciousness for more than 30 minutes, the brain injury is no longer considered "mild"; instead, it is considered "moderate" or "severe," depending upon how much beyond 30 minutes the loss of consciousness lasts. This threshold of 30 minutes is found in multiple mTBI definitions (Kaufman et al., 2019), indicating that it

DOI: 10.4324/9780367645090-4

Table 4.1 Conceptualizations of science from O'Donohue et al. (2007, pp. 9–23)

Conceptualization	*Explanation*
1. "Science as Error Correction"	Science is an ongoing process of hypothesis testing, identifying error, and welcoming constructive criticism about the theory's explanatory power.
2. "Science as Methodological Anarchy"	Science demands that scientists constantly question accepted methodologies, remain open to completely different methodologies, and appraise methodology by how much it contributes to the problem-solving enterprise.
3. "Science as Argument and Persuasion"	Science can ultimately be seen as a very sophisticated form of persuasion, both of the scientist about their own ideas and then of others (e.g., the public).

has gained considerable general acceptance. One might ask, however, why 30 minutes? Why not 15 minutes? Or ten minutes? A reasonable hypothesis, therefore, is that the boundary line between a truly mild brain injury, and one characterized by categorically more symptoms (i.e., enough to go from the category of "mild" to "moderate" or "severe"), has yet to be accurately demarcated.

That said, in the absence of compelling evidence to support a new hypothesis, asserting that 30 minutes should be replaced with some other length of time (15 minutes, 10 minutes, etc.), it is reasonable to proffer opinions in legal settings that color *inside* the lines of what is still generally accepted. But that is not the same stance as rigidly and inflexibly refusing to consider new, well-conducted research that leads to the falsification of how mTBIs are currently defined. Nor is it the same as proffering opinions in legal settings that extend beyond what is currently known about mTBIs, without having first falsified the dominant mTBI paradigm.

Science as Methodological Anarchy

Second, *science as methodological anarchy* comes from one of Karl Popper's students, Paul Feyerabend, who said scientific methods only matter if they lead to reliable results. This is an anything-goes approach to conducting science that "sees science as a radically creative enterprise, attempting always to see limits in any rule or prescribed method" (O'Donohue et al., 2007, p. 18), which is not to say that it is a seat-of-the-pants enterprise. This conceptualization of science constantly challenges the status quo and remains focused on how reliable and effective a particular method is at solving important problems. Under this definition of science, mTBI researchers would be encouraged to empirically dismantle current thinking (e.g., 30 minutes of unconsciousness as a fixed boundary between a mild and a moderate TBI) by designing studies that effectively lead to the construction of more nuanced definitions of mTBI, possibly involving shorter periods of unconsciousness.

Science as Argument and Persuasion

Third, *science as argument and persuasion* embraces the importance of convincing others as part of the scientific process. But first, the scientist must persuade or convince themselves that their ideas are correct through diligent attempts to control for bias. O'Donohue et al. (2007) explained this process as follows:

> The psychological experiment is an attempt at persuasion … Random sampling is a move designed to persuade those concerned by the claim that "The sample was biased and so therefore the results are unpersuasive due to their unrepresentativeness." Random assignment is a move designed to persuade those concerned by the claim "The groups might have been different from the start." The no-treatment control condition is a move designed to persuade those concerned by the claim "The problem would have spontaneously remitted." (p. 20)

This way of viewing science is noteworthy because it implies a responsibility for the scientist to go beyond the laboratory by promoting their scientific findings to non-scientists. It also draws attention to the connection between scientific findings and dissemination of those findings among those who stand to benefit—namely, the general public.

A Pragmatic View of Science

By challenging commonplace beliefs about science and breaking down various scientific myths, Goodstein (2011) offered a pragmatic discussion of science, which we will unpack. Considered one of the fathers of modern science, Galileo di Vincenzo Bonaiuti de' Galilei (i.e., "Galileo") is known to have put the scientific process above the influence of political and religious authority, suggesting that scientists purely operate in a vacuum of unbiased, rigorous thinking that is unaffected by social pressure. Goodstein (2011), in contrast, said that authority within the scientific community in fact *does* greatly influence how scientists operate. Similarly, Goodstein, after acknowledging Sir Francis Bacon as a key figure in scientific history, proceeded to question how applicable Bacon's ideas are today: "But Bacon's idea, that science proceeds through the collection of observations without prejudices, has been rejected by all serious thinkers" (p. 40). Likewise, rather than viewing scientists as open-minded about discarding established ideas, Goodstein described science as a competition among scientists, who "tenaciously cling to their ideas, even in the face of contrary evidence" (p. 48). Goodstein also critiqued the assertion that the peer-review process is infallible and that university-based research is unbiased and free of conflicts of interest. He pointed out that distinguishing real science from pseudoscience is easier said than done. And he asserted that even old theories, after having been proven wrong, can remain in play, if not outright useful. In short, Goodstein reminds us that science does not take place in a social vacuum; instead, it is impacted by social pressure.

Forensic Experts and Science

There is perhaps no simple answer for those asking what science is, which is important to consider whenever bold assertions about "the science" are used to justify opinions or decision-making. In other words, while most would likely agree that science is an epistemology—that is, a way of accumulating knowledge and understanding the world around us—involving intellectual competition and ongoing efforts to reduce bias and minimize error, precisely how science is carried out can vary considerably. Therefore, it is ironic when anyone, including mental health experts, justify their beliefs or actions using "the science" because "the science" is anything but fixed and established; rather, it is a dynamic, organic, living process that welcomes challenges and new good ideas.

Broad statements by experts about "the science" are problematic. When experts proffer scientific opinions, as they are allowed to do under *Daubert* v. *Merrell Dow Pharmaceuticals* (1993) and Federal Rule of Evidence (FRE) Rule 702 (or the state-level versions of these laws), it is reasonable to expect them to explain exactly the scientific foundation on which they are basing their opinions. The opinion might, for example, rest on the results of studies employing random assignment, which is scientific. The expert might cite peer-reviewed scientific literature in their report, to tether their statements to the established progress made by other scientists. Alternatively, the expert might utilize—and be able to testify about—tests with good psychometric characteristics, another tangible example of science. Whatever the case, it is not enough to say the opinion is based on "the science," because science encompasses too many things to justify such an oversimplification and because intellectual shortcuts like this invite sophistry, which does not improve legal decision-making by factfinders.

One way to know if a forensic mental health expert is relying on science is to consider the extent to which they are standing on the shoulders of scientific giants. This might sound trite, but, we believe, it is helpful. As will be explained next, pseudoscience is characterized by an "absence of connectivity," meaning that the ideas do not build on the good ideas of others. Real science, in contrast, slowly but surely progresses and improves over time. This progress was explained by Goodstein (2011) as follows:

> [Science] is one of the few areas of human endeavor that is genuinely progressive. There is no doubt that the quality of twentieth century science is better than nineteenth century science, and we can be absolutely

> confident that the quality of science in the twenty-first century will be better still. One cannot say the same about, say, art or literature. (p. 44)

Scientific Versus Pseudoscientific Methods

It is important to distinguish between methods that are in fact scientific, versus those that *seem* scientific on the surface, but—when considered more carefully—are not. In other words, we want to distinguish between science and pseudoscience whenever possible. To illustrate, social scientists have learned that the aggregation of delinquent youths with mental health challenges in an unstructured, inpatient treatment setting (e.g., a Residential Treatment Center [RTC] or group home) leads to the development of more antisocial behavior in this population (Chamberlain et al., 2007; Chamberlain & Reid, 1998; Dishion et al., 1999, 2001; Greenwood, 2008; Lipsey, 1995; Poulin et al., 2001), making RTCs, group homes, and other similar interventions iatrogenic (i.e., harmful). Stated plainly, the scientific studies just reviewed do not support these interventions, and yet they are still delivered on a regular basis in states like New Mexico, where judges frequently order them.

As another example, one of us recently testified in a hearing where the prosecution's expert had given a full-battery intelligence test, but had not corrected for the Flynn Effect (Flynn, 1984)—"a well documented phenomenon demonstrating score increases on IQ measures over time that average about 0.3 points per year" (Reynolds et al., 2010, p. 477). When cross-examined about this, the expert acknowledged that there is research "out there" on the Flynn Effect, but added that none of the psychologists she knew made the correction. In short, this expert was practicing forensic psychology without relying on the extensive scientific support for the Flynn Effect (Gresham, 2009; Gresham & Reschly, 2011; Trahan et al., 2014). Viewed from a slightly different vantage point, this expert was taking a position that, in order to be supported by science, should have at least been based on research that justifies *not* correcting for the Flynn Effect. Hence, the expert could have cited such research (e.g., Hagan et al., 2010), to offer a foundation for the opinion.

In their excellent book devoted entirely to distinguishing between science and pseudoscience in clinical psychology and related mental health fields, Lilienfeld et al. (2015) effectively captured the important distinction between science, on the one hand, and pseudoscience, on the other hand, as follows:

> The sprawling terrain of clinical psychology and allied disciplines (e.g., psychiatry, social work, counseling, school psychology, psychiatry nursing) houses two largely disconnected worlds. One world consists of researches and *practitioners* [emphasis added] who ground their work largely in *scientific* [emphasis added] evidence … Practitioners in this first world actively consume research findings and base their interventions and diagnostic methods largely on the best available published findings. The other world … consists of mental health professionals who routinely neglect research

> evidence … [and] commonly administer therapeutic and assessment methods that are either unsupported or inadequately tested. (p. 1)

In the foregoing quote are two important key words: *practitioners* and *scientific*. Practitioners are mental health clinicians who engage in face-to-face clinical work with real people, variously referred to as "patients," "clients," or—in the specific context of adult criminal and juvenile justice law—"defendants," "litigants," or "examinees." Scientists, in contrast to practitioners, are those who use the scientific method to generate and develop ideas and methods for practitioners to use in real-world settings. The methods used by the practitioners depend on the work of the scientists. When practitioners-in-training go to school to learn about their profession, they read articles and books written by scientists. Therefore, scientists and practitioners work together, each playing important roles in the delivery of mental health services to society. In reality, however, the scientists and the practitioners do not always work together, which can have two deleterious effects.

First, when practitioners cease to utilize the methods developed by the scientists, consumers of the mental health services delivered by the practitioners may suffer because they are receiving services that may not be effective. As explained by Lilienfeld et al. (2015) and others (Pennington, 2008), this can be *iatrogenic*, meaning harmful. It can also be a waste of the consumer's time and it can erode the public's trust in the services provided by the practitioner. The aforementioned example involving youths being ordered by judges to receive mental health treatment in RTCs, based on the assumption that such treatment is supported by social science, helps make this point.

The second deleterious effect, arising from the breakdown of healthy communication between scientists and practitioners, occurs when the scientists develop an arrogant, patronizing view of what practitioners do. Quite possibly this position, adopted by some scholarly scientists, is a result of spending all of their time in the proverbial ivory tower. What some of the scientists fail to appreciate is that their work is valuable, but only insofar as it leads to the delivery of improved mental health services—be it in treatment or forensic settings.

As makes logical sense, poor communication between the scientist and the practitioner can happen on both sides. Hence, the problem is not specific to wayward practitioners, who leave their textbooks behind upon receipt of their professional credentials and entry into the world of face-to-face service delivery. However, it is the methods of the wayward practitioner—i.e., those rendering specious forensic mental health services to litigants, attorneys, and judges—that we will draw attention to next.

Ten Pseudoscientific Red Flags

Lilienfeld et al. (2015) identified ten pseudoscience red flags, to be considered when trying to ascertain if a method is scientific, or pseudoscientific. As will become evident, a single theme is present in the following description of these pseudoscientific red flags. Namely, real science, not unlike the adversarial legal system in the United States, is highly competitive, in an intellectual sense. In contrast, pseudoscience is fearful of this intellectual competition, and finds ways to eschew exposure.

First is "overuse of ad hoc [i.e., band-aid] hypotheses designed to immunize claims from falsification" (p. 7). This basically means failures of the pseudoscientific method are explained away with after-the-fact reasoning that has itself not been tested. And this after-the-fact, band-aid reasoning prevents the hypothesis from ever being proven wrong. Ad hoc hypotheses have a "Yeah, but …" quality, which can be useful when trying to spot them. To illustrate this concept, Lilienfeld et al. (2015) use the following example: "some proponents of eye movement desensitization reprocessing (EMDR) have argued that negative findings concerning EMDR are almost certainly attributable to low levels of fidelity to the treatment procedure" (p. 7). Such reasoning represents a moving of the goalpost if it avoids taking on the negative research findings more directly.

Second is an "absence of self-correction" (p. 7), meaning the pseudoscientific method never matures because it never benefits from the self-correcting process inherent to competitive intellectual environments. By way of comparison, cross-examination is a competitive intellectual environment, the value of which is based on self-correction; experts making untenable assertions are more likely to be shut down, at some point, as a result of being challenged on cross-examination. Peer review, discussed next, functions much like cross-examination.

Third, the peer-review process cultivates a healthy, competitive intellectual environment, which is why "evasion of peer review" (p. 7) does not foster scientific development of a method. Pseudoscientific methods shy away from the scrutiny of thoughtful challenges from peers. If this is allowed, new—potentially better—ideas are stymied, while old—potentially worse—ideas stagnate.

To illustrate, the diagnosis of autism has increasingly become synonymous with the use of certain assessment methods described as "gold standards." In other words, if certain autism assessment instruments are not used during an autism assessment, the clinician becomes open to criticism for not having used the "gold standard" methods and the diagnostic results of the evaluation may be rejected as invalid. Similarly, "best practices" involving group decision-making about autism diagnosis are often encountered in the same literature. In other words, if a single clinician renders a clinical opinion about autism, it may be rejected because the decision was not made by a group or "team" of clinicians. However, as explained by Kaufman (2020), the scientific evidence for "gold standard" tests and "best practices" involving group diagnostic decision-making has not stood up to the rigors of scientific scrutiny, giving assertions about "gold standards" and "best practices" a strong *ipse dixit* (i.e., it-is-because-I-say-so) quality, a telltale sign of pseudoscience.

Fourth, a *confirmation bias* (Wason, 1960) occurs when there is an "emphasis on confirmation rather than refutation" (p. 8). This pseudoscientific red flag was discussed in Chapter 2.

Fifth, "reversed burden of proof" (p. 8) is easily appreciated by attorneys, who know that having the burden of proving something is more challenging than not having this burden. Criminal defendants in the state of NM, for instance, have the burden of proving to the court—by a preponderance of the evidence—that they are not competent to proceed through the adjudicative process (see *State v. Chavez*, 2007 in Section II of this book). The pseudoscientist, rather than accepting the burden of proving their claims, will "instead demand that skeptics demonstrate beyond a reasonable doubt that a claim (e.g., an assertion regarding the efficacy of a novel therapeutic technique) is false" (p. 8).

Sixth, "absence of connectivity" (p. 8) is when the pseudoscientific method does not build on existing knowledge. To illustrate, Ioannidis (2015) successfully challenged pseudoscientific assertions made by Elizabeth Holmes, then cheif executive officer (CEO) of Theranos, a new biotechnology company claiming to have developed cutting-edge methods for laboratory testing. Dr. Ioannidis' concerns arose out of a lack of connectivity between Holmes' assertions and existing scientific literature. When someone makes claims about new and superior methodology that do not build upon all of the good ideas already established by other deep thinkers (i.e., scientists), this is a red flag.

Seventh, "overreliance on testimonial and anecdotal evidence" (p. 9) invokes the concepts of *illusory correlation* (Chapman & Chapman, 1969) and *regression to the mean* (Campbell & Kenny, 1999), both described previously in Chapter 2. To illustrate, a method may seemingly work for an individual, causing that individual to offer a testimonial in favor of the method. But the method may have "worked" for other reasons, including reasons (e.g., illusory correlation or regression to the mean) having nothing to do with the effectiveness of the method. Hence, while it is nice to receive praise in the form of a testimonial, that praise may be empty if it is based on unsophisticated logic, used by the individual making the testimonial. Simply put, testimonials are logically vulnerable and, therefore, insufficient from a scientific standpoint.

Eighth, "use of obscurantist language" (p. 9) is when sophisticated-sounding language is used to describe a pseudoscientific method. Lilienfeld et al. (2015) cite Shapiro (1995), the developer of eye movement desensitization reprocessing (EMDR), who provides a good example of pseudo-scientific, obscurantist language:

> [The] valences of the neural receptors (synaptic potential) of the respective neuro networks, which separately store various information plateaus and levels of adaptive information, are represented by the letters Z through A. It is hypothesized that the high-valence target network (Z) cannot link up with the more adaptive information, which is stored in networks with a lower valence … The theory is that when the processing system is

> catalyzed in EMDR, the valance of the receptors is shifted downward so that they are capable of linking with the receptors of the neuro networks with progressively lower valances. (pp. 317–318)

Ninth, "absence of boundary conditions" means a method has no, or almost no, boundaries or limitations. It might, for example, be said to work for everyone, which would be a red flag. Scientific methods, in contrast to pseudoscientific methods, have limitations, which proponents are aware of and openly share.

Tenth, "the mantra of holism" is basically the idea that a method's effectiveness cannot be pinpointed, but that if one simply relaxes the rules and considers *all* of the information, cogent explanations will emerge. It is based on the idea that "the whole is greater than the sum of its parts," which avoids nailing down precisely what variable is having what effect. Stated another way, it is a loose way of thinking about cause and effect, which is the definition of unscientific. Lilienfeld et al. (2015) describe this pseudoscientific red flag as "heads I win, tails you lose" (p. 10) reasoning.

Scientific Versus Pseudoscientific Diagnosis

The foregoing ten pseudoscientific red flags are extremely helpful in rooting out problems with methods employed by forensic mental health experts, especially when these ten signs are considered with an active awareness of *Daubert v. Merrell Dow Pharmaceuticals* (1993), related case law (e.g., *State v. Alberico*, 1993), the FREs described in Chapter 2, or the state-level versions of these laws. Taken together, this framework can be applied to the results of forensic mental health evaluations, which often include a mental health diagnosis, condition, disease, or defect. Of particular importance, with specific regard to diagnosis, condition, disease, or defect, is the idea that forensic mental health clinicians are on much more solid scientific footing if they rely on the *DSM-5* (American Psychiatric Association, 2013). In contrast, the application of a mental diagnosis without adequate scientific support can be very problematic.

To illustrate, one of us was once asked by an attorney to see if her client had what the attorney was terming, "battered man syndrome," a condition not encountered in the scientific literature. The attorney was heavily invested in this theory of her case, and struggled to understand why there would likely be problems generating a scientific explanation for this disorder or condition. If forensic mental health experts rely on diagnoses, conditions, diseases, or defects that lack scientific support, they inject pseudoscience into the decision-making process. Not only can this damage the credibility of the expert, and their field, but it can lead to worse decision-making by the factfinders (i.e., judges and juries).

McCann et al. (2015) provide a more in-depth discussion of other pseudoscientific diagnoses, including the following: "rape trauma syndrome," "sexual addiction," "homosexual panic," "black rage," "road rage," "paraphilic coercive disorder," "codependency," "factitious disorder by proxy," "neonaticide/infanticide syndrome," "child sexual abuse accommodation syndrome," and "battered woman syndrome." Interestingly, premenstrual dysphoric disorder (PMDD) is now recognized in *DSM-5*, prompting McCann et al. (2015) to note that judges will now have to decide if PMDD can be the basis for a viable defense.

Pennington (2008) provided similar discussion in a chapter titled, *Less Well-Validated Learning Disorders*. In this chapter, he described central auditory processing disorder (CAPD) and sensory modulation disorder (SMD) as lacking scientific support and concluded that "ethical concerns" (p. 34) arise when such unvalidated diagnoses are used, in part because their use can delay or prevent a scientifically supported diagnosis and "appropriate treatment" (p. 34). It is difficult to imagine CAPD or SMD being used as a part of a criminal defense strategy, but the principles underlying their critique have high relevance to any criminal defense strategy that hinges on mental health conditions or diagnoses that lack scientific support.

While the *DSM-5* is widely relied upon by mental health clinicians, and includes valuable descriptive summaries of many disorders, it is not the only manual used to diagnose mental health disorders. An alternative is the ICD-10-CM (WHO, 2018), which includes diagnostic codes needed for billing of clinical (not forensic) mental health services. As touched on in Chapter 1, the *DSM-5* is not without limitations, which means that some diagnoses not specifically listed in the *DSM-5* are nonetheless valuable because they are based on a strong foundation of scientific scholarship. The diagnosis of mild cognitive impairment (Petersen, 2004) is one example. That said, there have been legal cases where a diagnosis *not* listed in the *DSM* is not recognized by the courts (see *State v. Alberico*, 1993, which is summarized in Section II).

The *DSM-5* includes some "Conditions That May Be a Focus of Clinical Attention," some of which do not have adequate scientific support. Borderline intellectual functioning (Ferrari, 2009) and malingering are two such conditions found in the *DSM-5*, but the scientific support for each varies drastically.

Whereas borderline intellectual functioning is as reliable as the intelligence test used to make this diagnosis/condition, which can be very high with full-battery intelligence tests, the condition of malingering has been heavily criticized by scholars who study malingering (Berry & Nelson, 2010; McDermott & Scott, 2015; Rogers & Shuman, 2006), making its use in the forensic setting ill-advised. Briefly, problems with the *DSM-5* conceptualization of malingering from Rogers and Bender (2013) include the following: Antisocial Personality Disorder is not a "distinguishing criterion" (p. 519) for malingering; "Any attempt to equate DSM-IV-TR [and DSM-5] with a 'diagnosis' of malingering is an egregious error" (p. 519); "all forensic evaluations include a forensic context; therefore, this item [i.e., being a criminal defendant] cannot distinguish between forensic examinees with genuine versus feigned disorders" (p. 520); and "the DSM-IV-TR [and DSM-5] screen is wrong 4 out of 5 times for identifying potential malingerers" (p. 520).

Simply stated, if a forensic evaluator opts to use a "Condition that May be a Focus of Clinical Attention," from the *DSM-5*, he or she should do so with awareness about the underlying scientific support for the condition. A diagnosis of borderline intellectual functioning based on a full-battery intelligence test, which has very low measurement error due to high test reliability (see Chapter 3), is defensible. But a *DSM-5* diagnosis of malingering is not.

"The Law"

What exactly is "the law"? In answering this important question, it is helpful to consider the different sources of law. In the United States, law is found at the federal and state levels. Broadly speaking, U.S. federal law govern the federal realm, including the federal courts, while state law governs within a given state, including in that state's courts. The federal government, as well as each state, has three main sources of law: (1) constitutional law; (2) statutory law; and (3) case or common law.

Constitutions are written collections of general protections and rights for individual citizens, and are the ultimate governing documents within that sovereign (either a state or the federal government). A constitution is a fundamental framework of directives that reflect the values of citizens, either within a state or within the entire country. For example, the New Mexico Constitution consists of multiple articles, which contain sections. Article II is the New Mexico Bill of Rights and comprises 24 sections (e.g., right to bear arms [Section 6]; Freedom of religion [Section 11]; Self-incrimination and double jeopardy [Section 15]; and due process, equal protection, and sex discrimination [Section 18]). A state's constitution only holds within that state, whereas the U.S. Constitution holds throughout the country. State constitutions must be in step with the U.S. Constitution, meaning that a state constitution can provide more protections for its citizens than is afforded under the U.S. Constitution, but not less. The U.S. Constitution is the prime governing document throughout the United States, and all other state and federal laws (e.g., statutes and case law) must comport with it, or those laws—even up to and including a state's constitution—could be struck down.

Statutory law is much more specific than constitutional law, which is broad in scope. Statutes, also called "codes," are enacted by state legislatures or by the U.S. Congress and catalogued according to topic. In New Mexico, for example, Criminal Offenses are largely listed within Chapter 30 of the New Mexico Statutes Annotated, most recently organized in 1978. They are further organized with multiple articles, and then have multiple sections within each article. Article 2, Homicide, begins with section 30-2-1. Murder, which is defined as follows:

> 30-2-1. Murder.
>
> A. Murder in the first degree is the killing of one human being by

another without lawful justification or excuse, by any of the means with which death may be caused:

1. By any kind of willful, deliberate and premeditated killing;
2. In the commission of or attempt to commit any felony; or
3. By any act greatly dangerous to the lives of others, including a depraved mind regardless of human life.

Whoever commits murder in the first degree is guilty of a capital felony.

B. Unless he is acting upon sufficient provocation, upon a sudden quarrel or in the heat of passion, a person who kills another human being without lawful justification or excuse commits murder in the second degree if in performing the acts which caused the death he knows that such acts create a strong probability of death or great bodily harm to that individual or another.

Murder in the second degree is a lesser included offense of the crime of murder in the first degree.

Whoever commits murder in the second degree is guilty of a second degree felony resulting in the death of a human being.

Statutory interpretation is one of the primary tasks that lawyers must perform. All of this codified information is highly structured and extremely specific, and each word and element of punctuation, or lack thereof, can be the source of debate that must be settled by the courts. Words like "and," "or," "willful," and "deliberate," are not simple descriptors. They are terms of art, encountered in *mens rea*/diminished capacity defenses, that can make or break the successful application of a charge to a defendant's criminal conduct.

Case law is the collection of published legal decisions made by courts, either at the state or federal level. For example, a court will hear arguments on two sides of a legal dispute and, ultimately, make a decision about that dispute. The decision, however, is not made in a vacuum; rather, it is made using constitutional and statutory law *and* an awareness of how other courts have handled similar legal disputes. Courts know how other courts have handled similar legal disputes because the most important decisions, or opinions, are meticulously documented and published. *Stare decisis* is a Latin term meaning "to stand by the things decided" (Clapp, 2007, p. 251), which means courts render opinions about legal disputes with an awareness of, and respect for, how other courts have rendered opinions about similar disputes.

As explained by DeMatteo et al. (2014), published legal opinions often include the following headings, to organize the case information: facts; procedural history; issue; *ratio decidendi* (Latin for "the reason for the decision"); and holding. In Section II of this book, we use the following headings to organize our summary of legal cases: case facts; main issue(s); court holding; court's reasoning; and quick summary.

Notably, not all cases are summarized in the body of case law; only those cases deemed to have significant precedential value are published, which is the vast minority of cases (Arnold, 1999). Also, published case law carries different weight for courts wrestling with a new decision, depending on where the published case originated. A prior ruling about a particular issue that is made by a higher court within the same jurisdiction (e.g., the NM Supreme Court is higher than the 13 NM District Courts) is said to have *binding authority* over the lower court. This means the lower court must follow the lead of the higher court. In contrast, courts wishing to not reinvent the wheel may look to the prior decision-making from a lower court within the same jurisdiction or a court from an entirely different jurisdiction. These rulings, however, only have *persuasive authority*, not binding authority. This means reasoning underlying the prior decisions can be relied upon for the purposes of persuasion. Hence, the court making the decision can more confidently deviate from the precedent set in these less influential courts, especially if it can support its reasoning. According to some legal scholars (Levi, 1992), legal decisions are more malleable than one would suspect, depending on how skilled the courts (or attorneys) are at drawing connections between existing case law and new decisions. It is also worth noting that exceptions to the foregoing apply (e.g., federal courts permit citation to unpublished opinions).

As stated previously, understanding the main sources of law—constitutional law, statutory law, and case law—helps answer the question, *What is meant by "the law"*? We see from the foregoing descriptions that "the law" is a very large body of rules, supported by reasoning, that reflects the values of a society. At one end of the continuum, these rules are relatively fixed, as is the case with a constitution, which is not amended regularly. Case law, in contrast, is alive and constantly evolving, to more accurately reflect the changing values of society. Statutes are also relatively fixed, but more malleable than constitutions.

Differences Between "Science" and "the Law"

Defense lawyers are advocates for their clients. Similarly, prosecutors advocate for the rights of the people in a community or jurisdiction (e.g., the state or the entire United States) and the truth. In contrast, scientific experts proffering opinions during legal proceedings are advocates for their scientific opinions. Implicit, here, is that the same word—"advocate"—has very different applications; attorneys advocate for individual defendants or large communities, but scientific experts advocate for opinions. Simply put, science and law differ with regard to the meaning and use of language.

Goodstein (2011), in making this point, explained how the words "force," "evidence," "theory," "law," and "error" have different meanings in the two fields. For example, *evidence* in law "has precise rules of evidence that govern what is admissible and what is not" (p. 51). In contrast, "The word evidence is used much more loosely in science than in law … In science, the word merely seems to mean something less than 'proof'" (p. 51). Similarly, "In law, and in common usage, error and mistake are more or less synonymous" (p. 51). In comparison, *error* in science means "uncertainty in the measured result" (p. 52).

One of us was involved in a case where the word "consultant" became a point of confusion. The retaining attorneys, a team of defense lawyers, interpreted "consultant" to mean that the mental health expert worked for the attorneys, with no distinction made between the role of "evaluating expert" and "consultant." The mental health expert, in contrast, interpreted the word "consultant" to mean that the mental health expert would not be operating as an expert witness in the case; rather, their role would be limited to be behind-the-scenes assistance to defense counsel in areas such as the following: generating questions for cross-examination; understanding the forensic reports written by the prosecution-retained expert; and understanding relevant topics in the expert's field. Because science and law differ with regard to language, effective communication between the two professions sometimes requires clarification about terms (see "Not preparing questions for cross-examination" in Chapter 2 for more on the five different roles mental health professionals can assume in forensic cases).

In addition to differences in use of language, Goodstein (2011) said that law and science have different objectives: "The objective of the law is justice; that of science is truth" (p. 52). Reinforcing this message, Justice Breyer (2011) wrote, "A court proceeding, such as a trial, is not simply a search for dispassionate truth. The law must be fair" (p. 5). Cole et al. (2017) also included justice as a primary objective of the criminal justice system, but they added *crime prevention* and *controlling crime* as additional objectives. Grimm (2012) pointed out that the law addresses idiosyncratic problems that are specific to each individual case, while science is concerned with more universal problems, and that the law must achieve its objective of justice relatively quickly, whereas solving problems in science is an ongoing endeavor with no deadlines. Overall, while attorneys and judges value scientific perspectives, the relatively swift delivery of just legal outcomes is perhaps ultimately what matters the most in the law.

Previously we stated that criminal defense attorneys are advocates for their clients. In fact, "lawyers ethically are charged with representing their clients' interests zealously" (Grimm, 2012, p. 15). Similarly, recall from earlier text that "legitimate courtroom practices and ethical attorney behavior would be considered unethical if practiced by a neuropsychologist" (Greiffenstein & Kaufman, 2012, p. 26). In contrast, scientific experts testifying in front of judges and attorneys are advocates for their opinions, not clients or communities. And these opinions are usually only presented because they happen to align with the advocacy goals of retaining counsel. In explaining the difference between the role of consultant and testifying expert witness, this important point was addressed by Drogin and Barrett (2013) as follows:

> Why professionals should not serve as both an expert witness and consultant ... is bound up in the way an expert arrives at and then

> conveys a valid and convincing opinion. This opinion must be the product of a two-stage process. The first stage requires the witness to approach the case with a tabula rasa or "blank slate" perspective, as free as possible of bias or preconception. An evaluation is then performed, resulting in a forensic conclusion. At the second stage, the expert is free to serve in an advocacy role. This "advocacy" is not for an examinee or a legal conclusion, but rather for the expert's own opinion, which would not be presented if it did not serve the retaining attorney's interests. (p. 650)

Given that attorneys are ethically required to zealously represent the interests of their clients, it is perhaps not surprising that they—if not also judges—become frustrated with testifying expert witnesses who do not join "the legal team" and who openly acknowledge the boundaries of the scientific findings upon which they are basing their opinions. Simply put, attorneys—and perhaps judges—think in terms of zealous advocacy for the rights of individual defendants or communities within jurisdictions; and it is expected that this advocacy be passionate and intense. But scientific experts are expected by their fields to acknowledge the limitations of their scientific knowledge and expertise (e.g., Guidelines 2.05, 6.02, and 10.02 of the Specialty Guidelines for Forensic Psychology, SGFP; APA, 2013), which can be misunderstood by attorneys and judges, if not exploited. To appreciate the potential for subtle sophistry from an enthusiastic and competitive attorney, consider the following from Meyer and Weaver (2006):

> By its very nature, empirical research rarely (if ever) resolves an issue with absolute certainty. There are always caveats and confounds when one tries to apply the results of empirical research to real life. A skilled attorney may be able to get a mental health clinician to focus on these uncertainties thereby undermining the clinician's credibility with the judge and/or jury. Yet, in the views of the mental health profession, a clinician who acknowledges the limitations of his or her knowledge is actually *more* credible than one who makes absolute claims in the absence of data. (p. 7)

Similarities Between "Science" and "the Law"

Despite the differences between science and law, there is an important, perhaps unexpected, parallel. Both fields are characterized by ongoing intellectual competition. While it is not difficult to recognize that lawyers compete with each other, with judges functioning a bit like a sports referee, it is important to appreciate that science too is a competitive enterprise:

> Science is, above all, an adversarial process. It is an arena in which ideas do battle, with observations and data the tools of combat. The scientific debate is very different from what happens in a court of law, but just as in

> the law, it is crucial that every idea receive the most vigorous possible advocacy, just in case it might be right. (Goodstein, 2011, p. 44)

Therefore, mental health experts working in forensic settings should appreciate that both science and the law, despite important differences, are connected by a heritage of intellectual competition. Correspondingly, attorneys and judges can expect of forensic mental health experts the capacity and willingness to opine vigorously and intelligently—but without going beyond the science underlying and supporting their opinions.

Conclusion

Science is many things. Therefore, it is inaccurate to state, or even imply, that science is a single monolithic enterprise. Hence, otiose statements about what "the science" supports, or does not support, demand more explicitness—especially from forensic experts. For example, studies employing random assignment to groups, one example of science, may support a particular expert opinion. Similarly, an expert may cite a body of peer-reviewed literature, established through the work of other scientists, to back up their testimony. The important takeaway message is that forensic experts are encouraged to anchor their professional opinions in established knowledge developed by scientists—and to do so as explicitly as possible.

Loyalty to scientific reasoning and methods by the forensic expert is not enough. It is equally important to diligently be on the lookout for bogus methods masquerading as science—that is, pseudoscience. Likewise, because abnormal human behavior—captured in treatment-oriented settings with a diagnosis—underlies forensic referral questions, it is crucial to know when a mental health diagnosis has adequate empirical support, versus being considered a pseudoscientific diagnosis.

Explicitness is equally important when referring to "the law," which can be different across federal and state jurisdictions. Moreover, "the law" originates from different sources, most notably the following: (1) constitutions; (2) statutes; and (3) cases. Hence, it is crucial for forensic experts to have a basic understanding of this. To illustrate, if asked to opine on a defendant's *mens rea* (i.e., the extent to which they had a guilty mind when committing the acts charged), it is extremely helpful to know which criminal charges require a high degree of guilty mind, also commonly described as specific intent. This necessarily demands knowledge of the statutory definition of the criminal charges, which can be examined for keywords like "willful" or "deliberate," thereby indicating whether or not a *mens rea*/diminished capacity defense even applies to a given charge.

Despite notable differences, careful consideration of what scientists and legal professionals do for a living leads to the conclusion that both fields are characterized by ongoing intellectual competition. Hence, while forensic experts define certain words differently than do legal professionals, experts and legal professionals both place high value on conclusions that can withstand serious-minded challenges. Arguably, the biggest difference between forensic mental health experts and legal professionals is *objective*: whereas attorneys are advocates of justice for their client (i.e., a criminal defendant or "the people"), forensic mental health experts are advocates of their scientifically supported opinions about abnormal human behavior. Stated another way, attorneys try to win cases, whereas forensic mental health experts aim to help factfinders (i.e., judges and juries) develop a more nuanced understanding of abnormal human behavior.

5 Ethical Considerations in Forensic Mental Health Practice

Foundation, cornerstone, bedrock, base – these are examples of terms used to convey the importance of professional ethics for effective forensic mental health services. Each aspect of the forensic evaluation process is informed by the ethical guidance of the profession, in concert with jurisdictional laws and the positions of professional organizations. Ethics, representing the shared values of the profession, guide the activities of all professionals governed by the profession's ethics code.

Intersection, crossroads, junction – these are examples of terms used to convey the influence of two professions or professional specialties on forensic mental health services. However, forensic mental health services can be characterized most accurately not as an intersection of professional ethics and law but as a traffic circle or roundabout fed by multiple professions and specialties. While law and the mental health disciplines are the primary professions, multiple specialties contribute to the science and practices used to inform triers of fact on matters before the court. Thus, sound ethical decision making, informed by input from multiple ethical, legal, and professional resources, is a foundational competency for effective forensic mental health practice (Bush et al., 2020).

In addition, as explained by ethical relativism (Brandt, 1967), cultural norms influence what is considered appropriate or inappropriate behavior, and such norms can differ considerably across professions. To use an example from the sporting world, in some sports it may be considered inappropriate or unethical to benefit from the efforts of a competitor, whereas in other sports, such as professional cycling where all athletes draft behind competitors to conserve their own energy, it is completely appropriate and widely practiced (i.e., it is ethical) (Vaughters, 2019). More specific to forensic mental health practice, attorneys understand that one of their primary obligations is zealous advocacy for their clients (American Bar Association, 1980, Canon 7), whereas forensic mental health professionals understand the importance of objectivity and avoidance of bias in their assessment of defendants (American Psychological Association [APA], 2013; Guideline 1.02, Impartiality and Fairness). Zealous advocacy for an examinee by a forensic expert would be ethically unacceptable.

Despite the frequent confluence of laws and ethics, what is legal is not always ethical. For example, in many jurisdictions, forensic examinees have a

DOI: 10.4324/9780367645090-5

legal right to have a representative (e.g., lawyer) be present during a mental health evaluation that involves psychometric testing; however, because of the empirically established influence of third parties on cognitive test performance (Howe & McCaffrey, 2010), it is generally considered professionally inappropriate to have third parties present during psychological or neuropsychological testing (American Academy of Clinical Neuropsychology, 2001; Lewandowski, et al., 2016; National Academy of Neuropsychology Policy and Planning Committee (2000a). This discrepancy underscores the value of considering multiple resources when establishing ethical practices and making decisions about ethical matters. The forensic mental health professional should understand not only that certain practices are unethical, but also *why* they are unethical.

Fundamental differences also exist between western justice systems and behavioral science in how human responsibility is viewed. Western justice systems tend to emphasize *free will* as the basis for personal actions, and personal accountability as the consequence for one's actions. In contrast, behavioral science tends to embrace a more *deterministic* perspective whereby human behavior is believed to have a cause (i.e., internal or external forces), is therefore predictable, and is not necessarily under one's control. Understanding differences among interacting professional disciplines is as important as understanding similarities for achieving a beneficial mental health contribution to criminal justice matters before the court.

Effective forensic mental health practice flows from ethical, legal, and professional resources. Effective practices advance the interests of justice. Although opinions differ with regard to the concept of justice, and it can be argued that justice is a much-abused term, ethical forensic mental health services facilitate legal outcomes that the criminal justice system deems fair. Professionals who are not competent, through education, training, and experience, to provide such services are likely to contribute to unjust legal determinations which can have significant implications for the lives of those involved, and reflect poorly on themselves and their profession.

Positive Ethics and the 4 A's of Ethical Practice

Ethics codes typically blend aspirational principles with enforceable standards of conduct. They outline minimum requirements that must be met to avoid sanctions by governing professional bodies. However, ethics codes are, by their nature, incomplete moral compasses. In contrast, *positive ethics* reflects a shift from an emphasis on misconduct and disciplinary action to the pursuit of highest ethical potential (Knapp et al., 2017). Although striving for highest ethical potential seems appealing at first blush, determining and pursuing such courses of action tends to require more effort and time. For example, releasing raw psychological test data to non-psychologists is permissible according the American Psychological Association (APA) (2017) ethics code (Standard 9.04a). In contrast, because of the many potential negative consequences of releasing raw test data to non-psychologists (see Bush et al., 2020), multiple professional organizations have taken the position that practitioners should strive to avoid releasing test data in such circumstances (Attix et al., 2007; Committee on Legal Issues, APA, 2006; National Academy of Neuropsychology Policy and Planning Committee, 2003). Thus, whereas releasing the data would be easily defensible by practitioners, following the recommendations of multiple professional organizations to safeguard the data, by educating the opposing counsel or the court about the drawbacks of such release, would require time and effort that some practitioners would prefer to avoid. However, such efforts would be consistent with higher standards of practices and positive ethics, and time and expense requirements are poor reasons for choosing not to pursue ethical ideals.

The *Four A's of Ethical Practice* provide a framework for conceptualizing ethical practice (Bush, 2009). The four A's are *Anticipate, Avoid, Address*, and *Aspire*. Forensic mental health practitioners can facilitate the establishment and maintenance of ethical practices by striving to (a) *anticipate* and prepare for ethical issues and challenges, (b) *avoid* ethical misconduct, (c) *address* ethical challenges when they are anticipated or encountered, and (d) *aspire* to the highest standards of ethical practice (see Figure 5.1). Consistent with a personal commitment to positive ethics, remaining mindful of the four A's of ethical practice can facilitate appropriate professional practices.

Ethical Issues and Challenges

The primary ethical requirement is that the mental health practitioner has the professional competence to perform the service being provided. If competence is lacking, the service provided or conclusions offered will be of little or no value to the trier of fact, and considerable harm to justice could ensue. Based on the assumption of professional competence, Bush (2015) described ten ethical and professional issues that are of primary importance in forensic mental health

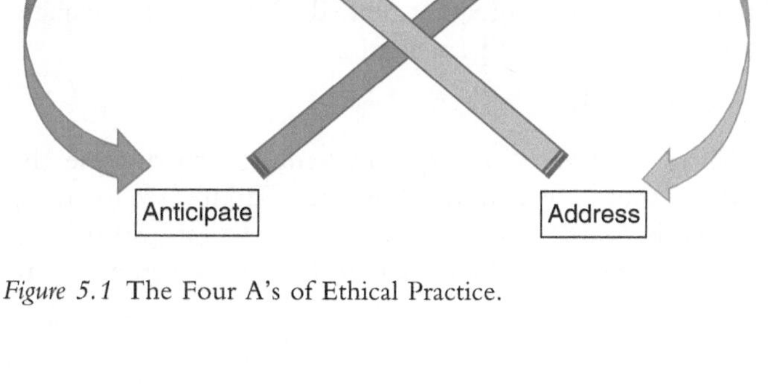

Figure 5.1 The Four A's of Ethical Practice.

practice. The order of importance of the issues will vary depending on the forensic practice context and activities performed, and issues not on this list may be of considerable importance to some forensic practitioners. Additionally, although each issue is presented with one primary risk and suggested solution, in practice there may be multiples risks and possible solutions. Some of these issues are covered in additional detail elsewhere in this chapter.

- Third-party requests for services
  - The risk: Direct or indirect influence from, or desire to please, the retaining party may result in a bias that favors the retaining party (i.e., advocacy for one side) rather than an objective presentation of findings and opinions.
  - Suggested solution: Consider how an opposing expert would describe the same evidence and the opinions that they would reach, and determine whether there is merit inn such an approach to the case.
- Multiple relationships/conflicts of interest
  - The risk: Having multiple relationships with any party involved in the case (e.g., treating and expert role with the examinee, expert witness and trial consultant with a retaining attorney) introduces or reflects conflicts of interest that may bias the practitioner and steer them away from a sole commitment to presenting opinions objectively.
  - Suggested solution: Reject offers for multiple relationships that lead to conflicts of interest.
- Informed consent/notification of purpose (including privacy and confidentiality)
  - The risk: Misunderstandings between practitioner and examinee about the nature and purpose of the forensic mental health service and/or a lack of willingness by the examinee to engage fully in an evaluation process can lead to invalid data and potentially harm to the examinee or the justice system if privacy expectations are not met or the information generated does not contribute to legal determinations that are just.
  - Suggested solution: All involved parties should be informed at the outset of their involvement in the forensic mental health service about the purpose and nature of the service and any other anticipated parameters that may contribute to their decision to participate, including consequences for not participating.
- Test security/release of test data
  - The risk: Forensic examiners are typically required to disclose the measures used in their evaluations; however, failure to maintain security of the psychological and neuropsychological test instruments, including answer sheets, used in mental health assessments can

invalidate their use in the future (e.g., examinees who have advanced access to test questions can skew their responses to their advantage).
- Suggested solution: Upon request for test materials or raw test data, forensic practitioners should first respond by educating the involved attorneys or court (support by position statements from professional organizations; e.g., Attix et al., 2007) about the risks to society of widespread dissemination of such materials and offer to provide a summary of test scores. If such efforts are unsuccessful, additional steps should be taken to maximize the security of the test materials and data (e.g., see National Academy of Neuropsychology Policy and Planning Committee, 2003).

- Explaining assessment results
  - The risk: Assessment results conveyed verbally and/or in written reports may be presented incompletely, inadequately, or inaccurately, thereby misleading attorneys and legal decision makers.
  - Suggested solution: Assessment results and conclusions/opinions should be conveyed clearly and concisely, minimizing or defining use of professional terms (i.e., jargon), based on the evidence obtained.
- Contingency fees
  - The risk: Fees based on a specific outcome of a case put the practitioner at considerable risk of bias toward the outcome that will get them paid.
  - Suggested solution: Do not accept cases when payment of fees is contingent upon a certain outcome in the case.
- Impartiality/bias
  - The risk: Forensic practice may have biases for or against a defendant for any number of reasons, thereby threatening the objectivity of their work and the accuracy of their findings and opinions and their usefulness by the trier of fact.
  - Suggested solution: Engage proactively in a systematic debiasing process for each case (see chapter 2 of this volume and resources cited in the next paragraph).
- Third-party observers
  - The risk: The presence of third parties, including recording devices, affects examinee performance on cognitive and motor tasks, thereby invalidating the results. Use of such results misleads triers of fact and can result in unjust legal determinations. Note that some exceptions, such as interpreters, may be necessary for evaluations to proceed; appropriate cautionary statements should be included in reports generated from such evaluations.

- Suggested solution: Whenever possible, do not allow third parties to be present during neuropsychological or other cognitive testing. Use the multiple position statements from professional organizations (e.g., AACN, 2001; Lewandowski et al., 2016; National Academy of Neuropsychology Policy and Planning Committee, 2000) to educate attorneys and courts.

- Accuracy and truthfulness in public statements (reports and testimony)
    - The risk: Inaccurate statements provided in reports, testimony, and other communications with parties involved in a legal case, as well as inappropriate omissions of important information, mislead triers of fact and can impact legal decisions in unfair ways.
    - Suggested solution: Forensic mental health professionals should provide accurate and truthful statements, consistent with highest ethical practices.
- Addressing ethical misconduct in colleagues
    - The risk: Contacting colleagues or filing ethics complaints against them during the course of a case can be perceived as witness tampering or a litigation tactic used to discredit the colleague in the eyes of the court, whereas failure to act on a severe ethical violation may leave others at risk of harm.
    - Suggested solution: If the perceived ethical misconduct is not so severe that considerable harm to another person is imminent, the preferred course of action is to wait until the matter before the court has been completed and then decide what action, if any, is necessary.

Many of the ethical and professional issues presented here and described by other authors (Murrie & Boccaccini, 2015; Richards et al., 2015; Zapf & Dror, 2017; Zapf et al., 2018) involve bias in various forms. Use of debiasing strategies, such as those described in chapter 2 of this volume and elsewhere (e.g., Lees-Haley, 1999; Neal & Brodsky, 2016; Sweet & Moulthrop, 1998) can help practitioners identify their own biases and manage or eliminate the impact of such biases on their forensic practices. Effective forensic practitioners understand the relevance of these issues in their professional activities, anticipate challenges, and establish procedures for addressing dilemmas when they arise. See Bush et al. (2020) for additional information on each of these issues in the context of forensic psychology.

A Systematic Decision-Making Process

Sound ethical practices and decision making are facilitated through use of systematic decision-making processes. Such processes guide practitioners through the steps of evaluating ethical issues. The mnemonic *CORE OPT* can help practitioners identify and give careful thought to the issues and arrive at an appropriate decision (Bush et al., 2017). At each step, the practitioner can consider and answer a specific question: (1) **C**larify the ethical issue. What is the ethical issue? (2) **O**bligations owed to stakeholders. Who are the stakeholders, and what are my obligations to them? (3) **R**esources - ethical and legal. What references can inform me about the issue? (4) **E**xamine personal beliefs and values. How might my values and beliefs affect my decisions? (5) **O**ptions, solutions, and consequences. What are my options? (6) **P**ut plan into practice. Which option should I choose? (7). **T**ake stock, evaluate outcome, and revise as needed. How did it work out, and is anything else needed?

Vignette

On December 24, a Saturday, Ms. L failed to show up to her parents' home for their traditional Christmas Eve dinner. Her family tried unsuccessfully to reach her by phone, with calls going directly to her voicemail. Very worried, they called her close friend and coworker and learned that Ms. L also had not shown up for work the day before. Calls by the friend and their supervisor also reached her voicemail. The friend had planned to call her family after Christmas if she still had not heard from her. Ms. L's family called the police and reported her missing.

Three months later, Ms. L was still missing. Family and police feared the worst. Ms. L had reported to friends and family that a coworker, Mr. P, was obsessed with her and was stalking her, and other coworkers confirmed this information. There was also considerable circumstantial evidence linking Mr. P and Ms. L's disappearance, which occurred shortly after she began dating another man. Mr. P who had a long psychiatric history and a prior arrest for harassment of a different woman, became a person of interest. Despite the lack of a body, murder weapon, and crime scene, Mr. P eventually was arrested and charged with her murder.

Although Mr. P protested his innocence, the public defender, after evaluating all of the evidence, was considering an insanity defense. The public defender was also considering arguing that Mr. P was amnestic for the crime, which was why he was protesting his innocence (Wilson v US, 1968). The public defender sought a psychological evaluation of her client from a psychologist who was very experienced in the evaluation and treatment of serious mental illness in clinical settings and was chair of psychology at a prestigious institution.

The psychologist discussed the case with the attorney, reviewed available records, and interviewed Mr. P. She then performed psychological testing similar to what she had done with more than one thousand prior patients in her career. She administered an intelligence test, on which Mr. P scored in the superior range. She administered the Minnesota Multiphasic Personality Inventory, second edition, restructured form (MMPI-2-RF) (a questionnaire commonly used by psychologists for diagnosis of mental disorders; Ben-Porath & Tellegen, 2008), which produced modest elevations on the Psychopathy

Total (Py-T), Impulsive-Antisociality (Py-IA), and Fearless-Dominance (Py-FD) scales. Finally, she administered two Rorschach cards, card 1 and card 10. Mr. P provided a very common response to card 1. However, upon seeing card 10, he stated:

> Ah, a love story…
>
> I sat alone on rolling golden hills,
> A piece of fresh-picked straw between my lips.
> With hands behind my head, I dreamt of thrills
> A woman gave to me by moving hips.
> The summer sun and warm relaxing breeze
> Engulfed my conscious thoughts with worlds of dreams
> But not in dreams she left for him with ease
> Until I brought her back to me. Those screams
> Began when I first bound her to the stake,
> Not ending as her face turned black and blue.
> There were no neighbors near who she could wake.
> I kept convincing her that we were through.
> I asked her who he was but got no names
> Above the screams and stake crackling in flames.

Mr. P's face had a faraway look, and a smile played over his lips as he recited the murder sonnet. He then returned his gaze to the psychologist and said, "Of course, I could never do anything like that" and winked. He then added, "Because this is just between you and me Doc, I want you to know that a classmate of mine in college also went missing, and I was a person of interest in that case too; I still think about her every now and then."

The psychologist, convinced that only a psychotic and dangerous person could generate such test results and that Mr. P was in desperate need of psychiatric help, produced a report explaining her opinion. She included the information about the missing college classmate. She concluded that Mr. P likely committed the crime while in a psychotic state and therefore had no memory for the event. She recommended that he be admitted for inpatient psychiatric care. The defense attorney thanked the psychologist for the report but asked the psychologist to remove the information about the disappearance of the classmate, reassuring her that "it would not be admissible anyway." The psychologist complied.

Ethical Issues in the Vignette

This vignette does not involve the type of situation in which a practitioner confronts competing ethical requirements and must determine the best way to address the dilemma; rather, it illustrates ethical problems that can arise when a practitioner gets into, or puts themselves into, a situation that they are not prepared to handle. The *CORE OPT* ethical decision-making model is applied to this case to illustrate the ethical problems that exist and actions that could have been taken to facilitate an ethical forensic mental health evaluation. The references to forensic practice guidelines (APA, 2013) are provided here as examples, with the understanding that different forensic mental health specialties have their own ethics codes and practice guidelines with somewhat different wording but sharing a commitment to the underlying values.

Clarify the Ethical Issue(s)

Multiple ethical problems are evident in this vignette. The primary problem is that, although the psychologist is experienced and skilled in clinical work, she lacks professional competence to provide forensic services, at least in the context presented in the vignette. Professional competence establishes the foundation upon which forensic mental health practitioners can provide services that are beneficial to the trier of fact. In this case, competence appears to have been lacking from the beginning and remained inadequate throughout the service, including (a) failure to make clear to the examinee the purpose of the evaluation and the limits to confidentiality, (b) inadequate selection of assessment procedures, (c) inappropriate use and interpretation of tests, and (d) altering the report at the request of the retaining attorney by removing information considered important for understanding the defendant's psychological functioning.

Obligations Owed to Stakeholders

The obligations owed by mental health professionals differ between clinical and forensic contexts, and sometimes within those contexts. Whereas a mental health professional providing clinical services typically forms a therapeutic alliance with the patient and is invested in promoting the well-being of that person, such an alliance with a forensic examinee is inappropriate because it introduces an element of bias for the examiner and may mislead the examinee. The forensic expert forms an alliance with the truth, with the primary obligation being to the trier of fact and, thus, justice. The investment in objectivity and justice can render the establishment of rapport between examiner and examinee problematic. The examinee may misconstrue rapport as a sign of advocacy, which may lead the examinee to disclose information that is not in the examinee's best legal interest. A posture of dispassionate respect, courtesy, and professionalism can be an effective posture to assume during forensic evaluations (Bush et al., 2020).

The mental health professional has an obligation to the examinee to be courteous and professional and to provide competent services. Similarly, the mental health professional has an obligation to the retaining party to address the psycho-legal question in an objective way and to present the findings with candor. Although the outcome of the legal matter may be influenced by that input, the practitioner fulfills their professional obligation by adhering to a commitment to appropriate evaluations and objective and dispassionate presentation of results and opinions.

The obligation to do no harm (nonmaleficence), which is a primary ethical responsibility in clinical practice, takes on a different focus in forensic practice. In most forensic contexts, one party or the other, and/or the notion of justice, is harmed by the outcome, and the work of forensic experts can contribute directly to such outcomes. Nevertheless, the practitioner's obligation is to the truth, obtained through scientific understanding, rather than to a particular party involved in the legal matter. If competent forensic services have been provided, it is not the services themselves that result in harm to any party; it is the trier of fact's ultimate determination that causes one side to "lose", with consequences that can be severe. In the present vignette, the psychologist had the obligations described in this section but seems to have failed to meet them because of her lack of professional competence.

Resources

The ethics codes of professional organizations are the primary resource for ethical practice. However, to be relevant for all members of a profession, an ethics code's directives must be general in nature. The more specialized a professional's practice activities become, the more the professional can, and should, turn to other resources for additional guidance. Major professional organizations in mental health disciplines have divisions or sections that specialize in various aspects of practice, and freestanding specialized organizations exist to promote effective practice of the specialty. Such organizations that focus on forensic practice commonly produce practice guidelines or position statements to direct practitioners in their professional activities (e.g., American Academy of Psychiatry and the Law, 2015; ABA, 2016; American Board of Forensic Psychology, 2015; APA, 2013). Position statements on various aspects of the forensic evaluation, such as psychometric testing, are also available and informative for practitioners. Such resources include the *Standards for Educational and Psychological Testing* (American Educational Research Association, American Psychological Association, & National Council on Measurement in Education, 2014), Practice Guidelines for Neuropsychological Assessment and Consultation (American Academy of Clinical Neuropsychology, 2007), Independent and Court-ordered Neuropsychological Assessment (Bush et al., 2005a), and position statements on the nature and value of validity assessment (Bush et al., 2005b; Heilbronner et al., 2009). Scholarly publications, experienced colleagues, and professional liability insurance carriers are also excellent sources of information in practice specialties. Of course, relevant laws provide essential information, ranging from privacy and confidentiality to record-keeping to copyright protections and beyond, for establishing and maintaining appropriate practices.

Once information from the various resources have been obtained and reviewed, the practitioner engages in *evidence synthesis*. As with clinical decision making, ethical decision making involves establishing a convergence of information that provides direction regarding the practice activities in question, as well as determining where the guidance diverges. Because *ethical issues* underlie all professional activities, identifying and understanding the issues relevant to one's specific practice activities and contexts is essential and is not necessarily problematic. *Ethical problems* exist when insufficient attention has been paid to the ethical issues, and the practitioner engages in unethical behavior. For example, it is an ethical problem when a practitioner engages in an activity that they are not qualified to perform. In contrast, *ethical dilemmas* arise when two or more ethical directives conflict with each other and/or laws, leaving the practitioner to determine which course to follow. For example, while federal courts generally prohibit third-party observers from being present during forensic mental health evaluations, and professional organizations oppose such presence during psychometric testing (American Academy of Clinical Neuropsychology, 2001; Howe & McCaffrey, 2010; Lewandowski et al., 2016; National Academy of Neuropsychology Policy and Planning Committee, 2000; Shindell et al., 2014), state courts have established differing rules regarding their permissibility, leaving practitioners with the dilemma of how to handle requests to have third parties be present during their evaluations.

When the conflict is between ethics and law, automatically following the law, while intuitively preferred to avoid stiff penalties, is not always the ideal option. In some circumstances, the practitioner can use the opportunity to educate the court about why following the law might be ethically contraindicated in a given case and seek a compromise or other solution that meets the needs of both the court and the mental health profession. For example, discovery law [FRCP 26(a)(2)(B)(ii)] requires experts to release the materials and data upon which their opinions are based. However, as previously described, multiple professional organizations emphasize the importance of protecting psychological test materials and data from dissemination and advise practitioners to strive to avoid releasing them, unless certain provisions are in place to safeguard against their broader dissemination (Attix et al., 2007; Committee on Legal Issues, APA, 2006; National Academy of Neuropsychology Policy and Planning Committee, 2003).

When conflicts emerge between ethical requirements or between ethics and law, general bioethical principles, which are commonly considered aspirational rather than remedial, can serve to inform practitioners about a preferred course of action. General ethical principles are based on fundamental human values that a society deems important, such as the right to self-determination, and are applied to specific industries and professions. Beauchamp and Childress (2013) offered a model of biomedical ethics that has been widely adopted by scholars and practitioners in a variety of health care and mental health specialties, including psychology. The model is comprised of moral principles: Respect for autonomy, nonmaleficence, beneficence, and justice. Although these principles are commonly applied in the context of routine clinical care of patients, by reconceptualizing the client as being the criminal justice system rather than the person being examined, the principles remain of value to ethical decision making in forensic practice. Despite such reconceptualization, the practitioner nevertheless has ethical obligations to all parties involved in the legal process.

In the present vignette, the psychologist, despite being an experienced and highly credentialed clinical psychologist, lacked professional competence to provide the service that she agreed to provide. The *Specialty Guidelines for Forensic Psychology* (SGFP) (APA, 2013) (Guideline 2.01, Scope of Competence) state, "When determining one's competence to provide services in a particular matter, forensic practitioners may consider a variety of factors including the relative complexity and specialized nature of the service, relevant training and experience, the preparation and study they are able to devote to the matter..." (p. 9). The psychologist, experienced in working with patients with serious mental illness in clinical settings, failed to consider the differences inherent in practicing in clinical and forensic settings.

As a manifestation of that lack of understanding, her selection and use of assessment measures was inadequate and inappropriate. Guideline 2.05 (Knowledge of the Scientific Foundation for Opinions and Testimony), states, "Forensic practitioners seek to provide opinions and testimony that are sufficiently based upon adequate scientific foundation, and reliable and valid principles and methods that have been applied appropriately to the facts of the case" (p. 9). Furthermore, Guideline 10.02 (Selection and Use of Assessment Procedures) states, "Forensic practitioners use assessment procedures in the manner and for the purposes that are appropriate in light of the research on or evidence of their usefulness and proper application" (p. 15). Although administration of only two Rorschach cards could possibly have some clinical value with some patients, use of the instrument in this manner, without the support of validity and reliability studies, raises significant concerns about its diagnostic usefulness and admissibility in the forensic case (Daubert v. Merrell Dow Pharmaceuticals, Inc., 1993).

Additionally, in addressing the use of the Rorschach "Comprehensive System" in forensic settings, Vitacco et al. (2012) drew the following conclusions: "Our analysis strongly suggests that the [Comprehensive System for scoring the Rorschach] does not meet *Daubert* standards for scientific admissibility. Because other Rorschach scoring and interpretive systems are on even shakier scientific footing than the [Comprehensive System], our negative verdict applies a fortiori to these other systems" (p. 350). Misuse of a measure that was heavily relied upon to inform her forensic opinions would likely result in the psychologist being discredited and her work rendered meaningless.

In addition, SGFP Section 6 (Informed Consent, Notification, and Assent), Guideline 6.03 (Communication with Forensic Examinees), notes the importance of informing examinees at the outset of the examination of the purpose, nature, and anticipated use of the examination; who will have access to the information; associated limitations on privacy, confidentiality, and privilege..." (p. 12). Such information allows the examinee to decide whether to participate in the examination and what to disclose during the examination, with the understanding that noncompliance may have stiff consequences, and providing such information is consistent with the ethical principle of respect for autonomy. Mr. P demonstrated a lack of understanding of these issues through his statement to the psychologist that what he was about to tell her was just between them. Thus, the psychologist seems to have failed in her responsibility at the outset and then did not stop him and clarify when he said, "Because this is just between you and me, Doc". These ethical issues and subsequent problems, while illustrated by sections from the SGFP, are also codified in the APA Ethics Code and described in other relevant resources.

Examine Personal Beliefs and Values

The psychologist in this case is very sensitive to the struggles and clinical needs of persons with serious mental illness. She has devoted her professional career to helping such persons. She is also invested in helping the trier of fact in this case understand the mental suffering of the defendant and the need for him to receive proper mental health care. Addressing the defendant's clinical needs would, she believes, serve the interests of both justice and the defendant.

Options, Solutions, and Consequences

Having considered the information from the various resources, practitioners have multiple possible solutions to choose from to establish ethical practices or resolve an ethical concern. Practitioners must weigh the anticipated advantages and disadvantages for the various solutions, consider the probable consequences of each solution, and then select a course of action. In the current vignette, the primary ethical question was whether it was appropriate to accept the case, given the psychologist's lack of forensic experience; however, the psychologist did not know enough to realize that she could be engaging in ethical misconduct, so she did not face that decision.

However, a qualified colleague retained by the prosecution who reviews this psychologist's work would identify the ethical problems and then need to decide how to address them. In clinical contexts, informal discussion with a colleague to point out concerns can result in meaningful changes that protect the psychologist and their patients. Attempts at informal resolution may also be indicated in forensic contexts (Guideline 7.03, Resolving Ethical Issues with Fellow Professionals). However, such efforts can be complicated, challenging, and risky (Behnke). Informal resolution efforts can require considerable time and energy, and even raising the possibility of an ethics violation can result in concerns about unfairly defaming a colleague's reputation, and, fair or not, invite retaliation. Additionally, informal contact with an opposing expert in a forensic context could be viewed as witness tampering and is therefore generally discouraged.

When attempts at informal resolution are not advisable or do not lead to the desired change, the concerned colleague can take more formal actions, such as reporting the ethical misconduct to an ethics committee or licensing board. However, filing a formal complaint against a colleague while involved in an ongoing legal matter can be viewed as a litigation tactic to discredit the colleague in the eyes of the court and, therefore, should also be avoided in most situations (American Academy of Clinical Neuropsychology, 2003; Sweet, 2005). If ethical concerns about a colleague persist after the legal matter has concluded, then addressing the matter formally or informally would be appropriate.

Put Plan into Practice

Related to this vignette, consider that the qualified colleague reviewed the psychologist's work and found it to be inadequate and therefore misleading to the trier of fact and thus harmful to the pursuit of justice. However, he elected not to address his concerns directly with the psychologist or to make a formal report of ethical misconduct. He believes that his own contribution to the matter will provide a competent contrast the psychologist's work and allow her weaknesses to come to light.

Take Stock, Evaluate Outcome, and Revise as Needed

Through the grueling cross-examination by the prosecutor, the psychologist was forced to confront her professional shortcomings in the forensic arena and vowed to limit her professional activities to familiar clinical settings. The qualified colleague, having learned of the events in the courtroom, decided not to pursue the matter with the psychologist unless he later learned that she was returning to forensic activities.

Conclusions

Competent forensic mental health professionals have much to offer triers of fact in their pursuit of justice. Such competence includes an understanding that professional competence is not a universal construct; effectiveness in one area of practice or with one set of skills does not necessarily translate into effectiveness in other contexts or activities. Ethical practice is best achieved in a proactive, versus reactive, manner. A structured, systematic ethical decision-making model can promote sound ethical decisions as forensic practices are established, issues are anticipated, challenges are avoided, and dilemmas are addressed. Forensic mental health professionals who aspire to high ethical standards are well positioned to serve the legal system through effective, ethical practices.

References

American Academy of Clinical Neuropsychology. (2001). Policy statement on the presence of 3rd party observers in neuropsychological assessments. *The Clinical Neuropsychologist, 15*, 433–439.

American Academy of Clinical Neuropsychology. (2003). Official position of the American Academy of Clinical Neuropsychology on ethical complaints made against clinical neuropsychologists during adversarial proceedings. *The Clinical Neuropsychologist, 17*, 443–445. 10.1076/clin.17.4.443.27943.

American Academy of Clinical Neuropsychology. (2007). American Academy of Clinical Neuropsychology (AACN) practice guidelines for neuropsychological assessment and consultation. *The Clinical Neuropsychologist, 21*, 209–231.

American Academy of Psychiatry and the Law. (2015). AAPL practice guideline for forensic assessment. *The Journal of the American Academy of Psychiatry and the Law, 43*(2 supplement), S3–S53.

American Bar Association. (1980). *ABA model code of professional responsibility*. Retrieved from https://www.americanbar.org/content/dam/aba/administrative/professional_responsibility/mrpc_migrated/mcpr.pdf.

American Bar Association. (2016). *Criminal justice standards on mental health*. Retrieved from www.americanbar.org/content/dam/aba/publications/criminal_justice_standards/mental_health_standards_2016.authcheckdam.pdf.

American Board of Forensic Psychology. (2015). *Core competencies in forensic psychology*. Retrieved from https://abpp.org/BlankSite/media/Forensic-Psychology-Documents/ABFP-Core-Competencies.pdf.

American Educational Research Association, American Psychological Association, & National Council on Measurement in Education. (2014). *Standards for educational and psychological testing*. American Educational Research Association.

American Psychological Association, Commission for the Recognition of Specialities and Profiencies in Professional Psychology. (2010a). *Clinical neuropsychology*. Retrieved from http:///www/apa.org/ed/graduate/specialize/neuro.aspx.

American Psychological Association, Commision for the Recognition of Specialities and Profiencies in Professional Psychology. (2010b). *Forensic psychology*. Retrieved from http://www.apa.org/ed/graduate/specialize/forensic.aspx.

American Psychological Association. (2013). Specialty guidelines for forensic psychology. *American Psychologist, 68*, 7–19.

American Psychological Association. (2017). *Ethical principles of psychologists and code of conduct*. Retrieved from www.apa.org/ethics/code/index.aspx.

Anastasi, A. (1986). Intelligence as a quality of behavior. In D. K. Detterman (Ed.), *What is intelligence?* (pp. 19–21). Ablex.

Arnold, R. S. (1999). Unpublished opinions: A comment. *The Journal of Appellate Practice and Process, 1*(2), 219–226.

American Psychiatric Association. (2013). *Diagnostic and Statistical Manual of Mental Disorders* (5th ed.) 10.1176/appi.books.9780890425596.

Atkins v. Virginia, 536 U.S. 304 (2002).

Attix, D.K., Donders, J., Johnson-Greene, D., Grote, C.L., Harris, J.G., & Bauer, R.M. (2007). Disclosure of neuropsychological test data: Official position of Division 40 (Clinical Neuropsychology) of the American Psychological Association, Association of Postdoctoral Programs in Clinical Neuropsychology, and American Academy of Clinical Neuropsychology. *The Clinical Neuropsychologist, 21*, 232–238.

Axelrod, B., Barth, J., Faust, D., Fisher, J., Heilbronner, R., Larrabee, G., … Silver, C. (2000). Presence of third party observers during neuropsychological testing: Official statement of the National Academy of Neuropsychology. *Archives of Clinical Neuropsychology, 15*(5), 379–380.

Axelrod, B., Heilbronner, R., Barth, J., Larrabee, G., Faust, D., Pliskin, N., … Silver, C. (2000). Test security: Official position statement of the national academy of neuropsychology. *Archives of Clinical Neuropsychology, 15*(5), 383–386.

Bagaric, M., & Gopalan, S. (2016). A Sober Assessment of the Link Between Substance Abuse and Crime-Eliminating Drug and Alcohol Use from the Sentencing Calculus. *Santa Clara Law Review, 56*, 243.

Bakker, R., Pluimgraaff, L. E., Steegers, E. A., Raat, H., Tiemeier, H., Hofman, A., & Jaddoe, V. W. (2011). Maternal alcohol consumption and fetal growth. *Maternal lifestyle and pregnancy complications* (pp. 169–191). Optima Grafische Communicatie.

Banich, M. T., & Compton, R. J. (2018). Executive function and higher-order thinking. *Cognitive neuroscience* (4th ed., pp. 332–366). Cambridge University Press.

Banich, M. T., & Compton, R. J. (2018). Motor control. *Cognitive neuroscience* (4th ed., pp. 100–135). Cambridge University Press.

Barr, A. M., Panenka, W. J., MacEwan, G. W., Thornton, A. E., Lang, D. J., Honer, W. G., & Lecomte, T. (2006). The need for speed: an update on methamphetamine addiction. *Journal of Psychiatry & Neuroscience, 31*(5), 301–313.

Beaver, K. M., & Wright, J. P. (2011). The association between county-level IQ and county-level crime rates. *Intelligence, 39*(1), 22–26.

Beauchamp, T. L., & Childress, A. F. (2013). *Principles of biomedical ethics*, 7th edition. Oxford University Press.

Behnke, S. (2006). *Responding to a colleague's ethical transgressions.* Retrieved from apa.org/monitor/mar06/ethics.

Ben-Porath, Y. S., & Tellegen, A. (2008). *Minnesota Multiphasic Personality Inventory-2-Restructured Form.* Pearson.

Ben-Porath, Y. S. (2012). *Interpreting the MMPI-2-RF.* University of Minnesota Press.

Berk, L., Castro, S., Brava, S., & Tapert, S. (2014). Adolescents. In D. Allen & S. Woods (Eds.), *Neuropsychological aspects of substance abuse disorders: Evidence-based perspectives* (pp. 598–632). Oxford University Press.

Berry, D. T., & Nelson, N. W. (2010). DSM-5 and malingering: A modest proposal. *Psychological Injury and Law, 3*(4), 295–303.

Blair, R. J. (2016). The neurobiology of impulsive aggression. *Journal of Child and Adolescent Psychopharmacology, 26*(1), 4–9.

Blumenfeld, H. (2014). *Neuroanatomy through clinical cases*. Sinauer.

Borum, R., Bartel, P., & Forth, A. (2006). *Structured assessment of violence risk in youth: Professional manual*. Psychological Assessment Resources.

Borum, R., Otto, R., & Golding, S. (1993). Improving clinical judgment and decision making in forensic evalution. *The Journal of Psychiatry & Law*, *21*(1), 35–76.

Boone, K.B. (2013). *Clinical practice of forensic neuropsychology: An evidence-based approach*. The Guilford Press.

Bowers, D. A., Ricker, J. H., Regan, T. M., Malina, A. C., & Boake, C. (2002). National survey of clinical neuropsychology postdoctoral fellows. *The Clinical Neuropsychologist*, 16(3), 221–231.

Brandt, R. (1967). Ethical relativism. In P. Edwards (Ed), *The encyclopedia of philosophy* (Vol. 3, pp. 75–78). Macmillan.

Breyer, S. (2011). Introduction. In N. R. Council (Ed.), *Reference manual on scientific evidence* (pp. 1–9). The National Academies Press.

Brodsky, S. L. (2004). *Coping with cross-examination*. American Psychological Association.

Bush, S.S. (2009). *Geriatric mental health ethics: A casebook*. Springer Publishing Company.

Bush, S.S. (2015). Ethical guidelines in forensic psychology. In R.L. Cautin & S.O. Lilienfeld (Eds.), *The encyclopedia of clinical psychology* (Vol. II, pp. 1115–1124). John Wiley & Sons, Inc.

Bush, S. S. (2017). Introduction. In S. S. Bush (Ed.), *APA handbook of forensic psychology* (pp. xvii–xxii). American Psychological Association.

Bush, S.S., Allen, R.S., & Molinari, V.A. (2017). *Ethical practice in geropsychology*. American Psychological Association.

Bush, S.S., Barth, J.T., Pliskin, N.H., Arffa, S., Axelrod, B.N., Blackburn, L. A., … Silver, C.H. (2005). Independent and court-ordered forensic neuropsychological examinations: Official statement of the National Academy of Neuropsychology. *Archives of Clinical Neuropsychology*, *20*, 997–1007.

Bush, S.S., Connell, M.A., & Denney, R.L. (2020). *Ethical practice in forensic psychology: A guide for mental health professionals* (2nd ed.). American Psychological Association.

Bush, S. S., Heilbronner, R. L., & Ruff, R. M. (2014). Psychological assessment of symptom and performance validity, response bias, and malingering: Official position of the Association for Scientific Advancement in Psychological Injury and Law. *Psychological Injury and Law*, 7(3), 197–205.

Bush, S. S., & Kaufman, N. K. (in press). Diagnostic testing: Rating scales and psychological and neuropsychological tests. In W. W. IsHak (Ed.), *Atlas of psychiatry*. Springer.

Bush, S.S., Ruff, R.M., Tröster, A.I., Barth, J.T., Koffler, S.P., Pliskin, N.H., … Silver, C.H. (2005b). Symptom validity assessment: Practice issues and medical necessity. Official position of the National Academy of Neuropsychology. *Archives of Clinical Neuropsychology*, *20*, 419–426.

Campbell, D. T., & Kenny, D. A. (1999). *A primer on regression artifacts*. Guilford Publications.

Chamberlain, P., Leve, L. D., & Degarmo, D. S. (2007). Multidimensional treatment foster care for girls in the juvenile justice system: 2-Year follow-up of a randomized clinical trial. *Journal of Consulting and Clinical Psychology*, *75*(1), 187–193.

Chamberlain, P., & Reid, J. B. (1998). Comparison of two community alternatives to incarceration for chronic juvenile offenders. *Journal of Consulting and Clinical Psychology*, *66*(4), 624–633.

Chapman, D. P., Whitfield, C. L., Felitti, V. J., Dube, S. R., Edwards, V. J., & Anda, R. F. (2004). Adverse childhood experiences and the risk of depressive disorders in adulthood. *Journal of Affective Disorders*, *82*(2), 217–225.

Chapman, L. J., & Chapman, J. P. (1969). Illusory correlation as an obstacle to the use of valid psychodiagnostic signs. *Journal of Abnormal Psychology, 74*(3), 271.

Chenneville, T., & Schwartz-Mette, R. (2020). Ethical considerations for psychologists in the time of COVID-19. *American Psychologist, 75*(5), 644–654.

Clapp, J. E. (2007). *Random House Webster's pocket legal dictionary* (3rd ed.). Random House Reference.

Cokkinides, V. E., Coker, A. L., Sanderson, M., Addy, C., & Bethea, L. (1999). Physical violence during pregnancy: maternal complications and birth outcomes. *Obstetrics & Gynecology, 93*(5, Part 1), 661–666.

Cole, G. F., Smith, C. E., & Dejong, C. (2017). *The American system of criminal justice* (15th ed.). Cengage Learning.

Committee on Legal Issues, American Psychological Association. (2006). Strategies for private practitioners coping with subpoenas or compelled testimony for client records or test data. *Professional Psychology: Research and Practice, 37*, 215–222.

Conners, C. (2014). *Conners CPT 3 & CATA technical manual*. Multi-Health Systems Inc.

Constantinou, M., Ashendorf, L., & McCaffrey, R. J. (2002). When the third party observer of a neuropsychological evaluation is an audio-recorder. *The Clinical Neuropsychologist, 16*(3), 407–412.

Constantinou, M., Ashendorf, L., & McCaffrey, R. J. (2005). Effects of a third party observer during neuropsychological assessment: When the observer is a video camera. *Journal of Forensic Neuropsychology, 4*(2), 39–47.

Cramer, R. J., Brodsky, S. L., & DeCoster, J. (2009). Expert witness confidence and juror personality: Their impact on credibility and persuasion in the courtroom. *Journal of the American Academy of Psychiatry and the Law Online, 37*(1), 63–74.

Cunningham, M. D. (2010). *Evaluation for capital sentencing*. Oxford University Press.

Dahlstrom, W. G. (1993). Tests: Small samples, large consequences. *American Psychologist, 48*(4), 393.

Das, J. P. (1973). Cultural deprivation and cognitive competence. In N. R. Ellis (Ed.), *International review of research in mental retardation* (Vol. 6, pp. 1–53). Academic Press.

Daubert v. Merrell Dow Pharmaceuticals, Inc., 509 U.S. 579 (1993).

Defoe, I. N., Dubas, J. S., Figner, B., & Van Aken, M. A. (2015). A meta-analysis on age differences in risky decision making: Adolescents versus children and adults. *Psychological Bulletin, 141*(1), 48.

Delis, D. C., Kramer, J. H., Kaplan, E., & Ober, B. A. (2000). *California Verbal Learning Test Manual*. Pearson.

DeMatteo, D., Murrie, D. C., Anumba, N. M., & Keesler, M. E. (2011) *Forensic mental health assessments in death penalty cases*. Oxford University Press.

DeMatteo, D., Keesler, M. E., & Strohmaier, H. (2014). Accessing the law and legal literature. In I. B. Weiner & R. K. Otto (Eds.), *The handbook of forensic psychology* (4th ed., pp. 57–83). Wiley.

Diamond, B., Morris, R. G., & Barnes, J. C. (2012). Individual and group IQ predict inmate violence. *Intelligence, 40*(2), 115–122.

DiPietro, J. A. (2004). The role of prenatal maternal stress in child development. *Current Directions in Psychological Science, 13*(2), 71–74.

Dishion, T. J., McCord, J., & Poulin, F. (1999). When interventions harm: Peer groups and problem behavior. *American Psychologist, 54*(9), 755–764.

Dishion, T. J., Poulin, F., & Burraston, B. (2001). Peer goup dynamics associated with iatrogenic effect in group interventions with high-risk young adolescents. *New directions for child and adolescent development* (pp. 79–92): Jossey-Bass.

Dubois, B., Feldman, H., Jacova, C., DeKosky, S., Barberger-Gateau, P., Cummings, J., … Scheltens, P. (2007). Research criteria for the diagnosis of Alzheimer's disease: Revising the NINCDS-ADRDA criteria. *Lancet, 6*, 734–746.

Drogin, E. Y., & Barrett, C. L. (2013). Trial consultation. In R. K. Otto (Ed.), *Handbook of psychology: Forensic psychology* (Vol. 11, pp. 648–663). John Wiley & Sons, Inc.

Drogin, E. Y. (2001). Utilizing forensic psychological consultation: A jurisprudent therapy perpsecitve. *Mental and Physical Disability Law Reporter, 25*(1), 17–22.

Drogin, E. Y., Barrett, C. L., & Goldstein, A. (2007). Off the witness stand: The forensic psychologist as consultant. In A.M. Goldstein (Ed.) *Forensic psychology: Emerging topics and expanding roles* (pp. 465–488): Hoboken, NJ: John Wiley & Sons.

Dube, S. R., Anda, R. F., Felitti, V. J., Chapman, D. P., Williamson, D. F., & Giles, W. H. (2001). Childhood abuse, household dysfunction, and the risk of attempted suicide throughout the life span: findings from the Adverse Childhood Experiences Study. *Journal of the American Medical Association, 286*(24), 3089–3096.

Dube, S. R., Anda, R. F., Felitti, V. J., Edwards, V. J., & Croft, J. B. (2002). Adverse childhood experiences and personal alcohol abuse as an adult. *Addictive behaviors, 27*(5), 713–725.

Dube, S. R., Felitti, V. J., Dong, M., Chapman, D. P., Giles, W. H., & Anda, R. F. (2003). Childhood abuse, neglect, and household dysfunction and the risk of illicit drug use: the adverse childhood experiences study. *Pediatrics, 111*(3), 564–572.

Dusky v. United States, 362 U.S. 402 (1960).

Estelle v. Smith, 451 U.S. 454 (1981).

Evergreen, S. (2017). *Presenting data effectively: Communicating your findings for maximum impact.* Sage Publications.

Fagan, J. (1990). Intoxication and aggression. *Crime and Justice, 13*, 241–320.

Fama, R., & Sullivan, E. (2014). Alcohol. In D. Allen & S. Woods (Eds.), *Neuropsychological aspects of substance use disorders: Evidence-based perspectives.* Oxford University Press.

Faust, D., Ahern, D., & Bridges, A. (2012). Neuropsychological (brain damage) assessment. In D. Faust (Ed.), *Coping with psychiatric and psychological testimony* (pp. 363–469).

Faust, D., & Ahern, D. C. (2012). Clinical judgment and prediction. In D. Faust (Ed.), *Coping with psychiatric and psychological testimony* (6th ed., pp. 147–208). Oxford University Press.

Faust, D., Grimm, P. W., Ahern, D. C., & Sokolik, M. (2010). The admissibility of behavioral science evidence in the courtroom: The translation of legal to scientific concepts and back. *Annual Review of Clinical Psychology, 6*, 49–77.

Fazel, S., Gulati, G., Linsell, L., Geddes, J. R., & Grann, M. (2009). Schizophrenia and violence: Systematic review and meta-analysis. *PLoS Medicine*, 10.1371/journal.pmed.1000120.

Felitti, V. J., Anda, R. F., Nordenberg, D., Williamson, D. F., Spitz, A. M., Edwards, V., & Marks, J. S. (1998). Relationship of childhood abuse and household dysfunction to many of the leading causes of death in adults: The Adverse Childhood Experiences (ACE) Study. *American Journal of Preventive Medicine, 14*(4), 245–258.

Ferrari, M. (2009). Borderline intellectual functioning and the intellectual disability construct. *Intellectual Developmental Disabilies, 47*(5), 386–389.

First, M. B., Williams, J. B. W., Karg, R. S., & Spitzer, R. L. (2016). *Structured Clinical Interview for DSM-5 disorders: Clinician version.* American Psychiatric Association.

Flynn, J. R. (1984). The mean IQ of Americans: Massive gains 1932 to 1978. *Psychological Bulletin, 95*(1), 29.

Forth, A. E., Kosson, D. S., & Hare, R. D. (2003). *Hare psychopathy checklist: Youth version (PCL: YV)*. Multi-Health Systems, Inc.

Frances, A. (2009). Whither DSM–V? *The British Journal of Psychiatry, 195*(5), 391–392.

Frances, A. (2010). The forensic risks of DSM-V and how to avoid them. *Journal of the American Academy of Psychiatry and the Law Online, 38*(1), 11–14.

Frank, R. G., & McGuire, T. G. (2010). Mental health treatment and criminal justice outcomes. In P. Cook, J. Ludwig, & J. McCrary (Eds.), *Controlling crime: Strategies and tradeoffs* (pp. 167–207). University of Chicago Press.

Fridell, M., Hesse, M., Jæger, M. M., & Kühlhorn, E. (2008). Antisocial personality disorder as a predictor of criminal behaviour in a longitudinal study of a cohort of abusers of several classes of drugs: relation to type of substance and type of crime. *Addictive Behaviors, 33*(6), 799–811.

Galatzer-Levy, I. R., & Bryant, R. A. (2013). 636,120 ways to have posttraumatic stress disorder. *Perspectives on Psychological Science, 8*(6), 651–662.

Gallagher, J., Otto, R. K., & DeMier, R. (2020). Conducting forensic evaluations using videoconferencing technology. *The Specialist, 46*(Summer), 13–18.

Galvan, A., Hare, T., Voss, H., Glover, G., & Casey, B. (2007). Risk-taking and the adolescent brain: Who is at risk? *Developmental Science, 10*(2), F8–F14.

Gardner, M., & Steinberg, L. (2005). Peer influence on risk taking, risk preference, and risky decision making in adolescence and adulthood: an experimental study. *Developmental Psychology, 41*(4), 625.

Gavett, B. E., Lynch, J. K., & McCaffrey, R. J. (2005). Third party observers: The effect size is greater than you might think. *Journal of Forensic Neuropsychology, 4*(2), 49–64.

Gawande, A. (2011). *The checklist manifesto: How to get things right*. Macmillan.

Glas, A. S., Lijmer, J. G., Prins, M. H., Bonsel, G. J., & Bossuyt, P. M. (2003). The diagnostic odds ratio: a single indicator of test performance. *Journal of Clinical Epidemiology, 56*(11), 1129–1135.

Goldberg, E. (2002). *The executive brain: Frontal lobes and the civilized mind*: Oxford University Press.

Goldstein, N. E. S., Zelle, H., & Grisso, T. (2014). *Miranda Rights comprehension instruments: Manual for juvenile and adult evaluations*. Professional Resource Press.

Goodstein, D. (2011). How science works. In N. R. Council (Ed.), *Reference manual on scientific evidence* (3rd ed., pp. 37–54). The National Academies Press.

Gowensmith, W. N., & McCallum, K. E. (2019). Mirror, mirror on the wall, who's the least biased of them all? Dangers and potential solutions regarding bias in forensic psychological evaluations. *South African Journal of Psychology, 49*(2), 165–176.

Graham v. Florida, 130 S.Ct. 2011 (2010).

Grant, B. F., & Dawson, D. A. (1997). Age at onset of alcohol use and its association with DSM-IV alcohol abuse and dependence: Results from the national longitudinal alcohol epidemiologic survey. *Journal of Substance Abuse, 9*, 103–110.

Green, L., Myerson, J., & Ostaszewski, P. (1999). Discounting of delayed rewards across the life span: age differences in individual discounting functions. *Behavioural Processes, 46*(1), 89–96.

Greenwood, P. W. (2008). *Changing lives: Delinquency prevention as crime-control policy*. University of Chicago Press.

Greiffenstein, M. F., & Kaufmann, P. M. (2012). Neuropsychology and the law. In G. Larrabee (Ed.), *Forensic neuropsychology: A scientific approach* (2nd ed., pp. 23–69). Oxford University Press.

Gresham, F. M. (2009). Interpretation of intelligence test scores in Atkins cases: conceptual and psychometric issues. *Applied Neuropsychology*, *16*(2), 91–97.

Gresham, F. M., & Reschly, D. J. (2011). Standard of practice and Flynn Effect testimony in death penalty cases. *Intellectual and Developmental Disabilities*, *49*(3), 131–140.

Grimes, D. A., & Shulz, K. F. (2002). Uses and abuses of screening tests. *Lancet, 359* (389), 881–884.

Grimm, P. W. (2012). Admissibility of expert testimony in fedral courts: A view from the bench. In D. Faust (Ed.), *Coping with psychiatric and psychological testimony* (6th ed., pp. 13–27). Oxford University Press.

Grisso, T. (2003). *Evaluating competencies: Forensic assessments and instruments* (2nd ed.). Plenum Publishers.

Grisso, T. (2005). *Evaluating juveniles' adjudicative competence: A guide for clinical practice.* Professional Resources Press.

Grisso, T. (2010). Guidance for improving forensic reports: A review of common errors. *Open Access Journal of Forensic Psychology*, *2*, 102–115.

Guilmette, T. J., Sweet, J. J., Hebben, N., Koltai, D., Mahone, E. M., Spiegler, B. J., … Participants, C. (2020). American Academy of Clinical Neuropsychology consensus conference statement on uniform labeling of performance test scores. *The Clinical Neuropsychologist*, *34*(3), 437–453.

Gumpert, C. H., Winerdal, U., Grundtman, M., Berman, A. H., Kristiansson, M., & Palmstierna, T. (2010). The relationship between substance abuse treatment and crime relapse among individuals with suspected mental disorder, substance abuse, and antisocial behavior: findings from the MSAC study. *International Journal of Forensic Mental Health*, *9*(2), 82–92.

Hackshaw, A., Rodeck, C., & Boniface, S. (2011). Maternal smoking in pregnancy and birth defects: a systematic review based on 173 687 malformed cases and 11.7 million controls. *Human Reproduction Update*, *17*(5), 589–604.

Hagan, L. D., Drogin, E. Y., & Guilmette, T. J. (2010). IQ scores should not be adjusted for the Flynn effect in capital punishment cases. *Journal of Psychoeducational Assessment*, *28*(5), 474–476.

Hamsher, K., Lee, G., & Baron, I. (2001). Policy statement on the presence of third party observers in neuropsychological assessments. *Clinical Neuropsychologist*, *15*(4), 433–439.

Hare, R. D. (2003). *Manual for the revised psychopathy checklist.* Multi-Health Systems.

Hare, T. A., Tottenham, N., Galvan, A., Voss, H. U., Glover, G. H., & Casey, B. (2008). Biological substrates of emotional reactivity and regulation in adolescence during an emotional go-nogo task. *Biological Psychiatry*, *63*(10), 927–934.

Harrison, P. L., & Oakland, T. (2015). *Adaptive behavior assessment system-III: Clinical use and interpretation.* Academic Press.

Heilbronner, R.L., Sweet, J.J., Morgan, J.E., Larrabee, G.J., Millis, S., & Conference Participants (2009). American Academy of Clinical Neuropsychology consensus conference statement on the neuropsychological assessment of effort, response bias, and malingering. *The Clinical Neuropsychologist*, *23*, 1093–1129.

Heilbrun, K. (1992). The role of psychological testing in forensic assessment. *Law and Human Behavior*, *16*(3), 257–272.

Hingson, R. W., Edwards, E. M., Heeren, T., & Rosenbloom, D. (2009). Age of drinking onset and injuries, motor vehicle crashes, and physical fights after drinking and when not drinking. *Alcoholism: Clinical and Experimental Research*, *33*(5), 783–790.

Hoffmann, N. G. (2013). *Comprehensive addictions and psychological evaluation-5 manual*. Evince Clinical Assessments.

Hoffmann, N. G., & Estroff, T. W. (2001). *Practical adolescent dual diagnosis interview manual*. Evince Clinical Assessments.

Hoge, R. D., & Andrews, D. A. (2011). *Youth level of service/case managment inventory 2.0 user's manual*. Multi-Health Systems, Inc.

Howe, L.L.S., & McCaffrey, R.J. (2010). Third party observation during neuropsychological evaluation: An update on the literature, practical advice for practitioners, and future directions. *The Clinical Neuropsychologist*, *24*, 518–537.

Ioannidis, J. P. (2015). Stealth research: is biomedical innovation happening outside the peer-reviewed literature? *Journal of the American Medical Association*, *313*(7), 663–664.

Iudicello, J., Bolden, K., Griglak, S., & Woods, S. (2014). Neuropsychology of methamphetamine use disorders. In D. Allen & S. Woods (Eds.), *Neuropsychological aspects of substance use disorders: Evidence-based perspectives* (pp. 276–307). Oxford University Press.

Kane v. United States, 399 F.2d 730 (1968).

Kaufman, N. (2020). Rethinking "gold standards" and "best practices" in the assessment of autism. *Applied Neuropsychology: Child*. doi: 10.1080/21622965.2020.1809414.

Kaufman, N., & Bush, S. S. (in press). Purposes of assessment in autism and pervasive developmental disorders. In J. L. Matson & P. Sturmey (Eds.), *Handbook of autism and pervasive developmental disorders*. Springer.

Kaufman, N., Holland, S, Bolshin, L. (2015). A Neuropsychological Framework for Diagnosing Intellectual Disability. *The New Mexico Trial Lawyer*, *XXXXVI*(4), 83–93.

Kaufman, N. K., & Bush, S. S. (2020). Concussion in pediatric neuropsychology. *Journal of Pediatric Neuropsychology*. doi:10.1007/s40817-020-00078-3.

Kaufman, N. K., & Bush, S. S. (in Press). Ethical issues in assessing malingering in head injury litigation. In C. R. Reynolds & A. M. Horton III (Eds.), *Detecting malingering in head injury litigation* (3rd ed.). Springer Publishing Company.

Kaufman, N. K., Bush, S. S., & Aguilar, M. R. (2019). What attorneys and factfinders need to know about mild traumatic brain injury. *Psychological Injury & Law*, *12*, 91–112.

Kaufman, N. K., Lyke, P. A., Walter, J. G., Bush, S. S., Tonarelli, S. B., Sandoval, H., … King, J. (2020). No free, appropriate, public education for most neuropsychologically referred outpatients. *Journal of Pediatric Neuropsychology*, *6*, 159–169.

Kiehl, K. A. (2014). *The psychopath whisperer: The science of those without conscience*. Crown.

Kim, B. E., Gilman, A. B., Kosterman, R., & Hill, K. G. (2019). Longitudinal associations among depression, substance abuse, and crime: A test of competing hypotheses for driving mechanisms. *Journal of Criminal Justice*, *62*, 50–57.

King, J. H., Rolin, S. N., & Frost, B. (2017). Moderate to severe traumatic brain injury. In S. S. Bush (Ed.), *APA handbook of forensic neuropsychology* (pp. 201–222). American Psychological Association.

Knapp, S.J., VandeCreek, L.D., & Fingerhut, R. (2017). *Practical ethics for psychologists: A positive approach*. (3rd ed.). American Psychological Association.

Kolb, B., & Whishaw, I. Q. (2009). *Fundamentals of human neuropsychology*. Macmillan.

Lally, S. J. (2003). What tests are acceptable for use in forensic evaluations? A survey of experts. *Professional Psychology: Research and Practice*, *34*(5), 491.

Lareau, C. R. (2012). The DSM-IV system of psychiatric classification. In D. Faust (Ed.), *Coping with psychiatric and psychological testimony* (6th ed., pp. 209–228). Oxford University Press.

Larner, A. J. (2016). *A dictionary of neurological signs* (3rd ed.). Springer.

Larrabee, G. J. (2012). Performance validity and symptom validity in neuropsychological assessment. *Journal of the International Neuropsychological Society, 18*, 1–7.

Lee, C. M., Fairlie, A. M., Ramirez, J. J., Patrick, M. E., Luk, J. W., & Lewis, M. A. (2019). Self-fulfilling prophecies: Documentation of real-world daily alcohol expectancy effects on the experience of specific positive and negative alcohol-related consequences. *Psychology of Addictive Behaviors, 34*(2), 327–334.

Lees-Haley, P. R. (1999). Commentary on Sweet and Moulthrop's debiasing procedures. *Journal of Forensic Neuropsychology, 1*(3), 43–47.

Lerner, M. D., Haque, O. S., Northrup, E. C., Lawer, L., & Bursztajn, H. J. (2012). Emerging perspectives on adolescents and young adults with high-functioning autism spectrum disorders, violence, and criminal law. *Journal of the American Academy of Psychiatry and the Law Online, 40*(2), 177–190.

Levi, E. H. (1992). *An introduction to legal reasoning*. University of Chicago Press.

Lewandowski, A., Baker, W. J., Sewick, B., Knippa, J., Axelrod, B., & McCaffrey, R. J. (2016). Policy Statement of the American Board of Professional Neuropsychology regarding Third Party Observation and the recording of psychological test administration in neuropsychological evaluations. *Applied Neuropsychology: Adult, 23*, 391–398.

Lexcen, F. J., Hawk, G. L., Herrick, S., & Blank, M. B. (2006). Use of video conferencing for psychiatric and forensic evaluations. *Psychiatric Services, 57*(5), 713–715.

Lieb, R., Merikangas, K. R., Höfler, M., Pfister, H., Isensee, B., & Wittchen, H.-U. (2002). Parental alcohol use disorders and alcohol use and disorders in offspring: a community study. *Psychological Medicine, 32*(1), 63.

Lilienfeld, S., Lynn, S., & Lohr, J. (2015). *Science and pseudoscience in clinical psychology* (2nd ed.). The Guilford Press.

Lilienfeld, S., Lynn, S., & Lohr, J. (2015). Science and pseudoscience in clinical psychology: Initial thoughts, reflections, and considerations. In S. Lilienfeld, S. Lynn, & J. Lohr (Eds.), *Science and pseudoscience in clinical psychology* (pp. 1–16). The Guilford Press.

Lipner, R. S., Hess, B. J., & Phillips, R. L. (2013). Specialty board certification in the United States: Issues and evidence. *Journal of Continuing Education in the Health Professions, 33*(S1), S20–S35.

Lipsey, M. W. (1995). What do we learn from 400 research studies on the effectiveness of treatment with juvenile delinquents? In J. McGuire (Ed.), *What works? Reducing Reoffending* (pp. 63–78). Wiley.

Lipsey, M. W., Wilson, D. B., Cohen, M. A., & Derzon, J. H. (2002). Is there a causal relationship between alcohol use and violence? A synthesis of the evidence. In M. Galanter (Ed.), *Recent developments inalcoholism* (Vol. 13, pp. 245–282). Plenum Press.

Little, B. B. G., L.H. (1998). *Drugs and Pregnancy*. Cambridge University Press.

Loeber, R. (1990). Development and risk factors of juvenile antisocial behavior and delinquency. *Clinical Psychology Review, 10*(1), 1–41.

Loeber, R., Wung, P., Keenan, K., Giroux, B., Stouthamer-Loeber, M., Van Kammen, W. B., & Maugham, B. (1993). Developmental pathways in disruptive child behavior. *Development and Psychopathology, 5*(1–2), 103–133.

Lord, C., Rutter, M., DiLavore, P. C., Risi, S., Gotham, K., & Bishop, S. (2012). *Autism diagnostic observation schedule* (2nd ed.). Western Psychological Services.

Lord, C., Rutter, M., & Le Couteur, A. (1994). Autism Diagnostic Interview-Revised: A revised version of a diagnostic interview for caregivers of individuals with possible pervasive developmental disorders. *Journal of Autism and Developmental Disorders, 24*(5), 659–685.

Loring, D. W. (1999). *INS dictionary of neuropsychology*. Oxford University Press.

Luxton, D. D., & Lexcen, F. J. (2018). Forensic competency evaluations via videoconferencing: A feasibility review and best practice recommendations. *Professional Psychology: Research and Practice, 49*(2), 124.

Maria, B. L. (2009). *Current management in child neurology*: PMPH-USA.

Marlowe, D. B. (1995). A hybrid decision framework for evaluating psychometric evidence. *Behavioral Sciences & the Law, 13*(2), 207–228.

Marra, D. E., Hamlet, K. M., Bauer, R. M., & Bowers, D. (2020). Validity of teleneuropsychology for older adults in response to COVID-19: A systematic and critical review. *The Clinical Neuropsychologist, 34*(7–8), 1411–1452.

McCann, J., Lynn, S., Lilienfeld, S., Shindler, K., & Natof, T. (2015). The science and pseudoscience of expert testimony. In S. Lilienfeld, S. Lynn, & J. Lohr (Eds.), *Science and pseudoscience in clinical psychology* (pp. 83–112). The Guilford Press.

McCrea, M. (2008). *Mild traumatic brain injury and postconcussion syndrome: The new evidence base for diagnosis and treatment.* Oxford University Press.

McDermott, B., & Scott, C. (2015). DSM-5 and malingering. In C. Scott (Ed.), *DSM-5 and the law: Changes and challenges* (pp. 242–267). Oxford University Press.

McWhirter, L., Ritchie, C. W., Stone, J., & Carson, A. (2020). Performance validity test failure in clinical populations—a systematic review. *Journal of Neurology, Neurosurgery & Psychiatry, 91*(9), 945–952.

Meade, C. S., Kershaw, T. S., Hansen, N. B., & Sikkema, K. J. (2009). Long-term correlates of childhood abuse among adults with severe mental illness: adult victimization, substance abuse, and HIV sexual risk behavior. *AIDS and Behavior, 13*(2), 207.

Meharg, S. (2017). Forensic neuropsychological reports. In S. S. Bush, G. J. Demakis, & M. L. Rohling (Eds.), *APA Handbook of Forensic Neuropsychology* (pp. 397–412). American Psychological Association.

Melton, G. B., Petrila, J., Poythress, N. G., Slobogin, C., Otto, R. K., Mossman, D., & Condie, L. O. (2017). *Psychological evaluations for the courts: A handbook for mental health professionals and lawyers* (4th ed.). Guilford Publications.

Merikangas, J. (2004). Commentary: Alcoholic blackout--does it remove mens rea? *The Journal of the American Academy of Psychiatry and the Law, 32*(4), 375–377.

Meyer, G. J., Finn, S. E., Eyde, L. D., Kay, G. G., Moreland, K. L., Dies, R. R., … Reed, G. M. (2001). Psychological testing and psychological assessment: A review of evidence and issues. *American Psychologist, 56*(2), 128–165.

Meyer, R. G., & Weaver, C. M. (2006). *Law and mental health: A case-based approach.* The Guilford Press.

Milberger, S., Biederman, J., Faraone, S. V., Guite, J., & Tsuang, M. T. (1997). Pregnancy, delivery and infancy complications and attention deficit hyperactivity disorder: Issues of gene–environment interaction. *Biological Psychiatry, 41*(1), 65–75.

Miller, T. R., Levy, D. T., Cohen, M. A., & Cox, K. L. (2006). Costs of alcohol and drug-involved crime. *Prevention Science*, 7(4), 333–342.

Moffitt, T. E. (1993). Adolescence-limited and life-course-persistent antisocial behavior: A developmental taxonomy. *Psychological review, 100*(4), 674.

Montana v. Egelhoff, No. No. 95-566, 518 37 (Supreme Court 1996).

Morey, L. C. (2007). *Personality Assessment Inventory Professional Manual.* Lutz, FL: Psychological Assessment Resources.

Morse, S. J. (2005). Brain overclaim syndrome and criminal responsibility: A diagnostic note. *Ohio State Journal of Criminal Law, 3*, 397.

Mulay, A. L., Gottfried, E. D., Mullis, D. M., & Vitacco, M. J. (2021). The use of videoconferencing in forensic evaluations: Moving forward in times of COVID-19. *Journal of Forensic Psychology Research and Practice, 21,* 338–354.

Murriel, D. C., & Boccaccini, M. T. (2015). Adversarial allegiance among expert witnesses. *Annual Review of Law and Social Science, 11*, 37–55.

Murphy, A., Steele, M., Dube, S. R., Bate, J., Bonuck, K., Meissner, P., ... Steele, H. (2014). Adverse childhood experiences (ACEs) questionnaire and adult attachment interview (AAI): Implications for parent child relationships. *Child Abuse & Neglect, 38*(2), 224–233.

National Academy of Neuropsychology Policy and Planning Committee. (2000). Presence of 3rd party observers during neuropsychological testing: Official statement of the National Academy of Neuropsychology. *Archives of Clinical Neuropsychology, 15*, 379–380.

National Academy of Neuropsychology Policy and Planning Committee. (2003). Test security: An update. *Official statement of the National Academy of Neuropsychology*. Retrieved from www.nanonline.org/docs/PAIC/PDFs/NANTestSecurityUpdate.pdf.

Neal, T. M. S., & Brodsky, S. L. (2016). Forensic psychologists' perceptions of bias and potential correction strategies in forensic mental health evaluations. *Psychology, Public Policy, and Law, 22*, 58–76.

Nellhaus, G. (1968). Head circumference from birth to eighteen years practical composite international and interracial graphs. *Pediatrics, 41*(1), 106–114.

Nelson, R. J., & Trainor, B. C. (2007). Neural mechanisms of aggression. *Nature Reviews Neuroscience, 8*(7), 536–546.

Nigg, J. T., Wong, M. M., Martel, M. M., Jester, J. M., Puttler, L. I., Glass, J. M., ... Zucker, R. A. (2006). Poor response inhibition as a predictor of problem drinking and illicit drug use in adolescents at risk for alcoholism and other substance use disorders. *Journal of the American Academy of Child & Adolescent Psychiatry, 45*(4), 468–475.

Nisbett, R. E., Zukier, H., & Lemley, R. E. (1981). The dilution effect: Nondiagnostic information weakens the implications of diagnostic information. *Cognitive Psychology, 13*(2), 248–277.

Norman, A. L., Pulido, C., Squeglia, L. M., Spadoni, A. D., Paulus, M. P., & Tapert, S. F. (2011). Neural activation during inhibition predicts initiation of substance use in adolescence. *Drug and Alcohol Dependence, 119*(3), 216–223.

Nurmi, J.-E. (1991). How do adolescents see their future? A review of the development of future orientation and planning. *Developmental Review, 11*(1), 1–59.

O'Donohue, W. T., Lilienfeld, S. O., & Fowler, K. A. (2007). Science is an essential safeguard against human error *The great ideas of clinical science: 17 principles that every mental health professional should understand* (pp. 3–27). Routledge.

Otto, R. K., DeMier, R., & Boccaccini, M. (2014). *Forensic reports and testimony: A guide to effective communication for psychologists and psychiatrists.* John Wiley & Sons.

Otto, R. K., & Goldstein, A. M. (2013). Overview of forensic psychology. In R.K. Otto (Ed.), *Handbook of psychology* (2nd ed., Vol. 11, 3–15). John Wiley & Sons.

Otto, R. K., & Krauss, D. A. (2009). Contemplating the presence of third party observers and facilitators in psychological evaluations. *Assessment, 16*(4), 362–372.

Packer, I. K. (2009). *Evaluation of criminal responsibility*. Oxford University Press.
Packer, I. K., & Grisso, T. (2011). *Specialty competencies in forensic psychology*. Oxford University Press.
Pagano, R. R. (1994). *Understanding statistics in the behavioral sciences* (4th ed.). West Publishing Company.
Parker, R., & Auerhahn, K. (1998). Alcohol, drugs, and violence. *Annual Review of Sociology*, *24*(1), 291–311.
Pennington, B. F. (2008). *Diagnosing learning disorders: A neuropsychological framework*. Guilford Press.
Pennington, B. F., McGrath, L., & Peterson, R. (2019). Autism spectrum disorder. *Diagnosing learning disorders* (3rd ed., pp. 258–311). The Guilford Press.
Petersen, R. C. (2004). Mild cognitive impairment as a diagnostic entity. *Journal of Internal Medicine*, *256*(3), 183–194.
Peterson, J. B., Rothfleisch, J., Zelazo, P. D., & Pihl, R. O. (1990). Acute alcohol intoxication and cognitive functioning. *Journal of Studies on Alcohol*, *51*(2), 114–122.
Pirelli, G., Gottdiener, W. H., & Zapf, P. A. (2011). A meta-analytic review of competency to stand trial research. *Psychology, Public Policy, and Law*. doi: 10.1037/a0021713.
Polanska, K., Jurewicz, J., & Hanke, W. (2015). Smoking and alcohol drinking during pregnancy as the risk factors for poor child neurodevelopment—A review of epidemiological studies. *International Journal of Occupational Medicine and Environmental Health*, *28*(3), 419–443.
Poulin, F., Dishion, T. J., & Burraston, B. (2001). 3-year iatrogenic effects associated with aggregating high-risk adolescents in cognitive-behavioral preventive interventions. *Applied Developmental Science*, *5*(4), 214–224.
Poythress, N. G., Nicholson, R., Otto, R. K., Edens, J., Bonnie, R. J., Monahan, J., & Hoge, S. (1999). *MacArthur competence assessment tool-criminal adjudication professional manual*. Psychological Assessment Resources.
Pressman, M. R., & Caudill, D. S. (2013). Alcohol-induced blackout as a criminal defense or mitigating factor: An evidence-based review and admissibility as scientific evidence. *Journal of Forensic Sciences*, *58*(4), 932–940.
Putnam, S.H., DeLuca, J.W., & Anderson, C. (1994). The second TCN salary survey: A survey of neuropsychologists Part II. *The Clinical Neuropsychologist*, *8*, 245–282.
Raine, A. (2013). *The anatomy of violence: The biological roots of crime*. Vintage.
Reavis, J. A., Looman, J., Franco, K. A., & Rojas, B. (2013). Adverse childhood experiences and adult criminality: How long must we live before we possess our own lives? *The Permanente Journal*, *17*(2), 44.
Reynolds, C. R., & Kamphaus, R. W. (2015). *Behavior assessment system for children manual* (3rd ed.). Pearson.
Reynolds, C. R., & Livingston, R. B. (2012). *Mastering modern psychological testing: Theory and methods*. Pearson Education.
Reynolds, C. R., Livingston, R. B., & Willson, V. (2009). *Measurement and Assessment in Education* (2nd ed.). Pearson
Reynolds, C. R., Niland, J., Wright, J. E., & Rosenn, M. (2010). Failure to apply the Flynn correction in ceath penalty litigation: Standard practice of today maybe, but certainly malpractice of tomorrow. *Journal of Psychoeducational Assessment*, *28*(5), 477–481.
Rice, M. E., Harris, G. T., & Lang, C. (2013). Validation of and revision to the VRAG and SORAG: The Violence Risk Appraisal Guide—Revised (VRAG-R). *Psychological Assessment*, *25*(3), 951.

Robin, A. L., Koepke, T., Moye, A. W., & Gerhardstein, R. (2009). *Parent adolescent relationship questionnaire*. Psychological Assessment Resources.

Roesch, R., Zapf, P. A., & Eaves, D. (2006). *Fitness interview test-revised. A structured interview for assessing competency to stand trial*. Professional Resource Press.

Rogers, R., & Bender, S. D. (2013). Evaluation of malingering and related response styles. In R. K. Otto (Ed.), *Handbook of psychology* (2nd ed., pp. 517–540). John Wiley & Sons.

Rogers, R., & Ewing, C. P. (1989). Ultimate opinion proscriptions: A cosmetic fix and a plea for empiricism. *Law and Human Behavior, 13*(4), 357.

Rogers, R., & Ewing, C. P. (2003). The prohibition of ultimate opinions: A misguided enterprise. *Journal of Forensic Psychology Practice, 3*(3), 65–75.

Rogers, R., & Shuman, D. (2006). *Fundamentals of forensic practice: Mental health and criminal law*. Springer Science & Business Media.

Rogers, R., & Shuman, D. W. (2006). Malingering and deception in criminal evaluations *Fundamentals of forensic practice: Mental health and criminal law* (pp. 21–55). Springer.

Rohling, M., Langhinrichsen-Rohling, J., & Axelrod, B. (2017). Mild Traumatic Brain Injury. In S. S. Bush (Ed.), *APA Handbook of Forensic Neuropsychology* (pp. 147–200). American Psychological Association.

Rohling, M. L., Lees-Haley, P. R., Langhinrichsen-Rohling, J., & Williamson, D.J. (2003). A statistical analysis of board certification in Clinical Neuropsychology. *Archives of Clinical Neuropsychology, 18*, 331–351.

Richards, P. M., Geiger, J. A., & Tussey, C. M. (2015). The dirty dozen: 12 sources of bias in forensic neuropsychology with ways to mitigate. *Psychological Injury and Law, 8*, 265–280.

Rompilla v. Beard, 545 U.S. 374 (2005)

Ropper, A. H. (2009). *Adams and Victor's principles of neurology*. McGraw-Hill Medical.

Rosenbaum, G. M., Venkatraman, V., Steinberg, L., & Chein, J. M. (2018). The influences of described and experienced information on adolescent risky decision making. *Developmental Review, 47*, 23–43.

Salvia, J., Ysseldyke, J. E., & Bolt, S. (2010). *Assessment in special and inclusive education* (11th ed.). Wadsworth.

Sardella, A. (2017). Mild cognitive impairment: Still a controversial stage between normal cognitive aging and dementia. *MOJ Geriatrics & Geriatrics, 2*, 215–216.

SAMSHA. (2019). *Results from the national survey of drug use and health: 2019*. Rockville, MD: Office of Applied Studies, DHHS.

Sattler, J. M. (2001). *Assessment of children: Cognitive applications* (4th ed.). Jerome M. Sattler, Publisher, Inc.

Scribner, R. A., MacKinnon, D. P., & Dwyer, J. H. (1995). The risk of assaultive violence and alcohol availability in Los Angeles County. *American Journal of Public Health, 85*(3), 335–340.

Shapiro, E. (1995). *Eye movement desensitization and reprocessing: Basic protocols, principles, and procedures*. The Guilford Press.

Sharp, L. K., Bashook, P. G., Lipsky, M. S., Horowitz, S. D., & Miller, S. H. (2002). Specialty board certification and clinical outcomes: the missing link. *Academic Medicine, 77*(6), 534–542.

Sher, K. J., Bartholow, B. D., & Wood, M. D. (2000). Personality and substance use disorders: a prospective study. *Journal of Consulting and Clinical Psychology, 68*(5), 818.

Sher, L., Rice, T., & WFSBP Task Force on Men's Mental Health. (2015). Prevention of homicidal behaviour in men with psychiatric disorders. *The World Journal of Biological Psychiatry, 16*(4), 212–229.

Sherer, M., & Madison, C. F. (2005). Moderate and severe traumatic brain injury. In G. Larrabee (Ed.), *Forensic neuropsychology: A scientific approach* (1st ed., pp. 237–270): New York, NY: Oxford University Press.

Shindell, M. R., McCaffrey, R. J., & Silk-Eglit, G. M. (2014). *Three's a crowd: The impact of third-party observers on neuropsychological exams.* Retrieved from https://www.americanbar.org/groups/litigation/committees/trial-practice/articles/2014/summer2014-0914-third-party-observers-neuropsychological-exams-at-trial/.

Siegel, D. M., & Kinscherff, R. (2018). Recording routine forensic mental health evaluations should be a standard of practice in the 21st century. *Behavioral Sciences & the Law, 36*(3), 373–389.

Smith, G. E., & Bondi, M. W. (2013). *Mild cognitive impairment and dementia: Definitions, diagnosis, and treatment.* Oxford University Press.

Spearman, C. E. (1923). *The nature of intelligence and the principles of cognition.* MacMillan.

Steinberg, L. (2009). Adolescent development and juvenile justice. *Annual Review of Clinical Psychology, 5,* 459–485.

Steinberg, L. (2013). The influence of neuroscience on US Supreme Court decisions about adolescents' criminal culpability. *Nature Reviews Neuroscience, 14*(7), 513–518.

Steinberg, L., Cauffman, E., Woolard, J., Graham, S., & Banich, M. (2009). Are adolescents less mature than adults?: Minors' access to abortion, the juvenile death penalty, and the alleged APA "flip-flop." *American Psychologist, 64*(7), 583.

Strauss, E., Sherman, E., & Spreen, O. (2006). Norms selection in neuropsychological assessment. *A compendium of neuropsychological tests. Administration, norms, and commentary* (pp. 44–58). Oxford University Press.

Sweet, J. (2003). Official Position of the American Academy of Clinical Neuropsychology on Ethical Complaints Made Against Clinical Neuropsychologists During Adversarial Proceedings. *The Clinical Neuropsychologist, 17*(4), 443–445.

Sweet, J. J. (2005). Ethical challenges in forensic neuropsychology, part IV. In S. S. Bush (Ed.), *A casebook of ethical challenges in neuropsychology* (pp. 51–61). Taylor & Francis.

Sweet, J. J., & Moulthrop, M. A. (1999). Self-examination questions as a means of identifying bias in adversarial assessments. *Journal of Forensic Neuropsychology, 1*(1), 73–88.

The Psychological Corporation. (1999). *Wechsler abbreviated scale of intelligence manual.* Hartcourt Brace & Company.

Thomas, T. A. (2010). *Predicting restoration of competence to stand trial: Demographic, clinical, and legal variables.* West Virginia University.

Thorndike, R., & Hagen, E. (1978). *Measurement and evaluation in psychology and education.* Wiley.

Tombaugh, T. N. (1996). *Test of memory malingering manual.* Multihealth Systems Inc.

Torres, L., Skidmore, S., & Gross, N. (2012). Assessment of post-traumatic stress disorder: Differences in standards and practice between licensed and board-certified psychologists. *Psychological Injury and Law, 5*(1), 1–11.

Trahan, L. H., Stuebing, K. K., Fletcher, J. M., & Hiscock, M. (2014). The Flynn effect: A meta-analysis. *Psychological Bulletin, 140*(5), 1332.

Tufte, E. (2001). *The visual display of quantitative information* (2nd ed.). Graphics Press.

Vaughters, J. (2019). *One-way ticket: Nine lives on two wheels.* Penguin.

Vitacco, M. J., Lilienfeld, S. O., Erickson, S., & Wood, J. M. (2012). Challenging personality testing: Objective and projective instruments. In D. Faust (Ed.), *Coping with psychiatric and psychological testimony* (6th ed., pp. 335–362). Oxford University Press.

Warren, J. I., Aaron, J., Ryan, E., Chauhan, P., & DuVal, J. (2003). Correlates of adjudicative competence among psychiatrically impaired juveniles. *Journal of the American Academy of Psychiatry and the Law Online, 31*(3), 299–309.

Wason, P. C. (1960). On the failure to eliminate hypotheses in a conceptual task. *Quarterly Journal of Experimental Psychology, 12*(3), 129–140.

Wechsler, D. (1944). *The measurement of adult intelligence.* Williams and Wilkins.

Wechsler, D. (1975). Intelligence defined and undefined: A relativistic appraisal. *American Psychologist, 30*(2), 135.

Wilens, T. E., Faraone, S. V., Biederman, J., & Gunawardene, S. (2003). Does stimulant therapy of attention-deficit/hyperactivity disorder beget later substance abuse? A meta-analytic review of the literature. *Pediatrics, 111*(1), 179–185.

Witt, P. (2010). Forensic report checklist. *Open Access Journal of Forensic Psychology, 2*, 233–240.

Youden, W. J. (1950). Index for rating diagnostic tests. *Cancer, 3*(1), 32–35.

Zapf, P. A., & Dror, I. E. (2017). Understanding and mitigating bias in forensic evaluation: Lessons from forensic science. *International Journal of Forensic Mental Health, 16*, 227–238.

Zapf, P. A., Kukucka, J., Kassin, S. M., & Dror, I. E. (2017). Cognitive bias in forensic mental health assessment: Evaluator beliefs about its nature and scope. *Psychology, Public Policy, and Law, 24*, 1–10.

Zapf, P., & Roesch, R. (2009). *Attorney CST Questionnaire.* Oxford University Press.

Zappala, M., Reed, A. L., Beltrani, A., Zapf, P. A., & Otto, R. K. (2018). Anything You Can Do, I Can Do Better: Bias Awareness in Forensic Evaluators. *Journal of Forensic Psychology Research and Practice, 18*(1), 45–56.

Zimring, F. E. (2013). American youth violence: A cautionary tale. *Crime and Justice, 42*(1), 265–298.

Section II

Legal Cases for the Forensic Mental Health Professional

Case Summaries

Ake v. Oklahoma
470 U.S. 68 (1985)
U.S. Supreme Court

Case Facts

Mr. Glen Burton Ake was an indigent defendant charged with first degree murder who was acting so bizarrely that the judge ordered a psychiatric evaluation sua sponte. The evaluator assessed that Ake was psychotic, rendered a diagnosis of paranoid schizophrenia, and opined that he was incompetent to stand trial. He was subsequently committed to a state hospital where he spent six weeks and eventually was found to be competent to stand trial (as long as he was given Thorazine). While the issue of competence was seemingly resolved, Ake's attorney requested that the court arrange a psychiatrist to conduct a sanity evaluation or provide funding for the defense to arrange it, but the trial judge denied the request. The sole defense at trial was insanity. The state hospital psychiatrists testified about dangerousness but not about the issue of sanity. The jury found Ake guilty, the state requested the death penalty, relied on the trial testimony provided by the state hospital psychiatrists about Ake's dangerousness, and sentenced him to death. On appeal, he argued that, as an indigent defendant, he should have been provided the services of a psychiatrist to evaluate his sanity. The Oklahoma Court of Criminal Appeals rejected his argument and stated that the state had no responsibility to provide psychiatric services to an indigent defendant charged with a capital crime. Certiorari was granted by the U.S. Supreme Court, which reversed.

Main Issue

Does the U.S. Constitution require that an indigent defendant have access to a forensic mental health examination and the legal assistance necessary to prepare an effective defense, when sanity at the time of the offense is in question?

DOI: 10.4324/9780367645090-102

Court Holding

Yes. When a defendant in a criminal matter makes a showing that sanity at the time of the offense is likely to be a significant factor at trial, the U.S. Constitution requires that the state provide the defendant access to a qualified forensic mental health professional if the defendant cannot otherwise afford one. A defendant is similarly entitled to the assistance of a forensic mental health professional at a capital sentencing proceeding regarding the defendant's future dangerousness; and the defendant's sanity was a significant factor at both the guilt and sentencing phases and the denial of psychiatric assistance constituted a deprivation of due process.

Court's Reasoning

The court focused on the protections of the 14th Amendment due process rights, specifically that a defendant cannot be restricted from a fair defense simply due to poverty. Indigent defendants must be provided "basic tools of an adequate defense or appeal." The court made it clear that the indigent defendant does not have a constitutional right to choose an expert of their personal liking or to receive funds to hire their own but that one must be provided at no cost to the defendant so that they can mount a relevant and fair defense.

Quick Summary

Indigent defendants have the right to be evaluated by a qualified mental health professional at no cost if sanity at the time of the offense is a significant factor at issue and if such an evaluation could affect the verdict or the sentencing.

Atkins v. Virginia
536 U.S. 304 (2002)
U.S. Supreme Court

Case Facts

Daryl Atkins was convicted of abduction, armed robbery, and capital murder and was sentenced to death by a Virginia jury. During the penalty phase of the trial, Atkins was evaluated by a forensic psychologist who concluded that Atkins was "mildly mentally retarded" with an IQ of 59. The jury nonetheless decided on the death penalty. Virginia Supreme Court ordered a second sentencing hearing because it had used a misleading verdict form. The forensic psychologist again testified regarding IQ, and the state presented an expert rebuttal witness who testified that Mr. Atkins was not "mentally retarded" (although no testing was administered) but rather was of "average intelligence, at least" and had antisocial personality disorder (ASPD). The jury again sentenced Mr. Atkins to death. On appeal, Atkins contended that he was mentally retarded and could not be sentenced to death. The court was unwilling to convert his sentence to life. When two Virginia justices strongly dissented, the U.S. Supreme Court granted certiorari.

Main Issue

Is the execution of "mentally retarded" individuals considered "cruel and unusual punishment" and, as such, prohibited by the Eighth Amendment to the Constitution?

Court Holding

The U.S. Supreme Court held that the death penalty is an "excessive" punishment for an intellectually disabled (ID) offender and that the constitution "places a substantive restriction on the State's power to take the life" of such an offender. It's up to the states to determine what constitutes intellectual disability.

Court's Reasoning

The court reasoned that there is a direction of change toward the prohibition of such executions and, in states that allow them, such executions are very rare. Professional and religious organizations oppose such executions, and data show "a widespread consensus by Americans against such executions." Retribution and deterrence, the main "basis" for invoking the death penalty, may not be applicable to such offenders based on differences in information processing, communication, and logical reasoning. With respect to retribution, "just deserts" depends on the culpability of the offender and, given that "only the most deserving of execution are put to death," excluding intellectual disability is appropriate. Regarding deterrence, the same deficits that make intellectually disabled offenders less culpable (e.g., diminished ability to process information and learn from experience) also make deterrence less likely to work. Non-ID offenders will not be negatively affected by excluding ID offenders from this penalty because they themselves are not excluded. ID offenders are at "special risk of wrongful execution" because they are less able to work effectively with counsel, are poorer witnesses, and can come off as lacking remorse for their crimes.

Quick Summary

The Supreme Court in this case concluded that the execution of offenders with intellectual disabilities is excessive and prohibited by the Eighth Amendment as cruel and unusual punishment.

Mary Berghuis v. Van Chester Thompkins
130 S.Ct. 2250 (2010)
560 U.S. 370
No. 08-1470.
Supreme Court of United States

Case Facts

On January 10, 2000, a shooting occurred outside a mall in Michigan. One victim died. The other victim recovered and later testified. Thompkins, who was a suspect, fled. About one year later, he was found in Ohio and arrested. Two police officers traveled to Ohio to interrogate Thompkins. At the beginning of the interrogation, one of the officers presented Thompkins with a form derived from the *Miranda* rule. After advising Thompkins of his rights, the officers interrogated him. At no point did Thompkins say that he wanted to remain silent, that he did not want to talk with the police, or that he wanted an attorney. He was largely silent, but near the end, he answered "yes" when asked if he prayed to God to forgive him for the shooting. He moved to suppress his statements, claiming that he had invoked his Fifth Amendment right to remain silent, that he had not waived that right, and that his inculpatory (incriminatory) statements were involuntary. The trial court denied the motion. At trial on first-degree murder and other charges, the prosecution called Eric Purifoy, who drove the van in which Thompkins and a third accomplice were riding at the time of the shooting. Thompkins' defense was that Purifoy was the shooter. Purifoy testified that he did not see who fired the shots.

The jury found Thompkins guilty, and he was sentenced to life in prison without parole. The federal district court denied his subsequent habeas request, reasoning that Thompkins did not invoke his right to remain silent and was not coerced into making statements during the interrogation, and that it was not unreasonable, for purposes of the Antiterrorism and Effective Death Penalty Act of 1996 (AEDPA), for the State Court of Appeals to determine that he had waived his right to remain silent. The Sixth Circuit reversed, holding that the state court was unreasonable in finding an implied waiver of Thompkins' right to remain silent. Thompkins argued that the police were not allowed to question him until they first obtained from him a waiver of his right to remain silent.

Main Issue

Can police interrogate a suspect without first obtaining a waiver of the right to remain silent?

Court Holding

The U.S. Supreme Court reversed and remanded. Police can infer a waiver of the right to remain silent when a suspect knowingly and voluntarily provides information to them.

Court's Reasoning

Thompkins' silence during the interrogation did not invoke his right to remain silent. A suspect's *Miranda* right to counsel must be invoked "unambiguously." If the accused makes an "ambiguous or equivocal" statement or no statement, the police are not required to end the interrogation. Had Thompkins said that he wanted to remain silent or that he did not want to talk, he would have invoked his right to end the questioning. He did neither. Thompkins waived his right to remain silent when he knowingly and voluntarily made a statement to police. The court noted that a waiver must be the product of a free and deliberate choice rather than intimidation, coercion, or deception and must be made with a full awareness of both the nature of the right being abandoned and the consequences of the decision to abandon it. Such a waiver may be "implied" through a "defendant's silence, coupled with an understanding of his rights and a course of conduct indicating waiver." If the state establishes that a *Miranda* warning was given and that it was understood by the accused, an accused's uncoerced statement establishes an implied waiver. The record here shows that Thompkins waived his right to remain silent. Any waiver, expressed or implied, may be revoked at any time, resulting in termination of further interrogation.

Quick Summary

Police can infer a waiver of the right to remain silent when a suspect knowingly and voluntarily provides information to them. If a *Miranda* warning was given and was understood by the suspected, the person's uncoerced statement establishes an implied waiver.

Boykin v. Alabama
395 U.S. 238 (1969)
U.S. Supreme Court

Case Facts

Edward Boykin, Jr. pled guilty to robbery that also involved the injury of one innocent person, resulting from a bullet that ricocheted off the floor. Boykin pled guilty to all five charges and no effort was made by the judge to assess whether or not Boykin's guilty plea was made knowingly and voluntarily. After Boykin was sentenced to death, the case was appealed to the Alabama Supreme Court, on the premise "that a sentence of death for common-law robbery was cruel and unusual punishment." While this argument was unanimously rejected, "four of the seven justices discussed the constitutionality of the process by which the trial judge had accepted petitioner's guilty plea." In their dissents, three of the justices maintained that Mr. Boykin may not have "intelligently and knowingly pleaded guilty." And a fourth justice wrote that "a trial judge should not accept a guilty plea unless he has determined that such a plea was voluntarily and knowingly entered by the defendant." On this basis, the U.S. Supreme Court granted certiorari.

Main Issue

Does a guilty plea need to be made knowingly, intelligently, and voluntarily?

Court Holding

Yes. The U.S. Supreme Court reversed the death sentence of Mr. Boykin on the basis that his guilty plea was not made knowingly, intelligently, and voluntarily.

Court's Reasoning

The Court reasoned that waiving one's Sixth Amendment right to counsel is so similar to waiving one's rights by pleading guilty that "the same standard must be applied to determining whether a guilty plea is voluntarily made." The Court also asserted that "it was error, plain on the face of the record, for the trial judge to accept [Boykin's] guilty plea without an affirmative showing that it was intelligent and voluntary," thereby emphasizing the importance of an intelligent and voluntary waiver of rights through a guilty plea. The Court also drew attention to the need for judges to actively seek evidence that guilty pleas are made with a full awareness of the consequences:

> What is at stake for an accused facing death or imprisonment demands the utmost solicitude of which courts are capable in canvassing the matter with the accused to make sure he has a full understanding of what the plea connotes and of its consequence. When the judge discharges that function, he leaves a record adequate for any review that may be later sought, and forestalls the spin-off of collateral proceedings that seek to probe murky memories.

Because, in this case, the record did not show that Mr. Boykin had "voluntarily and understandingly entered his pleas of guilty," the U.S. Supreme Court reversed the decision of the lower court, thereby underscoring the importance of a knowing, intelligent, and voluntary waiver of rights through a guilty plea.

Quick Summary

Edward Boykin Jr. was found guilty of "common-law robbery" and sentenced to death, so he appealed the case on the basis that it was a violation of his Eighth Amendment right against cruel and unusual punishment. While the

Alabama Supreme Court unanimously rejected this argument, enough of the dissenting justices raised concerns about the man's having "intelligently and knowingly" waived his constitutional rights by pleading guilty. And another justice expressed concern about how "voluntarily and knowingly" the plea of guilty was. Hence, the case was appealed to the U.S. Supreme Court, where the lower court decisions was reversed, on the basis that Mr. Boykin's guilty plea was not made knowingly, intelligently, and voluntarily.

Brady v. Maryland
373 U.S. 83 (1963)
U.S. Supreme Court

Case Facts

Defendant Brady and a partner, Boblit, were tried separately and convicted of first degree murder. Both were sentenced to death. At trial, Brady admitted his participation in the crime, but claimed that Boblit had done the actual killing. Prior to trial, Brady's counsel had asked the prosecution to allow him to examine Boblit's statements. Some statements were shown to him, but one—in which Boblit admitted the actual homicide—was withheld by the prosecution and did not come to Brady's notice until after trial. Brady appealed his conviction, and the Court of Appeals held that suppression of the evidence violated Brady's rights under the Due Process Clause of the 14th Amendment. The Supreme Court granted certiorari.

Issues

Does the suppression by the prosecution of evidence favorable to an accused violate due process, where the evidence is material to either guilt or punishment, regardless of the good or bad faith of the prosecution?

Court Holding

Yes.

Court's Reasoning

The court analyzed prior cases, in which it held that due process is violated when the state knowingly presents perjured testimony and, more broadly, where the state deliberately suppresses evidence favorable to the defendant. The court explained that these holdings represented not a punishment to society for the misdeeds of a prosecutor, but an "avoidance of an unfair trial to the accused." When a prosecutor withholds evidence that would tend to exculpate the defendant or reduce the penalty, this "helps shape a trial that bears heavily on the defendant." Accordingly, the court held that suppression of evidence favorable to an accused violates due process, whether the prosecution acts in good or bad faith.

Quick Summary

This is the seminal case that requires prosecutors to disclose evidence to a defendant, where it has any tendency to exculpate the defendant or reduce the penalty for the crime. If the prosecution fails to disclose such evidence—even if in good faith—it is a violation of the defendant's rights under the Due Process Clause of the 14th Amendment.

Brown v. Mississippi
297 US 278 (1936)
United States Supreme Court

Case Facts

Raymond Stewart, a white farmer, was murdered in 1934. Three defendants, who were all black tenant farmers, were arrested and interrogated for the murder. At trial, the prosecution introduced evidence of their confessions. However, witness testimony revealed that they only confessed after being subjected to brutal beatings. One of the men had also been strung up by the neck to a tree in addition to being whipped. The trial lasted one day and the only evidence the prosecution had was the so-called confessions. The defendants were convicted and sentenced to death. The convictions were affirmed on appeal by the Mississippi Supreme Court but one of the justices dissented saying that the testimony regarding the circumstances of the "confessions" was more akin to a medieval scene than anything in modern civilization. The United States Supreme Court granted certiorari after the former Mississippi governor appealed to it.

Main Issue

Are all confessions equal? Should confessions made involuntarily due to use of force by law enforcement be allowed as evidence at trial?

Court Holding

The Supreme Court of the United States unanimously voted to reverse the convictions of all three defendants. All confessions are not equal. A confession that is extracted from police by use of violence should not be allowed as evidence at trial.

Court's Reasoning

The use of coerced confessions violates the Due Process Clause of the Fourteenth Amendment. The trial court was aware of the manner in which the confessions were obtained as well as the lack of any additional evidence against the defendants. Confessions that are obtained through physical brutality violate the fundamental right to a fair trial, a right mandated by the Due Process Clause.

Quick Summary

Confessions that are involuntarily obtained through physical brutality and violence are prohibited by the Due Process Clause of the Fourteenth Amendment.

Budwin v. American Psychological Association
29 Cal. Rptr.2d 453 (Ct. App. 1994)
California Court of Appeal

Case Facts

Forensic psychologist, Dr. Howard Budwin, was working as a court-appointed child custody evaluator in Sacramento, California. During the course of a 1987 child custody proceeding, Dr. Budwin was found to have made false statements and to have withheld documents from one of the litigants and her attorney. In response, the litigant filed a complaint with the American Psychological Association (APA), who sustained the complaint and censured Dr. Budwin. Dr. Budwin responded by filing a petition for writ of mandate, seeking to overturn the APA censure, on the basis that his work was protected by the doctrine of quasi-judicial immunity (i.e., immunity from civil suits for those involved in legal proceedings, including mental health experts like Dr. Budwin). The doctrine of judicial immunity applies to judges, whereas quasi-judicial immunity is extended to those operating in a quasi-judicial capacity, which includes forensic mental health professionals. In 1993, Dr. Budwin was able to get a summary judgment in his favor, so the APA appealed the decision to the Court of Appeals of California, Third District.

Main Issue

Can the APA censure "one of its members for presenting false statements as a court-appointed expert in a child custody proceeding," thereby navigating around the doctrine of quasi-judicial immunity?

Court Holding

Yes. The Court of Appeals of California, Third District, reversed Dr. Budwin's successful summary judgment, thereby establishing that quasi-judicial immunity does not protect APA members from censure.

Court's Reasoning

Courts respect the autonomy of private organizations like the APA and tend to not get involved, unless a law has been broken. This was part of the reasoning as to why the doctrine of quasi-judicial immunity was independent of APA's censure process. The court reasoned further as follows:

> The reach of quasi-judicial immunity does not encompass disciplinary liability by a private, voluntary association. The decisions speak only in terms of protection from "civil actions," "civil suits," "damage claims," "civil liability," "subsequent suit," or "civil liability for various tort claims"... For this reason, we conclude the doctrine of quasi-judicial immunity does not bar the APA from disciplining Dr. Budwin for the false representations (noted previously) or the conduct (the wrongful refusal to produce documents) the APA claims he made or carried out.

Quick Summary

A forensic psychologist working as a court-appointed child custody evaluator was found to have made false statements and to have withheld documents from one of the litigants and her attorney. This ultimately led to the censure of the forensic psychology by the APA. The psychologist was initially able to use the doctrine of quasi-judicial immunity to obtain summary judgment in his favor. But the appeals court reversed the summary judgment, thereby establishing that quasi-judicial immunity does not protect forensic psychologists from censure by private organizations like the APA.

California v. Prysock
453 U.S. 355 (1981)
United States Supreme Court

Case Facts

Defendant Prysock was a juvenile who was arrested for murder in California. Before questioning Prysock, police notified his parents and, after they arrived, the interrogating officer advised Prysock of his rights. With regard to the right to counsel, the officer advised Prysock that he had "the right to talk to a lawyer before you are questioned, have him present with you while you are being questioned, and all during the questioning." After advising Prysock of his right to have his parents present, the officer returned to the right to counsel, advising Prysock that he had "the right to have a lawyer appointed to represent you at no cost to yourself." Prysock indicated that he understood his rights, and gave a recorded statement to police. At trial, he sought to have the statement suppressed, on the ground that he was not properly advised of his rights. The trial court denied the motion, and Prysock was convicted of first-degree murder with special circumstances. The California Court of Appeal reversed Prysock's convictions and ordered a new trial, on the basis that the police had failed to meet the requirements of *Miranda v. Arizona*, because they did not explicitly inform Prysock that he had the right to have an attorney appointed before questioning. The Supreme Court of California denied a petition for rehearing, and the U.S. Supreme Court granted cert to rule on the requirements of *Miranda*.

Main Issue

Were the warnings given to Prysock sufficient under *Miranda*, where police advised him that he had the right to counsel before questioning, and had the right to have an attorney appointed to him at no cost, but did not explicitly advise him that he had the right to have an attorney appointed before questioning?

Court Holding

Yes. No verbatim recitation of the *Miranda* warnings is required, so long as police convey their substance or equivalent.

Court's Reasoning

The court cited prior cases in which it held that there is no "talismanic incantation" required to satisfy *Miranda*, and that police are not required to strictly adhere to the form of the warnings. Rather, police satisfy the requirements of *Miranda* when they communicate the warnings or "their equivalent." The court also distinguished this case from other cases in which the reference to the right to counsel was linked to some future point in time after interrogation, such that the suspect was not advised that he had the right to appointed counsel before the interrogation began. According to the court, the warnings in this case did not place any such limitation on the right to counsel, and were adequate to inform Prysock that he had the right to appointed counsel before speaking with police.

Quick Summary

A defendant appealed his conviction for first-degree murder on the ground that the police had failed to properly advise him of his *Miranda* rights. The police advised the defendant that he had the right to have an attorney present before and during interrogation, and later informed him that he had the right to appointed counsel. The defendant argued that he was not clearly advised that he had the right to appointed counsel before interrogation. The Supreme Court held that the *Miranda* warnings were adequate, reaffirming that police need not strictly adhere to the form of the warnings, so long as they convey their substance or equivalent.

Clark v. Arizona
548 U.S 735 (2006)
U.S. Supreme Court

Case Facts

Eric Clark, a 17- year-old, was charged with the first-degree murder of a police officer who conducted a traffic stop of him in 2000. Mr. Clark had begun to exhibit signs and symptoms of a major mental illness a year and a half before the incident, with episodes of screaming and gibberish (at trial it was considered undisputed that he had paranoid schizophrenia). He asserted at trial that he did not intend to murder the officer and denied that he had knowledge that he was committing this act. He was prevented from introducing some of his mental health record. Arizona's insanity test is based solely on the second prong of the *M'Naghten* standard, which focuses on the defendant's ability to understand the wrongfulness of the act (see M'Naghten 8 Eng. Rep. 718 (1843) elsewhere in this section). The state argued that Clark knew that the victim was a police officer, that there was testimony indicating that Clark wanted to shoot officers, and that he lured the officer for the purposes of killing him. Clark had to prove by clear and convincing evidence that he was insane at the time of the murder, that he "did not know the criminal act was wrong." Clark offered lay testimony of his bizarre behavior and expert testimony that he could not appreciate the wrongfulness of his act due to his mental illness. The prosecution then offered expert testimony that Clark, despite his odd behaviors, did appreciate the wrongfulness of his actions. He was found guilty and sentenced to death. Clark argued that the insanity test in Arizona violated due process because of the state's elimination of the first prong in *M'Naghten* (knowingly) and only the application of the second prong (wrongfulness). Clark also argued that the case law in *State v. Mott*, which held that Arizona does not allow evidence of a defendant's mental disorder that does not rise to meet the sanity criteria, was too narrow and therefore violated his rights. Clark argued that it was a violation of his rights that he was not allowed to introduce mental health evidence that, while not specifically related to the question of his ability to appreciate the wrongfulness of his actions, still had what he felt was relevance to his mental state and mens rea. The trial court denied his motion and the Court of Appeals affirmed the decision U.S. Supreme Court granted certiorari.

Main Issue

Did Arizona's sanity statute violate the 14th Amendment (due process protection)?

Court Holding

No. The U.S. Supreme Court affirmed the lower court's rulings and further explained that Arizona's insanity statute (*capacity to appreciate whether a criminal act was right or wrong*) does not violate due process. The so-called *Mott* rule (psychologists/psychiatrists are precluded from offering testimony on mental disease/defect that addresses mens rea not specifically related to the sanity statute), does not violate due process.

Court's Reasoning

- The Court found that different states have different standards for insanity defenses, and therefore, "no particular formulation has evolved into a baseline for due process, and that the insanity rule … is substantially open to state choice." The court explained that states can adopt the sanity statute of their own choosing without violating due process rights.
- Under Arizona law, Clark had the burden of proving that his mental illness negated mens rea. Observation evidence was permitted (e.g., direct observations of behavior or thinking), but such evidence was applied solely toward the issue of insanity. Expert witnesses do not have the authority to offer opinions about association between mental disease/defect and mens rea as the court agreed that this issue should be decided by the trier of fact based on cases like *Mott* which governed in Colorado.

Quick Summary

States are permitted to make their own laws regarding sanity standards without violating due process. There is no one statute for sanity that must apply to all states. Psychologists and psychiatrists can provide observations about a defendant's mental health symptoms but they do not have the authority to form ultimate opinions regarding a defendant's intent to commit a crime; however, the use of ultimate opinions by experts also varies by state.

Billie Wayne Coble v. The State of Texas
131 S.Ct. 3030 (2011)
564 U.S. 1020
U.S. Supreme Court

Case Facts

Karen Vicha was Billie Coble's third wife. The relationship soon disintegrated, and, after a year, Karen told Coble to move out, that she wanted a divorce. Coble attempted to talk her out of this decision and randomly called her and showed up at her work place. He then kidnapped Karen as a further effort to convince her to forego the divorce. He was arrested for the kidnapping.

Nine days after being released on bail, Coble went to her house. As Karen's three daughters and her brother's son came home from school, Coble handcuffed them, bound their feet, and taped their mouths closed. Karen's oldest daughter testified that she heard Coble cut the telephone lines. Then he left and ambushed and shot and killed Karen's father, mother, and brother. Coble was convicted of capital murder and sentenced to death. The Texas Court of Criminal Appeals upheld his conviction and sentence, but the Fifth Circuit Court of Appeals granted habeas relief and remanded the case for a new trial on punishment. On retrial in 2008, a second jury sentenced Coble to death. Coble then appealed based on 25 points of error, including the sufficiency of the evidence to prove future dangerousness and the admissibility of a psychiatrist's expert testimony.

Coble argued that he experienced a character conversion while spending the last 18 years in prison, resulting in a spotless disciplinary record, which was proof that he no longer posed a threat of violence. The defense's expert forensic psychologist placed Coble in the lowest risk group for violence in prison. Coble agreed with the notion that prior actions are the best predictor of the future, relying on his positive prison record as the predictor of the future, insisting that he would not be a continuing threat to society. For that reason, he argued, his sentence must be vacated.

This is the same argument that Coble made during the trial. However, on retrial in 2008, the jury relied on multiple considerations, including the following: (1) Dr. Hodges's Austin State School psychiatric report from 1964, when Coble was 15, which stated that (a) Coble seemed paranoid and distant and extremely hostile to women; (b) he represented a sociopathic personality disturbance of the dissocial type; and (c) his long-term prognosis did not look good; (2) Coble's military medical record from a 1967 self-inflicted stabbing wound in his thigh after he had a fight with his girlfriend, in which the military doctor noted that Coble revealed evidence of lifelong maladjustment and that on the hospital ward, Coble was hostile and belligerent; (3) several sources described Coble's moods as mercurial; and (4) testimony that Coble, after all his time on death row, remained hostile to women.

The "future dangerousness" issue, in Texas statute, ensures that no defendant, regardless of how heinous his capital crime, will be sentenced to death unless the jury finds that he poses a real threat of future violence. The Court of Criminal Appeals of Texas case law construed the future-dangerousness issue to ask whether a defendant would constitute a continuing threat, in or out of prison, without regard to how long the defendant would actually spend in prison if sentenced to life. The focus was on the internal restraints of the individual, not only the external restraints of incarceration.

It had been the jury's duty to assess Coble's current character in the context of future dangerousness, and the Court of Criminal Appeals determined that there was ample evidence to support the jury's finding, beyond a reasonable doubt, that Coble had the same character for violence at age 60 that he did at younger ages, despite his impressive prison record.

Coble also contended that psychiatric expert testimony on the topic of future dangerousness was not admissible under Rule 702 because it was insufficiently reliable. At trial, Coble objected to that proposed testimony and requested a *Daubert/Kelly* (see *Daubert v. Merrell Dow Pharmaceuticals, Inc.*, 509 U.S. 579, 1993; *People v. Kelley*, Crim. No. 19028. Supreme Court of California, May 28, 1976) hearing outside the presence of the jury. At that hearing, the expert testified that he was board certified in general psychiatry and had been practicing forensic psychiatry for thirty-one years. Dr. Coons testified that psychiatric principles are commonly used when making determinations of a person's danger to themself or others in the context of involuntary psychiatric commitments. He said that he also relied upon psychiatric principles when evaluating defendants for "future dangerousness" for capital murder trials. He repeatedly stated that the best predictor of future behavior is the past behavior.

>Dr. Coons explained his standard methodology in assessing the issue of future dangerousness. He assessed the relevant factors based on information that he was given. That was his own personal methodology. He did not know whether others relied on this method, and he did not know of any psychiatry or psychology books or articles that use his factors. But, he noted, his procedures are those that are commonly discussed commonly at forensic meetings and among forensic psychiatrists. He doubted that his methodology was shared by everyone because different psychiatrists construct their own methodologies. Thus, his process was a subjective evaluation.

The court noted that although all of these factors (future dangerousness, attitudes about violence, circumstances of the offense, personality and behavior) overlap and blend, Dr. Coons knew of no book or article that discusses these factors or their overlap. He was not aware of any studies in psychiatric journals regarding the accuracy of long-term predictions into future violence in capital murder prosecutions or of any error rates concerning such predictions. He also was unaware of any psychiatric studies that support the making of such predictions. Dr. Coons had never gone back and reviewed records to try to check the accuracy of his "future dangerousness" predictions. He could not tell what his accuracy rate was. Based on this testimony, the trial judge found that Dr. Coons qualified as an expert witness. The Court of Criminal Appeals of Texas considered the appropriateness of the judge's determination.

Main Issue

Does psychiatric testimony satisfy admissibility requirements, and can it be used to inform the court regarding future dangerousness?

Court Holding

Forensic psychiatry is a legitimate field, predicting future dangerousness is within the scope of that field, and using education and experience to assess future dangerousness is a proper application of the principles involved in the field. These issues place forensic psychiatrists in a better position than the average juror to make such determinations. However, idiosyncratic methodology does not satisfy admissibility requirements for expert testimony.

The evidence was legally sufficient to support the jury's finding on the future dangerousness issue in this case (i.e., Coble remained a danger to others). Therefore, the court overruled Coble's objections on this point.

The prosecution did not satisfy its burden of showing the scientific reliability of the expert's methodology for predicting future dangerousness by clear and convincing evidence. Therefore, the trial judge abused his discretion by admitting the testimony.

Court's Reasoning

The court recognized in *Nenno* that expert testimony can be of the "nonscientific" variety, but that it might not be helpful to draw a strict distinction between "hard" science, "soft" sciences, or nonscientific testimony because the distinction between the various types of testimony is often blurred. The court noted that future dangerousness testimony can be provided by a mental health expert based upon the expert's specialized education and experience. However, consistent with *Daubert,* the judge must determine whether the evidence is genuinely scientific, rather than unscientific speculation offered by a genuine scientist.

The expert agreed that his methodology was idiosyncratic. Although there existed a significant body of scholarly literature concerning the empirical accuracy of clinical predictions versus actuarial and risk assessment predictions, he did not cite or rely upon any of those publications and was unfamiliar with the journal articles given to him by the prosecution. Thus, his methodology was insufficient to support admissibility of his testimony.

Quick Summary

Trial judges must serve as gatekeepers when addressing the reliability and relevance of expert testimony. When the subject of the expert's testimony is scientific knowledge, the basis of the testimony must be grounded in the accepted methods and procedures of science. When based on appropriate methodology, future dangerousness testimony can be provided by a mental health expert.

Coker v. Georgia
43 US 584 (1977)
United States Supreme Court

Case Facts

Erlich Anthony Coker escaped from prison where he was serving time for rape, kidnapping, and murder and broke into a private residence, raped one of the homeowners, and stole the family car. He was then captured, tried, and sentenced to death for the rape he committed when he escaped. The jury imposed death because he already convictions for prior felonies and the rape was committed during the commission of armed robbery. The jury found that the additional aggravating circumstances warranted the death penalty. The Supreme Court of Georgia upheld both the conviction and the death sentence. The United States Supreme Court granted certiorari.

Main Issue

Is the death penalty excessively harsh and a disproportionate punishment for a conviction of rape?

Court Holding

Yes. The United States Supreme Court held that the death penalty amounted to grossly disproportionate punishment for a conviction of rape and is therefore unconstitutional under the Eighth Amendment's prohibition against cruel and unusual punishment.

Court's Reasoning

The Eighth Amendment prohibits not only punishment that is barbaric but also punishment that is excessive in relation to the crime. A punishment is excessive if:

1. The sentence does not make a contribution to the goals of punishment and is nothing more than the needless infliction of pain and suffering
2. Is grossly out of proportion with the seriousness of the crime.

At the time, Georgia was the only state that allowed the death penalty for the crime of rape of an adult so the Court used that fact to highlight the rarity and severity of that punishment. At the time two other states only allowed the death penalty for the rape of a child. Although rape is a serious crime, the death penalty is unique in severity and reversibility and should be reserved for those who take a human life.

Quick Summary

Imposing the death penalty as punishment for a rape conviction is a violation of the Eighth Amendment's prohibition of cruel and unusual punishment and is therefore unconstitutional.

Colorado v. Connelly
479 U.S 157 (1986)
U.S. Supreme Court

Case Facts

In 1983, Francis Connelly, who suffered from psychotic symptoms such as auditory hallucinations and delusions, approached a Denver police officer and reported that he had murdered someone. The officer informed him of his *Miranda* rights (see *Miranda v. Arizona*, 384 US 436; 86 S. Ct. 1602; 1966 elsewhere in this section), at which time Mr. Connelly indicated that he understood these rights and continued to discuss the crime with the officer. A detective was then called who again informed him of his *Miranda* rights. Mr. Connelly explained that he had traveled from Boston to Denver so he could confess to the murder he committed. He spent the night in detention and was noted to be visibly disturbed, resulting in his admission to a state hospital for evaluation. The evaluating psychiatrist noted that Mr. Connelly was influenced by the "voice of God" and that his psychotic mental state prevented him from making free and rational choices. The psychiatrist also noted that although Mr. Connelly appeared to understand his rights, his symptoms of psychosis motivated him to confess. The Colorado trial court found that Mr. Connelly's confession, though obtained in the absence of police coercion, was in fact "involuntary" due to his mental illness. The Colorado Supreme Court affirmed this decision and noted that the constitution requires that a confession be suppressed when a defendant's "rational intellect" and "free will" is compromised by his mental state and that his mental state prevented him from making a valid waiver of *Miranda* rights. The U.S. Supreme Court granted certiorari and reversed.

Main Issue

The main issue for the U.S. Supreme Court's consideration focused on what constitutes a defendant's competence to confess to a crime and what is the correct burden of proof for a waiver of *Miranda* rights?

Court Holding

The Supreme Court found that a confession can only be considered "involuntary" if the police coerce the defendant. Although a defendant's mental state may be a "significant" factor in the voluntary nature of a waiver of *Miranda*, without police coercion, one's mental state is not enough for the confession to be considered "involuntary." Noting what the defendant says and admitting that statement into evidence does not constitute a violation of due process. Preponderance of the evidence is the standard of proof for a defendant's waiver of their *Miranda* rights.

Court's Reasoning

The Court cited *Brown v. Mississippi*, in which police brutality and coercion were used to extract a confession. Since then, police coercion has been a substantial element in determining whether or not a waiver of *Miranda* rights was valid. In Mr. Connelly's case, the court noted that there was no evidence of police misconduct; therefore, there is no reason to believe that the defendant was deprived of due process based solely on his mental state. The court ruled that confessions are considered "voluntary" if they are made in the absence of police coercion/misconduct.

Quick Summary

Absent police coercion, admission of a confession via waiver of *Miranda*, even by an individual with serious mental health symptoms, can be admissible without violating the accused's due process rights.

Commonwealth v. Stroyny
435 Mass. 635 (2002)
Supreme Judicial Court of Massachusetts, Bristol

Case Facts

Davud Stroyny and the murder victim were romantically involved, however, the relationship deteriorated quickly. Stroyny threatened and abused the victim verbally and physically and told others he might hurt or kill her, which he ultimately did via beating and stabbing. He testified that when he saw the stabbed victim lying on the ground, he cut his wrists, walked to a public telephone, and called his father, who took him to a hospital. Stroyny was apprehended at the hospital.

The primary contested issue at trial was Stroyny's intent at the time of the killing. He admitted to having killed the victim, but he claimed he could not recall delivering the killing blows. His defense was based mental impairment and lack of criminal responsibility.

1. Before trial, Stroyny stated his intention to bring a defense of lack of criminal responsibility, and a court-ordered psychiatric expert examined him. The expert then prematurely disclosed to the prosecutor, without permission from the judge, some of the defendant's statements. Stroyny moved to dismiss the indictments or suppress the expert's testimony. A Superior Court judge, who was not the trial judge, concluded that the expert's disclosures to the prosecutor had violated Stroyny's rights but denied the motion. The defendant later claimed in an appeal that both the disclosure and denial of his motion prejudiced his trial.
2. A licensed social worker that Stroyny met with once for counseling at a hospital six weeks prior to the murder testified at trial, without objection.

In his motion for a new trial, Stroyny claimed that his trial attorney was ineffective for failing to object to her testimony on grounds of privilege and relevancy. The motion judge concluded that counsel's failure to object did not constitute ineffective assistance of counsel, pointing to two exceptions to the social worker privilege and to the fact that the evidence was relevant to the defendant's defense.

Main Issues

1. Can a court-ordered psychiatric expert disclose to a prosecutor, without permission from the judge, statements made by the defendant?
2. Are there exceptions to social worker-patient privilege that allow a social worker to testify about statements made in a clinical context; specifically, is relevance of the information for the defendant's defense taken into account in determining whether such testimony can be admitted?

Court Holding

1. No. Information obtained by a court-appointed mental health expert and any report prepared by the expert should not be disclosed until a judicial determination is made that the defendant has waived his privilege against self-incrimination. However, in this case, there was no prejudice to the defendant from the sharing of the information.
2. Yes. When a defendant introduces their mental or emotional condition as an element of their defense, and the judge determines that disclosure of the information is more important to the interests of justice than protection of the relationship between the client and the social worker, the social worker may disclose the contents of the communication.

The order denying the motion for a new trial was affirmed.

Court's Reasoning

1. The court did not condone the sharing of the information by the Commonwealth's expert or the actions of the prosecutor. To the extent that the expert was unaware that information obtained from Stroyny could not be disclosed prematurely, the prosecutor should immediately have terminated any conversation with the expert when it became clear that he was divulging communications from Stroyny. The information provided by expert, however, had already been brought out in Stroyny's own direct testimony, so the prosecutor's cross-examination could have been based on Stroyny's statements at trial, rather than on the prosecutor's conversation with the expert several months earlier. Additionally,

Stroyny's own expert testified to an opinion that was based on the same statements that Stroyny had made to him. Even if the prosecutor's use at trial of Stroyny's statements to the expert was improperly based on his earlier conversation with the expert, there was no prejudice to Stroyny.

2. Stroyny's mental condition was a critical aspect of his defense, which was introduced by his counsel's opening statement to the jury. Therefore, the social worker's testimony was probative of Stroyny's contested mental state regarding the crimes with which he was charged. The social worker's statements illustrated not Stroyny's anger and thoughts about killing someone, as well as noting that he was coherent, oriented, and knew right from wrong. Had Stroyny objected at trial, it would have been appropriate for the judge to allow the social worker to testify.

Additionally, Stroyny's counsel used the social worker's testimony to advance his defense that he did not have the requisite mental state to commit murder. It was argued that the social worker's testimony was evidence of his loss of control in the weeks leading up to the murder and his efforts to obtain help. The tactic was found to be reasonable, and the admitted testimony was not able to be challenged on appeal.

Quick Summary

1. In the Commonwealth of Massachusetts, information obtained by a court-appointed mental health expert should not be disclosed until a judicial determination is made that the defendant has waived his privilege against self-incrimination.
2. A social worker may disclose during testimony the contents of otherwise privileged communication when a defendant introduces their mental condition as an element of their defense, and the judge determines that disclosure of the information is more important to the interests of justice than protection of the relationship between the client and the social worker.

Cooper v. Oklahoma
517 U.S. 348 (1996)
U.S. Supreme Court

Case Facts

Byron Cooper was charged with murder. Throughout the criminal proceedings, the issue of his competence to stand trial was raised five times. Pretrial, a psychologist examined him and found him to be incompetent, and he was sent to a mental health facility for treatment. After this hospitalization, two psychologists offered opposing opinions about his competence. Mr. Cooper acted bizarrely during trial (talking to himself, lying in a fetal position, etc.). Another competency hearing was held, and another psychologist testified that Mr. Cooper was incompetent to stand trial. Although the judge noted some uncertainty about Mr. Cooper's competence, he held that Mr. Cooper was competent. The judge ruled that the defense had failed to prove Mr. Cooper's incompetence by *clear and convincing evidence* (the standard then required by Oklahoma statute). Mr. Cooper was ultimately convicted and sentenced to death. The conviction was appealed to the Oklahoma Court of Criminal Appeals on the grounds that the clear and convincing standard of proof violated the Due Process clause of the 14th Amendment. The conviction was upheld, and the U.S. Supreme Court agreed to hear the case.

Main Issue

What is the proper standard of proof for competency determinations?

Court Holding

The U.S. Supreme Court reversed the appellate court's decision and remanded the case, holding that the Oklahoma law did violate the Due Process clause of the 14th Amendment by requiring a standard of clear and convincing evidence. The proper standard of proof for competency determinations shall be *preponderance of the evidence.*

Court's Reasoning

The court's reasoning was based on the premise that trying an incompetent defendant violates due process and that the Oklahoma law allowed the state to try a defendant who was *more likely than not* to be incompetent. The state is allowed to presume that a defendant is competent and to put the burden of proof on the defendant to show incompetence by a preponderance of the evidence; however, requiring a defendant to prove incompetence by clear and convincing evidence violates "fundamental fairness." That is, the risks to the defendant outweigh the state's interest in efficiently prosecuting criminal cases.

Quick Summary

There is a fundamental right to be competent at trial, the burden of proof may be placed on the defendant to show incompetence; however, requiring a higher standard of proof beyond preponderance of the evidence violates the 14th Amendment right to Due Process.

Crane v. Kentucky
476 U.S. 683 (1986)
U.S. Supreme Court

Case Facts

In 1981, a liquor store clerk was shot and killed in Louisville, Kentucky. Major Crane, a 16-year-old, was picked up by police on an unrelated robbery. Police said that Crane began spontaneously to confess to a number of other offenses and, while he initially denied any involvement in the liquor store murder, eventually confessed to that as well. He sought to suppress the confession, claiming that he had been held for a very long time in a windowless room, surrounded by up to six officers, denied the opportunity to contact his mother, and had been badgered into making a false confession. The court denied the motion to suppress the confession, having deemed that the interrogation was not coercive. At trial the prosecution's case was based mainly on the confession, which defense argued was full of admissions that did not match the facts of the case. The prosecutor sought for the court to prevent defense from being able to introduce evidence about the circumstances of the confession, and the defense argued that they wanted to be able to call into question the validity and credibility of the confession. Court granted prosecution's motion. The jury convicted, and Crane was sentenced to 40 years. The Kentucky Supreme Court affirmed. The U.S. Supreme Court granted certiorari.

Main Issue

Did the exclusion of testimony regarding the circumstances of the confession violate the defendant's rights under the 6th and 14th Amendments?

Court Holding

Yes. The exclusion of evidence pertaining to the circumstances of the confession violated the defendant's right to a fair trial. The jury should have been allowed to consider the circumstances of the confession, not just voluntariness, in determining its credibility.

Court's Reasoning

The court reasoned that even if a confession is determined by the court to have been made voluntarily, the defense should still be allowed to provide evidence to the court about the circumstances of the confession so that the credibility and reliability of the confession can be considered. The court differentiated between a voluntary confession legally and the right to present factual evidence of the circumstances surrounding the confession to address its credibility.

Quick Summary

There is a difference between the legal issue of a voluntary confession and the factual issue of the circumstances of the confession, and the jury should be able to consider the credibility and reliability of a confession even if it has been deemed voluntary.

Daubert v. Merrell Dow Pharmaceuticals, Inc.
509 U.S. 579 (1993)
U.S. Supreme Court

Case Facts

Two young children and their parents sued Merrell Dow because they argued that the drug, Bendectin, (for nausea during pregnancy), caused severe birth defects in the children. Merrell Dow called an expert who offered testimony that there was no relationship between Bendectin and birth defects. The petitioners called experts who testified that there was a relationship between the drug and birth defects as evidenced by test tube and live animal studies and other data. The district court granted summary judgment to respondent stating that the petitioners did not have the kind of evidence that met *Frye's* "general acceptance rule" so it was not admissible. The case went to the U.S. Court of Appeals for the Ninth Circuit, which also used *Frye* and affirmed the lower court's decision. The U.S. Supreme Court granted certiorari because courts were too often divided on the issue of admission of expert testimony.

Court Holding

The U.S. Supreme Court said that the *Frye* test of 1923 was superseded by the adoption of the Federal Rules of Evidence (FRE), which do not require "general acceptance" as an absolute prerequisite to admissibility. The court ultimately decided that it is up to the trial judge to decide whether the expert is proposing to testify to 1) scientific knowledge, and 2) if that knowledge will assist the trier of fact on the particular issue at hand. The court said it is then up to the factfinder (i.e., judge or jury) to determine the weight and credibility of the evidence based on the four key criteria established by the FRE:

1. Can the theory or technique be tested.
2. Has it been subjected to peer review.
3. what is the known or potential error rate.
4. General acceptance in the relevant field.

The court ordered the case to be retried under these rules.

Court's Reasoning

The court indicated that the *Frye* test had been superseded by the Federal Rules of Evidence, that it was too "rigid," and that under the FRE, "all relevant evidence is admissible." The court added that nowhere in the FRE does it state that "general acceptance" is a prerequisite to admissibility. Rather than basing admissibility on one rigid standard (as in *Frye*), the FRE considers the four criteria above to ensure that relevant and helpful information be allowed in for the trier of fact to consider.

Quick Summary

Whereas the Frye test looked at whether a theory was "generally acceptable" in the field to which it belonged in order to admit it into evidence, the FRE look at testability, peer review, error rate, and general acceptance of a theory/technique in determining the admissibility of scientific evidence/testimony. *Frye* criteria is but one factor to be considered in the more recent *Daubert* standards.

Deatherage v. Examining Board of Psychology
948 P.2d 828 (Wash. 1997)
Washington Supreme Court

Case Facts

Disciplinary proceedings in the state of Washington were brought by the Examining Board of Psychology against psychologist, Dr. Edward Deatherage, on the basis that he had practiced unethically when conducting child custody evaluations. Dr. Deatherage's license to practice psychology in the state of Washington was suspended for 10 years, so Dr. Deatherage filed a petition in Superior Court, but this court held that Deatherage did not have absolute immunity. The Court of Appeals then reversed the lower court's decision on the matter of absolute immunity, but still held that Dr. Deatherage could have his license suspended based on other conduct. The case then went to the Supreme Court of Washington.

Main Issue

"The question presented is whether an expert witness is absolutely immune from the disciplinary action of a state licensing board when the board initiates the proceeding based upon work performed as an expert witness in child custody cases." In other words, is a forensic psychologist immune from disciplinary action from the psychologist's state licensing board if their work as a forensic psychologist is deemed worthy of disciplinary action by the state licensing board?

Court Holding

The Supreme Court of Washington reversed the Court of Appeals with regard to witness immunity:

> Witness immunity is traditionally available in defamation cases and other related tort actions. However, the privilege is not so broad as to extend to a professional disciplinary proceeding. We reverse the Court of Appeals and hold absolute witness immunity does not exist in the context of a professional disciplinary proceeding.

In other words, this court held that a forensic psychologist is *not* immune from the disciplinary action of their state licensing board, if the licensing board deems the psychologist's work as a forensic psychologist to be worthy of disciplinary action.

Court's Reasoning

While the Supreme Court of Washington acknowledged that expert witness immunity from lawsuits *is* justified, in order to encourage experts to facilitate improved legal decision-making without fear of retaliatory lawsuits, it concluded that this doctrine should *not* be extended to state licensing board proceedings: "a disciplinary proceeding is not a civil suit against the expert, and the policies that underscore witness immunity do not apply. Disciplinary actions are different in character to civil actions." Hence, the reasoning is based on the difference between disciplinary actions of state licensing boards, which emphasize protecting the public and the reputation of the profession, as compared with a lawsuit, which seeks to right a civil wrong.

Quick Summary

A forensic psychologist tried to use the doctrine of witness immunity, available as a shield to expert witnesses when testifying in legal cases, as a shield from disciplinary action by his state licensing board. However, because "disciplinary actions are different in character to civil actions," the Supreme Court of Washington did not extend the protection of witness immunity to the forensic psychologist during the course of the disciplinary actions he was facing from his licensing board.

Dickerson v. United States
530 U.S. 428 (2000)
U.S. Supreme Court

Case Facts

Charles Dickerson was interviewed by law enforcement about one crime. During this interview, he admitted to involvement in other crimes. The exact timing of Dickerson's admission then became an issue: law enforcement said he confessed *after* they Mirandized Dickerson, but Dickerson said his confession occurred *before* he was Mirandized. In the ensuing legal proceedings, the government said that Dickerson's confession was admissible, even if he was Mirandized after confessing, because he made his confession voluntarily, the only necessary criterion under 18 USC Section 3501. An appeals court relied on Section 3501 as justification to admit Dickerson's statement, saying that voluntariness is all that is needed for a confession to be admitted. This was appealed to the U.S. Supreme Court via a writ of certiorari.

Main Issue

For a confession to be valid, must it only be made voluntarily? Or must it be made knowingly, intelligently, and voluntarily?

Court Holding

By reversing the decision of the Court of Appeals, the U.S. Supreme Court affirmed that its prior ruling in *Miranda v. Arizona* (1966) still held. Namely, confessions are valid only if made voluntarily, knowingly, and intelligently, not just voluntarily.

Court's Reasoning

The court reasoned that it would not go against its own prior decision in *Miranda v. Arizona*:

> We hold that *Miranda,* being a constitutional decision of this Court, may not be in effect overruled by an Act of Congress, and we decline to overrule *Miranda* ourselves. We therefore hold that *Miranda* and its progeny in this Court govern the admissibility of statements made during custodial interrogation in both state and federal courts.

Quick Summary

Miranda v. Arizona had previously established that confessions are only valid if a defendant in police custody knowingly, intelligently, and voluntarily waives their right to have an attorney present before making confessions. *Dickerson* reinforced in state and federal courts that all three of these elements are required before a confession can be admitted in as evidence. Hence, a law from Congress (i.e., Section 3501) could not be used to whittle away at *Miranda v. Arizona*, leaving only the voluntary element, which is what the government had successfully argued for in the lower courts.

Doe v. Roe
400 N.Y.S.2d 668 (Sup. Ct. 1977)
Supreme Court of New York

Case Facts

Jane Doe and her late husband were patients of a psychiatrist, Joan Roe, for many years. Eight years after terminating treatment, Dr. Roe published a book with her psychologist husband, Peter Poe, extensively detailing the Does' thoughts, feelings, sexual fantasies, and intimate details of their marriage. Ms. Doe brought a breach of privacy action for the unauthorized disclosure of her private matters in the book. The defendants alleged that they had obtained verbal consent although details in the book show that Dr. Roe seemed to have known that the consent she obtained was inadequate. The defendants asserted that there was no unlawful disclosure because the patient's identity was concealed; the book had scientific merit, which transcends the patient's right of nondisclosure; and the right to publication is protected by the First Amendment.

Main Issue

What is the proper scope of confidentiality when it comes to disclosures made in a psychiatrist-patient relationship even when efforts are made by the doctor to de-identify the patient, and the information is being used for scholarly purposes?

Court Holding

The court held that the psychiatrist and her husband violated the Doe's right of privacy. The court awarded them compensatory damages.

Court's Reasoning

The court cited various cases dealing with physicians' unauthorized disclosure of patient information including *in Re Lifschutz* in which the court stated that the effective practice of psychotherapy requires an absolute privilege of confidentiality. The court added that privacy is especially important for psychiatry because "[the] patient is called upon to discuss in a candid and frank manner personal material of the most intimate and disturbing nature … Patients will be helped only if they can form a trusting relationship with the psychiatrist." She was awarded $20,000 for suffering but, according to the court, the defendants' actions were not "willful, malicious or wanton – they were merely stupid," therefore punitive damages were not justified. Dr. Poe was deemed equally liable, despite there not being a doctor-patient relationship.

Quick Summary

A psychiatrist who enters into an agreement to provide treatment has a duty to keep relevant disclosures confidential, as well as all matters discovered by the physician in the course of examination or treatment that do not warrant a mandatory disclosure such as danger to self or others.

Drope v. Missouri
420 U.S. 162 (1975)
U.S. Supreme Court

Case Facts

Mr. Drope was indicted in 1969 for the rape of his wife and filed a motion for continuance to obtain a psychological examination. In this motion, he attached a recommendation from a mental health professional that he obtain treatment. The motion was denied, and his case went to trial. There was testimony about his odd behavior at trial, and Mr. Drope shot himself during the trial, which necessitated hospitalization. Trial continued on the notion that his absence was voluntary (via his own suicide attempt). He was found guilty and sentenced to life. He filed a motion for a new trial arguing that his absence was not voluntary, but it was denied.

Main Issue

This case considered the amount and type of evidence required to trigger a competency examination by a party to the trial.

Court Holding

Missouri Supreme Court affirmed the lower court's ruling, but the U.S. Supreme Court reversed and remanded for a new trial holding that there is a low bar for what triggers the need for an examination of a defendant's competence to stand trial and such an examination was not ordered despite sufficient evidence to warrant it.

Court's Reasoning

The U.S. Supreme Court unanimously reasoned that the lower court failed when it did not consider the evidence pertaining to Mr. Drope's competency. Without Mr. Drope present at trial, there was no way to properly evaluate his competency, so the proceedings should have paused until such an examination could be made. Even if he could have competently or voluntarily waived his right to be present, an evaluation was not conducted as to his ability to competently do so. It is not possible to assess whether he was competent retrospectively at the original trial, so a new trial in which his current competency can be assessed is the remedy.

Quick Summary

Competency to proceed with trial is a current state determination, and there should be a low bar for what triggers an examination of a defendant's competence. The court should consider any evidence regarding mental health, regardless of who raises it, and grant a motion for a competency examination where appropriate to not only ensure a fair process but also to avoid reversal by a higher court.

Durham v. United States
214 F. 2d 862 (D.C. Cir. 1954)
District of Columbia Circuit Court of Appeals

Case Facts

Monte Durham had a long history of psychiatric hospitalization and imprisonment. On July 13, 1951, after being discharged from his third hospitalization, he was charged with housebreaking. He was found incompetent to stand trial and committed to St. Elizabeth's Hospital. He was later found competent to stand trial and convicted by the District Court of D.C. Although the defense raised the issue of sanity at trial, the judge (despite testimony from a psychiatrist and Durham's mother about his mental state at the time of the offense) found: "There is no testimony concerning the mental state of the defendant as of July 13, 1951, and therefore the usual presumption of sanity governs." Durham was convicted and appealed. The U.S. Court of Appeals for D.C. reversed the lower court's ruling and remanded the case for a new trial.

Main Issue

Is there a more appropriate and better test of insanity than M'Naghten or the irresistible impulse test and, if so, what should that test be? What are the rules regarding the burden of proof for sanity/insanity?

Court Holding

The Court of Appeals held that the district court had not correctly applied the existing rules governing the burden of proof of the insanity defense. While there is the presumption of sanity, once "some evidence" is raised regarding the defendant's mental state at the time of the offense, it becomes the prosecution's burden to prove sanity beyond a reasonable doubt. Existing tests of criminal responsibility (i.e., M'Naghten and irresistible impulse tests) are obsolete and should be superseded. Mental disease can improve or deteriorate, while mental defect is not capable of change.

Court's Reasoning

"As soon as some evidence of mental disorder is introduced, sanity, like any other fact, must be proved beyond a reasonable doubt." The Court of Appeals for D.C. disagreed with the district court judge's opinion that the defense failed to find "some evidence," citing testimony from Durham's psychiatrist and, as such, the prosecution should have had the burden of proving that Durham was sane. The existing tests for determining criminal responsibility "are not satisfactory" and it is time for a new and broader test. Under the new test, "the accused is not criminally responsible if his unlawful act was the product of mental disease or mental defect." Under this rule, whenever there is "some evidence" that the defendant suffered from mental disease or defect at the time of the crime, the jury must be given guidelines for determining criminal responsibility. The court explained that the goal of broadening the criteria was to bring sanity statutes up to speed with burgeoning science pertaining to mental illness, to improve communication between courts and experts, and to give juries more psychological information to inform their deliberative process.

Quick Summary

This case created a new and broader test of criminal responsibility often referred to as the "product test" because of the requirement that the offense be the product of mental disease or defect. It also changed the burden of proof from the defendant to the state when "some evidence" of impaired mental state at the time of the offense has been raised.

Dusky v. United States
362 U.S. 402 (1960)
U.S. Supreme Court

Case Facts

In 1958, Milton Dusky was charged with kidnapping a 15-year-old girl, driving her across state lines, and attempting to rape her. His attorney raised the issues of competence to stand trial and criminal responsibility, and Dusky was hospitalized for evaluation. He was diagnosed with Schizophrenic reaction and determined to be "unable to understand the nature of the proceedings with reference to the charges against him" and "unable to properly assist counsel in his defense"; however, another evaluator had said he was "oriented to time, place, and person." The district court judge concluded that Mr. Dusky had sufficient mental competency to stand trial, saying, "Since he is oriented as to time and place and person, since he, in my opinion based on the limited evidence that has been presented so far, is able to assist counsel in his own defense, then it will be concluded that he is mentally competent to stand trial." Dusky was then convicted and asserted on appeal that the trial court erred in finding him competent to stand trial. The U.S. Court of Appeals upheld the lower court's ruling, arguing that how much mental capacity a defendant must have to be able to assist counsel was a question of fact for the trial court and that the judge was not bound by the conclusions of the expert.

Court Holding

The U.S. Supreme Court reversed the lower courts' decisions and held that the record was insufficient to support the conclusion that Dusky was competent to stand trial. The case was remanded to the district court for a new hearing to ascertain his competency to stand trial, and for a new trial if he was found competent.

Court's Reasoning

The U.S. Supreme Court took the position that "the record in this case does not sufficiently support the findings of competency to stand trial" and that to support the findings of competency to stand trial, the district judge would "need more information than this record presents." The Court further reasoned that it is not enough for the district judge to find that "the defendant [is] oriented to time and place and [has] some recollection of events." The Court asserted that the judge needed more information than what was available to decide the issue of competence and that the judge used inadequate criteria for determining Mr. Dusky's competence.

Quick Summary

The Supreme Court defined the test for competence to stand trial as: "the test must be whether [the defendant] has sufficient present ability to consult with his lawyer with a reasonable degree of rational understanding and whether he has a rational as well as factual understanding of the proceedings against him."

Estelle v. Smith
451 U.S. 454 (1981)
U.S. Supreme Court

Case Facts

In 1973, Mr. Ernest Smith was indicted for murder and Texas sought the death penalty. The district court ordered a competency to stand trial evaluation, which was performed by a psychiatrist, Dr. Grigson. Dr. Grigson did not inform Mr. Smith of the nature, purpose, limits to confidentiality, or that he could choose not to participate by remaining silent, and further did not inform defense counsel of the exam. Dr. Grigson opined that Mr. Smith was competent. Mr. Smith was tried by a jury and convicted. At sentencing, the jury had to decide whether Mr. Smith would be a "continuing threat to society" (dangerousness). Dr. Grigson testified at sentencing, relying on information gained during the competency examination to opine on dangerousness. Dr. Grigson referred to Mr. Smith as a "severe sociopath," stated that "his sociopathic condition will only get worse," and stated that "there is no treatment that in any way changes this behavior." The jury subsequently sentenced him to death.

Main Issue

What information must the defendant be provided before a court ordered mental health evaluation begins? Must the expert stick to the purpose of the evaluation and not opine on unrelated psycho-legal issues?

Court Holding

The Texas Court of Appeals affirmed the conviction and sentence. The U.S. district court for the Northern District of Texas vacated the death sentence. The U.S. Supreme Court held that Mr. Smith's Fifth and Sixth Amendment rights were violated and affirmed the decision to vacate the death sentence. The defendant should be informed of the nature and purpose of an evaluation as well as how it will be used and afforded an opportunity to consult with their lawyer prior to the examination. A mental health evaluator must not opine on matters outside of the nature and purpose of the evaluation.

Court's Reasoning

Mr. Smith's Fifth Amendment rights against self-incrimination were violated due to his not being informed that he had the right to refuse to participate, that he was allowed to terminate the exam, and that his statements and other findings from the evaluation would be used, possibly to his disadvantage, in court. The state (via Dr. Grigson) used Mr. Smith's unwarned disclosures as evidence against him in their efforts to obtain the death penalty. The use of unwarned statements made to Dr. Grigson in a competency evaluation could not be used to determine dangerousness. His rights were also violated because he was not given the assistance of counsel when deciding whether to submit to the exam and to what end the findings could be employed.

Quick Summary

Defendants must be sufficiently informed before a psychiatric evaluation of the right to decline participation, although other consequences may follow; to be able to end the evaluation at any time; and the anticipated uses of the examination. Evaluators must stick to the purpose of the requested evaluation, both in report and in testimony. Defendants must be informed of their right to the assistance of counsel and afforded an opportunity to consult with their attorneys prior to the examination.

Ex Rel. Edney v. Smith
425 F. Supp. 1038 (E.D.N.Y. 1976)
United States District Court for the Eastern District of New York

Case Facts

Herbert Edney was convicted of kidnapping and killing his former girlfriend's young daughter. He was convicted and sentenced to 25 years to life. At trial, the defense called a psychiatrist who opined that Mr. Edney was unable to appreciate the nature and quality of his actions and their wrongfulness due to his mental illness. The prosecution, in rebuttal, then called another psychiatrist who had previously met with the defendant at the defense's request but who defense elected not to call in trial. The defense objected, citing attorney-client and physician-patient privilege. Court denied the objection, and the psychiatrist testified for the prosecution that the defendant did not have a mental disease or defect and was able to appreciate the nature and wrongfulness of his actions. After his conviction, he appealed. The decision was affirmed by the Court of Appeals.

Main Issue

Can the prosecution call a mental health expert who was consulted by defense but not called to testify in an insanity trial?

Court Holding

The physician-patient privilege is not applicable because the defendant and his counsel sought an opinion from the psychiatrist specifically for legal purposes, not medical diagnosis or treatment purposes. The protection afforded is within the attorney-client privilege; however, once the defendant raises their mental health as an affirmative issue, the privilege is waived.

Court's Reasoning

When a defendant chooses to place his or her mental health at issue as in the affirmative defense of not guilty by reason of insanity (NGRI), the waiver to privilege is triggered. If the defendant makes the competent choice to assert mental health as a defense, maintaining privilege for psychiatric evaluations would be an obstruction to justice. While there is an important psychotherapist-patient privilege in place to promote the open sharing of diagnostic and treatment planning, there is also a waiver to it when a defendant relies on a mental condition as a defense. The privilege is qualified, not absolute, and may be infringed upon without violating constitutional rights in some situations like defendant's waiver.

Quick Summary

When a defendant raises the issue of insanity at trial, they effectively waive privilege to prior assessments regarding their mental state at the time of the instant offense, even if they do not specifically endorse that expert at trial.

Fare v. Michael C.
442 U.S. 707 (1979)
U.S. Supreme Court

Case Facts

Michael C. was 16 ½ years old with a history of juvenile offending and was on probation. His truck was found outside the home of a teen who had been murdered, and he was implicated in the murder, picked up by police, brought to the police station, and questioned. When the police gave him the Miranda warning, he asked for his probation officer. Police denied this request, went over the Miranda warning again with him, and he agreed to proceed with the interrogation. During the interrogation, he made self-incriminating statements, and he was subsequently charged with murder. He argued that his statements should be suppressed because they were obtained in violation of Miranda. He argued that prior cases had ruled that a juvenile asking for his parents was considered an invocation of his Fifth Amendment rights, so when he asked for his probation officer (a person he looked to for his care and protection), that should also be considered such an invocation. The trial court denied the motion, stating that the police had given Michael a clear Miranda warning, Michael had been through the process before, a probation officer is not the same as an attorney, and that he waived his Fifth Amendment rights knowingly and voluntarily. The Court of Appeals affirmed. The Supreme Court of California reversed, stating that (a) asking for his probation officer should have been taken as a sign that he had reservations about proceeding, (b) the officer is "a trusted guardian figure" to Michael, and (c) Michael may not have known the probation officer functioned different from an attorney. The U.S. Supreme Court granted certiorari.

Main Issue

Which situations should be considered a per se invocation of Fifth Amendment rights when interrogating juveniles? Specific to this case, should the juvenile's request for the presence of his probation officer necessarily invoke his Fifth Amendment rights?

Court Holding

It depends on the case, and a *totality-of-the-circumstances* assessment is best. Specific to this case, just because Michael asked for his probation officer does not mean that he was invoking his Fifth Amendment rights or that his statements should have been suppressed.

Court's Reasoning

The Supreme Court agreed with the trial court and said that the police did a thorough and careful job of explaining the Miranda warning to the juvenile, and there was evidence from the transcript that he understood it. Further, this is not a "young, naïve minor with no experience with the courts." The court noted that Michael had been in the juvenile justice system since age 12 and is aware of the process. Attorneys are in the unique position of helping their clients not to incriminate themselves, and asking for a probation officer is not the same as asking for an attorney. The probation officer is not trained in the law and cannot act on behalf of the minor. Comments made to the probation officer are not protected, and the officer is an employee of the state and actually has a duty to report when the juvenile gets in trouble. If courts start conceding that any request other than an attorney should be taken as an invocation of the Fifth Amendment right, then "a juvenile's request for almost anyone he considered trustworthy enough to give him reliable advice would trigger the rigid rule of Miranda." A consideration of the totality-of-the-circumstances (e.g., child's age, educational level, maturity level, history of involvement with the courts) is necessary, and there may potentially be some cases in which a request for a trusted guardian would mean the juvenile is invoking their Fifth Amendment rights, but this is not the case here.

Quick Summary

A juvenile's request for someone other than an attorney during a police interview is not a per se invocation of their Fifth Amendment rights but should be considered as part of a *totality-of-the-circumstances* approach to deciding when the right should be invoked for such juveniles.

Faretta v. California
422 U.S. 806 (1975)
U.S. Supreme Court

Case Facts

Anthony Faretta was charged with grand theft in California. He requested to represent himself at trial. The judge initially allowed him to proceed pro se but reversed his decision after an inquiry about a hearsay rule and a law regarding jury selection. The judge determined that Mr. Faretta had not made a knowing, intelligent waiver of counsel and ruled that the defendant had no constitutional right to represent himself; he appointed a public defender to represent him. The defendant was convicted, sentenced to life, and on appeal the appellate court affirmed the lower court judge's ruling that Mr. Faretta had no constitutional right to represent himself. The Supreme Court of California denied review, and the U.S. Supreme Court granted certiorari.

Main Issue

Can a court refuse to permit a defendant to represent themselves at trial, or does a defendant have a constitutional right to represent themselves?

Court Holding

The court held that it is not permissible for a court to force a lawyer on a defendant if the defendant chooses to waive counsel voluntarily and intelligently. The court indicated that while defendants have the right to representation by counsel, counsel may not be thrust upon a defendant who competently refuses the assistance.

Court's Reasoning

The court reasoned that while effective assistance of counsel is a right afforded to defendants, counsel may not be forced upon a defendant who voluntarily and intelligently waives such assistance. However, the defendant may not later claim ineffective assistance of counsel.

Quick Summary

A defendant who is competent to do so has the right to waive counsel and represent themselves. Counsel may not be forced on a defendant who intelligently and voluntarily waives their assistance. They may not, however, claim ineffective assistance of counsel once the waiver is competently made.

Farmer v. Brennan
511 U.S. 825 (1994)
U.S. Supreme Court

Case Facts

Dee Farmer was an inmate serving time for credit card fraud at the Federal Correctional Institution in Wisconsin. Farmer was born biologically male, but identified as female, wore women's clothing, and had silicone breast implants.

Farmer was transferred to a penitentiary in Indiana for higher security due to disciplinary issues and placed in general population, and was subsequently beaten and raped. Farmer filed a *Bivens complaint*, which allows a person to collect damages for constitutional violations by federal agents. Farmer claimed that the officers knew of the vulnerability to sexual attack as a transexual inmate and especially at that facility. The district court granted summary judgment in favor of the penitentiary, stating that there had been no "deliberate indifference" and that the officers were not "reckless in a criminal sense" and had no "actual knowledge" that harm would come to Farmer. The Court of Appeals affirmed the lower court's ruling, and the U.S. Supreme Court granted certiorari to finally arrive at a clear definition of *deliberate indifference*, which had not been clear in prior case law.

Main Issue

What constitutes deliberate indifference, and how shall it be defined?

Court Holding

Prison officials can be held liable if they know an inmate is at "substantial risk of serious harm" and fail to take measures to prevent it. A constitutional violation has occurred when the deprivation is "sufficiently serious," and the prison official knew or should have known that harm was likely. The court explained that the lower court erred by placing the responsibility on farmer for not having specifically told prison staff about the fear for safety. The official can or should know of the reasonable likelihood of harm without an inmate's direct expression, and the degree of culpability is for a fact finder to decide.

Court's Reasoning

According to the court, deliberate indifference is "somewhere between the poles of negligence at one end and purpose or knowledge at the other." The Eighth Amendment requires prison officials to provide humane conditions of confinement and "a punishment is simply no less cruel or unusual just because its harm is unintended." The inmate does not need to prove that the official knew harm would occur, just that they acted or failed to act "despite his knowledge of a substantial risk of serious harm." The court added then when an individual's civil liberties are taken away as a result of incarceration, their ability to protect themselves is compromised, and they are reliant on the prison system for adequate protection.

Quick Summary

In this case, the U.S. Supreme Court defined deliberate indifference as occurring when (a) a prison official is aware that an inmate is at substantial risk of serious harm and ignores that risk, (b) the official knew or should have known of the risk (culpable state of mind), and (c) the deprivation is sufficiently serious.

Ford v. Wainwright
477 U.S. 399 (1986)
U.S. Supreme Court

Case Facts

Alvin Bernard Ford was convicted of murder in a Florida State Court and sentenced to death. He appeared to be competent at the time of the offense, trial, and sentencing. Around 1982, he began to show signs of psychosis (delusions that (a) family members were being tortured, (b) there was a conspiracy with the KKK to have him commit suicide, (c) prison guards were killing people, and (d) he appointed 9 new justices to the Fl. S. Ct., etc.). Defense counsel had him examined by two psychiatrists, one of whom believed he was incompetent to be executed. The state had him examined, according to their standard procedure, by three psychiatrists. Although they all thought he was mentally ill, they agreed that he was competent to be executed (i.e., "had the mental capacity to understand the nature of the death penalty and the reasons why it was imposed upon him"). The governor in Florida was responsible for making the decision regarding competency at the time, and he signed the death warrant without giving his reasoning. No formal hearing was done, which meant no chance for cross examination of experts. Mr. Ford petitioned in the state courts to have a hearing on his competency but was denied. He also filed for habeas corpus in Federal District Court but was denied. The Court of Appeals also denied. The U.S. Supreme Court granted certiorari to consider the Eighth Amendment's prohibition against cruel and unusual punishment and its application to the execution of the mentally ill.

Main Issues

1. Does the Eighth Amendment bar execution of the "insane"?
2. Was Florida's statutory procedure constitutionally adequate?

Court Holding

1. Yes, the Eight Amendment's prohibition against cruel and unusual punishment does bar the execution of those determined to be insane (incompetent).
2. Florida's statutory procedure was not constitutionally adequate and, therefore, Mr. Ford is entitled to a new evidentiary hearing in the district court to decide his competence to be executed.

Court's Reasoning

1. Execution of the insane is barred because it provides no deterrent value, no retributive value, and is offensive to humanity.
2. The procedures were unsatisfactory because Mr. Ford was denied a fact-finding procedure "adequate to afford a full and fair hearing." The court opined that Ford should have the right to present a defense, provide data in support of his position (e.g., reports of the two private psychiatrists), and cross examine the state-appointed psychiatrists. The governor could be biased and should not be making the final decision on competency/sanity to be executed; rather, a neutral party should be used.

Quick Summary

The Eight Amendment bars the execution of those found "insane" or incompetent. Also, a "full and fair hearing" must occur to decide the issue of competency/sanity to be executed. The defendant must know that they are being executed as well as why.

Foucha v. Louisiana
504 U.S. 71 (1992)
U.S. Supreme Court

Case Facts

Terry Foucha was charged with aggravated burglary and illegal discharge of a firearm and was found not guilty by reason of insanity after evidence was presented of a drug-induced psychosis. He was confined beyond the time required to successfully treat his psychosis. He also carried a diagnosis of ASPD, which is not a qualified mental illness responsive to treatment. He appealed, but the appellate court denied. Supreme Court of Louisiana affirmed the denial, although they acknowledged that he no longer had a qualified mental illness and that dangerousness alone would not meet commitment criteria. The U.S. Supreme Court granted review.

Main Issue

What are the proper criteria for the ongoing commitment of an individual adjudicated not guilty by reason of insanity (NGRI)? Is it a violation of the 14th Amendment to allow an NGRI acquittee to be held in a psychiatric hospital even if they are no longer mentally ill?

Court Holding

Potential dangerousness without ongoing mental illness is insufficient commitment criteria for an insanity acquittee. The court held that if the mental disease or defect that qualified the person for the initial insanity commitment no longer applies, the acquittee must be released. The court reversed the ruling of the lower courts.

Court's Reasoning

If the reason for an NGRI commitment was the presence of mental illness (and dangerousness as a result of that mental illness) and the mental illness is resolved, ongoing dangerousness alone does not warrant ongoing psychiatric commitment. If there is no ongoing mental illness, there is no justification for ongoing commitment. Dangerousness alone is insufficient for psychiatric commitment following an NGRI acquittal. If it was acceptable for Louisiana to hold a person just based on dangerousness, there would be no difference between insanity acquittees and any convicted criminal, even if they have completed their prison sentence.

Quick Summary

The U.S. Supreme Court found it unconstitutional to continue the involuntary commitment of persons who were adjudicated NGRI if the mental disease or defect that qualified them for that adjudication has resolved. As in civil commitment, dangerousness alone was found to be insufficient criteria for ongoing commitment. If an NGRI acquittee no longer meets civil commitment criteria, they must be released. Commitment requires meeting the criteria of mental illness and dangerousness and not just an automatic indefinite process following an NGRI acquittal.

Frazier v. Cupp
394 U.S. 731 (1969)
Supreme Court of United States

Case Facts

Martin Frazier was convicted of second-degree murder after making a confession to police. The confession, however, was a result of deception used by the police during the interrogation: "At this point, the officer questioning petitioner told him, falsely, that [the co-defendant] had been brought in and that he had confessed." The Supreme Court of Oregon affirmed Frazier's conviction, so Mr. Frazier successfully filed a writ of habeas corpus to the U.S. District Court for the District of Oregon. However, the Court of Appeals for the Ninth Circuit reversed the decision, so the case was then appealed via a writ of certiorari to the U.S. Supreme Court.

Main Issue

Can police use deception during a custodial interrogation to elicit a confession?

Court Holding

Yes. The Supreme Court of the United States affirmed the decision from the lower court, thereby reinforcing the use of police deception during custodial interrogations.

Court's Reasoning

The Court reasoned that a totality-of-the-circumstances analysis allows room for police deception in *some* cases:

> The questioning was of short duration, and petitioner was a mature individual of normal intelligence. The fact that the police misrepresented the statements that [the co-defendant] had made is, while relevant, insufficient in our view to make this otherwise voluntary confession inadmissible. These cases must be decided by viewing the "totality of the circumstances," and on the facts of this case we can find no error in the admission of petitioner's confession.

Quick Summary

A murder defendant confessed to police, after police "misrepresented the statements that the [co-defendant] had made," by saying that the codefendant had already confessed. The confession was appealed on the basis that police cannot use deception during custodial interrogations to elicit confessions. But the Supreme Court of the United States held that a totality-of-the-circumstances standard allows room for deception in some cases, including this one, where the defendant "was a mature individual of normal intelligence."

Frendak v. United States
408 A.2d 364 (D.C. Cir. 1979)
District of Columbia Circuit Court of Appeals

Case Facts

Paula Frendak fatally shot Willard Titlow in Washington, D.C. and was indicted for first-degree murder and carrying a pistol without a license. Ms. Frendak participated in several competency to stand trial evaluations and was found by the trial judge to be competent. During the competency proceedings, Ms. Frendak refused to raise the insanity defense, despite evidence indicating that the defense may be relevant, so an *amicus curia* (uninterested party) was appointed and a criminal responsibility evaluation was ordered anyway. The trial judge found that *if* a higher degree of competence is not required for the defendant to make a decision regarding the insanity defense, then Ms. Frendak was able to appreciate her decision to refuse such a defense. However, the judge also noted that there was "sufficient question" regarding her criminal responsibility. Despite her oppositions, per the *Whalem* rule (the assertion of a sanity defense over the objection of the defendant), the trial judge imposed the insanity defense. During the trial, three psychiatrists testified and offered varying opinions regarding Ms. Frendak's criminal responsibility. The jury found her not guilty by reason of insanity (NGRI), which could carry a longer civil commitment than incarceration if found guilty. On appeal, Ms. Frendak asserted that the *Whalem* rule afforded the trial judge too much discretion to force an unwanted insanity defense over a competent person's wishes.

Main Issue

To what extent may a trial judge make decisions on their own regarding the imposition of the insanity defense without prompting by a party (i.e., *sua sponte*), particularly when a defendant is competent to stand trial and opposes such a defense?

Court Holding

The Court of Appeals held that the trial court may not force the insanity defense on a defendant who has been determined competent to stand trial and who intelligently and voluntarily declines to implement that defense.

Court's Reasoning

1. A defendant may refuse an insanity defense due to fear of a longer civil commitment than incarceration if found guilty, the quality/type of treatment and/or confinement in the mental institution, or to avoid the stigma of mental illness.
2. A trial judge still has the discretion to enforce *Whalem,* but if the defendant is "voluntarily and intelligently making the choice," then the defendant's decision should be respected. If there is question regarding the voluntary and intelligent nature of the defendant's decision, the trial judge does have the discretion to raise that defense *sua sponte.*

Quick Summary

A voluntary and intelligent decision made by a competent defendant regarding to their own defense, particularly whether to utilize the NGRI defense, should be respected by the trial judge. Despite evidence that may exist that the defendant was suffering from a requisite mental disease or defect at the time of the offense, it should be up to the competent defendant whether they choose to pursue that defense or not.

Frye v. United States
293 F. 1013 (D.C. Cir. 1923)
District of Columbia Circuit Court of Appeals

Case Facts

The defendant, Mr. James A. Frye, was a patient of Dr. R.W. Brown, a physician. When Mr. Frye did not have enough money to pay for the medications prescribed by Dr. Brown, he offered his pistol as the additional payment. That offer was declined. Dr. Brown was later shot and killed. On the day Dr. Brown was killed, there were four missed calls made to him, and then Dr. Brown's houseguest (another doctor) admitted a man into the home where Dr. Brown (a widower) lived with his two daughters. Four gunshots were fired, and the gun was left next to Dr. Brown's body. The case went unsolved for more than a year. Mr. Frye was identified as a suspect in other criminal acts and indicated. When interviewed, he offered that he shot Dr. Brown in self-defense after the doctor assaulted him. Mr. Frye was charged, tried, and convicted of second-degree murder and sentenced to life in prison. He argued on appeal that the trial court erred by refusing to allow an expert witness to testify as to the result of a systolic blood pressure deception test taken by Mr. Frye. The systolic blood pressure test was a novel test, invented by Dr. William Maulton Marston, which was supposed to be able to distinguish between those who told the truth and those who were lying on the basis of changes in blood pressure. Prior to the trial, the defendant had taken the test, and counsel offered the psychologist who conducted the test as an expert to testify to the results. The testimony was objected to by the prosecution, and the court sustained the rejection because lie detection was not yet "a matter of common knowledge" and was not generally accepted in the field.

Main Issue

What is the proper standard for the admissibility of evidence through expert testimony?

Court Holding

The conviction was affirmed. The court held that, given that the science on the device had not yet achieved standing, (i.e., was not generally accepted within the field to which it belongs), the testimony derived from it must be excluded.

Court's Reasoning

The court reasoned that the expert testimony regarding the systolic blood pressure test was properly excluded at trial because the defense counsel did not establish that the test was not merely experimental. The court held that the admissible expert testimony should be based on scientific principles that are sufficiently established to have gained general acceptance in the particular field in which it belongs. In the court's opinion, the systolic blood pressure deception test had not gained sufficient standing and scientific recognition.

Quick Summary

This case led to the "Frye test" for admissibility of scientific evidence based on the general acceptance of the methodology by the scientific community (also known as the "general acceptance" test).

Furman v. Georgia
408 U.S. 238 (1972)
U.S. Supreme Court

Case Facts

William Henry Furman unlawfully entered a home and was in the process of committing burglary when he claimed he tripped and discharged a firearm, killing the resident (although this statement was inconsistent with another he had made indicating that he had fired a shot randomly while attempting to escape). He was convicted in Georgia for murder. The jury was not mandated to elect the death penalty but did choose this as the punishment. This punishment was affirmed on appeal. The U.S. Supreme Court granted certiorari to review the constitutionality of not just his punishment but also the imposition of the death penalty for two other unrelated death penalty cases (Lucius Jackson and Elmer Branch both convicted of rape). The U.S. Supreme Court reversed the sentences of all three.

Main Issue

Is the death penalty cruel and unusual punishment and therefore a violation of the 8th and 14th Amendments, and as such unconstitutional?

Court Holding

Yes. The justices wrote nine different opinions and voted five to four that the death penalty constituted cruel and unusual punishment. The court reversed the death penalty sentences of the three appellants. The Furman decision stopped all pending executions across the country (applicable to approximately 600 people at the time), commuting them to life sentences.

Court's Reasoning

The court stated that the death penalty was "wantonly and freakishly imposed" in these cases and was "cruel and unusual in the same way that being struck by lightning is cruel and unusual." The court explained that death is "different" from other punishments and there should be clear rules for its application if at all. The way the penalty had been imposed to that point, the Court explained, was haphazard and discriminatory, was applied infrequently and randomly, and was applied mostly to minority defendants. The court reasoned that death as a penalty is inherently cruel and unusual and incompatible with the evolving standards of a civilized society. States had to change the circumstances under which the death penalty could be enforced, either by making certain crimes carry a mandatory death sentence or creating certain aggravating factors that could qualify a crime for the death penalty, or they had to abolish the death penalty altogether.

Quick Summary

In this case, the U.S. Supreme Court voted to overturn and remand the death sentences in three cases due to the arbitrary and discriminatory process of the penalty's imposition. The death penalty was determined to be cruel and unusual punishment under the eighth amendment. This case led to the revision of capital punishment laws across the country.

Godinez v. Moran
509 U.S. 389 (1993)
U.S. Supreme Court

Case Facts

In 1984, Mr. Richard Moran entered a saloon in Nevada, shot and killed the bartender and a customer and robbed the register, then later shot his ex-wife and himself. He was taken to a hospital where he asked police to come to his bedside, and he confessed the killings. He was charged with murder. He was evaluated by two mental health professionals who opined that he was competent to stand trial but depressed. The prosecution sought the death penalty; Mr. Moran pled not guilty. After a couple of months, however, he wanted to change his plea to guilty and waive his right to counsel. He was found guilty and sentenced to death. He then appealed, arguing that he was not competent to represent himself, but the appeal was rejected by the court. The Nevada Supreme Court dismissed his claim, but the Court of Appeals reversed, indicating that the lower court needed to hold a hearing to determine if the defendant was competent to waive counsel and plead guilty *and* that the level of competency should be higher to waive counsel and plead guilty than it is to stand trial. More specifically, the appellate court held that while competence to stand trial requires a defendant to have a factual and rational understanding of the proceedings and the ability to consult effectively with counsel, pleading guilty and waiving counsel require the ability to have reasoned choice. The U.S. Supreme Court granted certiorari.

Main Issue

Should there be a different level of competency when it comes to a defendant's ability to competently stand trial versus to competently plead and waive counsel?

Court Holding

No. Competency to stand trial, competency to plead guilty, and competency to waive counsel are the same competencies.

Court's Reasoning

The court reasoned that there is no differentiation between different phases of a trial and the decisions a defendant is required to think through. If a defendant is competent to stand trial, they are also competent to plead guilty and to make other case-related choices. The court reasoned that there should be a single standard of competency that is applied throughout a criminal proceeding. Further, identifying different competencies for different stages and decisions that may arise during a trial is disruptive and creates endless appellate issues. Competency to waive counsel should be a part of a competency to stand trial forensic mental health evaluation going forward.

Quick Summary

The U.S. Supreme Court decided in this case that there is a single standard for competency to stand trial, competency to plead, and competency to waive counsel and that all should be included in a forensic assessment of a defendant's competency.

General Electric Company v. Joiner
118 S.Ct. 512 (1997)
U.S. Supreme Court

Case Facts

Robert Joiner was an electrician who worked on city transformers that contained dielectric fluid. In 1983, it was discovered that the fluid was contaminated with polychlorinated biphenyls (PCBs), which are considered hazardous to human health. In 1991, Joiner developed small cell cancer of the lung. He sued stating that there was a link between the exposure to the PCBs and the cancer. He had expert witness testimony supporting the link between the exposure and the cancer. The district court decided that the expert opinions were not admissible due to the studies either being dissimilar or failing to show the link. The court believed that the expert opinions did not rise above "subjective belief or unsupported speculation." The Court of Appeals said the lower court erred because they should have relied on deciding "legal reliability" of the expert opinion and leave deciding the "correctness" of the opinion to the jury. The U.S. Supreme Court reversed this decision.

Court Holding

The U.S. Supreme Court wanted to decide what standard the appellate court should use in reviewing a trial court's decision to admit or exclude evidence. It was determined that "abuse of discretion" is the appropriate standard of review. The U.S. Supreme Court ruled that the district court did not abuse its discretion when it kept the expert opinions out.

Court's Reasoning

The U.S. Supreme Court decided that the district court used the proper methods to exclude the expert opinions. They noted that the trial judge has a "gatekeeper" role that allows them to screen evidence to ensure it is not only relevant but reliable. Joiner argued that under the *Daubert* ruling, the focus should have been on methodology, not the conclusions (in determining whether the expert testimony was admissible) and therefore the court should not have excluded the expert opinions/conclusions. The U.S. Supreme Court indicated that neither *Daubert* nor the Federal Rules of Evidence (FREs) say that a judge is required to admit evidence based on the "ipse dixit" (i.e., it-is-so-because-I-said-so logic) of the expert and that the lower court judge was properly playing the gatekeeper role with the experts in the *Joiner* matter.

Quick Summary

The significance of the Joiner decision is that testimony by an expert can be excluded by the judge if an expert's opinion does not flow in a reasonably causal way from the expert's data ("Nothing in either *Daubert* or the Federal Rules of Evidence requires a district court judge to admit opinion evidence that is connected to existing data only by the ipse dixit [i.e., it-is-so-because-I-said-so logic] of the expert. A court may conclude that there is simply too great an analytical gap between the data and the opinion proffered."). Moreover, lower court serves a gatekeeping function for what evidence is allowed to be considered. And as long as the court does not abuse its power, it is not a violation of due process. The appellate court is to use the standard of abuse of power when reviewing excluded evidence claims. The evidence must be "reliable and relevant" and the appellate court will not reverse unless there was a major error that rose to abuse of discretion.

Graham v. Florida
560 U.S. 48 (2010)
U.S. Supreme Court

Case Facts

Terrance Graham was 16 years old in 2003 when he attempted to rob a restaurant in Florida. He was charged as an adult, pled guilty, and, placed on probation. Despite a letter he wrote vowing he would never get in trouble again, he violated the conditions of his plea agreement when he was arrested again for home invasion. After expressing sadness and dismay at the situation (he had been given opportunities to turn his life around, including the initial plea deal), the judge sentenced him to life in prison in 2006. However, in Florida, parole had been abolished, so it essentially became a life without parole sentence. Graham appealed, citing the Eighth Amendment, but the appellate court affirmed, holding that the sentence was not disproportionate to his crimes. Florida Supreme Court denied review. The U.S. Supreme Court granted certiorari, reversed the decision, and remanded the case for additional proceedings, consistent with the ruling that it is prohibited by the constitution to sentence a juvenile to life in prison without the possibility of release in non-homicide offenses. Graham was later resentenced to 25 years.

Main Issue

Was it a violation of the constitution to sentence a non-homicide offending juvenile to life without the possibility of parole given that Florida had abolished parole?

Court Holding

Yes. If a state sentences a juvenile who was convicted for a non-homicide offense to life in prison, there has to be some "realistic opportunity" for release.

Court's Reasoning

The standard of extreme cruelty is a moral judgment, and the state must respect the human attributes of even the most serious offenders. The court pointed out the necessity of looking beyond the barbaric nature of a punishment and more at the proportionality of the punishment to the crime, both in terms of length and related to categorical exceptions to the death penalty. The court cited other jurisdictions that, at the time, were divided between forbidding life in prison without parole for juveniles convicted of non-homicide offenses, permitting it for homicide offenses, and permitting it for some non-homicide offenses. It concluded that there is no national consensus on the issue. The court further looked at Florida's abolition of parole in addition to its liberal waiver of youth to adult court and reasoned that a five-year-old could, theoretically, be waived to adult court and sentenced to life in prison, and, because of the absence of parole, receive a life without the possibility of parole sentence. Prior case law established that juveniles differ from adults and are more likely to be reformed. The court also discussed the difference between non-homicide and homicide offenses, reasoning that although non-homicide offenses can cause great pain and suffering, they "cannot be compared to murder in their severity and irrevocability." However, life without parole is the second most severe penalty permitted by law and is especially harsh for a juvenile who will, on average, serve more years and a greater percentage of life in prison compared with an adult. The principles of punishment do not serve the same function for juveniles as for adults. Life in prison without the possibility of parole for juvenile non-homicide offenders constitutes cruel and unusual punishment.

Quick Summary

It is unconstitutional to sentence a juvenile non-homicide offender to life in prison without the possibility of parole.

Hedlund v. Super. Ct.
669 P.2d 41 (Cal. 1983)
Supreme Court of California

Case Facts

Psychologists Dr. Bonnie Hedlund and Dr. Peter Ebersole provided psychotherapy to Mr. and Ms. Wilson. During the course of this psychotherapy, Mr. Wilson made threatening statements concerning Ms. Wilson, but the threatening statements were not shared by Dr. Hedlund or Dr. Ebersole with Ms. Wilson. Following this psychotherapy, Mr. Wilson "used a shotgun to inflict serious bodily injury on [Ms. Wilson]." And because Ms. Wilson was with her son, Darryl, at the time of the shooting, it was later asserted that Drs. Hedlund and Ebersole had a duty to warn her to prevent harm to her, as well as to her son, who went on to experience psychological trauma:

> He was seated next to his mother when she was shot by [Mr. Wilson]. She threw herself over him thereby saving his life and preventing serious physical injury to him, but, as a result of the attack he has suffered serious emotional injuries and psychological trauma. Darryl alleges that because it was foreseeable that [Mr. Wilson's] threats, if carried out, posed a risk of harm to bystanders and particularly to those in close relationship to [Ms. Wilson], petitioners' duty extended to him, and that this duty was breached when they failed to act to protect [Ms. Wilson] and such foreseeable individuals.

Drs. Hedlund and Ebersole petitioned the Supreme Court of California via a writ of mandate (i.e., a court order for the lower court to correct its prior action) in an attempt to compel the superior court to vacate an order, which had already overruled their objection to "two counts of a complaint by [Ms. Wilson and her son, Darryl]."

Main Issues

1. Do mental health professionals have a duty to "warn a potential victim of a threat to the victim made by the [mental health professional's] patient"? And if so, is there a statute of limitations on such a duty?
2. Do mental health professionals have a responsibility to protect others who might be harmed as a result of their failure to warn potential victims of threat, when the threat was made by the mental health professional's patient?

Court Holding

1. Yes. Mental health professionals *do* have a duty warn potential victims about threats made by their patients and there is no statute of limitations on such a duty.
2. Yes. Mental health professionals *do* have a responsibility to protect others who might be harmed as a result of their failure to warn potential victims of threat, when the threat was made by the mental health professional's patient.

For these two reasons, the Supreme Court of California denied the petition by Drs. Hedlund and Ebersole.

Court's Reasoning

The Supreme Court of California reasoned that Drs. Hedlund and Ebersole had a duty to warn *at the time* the threats were made: "the duty arose and the omission to act occurred during the time that defendants were rendering professional services to [Mr. Wilson]." So even though the shooting took place sometime after the services were provided, the Court reasoned that the prior failure to warn Ms. Wilson may have played a causative role in the subsequent shooting. That is, Ms. Wilson and her son may have been able to avoid the shooting, had Ms. Wilson been informed of the threats made during psychotherapy. The Court also reasoned that Drs. Hedlund and Ebersole had a responsibility to diagnose or recognize the threat posed by Mr. Wilson:

> [Ms. Wilson] argues that … because the duty imposed on a therapist in that case is first to diagnose or recognize the danger posed by the patient and only then to warn. The warning aspect of this duty, she claims, is inextricably interwoven with the diagnostic function. We agree..

Quick Summary

Two psychologists providing psychotherapy to a couple failed to share threatening statements made by the husband, directed at his wife. Sometime later, the husband followed through on his threats by shooting his wife with a shotgun, while her son was seated next to her in a vehicle. The psychologists unsuccessfully attempted to avoid responsibility for this violent outcome. Instead, the Supreme Court of California held them responsible for the harm brought to both the wife and her son, despite a lapse of time between the threatening statements and the shooting. This court held that it is the responsibility of the psychotherapist to diagnose or recognize the threats posed by their patients and to then warn potential victims..

Henderson v. Morgan
426 U.S. 637 (1976)
U.S. Supreme Court.

Case Facts

A 19-year-old man—with a history of being "committed to the Rome State School for Mental Defectives [in seventh grade] where he was classified as 'retarded.'"—killed his boss not long after getting into an argument with her because "she threatened to return him to state custody." Following the argument, the man "decided to abscond" and "during the night he entered [the victim's] bedroom with a knife, intending to collect his earned wages before leaving." However, the victim "awoke, began to scream, and he stabbed her." Shortly thereafter, the defendant was found with the murder weapon "in the glove compartment of [the victim's] car." The defendant, described as "substantially below average intelligence," was quickly arrested, he made a statement to police, he was later found competent to stand trial, he pled guilty to second-degree murder, and he received a sentence carrying a minimum of 25 years in prison.

However, he later appealed on the basis "that his guilty plea was involuntary because he was not aware (1) of the sentence that might be imposed upon conviction of second-degree murder, or (2) that intent to cause death was an element of the offense." After reviewing all of the evidence, the district court held that the defendant was in fact adequately advised about the likely sentence associated with pleading guilty to second-degree murder. But, "the court found that respondent 'was not advised by counsel or court, at any time, that an intent to cause the death or a design to effect the death of the victim was an essential element of Murder 2nd degree.'"

Based on this finding, the district court concluded that "the plea of guilty was involuntary and had to be set aside." The court of appeals affirmed this decision, so the case was appealed to the U.S. Supreme Court.

Main Issue

Must guilty pleas be made voluntarily?

Court Holding

Yes. Because "There was no discussion [between defense counsel and the defendant] of the elements of the offense of second-degree murder, no indication that the nature of the offense had ever been discussed with respondent, and no reference of any kind to the requirement of intent to cause the death of the victim," the U.S. Supreme Court affirmed the lower court's decision.

Court's Reasoning

In explaining this decision, the Court acknowledged that the "respondent's unusually low mental capacity provide[d] a reasonable explanation for counsel's oversight [in not fleshing out the details of the plea deal with the defendant]." However, the Court also underscored the likely role of the defendant's low IQ in forming the necessary intent to commit murder: "[the defendant's low IQ] lends at least a modicum of credibility to defense counsel's appraisal of the homicide as a manslaughter rather than a murder." Ultimately, the court concluded its decision to affirm the lower court's ruling as follows: "Since respondent did not receive adequate notice of the offense to which he pleaded guilty, his plea was involuntary and the judgment of conviction was entered without due process of law."

Quick Summary

A 19-year-old with limited intellectual functioning killed his boss shortly after getting into an argument with her. After being found competent to proceed, he pled guilty to second-degree murder and was sentenced to a minimum of 25 years in prison. The case was later appealed on the basis that the plea was not made voluntarily.

This case is relevant because it highlights what must go into a valid guilty plea; namely, a guilty plea can only be voluntary if the defendant is made fully aware of the crime they are agreeing to have committed. In this case, the defendant had not been adequately informed by his lawyers that second-degree murder included an element of intent, which the defendant did not agree was behind his motivation to kill his boss. Because of this oversight by his attorneys, the U.S. Supreme Court affirmed the lower court's decision that the guilty plea was not valid.

Ibn-Tamas v. U.S.
407 A.2d 626 (D.C. Cir. 1979)
District of Columbia Circuit Court of Appeals

Case Facts

In 1977, Mrs. Beverly Ibn-Tamas was convicted of second-degree murder in D.C. Superior Court after shooting and killing her husband, Dr. Yusef Ibn-

Tamas. During the trial, evidence was presented that Dr. Ibn-Tamas had been repeatedly violent towards his wife and others and that on the morning of the shooting, he had beaten his wife. The defense proffered Dr. Lenore Walker, a clinical psychologist, as an expert witness on the subject of "battered women." The defense wanted Dr. Walker to describe the phenomenon of "wife battering" and to give her opinion of the extent to which Mrs. Ibn-Tamas' personality and behavior corresponded to other battered women. The defense argued that the expert's testimony was relevant because it would help the jury appraise the credibility of Mrs. Ibn-Tamas' argument that she had perceived herself in such imminent danger that she had shot her husband in self-defense. The trial court refused to permit this evidence because (1) it would include past violent acts that the jury was not entitled to hear about, (2) "invade the province of the jury, who are the sole judges of the facts and triers of the credibility of the witnesses, including the defendant," and (3) the expert would necessarily infer that the victim was a batterer by the nature of that testimony. Mrs. Ibn-Tamas appealed her conviction, claiming that the trial court erred in excluding Dr. Walker's testimony.

Court Holding

The Court of Appeals held that the trial court erred in precluding Dr. Walker's testimony. The court further held that the record was insufficient to ultimately determine if the testimony was admissible because of insufficient information regarding Dr. Walker's qualifications, methodologies for studying battered women, and general acceptance of her research. The case was remanded to the trial court to gather more information about the admissibility of Dr. Walker's testimony.

Court's Reasoning

The Court of Appeals held that the expert testimony was not, in principle, inadmissible. Expert testimony can invade the province of the jury by either addressing the ultimate issue (guilt/innocence) or by speaking about subjects that "the jury is just as competent as the expert to consider and weigh" in drawing the necessary conclusions. The court held that the expert in this case would not give ultimate issue testimony. Regarding the issue of whether the expert would testify to matters which the jury is just as competent to consider, the court applied the threefold "Dyas" test for admissibility:

1. The subject matter must be "beyond the ken of the average layman."
2. The expert must have sufficient skill, knowledge, or experience.
3. The state of the pertinent art allows a reasonable opinion to be asserted.

The court held that the expert testimony was "beyond the ken of the average layman," but that the record was insufficient to determine if Dr. Walker was qualified and if her methods for evaluating battered women had gained general scientific acceptance.

Quick Summary

Expert testimony invades the province of the jury if it speaks to the ultimate issue or if it addresses matters that are not "beyond the ken of the average layman."

Illinois v. Heral
62 Ill.2d 329 (1976)
342 N.E.2d 34
No. 47443.
Supreme Court of Illinois

Case Facts

On August 2, 1972, Carrie Jean Heral, who was then 19 years old, was arrested and charged with the murder of Rodney Stewart Collison, a 14-month-old child. The public defender who represented Heral requested that she examined to determine her competency to stand trial. Two psychiatrists determined that Heral showed severe remorse and was depressed and suicidal; however, both stated that she understood the nature of the charges against her and was willing and able to cooperate in her defense. A matron (chief nurse) at the county jail also testified regarding Heral's behavior in jail, stating that Heral had made two suicide attempts in jail. Heral was found competent to stand trial.

Three months later, as a result of plea negotiations, Heral withdrew her plea of not guilty and entered a plea of guilty. During the proceedings, the State's Attorney introduced into evidence additional reports of the two psychiatrists, two psychologists, and a neurosurgeon, as well as psychological test results and a lengthy psychotherapy progress report concerning her treatment.

Heral later appealed, challenging the trial judge's determination that she was competent to enter a guilty plea. She claimed that, based on her history of profound psychological disturbance, a possible insanity defense, and her recent suicide attempt, a second competency hearing was indicated. She contended that competence to stand trial and competence to plead involve two different levels of capacity, with the required level of the latter exceeding the level of the former. She further contended that she had a constitutional right to a separate and specific determination that she is competent to enter a guilty plea.

Main Issue

Are there different standards for competency to stand trial and competency to plead guilty?

Court Holding

No. The Court determined that the test of competency must be the same whether the defendant is standing trial or pleading guilty. The Court found that the trial court did not err in accepting Heral's plea of guilty.

Court's Reasoning

The court noted that the trial judge who conducted Heral's plea-change proceedings was the same one who had conducted the competency to stand trial hearing. Thus, at the time the plea of guilty was entered and accepted by the court, the judge had the benefit of the preliminary reports of the two psychiatrists, the prior testimony of the psychiatrists and the matron, updated reports from the two psychiatrists, and the reports of two psychologists, a neurosurgeon, and psychotherapy progress reports. Thus, the court had adequate information upon which to base a determination of competency to change the plea.

The court noted that a dual standard of competency might "create a class of semi-competent defendants who are not protected from prosecution because they have been found competent to stand trial, but who are denied the leniency of the plea-bargaining process because they are not competent to plead guilty." It also noted that a mere history of psychological disturbance does not necessarily equate to incompetence.

Quick Summary

The test of competency must be the same whether the defendant is standing trial or pleading guilty.

In re Gault
387 U.S. 1 (1967)
U.S. Supreme Court

Case Facts

Fifteen-year-old Gerald Francis Gault was on a six-month probation when his female neighbor complained that he was making lewd phone calls to her. He was picked up by the police and taken to the children's detention home. His parents were not notified by police as to his whereabouts. The superintendent of the detention home eventually told Gault's mother why her son was detained and that a hearing was scheduled for the next day. At the hearing, the superintendent filed a petition that made no reference to any factual basis for the judicial action they were taking, just that, "minor is under the age of 18 years, and is in need of the protection of this Honorable Court … said minor is a delinquent minor." The Gaults were never served with this petition. During the hearing, Gault's father was out of town, and the

Superintendent was not present. No one at the hearing was sworn in, and no transcription was made of the proceedings. During the hearing, inconsistent information was presented about Gault's role in the incidents. The judge made no decision and stated that he would think about the case some more. Gault returned to the Detention Home for a few days before he was released. His mother received a letter from the superintendent stating that another hearing was scheduled the following week. At that hearing, the judge again heard conflicting stories about which boy actually made the lewd remarks. The female neighbor who initially brought the complaint was not present. When Gault's mother requested to confront the neighbor about which boy said what, the judge said that the complainant did not have to be present. The judge then committed Gault as a juvenile delinquent to the State Industrial School "for the period of his minority [until 21] unless sooner discharged by due process of law." In Arizona, adults convicted of the same offense received a sentence of $5 to $50 or no more than two months imprisonment. There was also no appeal process in Arizona juvenile cases, so Gault's parents filed a writ of habeas corpus (petition claiming unlawful detention) with the Arizona Supreme Court. They asked that the court find the Juvenile Code of Arizona to be unconstitutional under the Due Process Clause with regard to (1) adequate notice of the charges, (2) right to counsel, (3) right to confrontation/cross-examination, (4) privilege against self-incrimination, (5) right to a transcript of the proceedings, and 6) right to appellate review. The U.S. Supreme Court granted certiorari to examine the adequacy of Due Process within Arizona's delinquency hearings.

Main Issue

Were Arizona's juvenile commitment procedures constitutional under the Due Process Clause of the 14th Amendment? Should juveniles be allowed the same procedural due process safeguards afforded to adults in criminal matters?

Court Holding

Arizona Juvenile Court hearings were unconstitutional because they failed to comply with the requirements of the 14th Amendment. Juveniles should be afforded due process protections.

Court's Reasoning

The court reviewed the history of the Juvenile Court System and the focus on rehabilitation rather than guilt, innocence, and punishment. Under parens patriae, the state may deny a child procedural rights given to adults because children, unlike adults, can be made to do certain things (i.e., go to school), and the state may intervene if the parents are delinquent in their duties. The court noted that this is not a deprivation of rights, because the child does not have any rights. The court referred to *Kent v. U.S. (1966),* in which the court ruled that juveniles are entitled to fundamental fairness and the elements of due process (adequate notice of charges, notification to parents and the child of the juvenile's right to counsel, opportunity for confrontation and cross-examination, and safeguards against self-incrimination). The court noted that Gault and his parents should have been notified of the specific charges and the factual allegations of the case at the earliest possible time. Also, given that Gault's freedom was at stake, he and his parents must be informed of their right to counsel. The court held that the procedures used in Gault's case met none of the requirements set forth in *Kent.*

Quick Summary

Juveniles are entitled to criminal due process protections (i.e., notice of charges, the right to counsel, the right to confront witnesses, to appeal, and privilege against self-incrimination).

In re Subpoena Served Upon Jorge S. Zuniga, M.D., et al.
714 F.2d 632 (1983)
Nos. 82-1906, 82-1907 and 82-1964.
United States Court of Appeals, Sixth Circuit

Case Facts

Zuniga, a psychiatrist licensed in Michigan, had a practice organized as a professional corporation. On March 30, 1982, the Grand Jury for the Eastern District of Michigan issued a subpoena commanding Zuniga, or an authorized custodian of his records, to appear before the grand jury and produce patient and office records, essentially limited to patients' names, dates of service, and type of service provided. Zuniga filed a motion to quash the subpoena, which was denied but limited the subpoena to the production of records for 75 of the original 268 patients and confined the scope of the subpoena to the prior five years. On July 15, 1982, the grand jury issued a new subpoena ordering the production of additional documents. Zuniga moved to quash the second subpoena, but the motion was denied again. Zuniga persisted in his refusal to comply and the district Court found Zuniga in contempt and remanded him to the custody of the U.S. Marshal until he complied with the subpoena. Execution of the order was stayed pending this appeal.

Zuniga contended on appeal that the documents sought by the grand jury are protected from disclosure for three reasons: (1) a psychiatrist-patient privilege, (2) the patients' constitutional privacy right, and (3) the Fifth Amendment's privilege against self-incrimination.

Two preliminary observations were necessary. First, because the subpoenas came from a federal grand jury investigation into alleged violations of federal criminal law, questions of privilege were governed by federal law. Second, although subpoena powers of a grand jury are very broad, a grand jury may not use its authority to violate a valid privilege, whether it was established by the constitution, statutes, or common law. Thus, the court must determine if federal law recognizes a psychiatrist-patient privilege and, if so, whether enforcement of the grand jury subpoenas would violate that privilege. Although reception of psychotherapist-patient privilege in federal courts has been mixed, it was determined that the court has the authority to recognize a psychiatrist-patient privilege, but the authority must be exercised with caution.

Main Issue

Are psychiatrist-patient records, limited to (a) the identity of the patients, (b) the treatment dates, (c) and the length of the treatment on each date, protected from federal grand jury subpoena?

Court Holding

No. The U.S. Court of Appeals for the Sixth Circuit concluded that Zuniga's refusal to comply with the grand jury subpoenas in order to protect patient privacy was unjustified, and the lower courts' judgments of contempt were therefore proper.

Court's Reasoning

Regarding the first argument (psychiatrist-patient privilege), the court determined that patient privacy interests, in general, outweigh the need for evidence in the administration of criminal justice. However, in the case of Zuniga, the information sought by the grand jury subpoenas was limited and not considered to fall within the psychiatrist-patient privilege. Therefore, the balance tipped in favor of disclosure. The court reasoned that while the essential element of the psychotherapist-patient privilege is its assurance to patients that they may express their innermost thoughts without fear of disclosure, mere disclosure of the patient's identity does not negate this element. Thus, the court concluded that the identity of patients or the fact and times of their treatment does not, in general, fall within the scope of the psychotherapist-patient privilege. Accordingly, the information sought by the grand jury subpoenas was considered not privileged. Additionally, in this case, the patients had already disclosed their identities to a third party (i.e., Blue Cross/Blue Shield), thereby waiving the privilege regarding their identity.

In their second argument (the patients' constitutional right to privacy), the court noted that the grand jury was seeking limited information pertaining to individual patients, and the identity of the patients was already known to the grand jury from the insurance forms in its possession. Additionally, the information would be protected by the veil of secrecy attending grand jury proceedings. In sum, weighing the slight intrusion on the patients' privacy interest against the need for the grand jury to conduct an effective and comprehensive investigation into alleged violation of the law, the court concluded that enforcement of the subpoenas does not unconstitutionally infringe on the privacy rights of the patients.

Regarding the third argument (Fifth Amendment's privilege against self-incrimination), the court noted that Zuniga's practice was maintained as professional corporation and, as such, the billing records were corporate rather than private records. As a result, the Fifth Amendment could not be used to deny production of the subpoenaed information.

Quick Summary

In the context of federal investigations into billing fraud, the identities of patients, their dates of service, and the services they received may be subpoenaed by a grand jury. Such records are not subject to psychiatrist-patient privilege; therefore, failure to supply the records can result in the practitioner being charged with contempt of court.

In re Winship
387 U.S. 358 (1970)
U.S. Supreme Court

Case Facts

Samuel Winship was 12 years old when he stole $112 from a woman's wallet. The petition that charged him indicated that similar crimes committed by an adult would constitute larceny. The judge relied on the New York Family Court Act, which stated that the burden of proof for juvenile hearings was a preponderance of the evidence. Winship was sent to a training school for 18 months, which could be extended with review until his 18th birthday. The appellate court affirmed without opinion. The U.S. Supreme Court granted certiorari to examine the proper standard of proof for juvenile criminal court hearings.

Main Issue

What is the appropriate standard of proof for juvenile criminal trials?

Court Holding

The U.S. Supreme Court reversed and held that the standard of preponderance of the evidence in juvenile criminal court is unconstitutional.

Court's Reasoning

Proof beyond a reasonable doubt is required in the interest of due process for adults and should be guaranteed for juvenile defendants as well. Due Process mandates that each element be proven beyond a reasonable doubt to ensure proper protections against false or erroneous convictions. The court cited the protections decided in Gault, including notice of charges, right to counsel, and the right to confrontation and cross-examination, when it reasoned that another right juveniles should be afforded is the same standard of proof as in adult court.

Quick Summary

Juvenile criminal defendants who are charged with an offense that would be considered a crime if they were adults should be afforded a standard of proof beyond a reasonable doubt rather than a preponderance of the evidence in accordance with the constitutional requirements of due process. Further, every element of a charged offense must be proven beyond a reasonable doubt.

Indiana v. Edwards
554 U.S. 164 (2008)
U.S. Supreme Court

Case Facts

Ahmad Edwards, a man with schizophrenia, attempted to shoot at a security guard in a store and ended up injuring an innocent customer. He was charged with attempted murder, battery, and other charges. He was evaluated and determined to be incompetent to stand trial. He was hospitalized for treatment and was determined eventually, after approximately seven months, to be restored to competency, but his attorneys soon requested another evaluation. He was again deemed competent to stand trial, although noted to be mentally ill. As his defense team prepared for trial, they again noticed challenges in effectively working with Mr. Edwards and requested a third competency evaluation in which he was found to be incompetent to proceed and was again hospitalized. Eight months later he was considered competent to proceed with trial. Mr. Edwards requested to represent himself, but the request was denied, and he was convicted on some charges, although the jury could not reach a decision on the attempted murder charge. Before the second trial, Mr. Edwards again requested to waive counsel, but the judge denied the request based on Mr. Edwards' long history of mental illness. Counsel was appointed for trial, and he was convicted on the attempted murder charge. He appealed, arguing that his right to represent himself was violated. Both the appellate court and the Supreme Court of Indiana agreed with Edwards and remanded for a new trial. Indiana asked for U.S. Supreme Court review, which was granted.

Main Issue

Should the standard for competency to stand trial be the same as the standard for competency to waive counsel and represent oneself?

Court Holding

No. The court here held that the abilities required to represent oneself are more complex than those involved in, for example, deciding how to plead. The standard for competency to represent oneself at trial should be higher than competency to stand trial or to plead.

Court's Reasoning

The court acknowledged that prior cases had decided that the skills required to plead are subsumed in the competency to stand trial assessment but that the skills required to conduct proceedings oneself is higher. The court further reasoned that the perception of a fair trial is also important and that a defendant with mental illness would likely struggle to effectively navigate a trial successfully. Therefore, counsel may be appointed by the court even if a defendant has been found competent to stand trial if they have not been deemed competent to represent themselves. No standard was established to specify the competencies required to meet this higher bar; it is left up to states and lower courts to decide.

Quick Summary

There is now a different standard for competency to stand trial and competency to waive counsel and represent oneself at trial. While the court noted that competency to plead is subsumed under a general competency to proceed assessment, competency to represent oneself is a more complex task requiring more advanced skills. The specific skills required for representing oneself were undefined and left to states to determine.

Ira v. Janecka
419 P.3d 161 (N.M. 2018)
New Mexico Supreme Court

Case Facts

Defendant Joel Ira "pled no contest to ten counts of criminal sexual penetration, one count of aggravated battery (great bodily harm), one count of aggravated battery against a household member, and one count of intimidation of a witness. Ira committed these crimes when he was 14 and 15 years old. The victim of Ira's criminal sexual penetration and intimidation of a witness offenses was his stepsister, who was six years younger than Ira." Ira was sentenced as an adult under NMSA 32A-2-20(B)(1)-(2), because he was "not amenable to treatment or rehabilitation as a child in available facilities" and was "not eligible for commitment to an institution for the developmentally disabled or mentally disordered." Ira's adult sentence was 91 ½ years in the New Mexico Department of Corrections. Upon appeal, the Court of Appeals affirmed this sentence on the basis that it was not in violation of the Eighth Amendment right against cruel and unusual punishment. Ira then filed a writ of habeas corpus in the district court. In the writ, "he argued that (1) his sentence constitutes cruel and unusual punishment in violation of the Eighth Amendment and Article II, Section 13 of the New Mexico Constitution; (2) the trial court erred in failing to set aside his plea agreement; and (3) he was denied effective assistance of counsel." The New Mexico Supreme Court granted Ira certiorari to hear his case.

Main Issues

Do the U.S. Supreme Court decisions, *Roper v. Simmons* (2005), *Graham v. Florida* (2010), and *Miller v. Alabama* (2012) support the argument in defendant Ira's writ of habeas corpus? In other words, does the exculpatory neurodevelopmental evidence from these cases warrant reconsideration of Ira's 91-½-year sentence for crimes he committed at ages 14 and 15?

Court Holding

The Supreme Court of New Mexico affirmed the district court's denial of defendant Ira's habeas corpus petition. In other words, this court held that Ira's Eighth Amendment rights were *not* in violation, even in light of recent U.S. Supreme Court decisions that acknowledged the relationship between brain development, on the one hand, and culpability and amenability to treatment and positive change, on the other hand.

Court's Reasoning

Ultimately, this court reasoned that defendant Ira was not "deprived of a meaningful opportunity to obtain release by demonstrating his or her maturity and rehabilitation" because "Ira can be eligible for a parole hearing when he is 62 years old if he demonstrates good behavior." However, this court also acknowledged the significance of *Roper*, *Graham*, and *Miller*, as they pertains to juvenile sentencing as follows: (1) "juveniles' developmental immaturity makes them less culpable than adults"; (2) "juveniles have a greater potential to reform than do adults criminals which makes it essential that they have a meaningful opportunity to obtain release based on demonstrated maturity and reform"; and (3) "no penological theory—retribution, deterrence, incapacitation, and rehabilitation—justifies imposing a sentence of life without parole on a juvenile convicted of a non-homicide crime because juveniles are less culpable and more amenable to reformation."

Quick Summary

Defendant Joel Ira was sentenced to 91½ years as an adult after pleading no contest to ten counts of criminal sexual penetration, among other similar charges. After unsuccessfully appealing his sentence, his case went to the Supreme Court of New Mexico through a writ of certiorari, on the basis that newer neurodevelopmental evidence, and U.S. Supreme Court decisions (*Roper v. Simmons*, 2005; *Graham v. Florida*, 2010; and *Miller v. Alabama*, 2012) justified reconsideration of Ira's lengthy adult sentence. However, the New Mexico Supreme Court affirmed the district court's denial of the petition, on the basis that Ira was not being deprived of opportunities to obtain release at age 62 years, through demonstration of his maturity and rehabilitation.

Jablonski v. United States
712 F. 2d 391 (9th Cir. 1983)
Ninth Circuit Court of Appeals

Case Facts

On July 7, 1978, Phillip Jablonski agreed to psychiatric treatment in a Veterans Affairs (VA) facility after attempting to rape his girlfriend's mother. Police called the VA hospital and told the head of psychiatry about Mr. Jablonski's criminal history and that he should be admitted to their inpatient unit. The head of psychiatry said he would relay the message to Mr. Jablonski's treating psychiatrist but he never did. A few days later, Mr. Jablonski went to the VA for psychiatric evaluation and revealed that he had previously raped his wife and attempted to rape his new girlfriend's mother. The psychiatrist recommended that Jablonski voluntarily admit himself into the hospital, but he refused. The psychiatrist believed that there was no basis for involuntary hospitalization at that time, despite what he had heard and the girlfriend indicating to the doctor that she felt insecure around Jablonski. On July 14, 1978, Mr. Jablonski and his girlfriend returned to the VA where he again refused voluntary admission, and again the psychiatrist saw no basis for involuntary admission. Mr. Jablonski's girlfriend told another doctor how unsafe she felt around Mr. Jablonski, and that doctor told his psychiatrist and also told her to stay away from him. The psychiatrist still did not see a need to hospitalize him involuntarily. He also never sought to review prior treatment records. On July 16, 1978, Mr. Jablonski killed his girlfriend. Their daughter brought a wrongful death suit against the VA alleging that the doctors committed malpractice that was directly proximate to her mother's death. The district court ruled in her favor, and the government appealed.

Main Issue

What is the scope of Tarasoff (see *Tarasoff v. Regents of University of California 17 Cal 3d. 425 1976*) and should it extend to a foreseeable victim even if the patient has not made specific threats?

Court's Holding

The appellate court affirmed the lower court's ruling in favor of the daughter. There is a duty to warn a foreseeable victim of an offense even in the absence of specific threats.

Court's Reasoning

The court applied *Tarasoff* to this case and found:

1. A psychotherapist-patient relationship existed.
2. The psychiatrist knew or should have known that Mr. Jablonski was dangerous.
3. The girlfriend was a foreseeable victim.
4. The psychiatrist did not take the necessary steps in discharging his duty.

The court also agreed with the daughter that the proximate cause of the victim's death was the VA's negligence. The court also opined that there was sufficient evidence in Mr. Jablonski's history that even without a direct threat to his girlfriend, she was a reasonably foreseeable target and potential victim of his violence and that vague advice to avoid Mr. Jablonski was inadequate.

Quick Summary

This case extended *Tarasoff* warnings to foreseeable victims even in the absence of specific threats.

Jackson v. Indiana
406 U.S. 715 (1972)
U.S. Supreme Court

Case Facts

In 1968, Theon Jackson was charged with two robberies, one amounting to $4 and the other amounting to $5. Mr. Jackson was deaf and mute, and what the court referred to as a "mental defective." The district court ordered a competency to stand trial evaluation, Mr. Jackson was found incompetent, and the evaluators argued that his chances of ever being competent were "rather dim." An interpreter from a school for the deaf testified that the state had no facilities that could help Mr. Jackson learn even minimal communication skills. Mr. Jackson was committed to the Department of Mental Health until such time that he became "sane" (which meant competent) and could return to court to face his charges. Mr. Jackson asked for a new trial, arguing that if he was going to be committed, it should be done under one of the state's two other commitment statutes (for those with mental illness or "feeble-minded"). The U.S. Supreme Court heard this case.

Main Issue

Is the indefinite involuntary commitment of a defendant solely because they have been deemed incompetent to stand trial unconstitutional?

Court Holding

Yes. The U.S. Supreme Court reversed the district court's decision based on violations of the equal protection clause of the 14th Amendment: 1) The commitment for incompetency was a more lenient commitment standard and a more stringent standard for release than those provided to others who have not been charged with an offense, and 2) the commitment was indefinite and based only on his incompetence to stand trial.

Court's Reasoning

The Supreme Court held that Indiana cannot commit a person for an indefinite amount of time solely based on their incompetence to stand trial. In Indiana, there was no statutory provision for periodic review of the defendant's competency and, given that Jackson would likely never become competent, this amounted to a life sentence. The standard required to commit a person under the mentally ill or "feeble-minded" statute entailed (1) a showing of mental illness, and (2) a showing that the person needs care, treatment, training, or detention (which includes dangerousness). Further, under those statutes, the person is eligible for release when their condition "justifies it" rather than having to become competent ("sane") to be released. Mr. Jackson may have been eligible for release under the other two statutes, given that he may not have met the standard. Under the competency statute, he would never have been entitled to release at all given his inability to become competent to stand trial.

Quick Summary

The Supreme Court in this case found it unconstitutional to commit a person indefinitely due solely to incompetence to stand trial and instead argued that, without a finding of dangerousness, a person can only be held for "a reasonable period of time" necessary to determine if there's a chance that they will attain competence in the foreseeable future. If the defendant does not meet civil commitment criteria, and restoration to competence is unlikely, they must be released or given a hearing.

Jaffee v. Redmond
518 U.S. 1 (1996)
United States Supreme Court

Case Facts

In June 1991, Officer Mary Lu Redmond was the first to respond to a fight in progress. According to her testimony, when she arrived on the scene, two of Ricky Allen's sisters ran out of the apartment screaming that someone had been stabbed. Allen had a butcher knife in his hands and disregarded Redmond's commands to drop it. Redmond believed that Allen was going to stab one of the men, so she shot him. Allen died on the scene. In federal district court, Jaffee (acting for the deceased Allen) filed suit alleging that Redmond used excessive force and thus violated Allen's constitutional rights. After the incident, Redmond participated in 50+ therapy sessions with a licensed social worker. Jaffee wanted access to the mental health records for use in cross examination. While the social worker and Redmond asserted that the records were protected by psychotherapist-patient privilege, the district judge disagreed. Redmond and the clinician continued to refuse to turn over the records. The judge advised the jury that they were permitted to draw an adverse inference from their refusal and to presume that the records would have been unfavorable to the defendant. The Court of Appeals reversed and remanded under FRE Rule 501 pertaining to privilege ("reason and experience"). It stated that the "ability to communicate freely without the fear of public disclosure is the key to successful treatment." The court noted that psychotherapist-patient privilege requires a weighing of conflicting interests; specifically, the evidentiary need for disclosure of the patient's counseling weighed against the patient's privacy. The court indicated that there was no evidentiary need due to the eyewitnesses' accounts provided at trial and that Redmond's privacy was more important.

Main Issue

Are statements made between patient and therapist during counseling sessions protected from disclosure in federal action cases?

Court's Holding

Yes. Confidential communications between licensed psychotherapists (including social workers) and their patients in the course of diagnosis or treatment are protected from disclosure under FRE Rule 501.

Court's Reasoning

- "[Rule 501] is not immutable but flexible, and by its own principles adapts itself to varying conditions."

- Rule 501 is meant to reflect the importance and privilege of a confidential relationship between therapist and patient and should be determined on an individual basis.
- Not much evidence would be lost by the implementation of privilege because, with the limits of confidentiality warning, litigants would not offer incriminating or otherwise prejudicial information that would be useful in court. The court agreed with state legislatures and the Judicial Conference Advisory Committee that the mere possibility of disclosure may impede the therapeutic relationship and thus interfere with treatment; therefore, exceptions to the rule must be justified and done in an effort to find the truth because.
- The primary concern is to promote the public's interest. The psychotherapist-patient privilege promotes treatment and therefore is in the public's interest. In giving patients the limits to confidentiality, both parties "must be able to predict with some degree of certainty whether particular discussions will be protected." All 50 states recognize psychotherapist-patient privilege and agree that "reason and experience" support privilege.

Quick Summary

This important case in mental health law was the first to look at the psychotherapist-patient privilege. Confidential communication between therapist and patient is protected under Federal Rules of Evidence, Rule 501.

Jenkins v. United States
307 F.2d 637 (D.C. Cir. 1962)
District of Columbia Circuit Court of Appeals

Case Facts

In September 1959, Mr. Vincent Jenkins was committed to the District General Hospital (DGH) for an examination to determine his competency to stand trial and his sanity at the time of the offense of sexual assault. He participated in numerous psychological tests including intelligence testing (IQ = 63, extremely low) and clinical interviews by both psychiatrists and psychologists. The DGH examiners opined that Jenkins was "suffering from an organic brain defect resulting in mental deficiency and impaired judgment." They also concluded that Jenkins was psychotic and incompetent to stand trial. The court committed him to St. Elizabeth's Hospital until his competency was restored. During Jenkins' commitment period, the examiners at St. Elizabeth's had different opinions regarding his diagnosis, which included schizophrenia, no mental disease or defect, and borderline intelligence (IQ = 74). It was noted that Jenkins did not suffer from mental illness, but rather only had borderline intelligence and was competent to proceed. The court agreed, but the DGH examiners were asked to examine his criminal responsibility at the time of the offense. Upon the review of all data, the DGH examiners concluded that Jenkins "is psychotic and schizophrenic" and changed their original diagnosis to schizophrenia. At trial, the jury was instructed to disregard the testimony of the St. Elizabeth's psychologists who opined on Jenkins' mental state at the time of the alleged offenses. The court held that psychologists were not qualified to testify as an expert witness on issues related to the presence or absence of a mental disease or defect. Mr. Jenkins was subsequently convicted of the charges and appealed the court's finding on grounds that the psychologists' testimonies should not have been disregarded.

Main Issue

Are psychologists permitted to offer opinions about the nature and existence (or non-existence) of mental disease or defect and testify as expert witnesses about those issues?

Court Holding

Yes. The U.S. Court of Appeals for the D.C. Circuit held that psychologists are qualified to provide expert testimony in the matter of the presence or absence of mental disease or defect. The court reversed Jenkins' conviction and ordered for a new trial.

Court's Reasoning

The U.S. Court of Appeals found that expert testimony is based on two essential elements:

- The witness must be distinctively related to some science, profession, business, or occupation.
- The witness must have such skill, knowledge, or experience in that field so it will aid the trier of fact in finding the truth of the matter.

The court referenced other cases in which nonmedical professionals served as expert witnesses, such as doctoral-level toxicologists. The court recognized that the training and experiences of psychologists varies greatly and that determining a psychologist's qualification to provide expert testimony must depend on the nature and extent of their knowledge.

Quick Summary

In this important case, the U.S. Court of Appeals for the D.C. Circuit decided that psychologists who have completed the doctoral educational and training requirements as determined by the American Psychological Association or who have achieved board certification have meet the qualifications necessary to be considered an expert witness in cases involving the absence/presence of mental disease or defect.

Johnson v. Texas
509 U.S. 350 (1993)
U.S. Supreme Court

Case Facts

Defendant Johnson, who was 19 years old at the time of the offense, robbed a convenience store. During the commission of the robbery, Johnson took the store clerk to the store's cooler and shot him in the back of the neck, killing him. Upon arrest, Johnson confessed to the robbery and shooting, and was tried and convicted of capital murder. Under Texas's capital sentencing statute, the trial court instructed the jury to answer two special issues: (1) whether Johnson's conduct was deliberate and with the reasonable expectation that the death of the victim would result; and (2) whether there was "a probability that the defendant … would commit criminal acts of violence that would constitute a continuing threat to society." In mitigation, Johnson presented his father as his only witness. Johnson's father attributed Johnson's criminal activities to his drug use and his youth, citing his "undeveloped mind" and immaturity. Johnson's trial counsel emphasized that, given Johnson's youth, there was a possibility that he could change. The jury found that the answer to both special issues was yes, and the trial court sentenced Johnson to death. On direct appeal, Johnson argued that the special issues did not allow for adequate consideration of his youth. The Texas Court of Criminal Appeals affirmed the trial court. Johnson petitioned for certiorari, and the Supreme Court granted review.

Main Issue

Does the Texas sentencing system violate the Eighth Amendment, because it does not allow the jury to give adequate mitigating effect to evidence of a defendant's youth?

Court Holding

No.

Court's Reasoning

Under the second special issue, the jury was instructed to decide whether there was "a probability that the defendant … would commit criminal acts of violence that would constitute a continuing threat to society." The jury was also told that it could consider all the mitigating evidence that the defendant had presented during the guilt and punishment phases of trial. Under *Graham v. Collins* and other Supreme Court cases evaluating Texas's capital sentencing scheme, so long as mitigating evidence is within "the effective reach of the sentencer," the requirements of the Eighth Amendment are satisfied. The jury's instructions, coupled with the testimony of Johnson's father regarding Johnson's youth, provided a meaningful basis for the jury to consider youth as a mitigating factor. No additional instruction or vehicle for consideration of his youth was required.

Quick Summary

A 19-year-old defendant was sentenced to death for capital murder under Texas's capital sentencing scheme. Texas's capital sentencing jury instructions directed the jury to consider the "probability" that the defendant would commit future violent acts and pose a threat to society, but did not provide any additional instruction for consideration of the defendant's youth as a mitigating factor. The Supreme Court held that the jury instructions were consistent with the Eighth Amendment, and no special instructions for consideration of a defendant's youth were required.

Johnson v. Zerbst
304 U.S. 458 (1938)
U.S. Supreme Court

Case Facts

Mr. Johnson was arrested and charged with "feloniously uttering and passing four counterfeit twenty-dollar Federal Reserve notes and possessing twenty-one such notes." Johnson was unable to post bail, so he remained in jail, until the indictment, at which time he and an accomplice "immediately were arraigned, tried, convicted and sentenced that day to four and one-half years in the penitentiary." Mr. Johnson and his codefendant had legal counsel during the preliminary hearings, but they had no legal counsel for the trial. The men both pled not guilty, but were tried, convicted, and sentenced—without legal representation. Mr. Johnson filed a writ of habeas corpus on the basis that his Sixth-Amendment right to counsel had been denied at the federal district court and then the court of appeals. The U.S. Supreme Court granted Mr. Johnson's writ.

Main Issue

Does a criminal defendant have a right to legal representation during a trial?

Court Holding

Yes.

Court's Reasoning

The court reasoned that it is a violation of the Sixth Amendment to not have legal representation during a criminal trial, unless the defendant has intelligently waived their right to counsel. Moreover, the Court reasoned that an intelligent waiver of Sixth Amendment rights depends on case-specific facts and circumstances: "The determination of whether there has been an intelligent waiver of the right to counsel must depend, in each case, upon the particular facts and circumstances surrounding that case, including the background, experience, and conduct of the accused."

Quick Summary

Mr. Johnson was arrested and charged with counterfeiting. Despite having some legal representation earlier in the legal proceedings, he had no legal counsel during the trial, where he and a codefendant were found guilty and sentenced to 4 ½ years in the penitentiary. After unsuccessful attempts at the federal district court and court of appeals, the U.S. Supreme Court granted Mr. Johnson's writ of habeas corpus and concluded that the lower courts had erred. This case is significant because it emphasizes the Sixth Amendment right to counsel during criminal proceedings, unless a defendant intelligently waives that right.

Jones v. Mississippi
141 S. Ct. 1307 (2021)
U.S. Supreme Court

Case Facts

Defendant Brett Jones was convicted of murder for killing his grandfather when he was 15 years old. Under Mississippi law at the time, murder carried a mandatory sentence of life without parole, and the trial court imposed that sentence. Subsequently, the Supreme Court decided *Miller v. Alabama*, which held that the Eight Amendment permits a sentence of life without parole for juvenile offenders, but only if the sentence is not mandatory. The Mississippi Supreme Court ordered that Jones be resentenced in accordance with *Miller*. At resentencing, the trial court acknowledged that he had discretion to impose a lesser sentence, but determined that life without parole was the appropriate sentence. Jones appealed, citing both *Miller* and the more recently decided case of *Montgomery v. Louisiana*, which held that *Miller* applied retroactively on collateral review. Jones argued that under *Miller* and *Montgomery*, the court must make a separate factual finding of permanent incorrigibility before sentencing a juvenile defendant to life without parole.

Main Issue

Under the Eighth Amendment, must a sentencer make a separate factual finding of permanent incorrigibility before sentencing a juvenile defendant to life without parole?

Court Holding

No. The fact that a sentencing system is discretionary is constitutionally sufficient.

Court's Reasoning

The court held that under *Miller*, sentencers need only follow a certain process—considering an offender's youth and attendant characteristics—before imposing a life-without-parole sentence. And in *Montgomery*, the court stated that "a finding of fact regarding a child's incorrigibility ... is not required." Accordingly, *Miller* and *Montgomery* require consideration of an offender's youth, but not any particular factual finding. The court held that Jones' re-sentencing complied with *Miller* and *Montgomery* because the court had discretion to impose a sentence less than life without parole in light of Jones' youth.

Quick Summary

Defendant was sentenced as a juvenile to life without parole, and appealed on the ground that more recent Supreme Court authority required the trial court to make a separate factual finding of permanent incorrigibility before it could issue a life-without-parole sentence. The Supreme Court held that neither the Eighth Amendment nor its precedents require a factual finding of permanent incorrigibility. Rather, it is sufficient that a sentencing system is discretionary and allows consideration of an offender's youth and attendant characteristics.

Jones v. United States
463 U.S. 354 (1983)
U.S. Supreme Court

Case Facts

In 1975, Mr. Michael Jones was found not guilty by reason of insanity (NGRI). Under D.C. Code, a defendant may be acquitted NGRI if it is proven by a preponderance of the evidence. He was committed to St. Elizabeth's Hospital for treatment. D.C. Code also provides NGRI acquittees with a 50-day hearing and a hearing every six months, allowing for the opportunity to show recovery and consequently, release. At the hearing, a psychologist testified that Mr. Jones' illness is "still quite active," and he is "still a danger to himself and to others." At a second release hearing, he demanded to be released unconditionally or recommitted pursuant to civil commitment standards, which included a jury trial and a standard of proof of clear and convincing evidence of ongoing mental illness and dangerousness. His motion was denied. Mr. Jones' commitment was then extended because he did not meet the preponderance of the evidence threshold, indicating that he was no longer mentally ill and dangerous. Mr. Jones appealed to the D.C. Court of Appeals, which affirmed and rejected his arguments that the length of the prison sentence had he been incarcerated would have allowed for him either to be released or civilly committed (via clear and convincing burden of proof). The D.C. Court of Appeals found "various statutory differences between civil commitment and commitment of insanity acquittees under the equal protection clause of the Fifth and Fourteenth Amendments," which allowed for his continued hospitalization because he did not meet the burden of proof for his release. U.S. Supreme Court granted certiorari.

Main Issue

Is a finding of NGRI, in and of itself, a constitutionally adequate reason for the involuntary and indefinite commitment of a defendant to a psychiatric hospital and by what burden of proof? Is there a difference regarding burden of proof and standards for civil commitment versus commitment of those adjudicated NGRI?

Court Holding

NGRI acquittees may be involuntarily and indefinitely committed to a psychiatric hospital until they are able to prove by a preponderance of the evidence that they are no longer mentally ill and/or no longer a danger to self or others. The burden of proof for commitment to a hospital following an adjudication of NGRI is permissibly lower (preponderance of the evidence) than a civil commitment burden (clear and convincing).

Court's Reasoning

NGRI acquittees may be hospitalized given that their mental illness caused them to commit a criminal act. The government's interest in avoiding a commitment hearing after every NGRI acquittal outweighs the acquittee's interest in avoiding an unjustified psychiatric hospitalization. NGRI acquittees have a mental illness that is "presumed to continue" and thus they "should automatically be confined for treatment until it can be shown that they have recovered." The criminal act (regardless of severity) is an indication of "dangerousness" and meets the criteria for commitment. *Clear and convincing* is not the standard required in NGRI cases for commitment because the "risk of errors" in committing NGRI acquittees are less than those in civilly committed cases. An NGRI adjudication establishes that the defendant is dangerous due to a legitimate illness and hospitalization is for treatment not punishment. The length of the acquittee's possible sentence is unrelated to the purposes of NGRI commitment because "there simply is no necessary correlation between severity of the offense and length of time for recovery."

Quick Summary

Preponderance of the evidence is constitutionally permissible as a standard for the confinement of NGRI acquittees because they have already established a mental illness (insanity) and dangerousness (a criminal act). The successful NGRI adjudication serves as mentally ill and dangerous criteria. There are statutory differences between civil commitment and commitment of insanity acquittees under the equal protection clause of the 5th and 14th Amendments. Length of hospitalization may exceed the length of the maximum sentence if found guilty of the offense.

Jurasek v. Utah State Hospital
158 F.3d 506 (1998)
No. 97-4082.
U.S. Court of Appeals, Tenth Circuit

Case Facts

Jan Jurasek, with a history of paranoid schizophrenic, was civilly committed to the Utah State Hospital on April 12, 1991. At the commitment hearing, a Utah state court determined (1) Jurasek suffered from a mental illness, (2) Jurasek posed an immediate physical danger to himself and others because of his mental illness, (3) Jurasek lacked the ability to engage in rational decision-making regarding the acceptance of mental treatment, (4) there was no appropriate less-restrictive alternative to court-ordered inpatient care, and (5) the hospital could provide Jurasek with adequate and appropriate treatment. Jurasek was examined by an independent psychiatrist prior to the commitment hearing and was represented by counsel. The original commitment was for six months. At the conclusion of that period, a Utah state court reviewed Jurasek's commitment and extended it for an indeterminate period. Jurasek was treated with psychotropic drugs from the time he was admitted to the hospital. He continuously objected to the treatment, so it was administered against his will. In deciding to forcibly medicate Jurasek, the hospital committee determined Jurasek was "gravely disabled."

Jurasek filed a lawsuit in federal district court seeking injunctive relief and damages based on the premise that being subjected to forced medication violated his 14th Amendment due process and First Amendment free expression rights. The defendants responded they had not violated Jurasek's constitutional rights, but, even if they had, the doctrine of qualified immunity absolved them of liability. The district court denied Jurasek's request for injunctive relief and granted the defendants' motion for summary judgment. Jurasek appealed.

Main Issue

Can a patient who has been involuntarily committed to psychiatric hospital because he or she is gravely disabled be forcibly administered antipsychotic medications if it is in his or her best interests clinically?

Court Holding

The Court of Appeals affirmed the district court's order granting summary judgment in favor of defendants. Because Jurasek had been adjudicated gravely disabled, and treatment with psychotropic drugs has been found to be in his medical best interests, the hospital may treat him with psychotropic drugs without employing further substantive due process protections.

Court's Reasoning

Individuals have a personal liberty interest in avoiding the unwanted administration of antipsychotic drugs under the Due Process Clause of the 14th Amendment. When an individual is confined in a state institution, individual liberties must be balanced against the interests of the institution in preventing the individual from harming themself or others who reside or work in the institution.

The parties in this case disagreed over how to balance Jurasek's due process rights with the hospital's interests in health and safety. The Court of Appeals concluded that the standards established in *Harper* for involuntarily medicating prisoners strike the appropriate balance. Accordingly, the Due Process Clause allows a state hospital to forcibly medicate a mentally ill patient who has been found incompetent to make medical decisions if the patient is dangerous to himself or others and the treatment is in the patient's medical interests.

The court noted that treatment with psychotropic drugs is not punishment, and the lack of punishment in the context of forced medication removes any need to provide involuntarily-committed patients with greater due process protection than prisoners. Moreover, unlike prisoners, involuntarily-committed patients have been adjudicated incompetent in a prior formal proceeding, thereby minimizing the potential for abuse of rights.

The court further noted that an individual's classification as "gravely disabled" provides sufficient overriding justification for involuntary medication. However, a hospital may not rely on a commitment court's determination unless such determination was made close in time to the hospital's decision to medicate.

Although the hospital may treat him with psychotropic drugs without employing further substantive due process protections, the hospital must afford him procedural due process before administering such treatment. Such procedures require (a) a committee of independent medical personnel to examine whether the patient should be treated with psychotropic drugs, (b) permit the patient to appeal the committee's decision to a hospital official, (c) authorize the patient to be present at the hearing with an advisor, and (d) allow the patient to present evidence and cross-examine witnesses. Further, if the committee determines that the patient should be medicated, the policies require that the committee support its decision with adequate documentation. The Court of Appeals concluded that the Hospital provided Jurasek with procedural due process.

Jurasek also insisted that his due process rights were violated because he was not found to be incompetent to make medical decisions on his own behalf. However, the Court of Appeals noted that here could hardly be a clearer finding of Jurasek's inability to make medical decisions on his own behalf than that found by the commitment court. The court also noted that if Jurasek believed the commitment court's determination was wrong or became obsolete because of changed circumstances, he could request a review hearing.

Jurasek further argued that a mentally ill person who is involuntarily committed under the Utah Mental Health Code has a right to have a legal guardian make medical decisions that are inconsistent with treatment determined appropriate by the hospital. However, the court determined that Jurasek had no absolute right to the "substituted judgment" of a guardian under Utah law and found that the district court correctly rejected Jurasek's due process claim.

The Court of Appeals also agreed with the district court that the defendants were protected from liability pursuant to the qualified immunity doctrine, which shields government officials "performing discretionary functions … from liability for civil damages insofar as their conduct does not violate clearly established statutory or constitutional rights of which a reasonable person would have known."

Quick Summary

Balancing a patient's due process rights with a hospital's interests in the health and safety of its patients and employees can be challenging and may require some patients to be medicated against their wishes. Patients who have been involuntarily committed to psychiatric hospital because they are gravely disabled can be forcibly administered antipsychotic medications if it is in their best interests.

Jurek v. Texas
428 U.S. 262 (1976)
U.S. Supreme Court

Case Facts

Defendant Jurek was convicted of capital murder, after kidnapping, strangling, and drowning a ten-year-old girl in the course of attempting to commit forcible rape. During the sentencing phase of Jurek's trial, the jury heard testimony from the state, and Jurek's father testified on Jurek's behalf. The jury then considered two questions required by Texas's capital sentencing statute: (1) whether the evidence established beyond a reasonable doubt that the murder of the deceased was committed deliberately and with the reasonable expectation that the death of the deceased or another would result; and (2) whether the evidence established beyond a reasonable doubt that there was a probability that the defendant would commit criminal acts of violence that would constitute a continuing threat to society. The jury unanimously answered "yes" to both questions and the judge, in accordance with the statute, sentenced Jurek to death. The Texas Court of Criminal Appeals affirmed, and the Supreme Court granted cert to review the judgment.

Main Issue

Does the imposition of the death sentence for the crime of murder under Texas law violate the 8th and 14th Amendments to the constitution?

Court Holding

No.

Court's Reasoning

In order to be constitutional, a capital sentencing scheme must allow the jury to consider all relevant evidence as to why a death sentence should be imposed, and also why it should not be imposed—that is, aggravating and mitigating circumstances. Texas addresses aggravating circumstances by narrowing its definition of capital murder to five types of crimes, in essence requiring that at least one aggravating circumstance must be met before a defendant can be charged with a capital crime. Although the Texas statute does not directly speak to mitigating circumstances, in asking the second statutory question to juries—whether there is a probability that the defendant would commit criminal acts of violence that would constitute a continuing threat to society—the statute allows consideration of particularized mitigating factors. In Jurek's case, the Court of Criminal Appeals indicated that it would interpret that second question so as to allow a defendant to bring to the jury's attention whatever mitigating evidence he could show. Because Texas law allows consideration of both aggravating and mitigating factors, and because it also provides for prompt judicial review through the Court of Criminal Appeals, its capital sentencing procedure is constitutional.

Quick Summary

Defendant sought review of Texas's capital sentencing scheme, claiming it violated the 8th and 14th Amendments. The Supreme Court held that although Texas does not explicitly direct juries to consider mitigating circumstances, the statutory questions directed to juries in death penalty deliberations allow consideration of mitigating factors. Because the Texas statute allows defendants to present mitigating evidence to juries, it is consistent with the requirements of the constitution.

Kane v. United States
399 F. 2d 730 (9th Cir. 1969)
Ninth Circuit Court of Appeals

Case Facts

In 1966, Coe Kane shot and killed his wife within the boundaries of the Fort Apache Indian Reservation in Arizona. Prior to the shooting, he had suffered several head injuries with substantial periods of loss of consciousness. He testified that he was drunk and blacked out during the shooting. He also testified that he was aware that alcohol was causing him to become unconscious following the most recent head injury. Four qualified forensic mental health experts testified at trial. Only one of them opined that the defendant had chronic and undifferentiated schizophrenic disorder and was insane at the time of the offense due to the combination of stress in the moment, plus the drinking. The other three experts disagreed and opined that he had pathological intoxication, which is a latent mental condition caused by head injuries that lowers the tolerance for, and increases reaction to, alcohol. The experts agreed that Kane did not have this condition when sober, only when he drank, and that he was aware of this condition. The jury found him guilty of the included offense of voluntary manslaughter and sentenced him to ten years in prison. He appealed, arguing that his mental condition did warrant an instruction on insanity. The Court of Appeals affirmed the lower court's findings.

Main Issue

Is pathological intoxication considered a mental disease or defect for the purposes of an insanity defense?

Court Holding

There is no judicial recognition of pathological intoxication rising to meet the definition of mental disease or defect, but, even if there were, it would be predicated on the pathological reaction being idiosyncratic as opposed to previously known by the defendant.

Court's Reasoning

Although there is no judicial precedent that recognizes pathological intoxication as an affirmative defense, even if one existed, it would require that the defendant not know they are uniquely and especially susceptible to the intoxication. In this case, the defendant admitted that he knew he had severe reactions to alcohol intoxication, such as blackout and loss of consciousness, and that they were increasing in frequency over time. His alcohol use was not such that he could not prevent an episode of drinking. Therefore, the effects to his mental state were previously known and avoidable.

Quick Summary

Pathological intoxication that results from a previously existing latent condition, such as brain damage, is not judicially recognized. An important consideration, if it were, would be the extent of the defendant's knowledge of that individualized reaction and sensitivity (i.e., idiosyncratic or repetitive).

Kansas v. Crane
534 U.S. 407 (2002)
U.S. Supreme Court

Case Facts

Michael Crane pleaded guilty to aggravated sexual battery after he exposed himself to a tanning salon attendant, and 30 minutes later he exposed himself to a clerk in a video store. In the second incident, he grabbed the clerk by the neck and forced her to perform oral sex on him. He threatened to rape her before running out of the store. The state filed a petition to have Mr. Crane evaluated and adjudicated a sexual predator under the Kansas Sexually Violent Predator Act (SVPA). According to SVPA, a person with prior sexual offenses must be proven beyond a reasonable doubt to have a "mental abnormality" or a "personality disorder" that makes the person "likely to engage in repeat acts of sexual violence," and the person "cannot control their dangerous behavior." Crane was evaluated by psychologists who opined that he was an exhibitionist and had ASPD but agreed that his mental disorder "did not impair his volitional control to the degree he cannot control his dangerous behavior." Mr. Crane argued that the state must prove that he is unable to control his dangerous behavior. The jury found that Mr. Crane was a sexual predator per SVPA. The Kansas Supreme Court reversed, saying that the probability of violent recidivism, as well as lack of control over violent behavior, is required for a finding of sexually violent predator status. The state argued that the Kansas Supreme Court was too rigid in its interpretation of the prior precedent set in *Kansas v. Hendrix, 1997*. The U.S. Supreme Court granted certiorari.

Main Issue

Was the SVPA in Kansas unconstitutionally applied in this case because the defendant only had an emotional or personality disorder?

Court Holding

No. The U.S. Supreme Court agreed that the Kansas Supreme Court's interpretation of *Hendrix* was too rigid. The ability to control dangerous behaviors is not an absolute construct.

Court's Reasoning

The Supreme Court reasoned that the nature and severity of the mental abnormality must be sufficient to distinguish between dangerous sexual offenders whose mental illness/abnormality/disorder subjected them to civil commitment and other dangerous recidivists whose case could be resolved in criminal proceedings. *Hendrix* referred to the SVPA as requiring the presence of some sort of mental abnormality that makes it "difficult" to control dangerous behaviors. In *Hendrix*, it was implied that an absolute and complete lack of control was needed in order to civilly commit a sexually violent person. The problem with this interpretation is that any sexually violent recidivist who had some sort of mental abnormality but did not demonstrate a complete lack of control over his behaviors would not meet the SVPA criteria for civil commitment. Thus, the Supreme Court reconsidered *Hendrix*. It was noted that the term "difficult" suggests that a person's ability to control his dangerous behavior may be judged on a continuum. Behavioral control is not an absolute construct.

Quick Summary

Sexual offenders do not need to have a complete lack of control over their dangerous behaviors in order to be civilly committed as sexually violent predators under the act.

Kansas v. Hendricks
521 U.S. 346 (1997)
U.S. Supreme Court

Case Facts

The SVPA was enacted in Kansas in 1994. This law made it legal to civilly commit individuals who had either a "mental abnormality" or a "personality disorder" and were deemed likely to commit "predatory acts of sexual violence" in the future. It was first applied to Mr. Leroy Hendricks, "who had a long history of sexually molesting children, and who was scheduled for release from prison." Mr. Hendricks had already served his sentence for sexually molesting children, but was going to be forcibly civilly committed on the basis that he had a "mental abnormality" or a "personality disorder" and was likely to commit more "predatory acts of sexual violence." Mr. Hendricks opposed the commitment and argued that his due process rights were being violated because "mental illness" (a mental health term) is different from "mental abnormality" (a legal term). He further claimed that he was being sentenced twice for the same crime (a double-jeopardy violation) because he not only had to serve time in prison, but he then had to serve time in a psychiatric facility. Kansas Supreme Court invalidated the act because a "mental abnormality" was not the same as the requirement of "mental illness" for civil commitment. This case went to the U.S. Supreme Court.

Main Issue

Was Kansas's SVP Act—a legal mechanism to force individuals into a psychiatric facility after serving prison time for sex crimes—in violation of due process as well as the Double Jeopardy Clause of the U.S. Constitution?

Court Holding

No. The U.S. Supreme Court reversed and held that Kansas's SVP Act was *not* unconstitutional:

Court's Reasoning

Using the legal term, "mental abnormality," to characterize Mr. Hendricks's sexually violent behavior instead of the mental health term, "mental illness," was not viewed as a violation of due process: "Contrary to Hendricks' assertion, the term 'mental illness' is devoid of any talismanic significance. Not only do 'psychiatrists disagree widely and frequently on what constitutes mental illness,' … but the Court itself has used a variety of expressions to describe the mental condition of those properly subject to civil confinement." There was no meaningful difference between having a "mental abnormality" and having a "mental illness" in the context of sexually violent predators. Double jeopardy rights were not invoked because the civil commitment was part of civil proceedings, not criminal proceedings, part of treatment not punishment.

Quick Summary

Civil commitment of sexually violent predators, following their prison term, is not unconstitutional. As long as ongoing dangerousness is linked with a mental condition, the State can set their terminology for that condition (i.e., mental illness vs abnormality). Pedophilia (and potentially other paraphilias) can meet criteria for a mental condition requiring commitment if the person is thought to pose a danger to society.

Kent v. United States
383 U.S. 541 (1966)
U.S. Supreme Court

Case Facts

Sixteen-year-old Morris Kent was arrested in Washington, D.C. after it was suspected that he broke into a woman's apartment, raped her, and stole her wallet. Kent confessed to police about the incident as well as other similar offenses. As a result of his age, he would be under the jurisdiction of the juvenile court unless there was to be a waiver to adult court. He was waived to adult court but without reason, "full investigation," or hearing. Kent claimed the waiver was invalid, but the court overruled, and he was tried in adult court. He was convicted on some counts and found not guilty by reason of insanity on others. He was committed to a psychiatric hospital and also to prison for 30 to 90 years. The U.S. Court of Appeals for the D.C. circuit affirmed the waiver. The U.S. Supreme Court granted certiorari.

Main Issue

What Due Process protections should apply to juveniles in the criminal justice process, and what are the criteria for waiver to adult court for juvenile defendants?

Court Holding

The waiver to adult court was invalid. The juvenile defendant was not granted a hearing, the defense attorney was not provided with requested records, and there was no articulation of the reasons for waiver. The case was remanded to district court to be vacated if it found that the waiver was inappropriate.

Court's Reasoning

The court noted concerns that juveniles were being afforded far fewer rights and protections than adult defendants, especially once they were waived out of the normally more protective juvenile system. While the D.C. Juvenile Court Act allowed a juvenile's waiver to adult court after a "full investigation" for any child 16 years of age and older, no standards for that waiver determination were ever detailed. The court reasoned that this process should not be arbitrary and is a very important decision for the statutory rights of the juvenile. The parens patriae spirit governing juvenile procedures are not a substitute for, nor permission granting, "an invitation for procedural arbitrariness." A juvenile is entitled to counsel, and that counsel is allowed to receive and review social service records. If the court approves a waiver to adult court, there must be a hearing in which the reasons are clearly articulated for the transfer. The court also pointed out factors to be considered by the Juvenile Court when making transfer decisions, such as the type and seriousness of the offense, the manner in which the offense was committed, the age and maturity level of the defendant, the juvenile's criminal record, and the likelihood for rehabilitation.

Quick Summary

This case identified the importance of ensuring due process protections for juvenile defendants, especially when it comes to waiver to adult court. The court cited the importance of taking arbitrariness out of waiving juveniles to adult court and required appointment of counsel and a hearing with clear factors to be addressed.

Kumho Tire Co. v. Carmichael
526 U.S. 137 (1999)
U.S. Supreme Court

Case Facts

In 1993, Patrick Carmichael was driving his used minivan when the right rear tire blew out, resulting in a serious accident. The Carmichaels sued the tire company, Kumho Tire, claiming the blow out was due to a defective product. Their case relied mainly on the expert testimony of the tire failure analysis conducted by a Mr. Carlson. Some of the testimony he offered was considered widely accepted in the field. He also testified that there was a manufacturer defect, which caused the tire to blow out. Kumho Tire argued that Mr. Carlson's testimony should be excluded because it did not meet the Daubert criteria and that it should be excluded under FRE 702. The trial court agreed, and the testimony was excluded. The Carmichaels appealed, arguing that the court was too rigid when applying Daubert, and the 11th Circuit agreed and reversed the district court's ruling. The appellate court indicated that Daubert only applied to scientific expert testimony and not to "skill or experienced-based observation" and that the trial court judge should have allowed the testimony in under unscientific "observation and experience" considerations rather than just the scientific validity of the testimony. Kumho Tire then petitioned the court to ask if a trial court is allowed to admit evidence that is based on "technical or other specialized" knowledge under Daubert. The U.S. Supreme Court heard the case.

Main Issue

Should the Daubert factors apply to all types of expert testimony to include "technical" or "other specialized knowledge" that may be garnered through experience or just applied to scientific knowledge testimony?

Court Holding

Daubert criteria and analysis should apply to all types of expert testimony that would typically be outside the grasp of the average juror and assessed under FRE 702. The U.S. Supreme Court agreed with district court and reversed the appellate court's decision.

Court's Reasoning

It is often difficult for trial judges to clearly differentiate what constitutes "scientific" versus "other specialized or technical knowledge" and there is no reason to differentiate them because in both cases, the testimony is being used to assist the court in understanding information that is beyond common knowledge. The U.S. Supreme Court agreed with the district court that the reliability of the tire expert's testimony could not be assessed because it was based on the expert's assertions and not scientific merit. The district court acted within its discretion as gatekeeper when it excluded the tire expert's testimony.

Quick Summary

A trial court judge's role as gatekeeper allows them to apply the Daubert factors not only to scientific testimony but to all types of expert testimony, scientific or not.

Lipari v. Sears, Roebuck & Co.
497 F. Supp. 185 (D. Nebr. 1980)
United States District Court for the District of Nebraska

Case Facts

Ulysses Cribbs, Jr. began psychiatric day treatment program in 1977 at a Veterans Administration (VA) Hospital in Nebraska. While in the program he purchased a shotgun from Sears, Roebuck & Co., although he never gave his providers any indication of dangerousness. Approximately one month after initiating treatment at the VA, Cribbs terminated his mental health treatment against medical advice. In late November 1977, Cribbs went to a nightclub with the shotgun and opened fire into the crowd. During his rampage, he shot and killed Dennis Lipari and seriously injured his wife, Ruth Ann Lipari. Lipari sought damages for the wrongful death of her husband and for her personal injuries. She alleged that Sears should have known that Cribbs was mentally ill or that he had been committed, and thus Sears was negligent in selling a gun to such a person. Sears filed a complaint against the United States (representing the VA Hospital) for negligence. Sears alleged that the VA should have known that Cribbs was mentally ill and posed a risk for violence to self and others and should have taken the necessary precautions to minimize the risk. Lipari filed a similar complaint against the United States, claiming that the VA was negligent in failing to detain or civilly commit Cribbs. The U.S. filed a motion to dismiss, claiming that a therapist cannot accurately predict dangerous and therefore should not be held liable and that mentally ill patients have a right to be in the least restrictive environment.

Main Issue

Should Nebraska law impose a duty on a therapist to take "reasonable precautions to protect potential victims" of the patient when the therapist knows that the patient poses a risk of violence to others?

Court Holding

The U.S. district court for the district of Nebraska held that therapists do have a duty to control the conduct of their patients and to protect potential victims only when the therapist knows (or should know) that the patient poses a risk of harm to others. Regardless of therapists' inaccurate "predictions" of violence, the risk of violence is typically uncovered when exercising "reasonable care" of a patient.

Court's Reasoning

The Nebraska Supreme Court had never addressed the issue of a therapist's duty to protect third persons, so it considered other analogous issues that have been raised in other Nebraska courts and the case law of other jurisdictions. There was no relationship between the VA and Mr. & Mrs. Lipari, thus the court only considered the relationship between Mr. Cribbs and the VA treatment team. The court referred to Tarasoff and other cases that found the doctors/hospitals are responsible for their patients' actions and thus may be held liable if dangerous patients are negligently released. The court adopted the "special relationship" rule and found that a therapist-patient relationship fits under this rule (e.g., a doctor preventing the spread of contagious disease). The court indicated that therapists who use "proper psychiatric procedures" in their care of a patient cannot be found negligent even if their opinions/recommendations were incorrect. Finally, the court agreed with the passage in Tarasoff, which states that a therapist should "warn the intended victim of the danger, notify the police, or take whatever other steps are reasonably necessary under the circumstances."

Quick Summary

Therapists have a duty to take reasonable steps to protect potential victims of their clients when the therapist knows or should know of the client's dangerousness.

> ***Lockett v. Ohio***
> **438 U.S. 586 (1978)**
> **U.S. Supreme Court**

Case Facts

Sandra Lockett drove a getaway car during the commission of a robbery that ended in murder. In Ohio, her offense was punishable by death if convicted, which she was. After her sentencing, she appealed, seeking relief because she had not been given an opportunity to present mitigating evidence at the penalty phase, which, she argued, violated her 8th and 14th Amendment rights. The Ohio Supreme Court affirmed the conviction and sentence, and the U.S. Supreme Court granted certiorari.

Main Issue

Was Ohio's death penalty law unconstitutional because it prevented the sentencer from being able to consider all mitigating evidence at the sentencing phase of a capital trial?

Court Holding

Yes. The state statute was unconstitutionally narrow. While the statute did allow the sentencing body to consider several factors, including whether (a) the victim of the murder induced the crime, (b) the defendant was under duress or coercion at the time, or (c) the defendant was mentally ill at the time, it prevented the introduction of further mitigating evidence. The prevention of additional available mitigation was unconstitutional.

Court's Reasoning

The court reasoned that in order for the Ohio death penalty statute not to violate cruel and unusual punishment standards, it had to permit mitigating evidence pertaining to the defendant's age, character, or details of the offense at sentencing. The Ohio statute did not permit a sentencing body to consider evidence that the defendant had not intended to kill the victim, played a minor role in the murder, or other potentially mitigating information that could have altered her sentence. The 8th and 14th Amendments provide for a defendant to introduce more mitigating evidence than the Ohio statute permitted. There were psychiatric reports about Ms. Lockett's rehabilitation potential, intelligence level, participation in substance abuse treatment, and lack of prior major offenses. This information, according to the Court, should have been before the lower court for consideration at sentencing.

Quick Summary

It is unconstitutional to place such serious restrictions on the mitigating evidence a sentencing court can consider in a capital trial as was done in this Ohio case. The U.S. Supreme Court held that a sentencer should be able to consider a wider range of mitigating factors in in capital trials to prevent a constitutional violation.

Madison v. Alabama
139 S. Ct. 718 (2019)
U.S. Supreme Court

Case Facts

Vernon Madison was convicted of capital murder of a police officer and sentenced to death. While in prison he suffered a series of strokes and was diagnosed with vascular dementia. He petitioned the court for a stay of execution because, he argued, he could not remember the events of the crime he committed. The state claimed he understood the rational reasons for his execution despite being unable to remember the crime and was not delusional (as implicated in *Ford v. Wainwright* and *Panetti v. Quarterman)*. The trial court found him competent to be executed. Court of Appeals reversed and granted the stay, and the U.S. Supreme Court granted review.

Main Issue

Is it a violation of the Eighth Amendment to execute a prisoner because they have amnesia for the crime for which they were sentenced to death? Does the Eight Amendment apply to amnesia the same way it does to psychotic delusions?

Court Holding

No, it is not a per se violation of the Eighth Amendment to execute a prisoner who lacks memory for the crime. Yes, the Eighth Amendment applies to amnesia the same way it does to issues of psychotic illness. The U.S. Supreme Court reversed the Court of Appeals stay of execution. Amnesia for the crime does not, alone, prohibit the execution of a prisoner who was sentenced to death for that crime. A person who lacks memory for the crime he or she has committed still may have a rational understanding for the reasons for the execution.

Court's Reasoning

Prior rulings, for example in *Ford v. Wainwright* and *Panetti v. Quarterman,* permit the execution of a prisoner who does not recall the crime. *Panetti* asks only about the inmate's comprehension of the reasons for the execution not about memory of the offense. If loss of memory is one symptom of a larger set of symptoms that interferes with competence, it may be implicated but it is not sufficient alone. Both cases hinge on the prisoner's incomprehension of the reason they have been singled out for execution. The focus is on the effect of the impairment, not the cause. The court was not satisfied with the lower court's reasoning that Madison did not prove "insanity" and noted that there should have been a discussion about amnesia and dementia specifically. Whether the defendant presents with amnesia or delusions or another mental condition, the issue really is the effect on competence. Amnesia or psychosis similarly may or may not impact competency (the ability to have a rational understanding of the reason for execution). In both the *Ford* and *Panetti* decisions, the fundamental issue was that the prisoner has a rationale for the punishment and that if there were a mental illness or mental disease that impeded that understanding, execution would serve no retributive purpose. The court, in those cases, emphasized the importance of the offender being able to grasp the link between his crime and the punishment. What matters is the ability to appreciate and rationally understand the reason for the execution and its relation to the crime, not the specific mental disorder present.

Quick Summary

This case fleshed out what it means to be competent to be executed and focused on capacity and the inmate's ability to rationally apply the punishment to the crime rather than narrowing the specific mental disorder to delusions or other symptoms of psychosis alone. Competency to be executed is based on functioning, impairments, and abilities rather than a specific diagnosis.

Maryland v. Craig
497 U.S. 836 (1990)
U.S. Supreme Court

Case Facts

Sandra Ann Craig, who operated a preschool and kindergarten, was accused of having sexually abused a six-year-old child. The child was permitted, despite Craig's objections, to testify via a closed-circuit television rather than in live court to avoid the potential for emotional distress for the child. Although the child testified outside of the courtroom, the defendant and her attorney were allowed to object, and the judge and jury watched the testimony from in the courtroom. The trial court convicted her, but the court of appeals reversed it, and the U.S. Supreme Court granted certiorari.

Main Issue

Is it a violation of the Confrontation Clause of the Sixth Amendment to allow a child to testify outside of the courtroom via closed-circuit television?

Court Holding

No. The Confrontation Clause of the Sixth Amendment is not absolute and, in certain circumstances, removing confrontation may be warranted at trial.

Court's Reasoning

The court reasoned that the state has an interest in protecting the welfare of a child and that the need to protect the physical and psychological welfare of a child could be sufficiently important to outweigh the confrontation rights of the accused. The importance of protecting a child witness from the trauma of testifying in a child abuse case may warrant, in a given case, a special procedure that supersedes the right of the accused to confront witnesses. This decision should be made on a case-by-case basis with a hearing to address whether the child would be traumatized by the defendant's presence, and whether the trauma would be more than *de minimis* (too trivial to justify consideration or special accommodations). The Maryland statute went beyond the minimal criteria of *de minimis* and required a showing that the child would suffer severe emotional distress, which the court indicated clearly met constitutional standards. Additionally, the child was placed under oath, subjected to cross examination, and able to be observed by the judge and jury, so there was no serious deprivation of due process.

Quick Summary

A state's procedure for the remote (closed-circuit television or similar accommodations) testimony of a child witness in a child abuse case does not violate the Confrontation Clause of the Sixth Amendment, provided minimal standards are met during a hearing prior to the testimony.

McClesky v. Kemp
481 U.S. 279 (1987)
U.S. Supreme Court

Case Facts

McClesky was a black defendant convicted in Georgia of armed robbery and murder, arising from the killing of a white police officer during a store robbery. The jury recommended the death penalty and the trial court followed the recommendation. McClesky appealed and the Georgia Supreme Court affirmed. After unsuccessfully seeking postconviction relief in the state courts, McClesky filed a habeas petition. His petition included a claim that the Georgia capital sentencing process was administered in a racially discriminatory manner, in violation of the 8th and 14th Amendments. In support of his claim, McClesky offered a statistical study (the Baldus study) that showed a disparity in the imposition of the death sentence in Georgia based on the murder victim's race and the defendant's race. The Baldus study indicated that black defendants who killed white victims, as in McClesky's case, had the greatest likelihood of receiving the death penalty. The federal district court denied McClesky's petition and the Court of Appeals affirmed. The Supreme Court granted cert.

Main Issue

Is the Georgia capital punishment system unconstitutional under the 8th and 14th Amendments?

Court Holding

No. The Baldus study, while valid, does not show that the administration of Georgia's capital punishment system constitutes unconstitutional discrimination in the 14th Amendment context, or irrationality, arbitrariness, and capriciousness under the Eighth Amendment.

Court's Reasoning

In order to prevail under the Equal Protection Clause of the 14th Amendment, a petitioner must prove that the decision-makers in his case acted with discriminatory purpose. Here, McClesky offered no evidence specific to his own case that would support an inference that racial considerations played a part in his sentence, and the court held that the Baldus study was insufficient to support that inference. McClesky's related argument that Georgia violated the Equal Protection Clause by adopting and allowing the capital sentencing statute despite its discriminatory application also failed. To prevail, McClesky would have to show that the legislature enacted the statute for a discriminatory purpose, or maintained it because of its racially disproportionate impact. The court held that McClesky offered no support for such a claim. With regard to the Eighth Amendment claims, the court held that the Baldus study did not show that Georgia's capital punishment system is arbitrary and capricious in its application. According to the court, the statistics in the Baldus study did not prove that race enters into any capital sentencing decisions in Georgia, or that race was a factor in McClesky's case.

Quick Summary

A defendant challenged his death sentence in Georgia, on the basis of a study that showed a disparity in the imposition of the death sentence, based on the races of the murder victim and the defendant. According to the study, black defendants who killed white victims had the greatest likelihood of receiving the death penalty. The defendant argued this racial disparity showed that Georgia's capital punishment system was unconstitutional under the 8th and 14th Amendments. While the Supreme Court acknowledged that the study was valid, it held the defendant had to prove that the decision-makers in *his* case had acted with a discriminatory purpose, and that Georgia's capital punishment system was arbitrary and capricious in its application. According to the court, the study was insufficient to prove either point. The court affirmed the death sentence.

McCoy v. Louisiana
138 S.Ct. 1500 (2018)
No. 16-8255
Supreme Court of United States

Case Facts

Robert McCoy was charged with murdering his estranged wife's mother, stepfather, and son. McCoy pleaded not guilty to first-degree murder, insisting that he was out of state at the time of the killings and that corrupt police officers killed the victims when a drug deal went wrong. At defense counsel's request, a court-appointed sanity commission examined McCoy and found him competent to stand trial. Although McCoy insisted on his innocence and strongly objected to any admission of guilt, the trial court permitted his counsel to tell the jury, during the trial's guilt phase, that McCoy committed the murders. The strategy was to concede, over McCoy's repeated objections, that McCoy committed the murders but that McCoy's mental state prevented him from forming the specific intent necessary for first-degree murder.

McCoy testified in his own defense, maintaining his innocence and pressing an alibi that was difficult to believe. The jury returned a verdict of guilty of all three counts of first-degree murder. At the penalty phase, his counsel again conceded McCoy's guilt, but urged mercy in view of McCoy's mental and emotional issues. However, the jury returned three death sentences. Represented by new counsel, McCoy unsuccessfully sought a new trial. The Louisiana Supreme Court affirmed the trial court's ruling that the original counsel had authority to concede guilt, despite McCoy's opposition. The U.S. Supreme Court granted certiorari in view of a division of opinion among state courts of last resort on the question whether it is unconstitutional to allow defense counsel to concede guilt over the defendant's intransigent and unambiguous objection.

Main Issue

Does a criminal defendant have the right to insist that their attorney argue their innocence with respect to all charged offenses?

Court Holding

Yes. Counsel may not admit a client's guilt over the client's objection to that admission. The judgment of the Louisiana Supreme Court was reversed, and the case was remanded for further proceedings.

Court's Reasoning

The Sixth Amendment guarantees a defendant the right to choose his or her defense and to insist that his or her counsel refrain from admitting guilt, even when counsel's perspective is that confessing guilt offers the defendant the best chance of avoiding the death penalty. The lawyer's province is trial management, but some decisions are reserved for the client, including whether to plead guilty, waive the right to a jury trial, testify on one's own behalf, and forgo an appeal. Autonomy to decide that the objective of the defense is to assert innocence belongs in this reserved-for-the-client category.

Quick Summary

Counsel may not admit a client's guilt of a charged crime over the client's objection to such admission.

McDonald v. United States **312 F. 2d 847 (D.C. Cir. 1962)** **District of Columbia Circuit Court of Appeals**

Case Facts

Ernest McDonald was convicted of manslaughter for aiding and abetting his employer in a shooting. A psychiatrist and a psychologist both testified that the defendant had a "mental defect" primarily because of an IQ score of 68, which, the psychiatrist explained, probably prevented him from progressing past the sixth grade. The psychologist also testified about an impaired state of development and its relationship to the ability to appreciate right and wrong. The court failed to include not guilty by reason of insanity for the jury to choose from regarding verdict. Although defense did not object to the jury instructions, Mr. McDonald, on appeal, cited *Durham v. U.S.* claiming that there was enough evidence of mental disease or defect raised in trial to instruct the jury on other available mental health adjudications.

Main Issue

What constitutes "some evidence" or enough evidence to require the affirmative defense of sanity, and what does mental disease or defect mean?

Court Holding

The D.C. appellate court held that what psychiatrists and psychologists may consider mental disease or defect clinically may be different from what courts are to consider for the purposes of determining criminal responsibility. The jury should be told, regardless of what mental health experts may discuss for the purposes of treatment, that *a mental disease or defect should be any abnormal condition of the mind which substantially affects mental or emotional processes and substantially impairs behavior controls.* It is up to the jury, not an expert, to decide if a defendant had a mental disease or defect, and they may consider lay and expert testimony in arriving at that decision. The court held that the defendant did not waive an instruction on insanity for the jury to consider and that the case should be retried with those instructions.

Court's Reasoning

Juries should receive instructions on a sanity adjudication if the evidence has raised the issue of mental disease or defect that may have impacted the defendant's ability to distinguish right from wrong. The court reasoned that the conviction should be reversed for Mr. McDonald because the judge did not instruct the jury on a verdict of not guilty by reason of insanity.

Quick Summary

The court here provided a definition of mental disease or defect and held that it is up to the court, not the experts, to decide whether the defendant met the criteria. Legal and clinical definitions of mental disease are distinct.

Medina v. California
505 U.S. 437 (1992)
U.S. Supreme Court

Case Facts

In 1984, Mr. Teofilo Medina was charged with a number of offenses, including murder. At a defense-requested competency hearing, the presumption in California was that the defendant was competent to stand trial and had the burden to prove incompetence by a preponderance of the evidence. He was found competent to stand trial, convicted, and sentenced to death. He appealed. The Supreme Court of California upheld the conviction and held that it was not a violation of his due process rights to place the burden to demonstrate incompetence on the defendant by a preponderance of the evidence. The U.S. Supreme Court agreed to review the case.

Main Issue

Is it constitutional for a state to presume a defendant is competent to stand trial and place the burden to prove incompetence to stand trial on the defendant, or is it a violation of due process rights?

Court Holding

It is constitutional for a state to presume that defendants are competent and to place the burden of demonstrating incompetence to stand trial on the defendant by a preponderance of the evidence.

Court's Reasoning

The court reasoned that it was permissible to place the burden on the defendant to show incompetence by a preponderance of the evidence for the following reasons:

1. Placing the burden on the defendant does not offend a fundamental principle of justice.
2. The defendant's potential inability to assist counsel in proving incompetence can be further evidence of incompetence, and defense counsel can best articulate that.

3. Although psychiatry is not an exact science, there are still ways to demonstrate incompetence, even placing the burden on the defendant.
4. Placing the burden on the prosecution would not deter lawless conduct by the government.
5. There was no reason to disagree with the State Supreme Court's opinion that presumption of competence is a restatement of the burden of proof.

Quick Summary

It is not a violation of due process to place the burden on the defendant to prove their incompetence to stand trial by a preponderance of the evidence. It is acceptable to presume competence and place the burden on the defendant to prove their incompetence.

Menendez v. Super. Court
834 P.2d 786 (Cal. 1992)
California Supreme Court

Case Facts

Jose and Mary Louise Menendez were killed in their Beverly Hills, California, home in 1989. Their sons reported the murders and were arrested and charged with murder. The sons had been in therapy with a psychologist prior to the murders and had revealed homicidal thoughts to him. A search warrant was executed for the psychologist's office and residence. The psychologist claimed the psychotherapist-patient privilege when refusing to allow access to three audiotapes, which contained information related to the charges. The defendants also filed papers in support of the privilege.

Main Issue

Does the psychotherapist-patient privilege extend to the case-related audio tapes in the psychologist's possession, or is there a "dangerous patient" exception to privilege? What information is still privileged when there is a Tarasoff duty?

Court Holding

The Supreme Court of California said the privilege does not apply in all situations. It does apply to confidential patient-therapist communications, but that there are times when it can be broken due to a "dangerous patient" situation, which some of the information contained in the audiotapes could reveal. The court ruled that the information that was focused on therapy alone was privileged, but it ruled that other information from other sessions, including threats of harm made by the defendants, were not privileged.

Court's Reasoning

The court recognized the importance of privileged communications but also the importance of breaking that privilege if information contained therein contains threats of harm. If there is information provided to the psychologist, such as in this case, that could prevent harm (e.g., threats to kill their parents), that information can and should be released. "To the extent that the Menendez's argue that the 'dangerous patient' exception requires something more than reasonable cause for belief by the psychotherapist in the dangerousness of the patient and the necessity of disclosure, they are unpersuasive." The psychologist should have disclosed the threats of harm revealed to him even though they were made in the context of a psychotherapist-patient relationship.

Quick Summary

In this case, the court considered the balance between protecting the psychotherapist-patient privilege and preventing harm. The psychotherapist who receives risk-related information must have reasonable cause to believe that (1) the patient is dangerous and (2) disclosure is necessary to prevent any harm. Only the information necessary to prevent the harm should be disclosed rather than all communications.

Miller v. Alabama
567 U.S. 460 (2012)
U.S. Supreme Court

Case Facts

In 2003, 14-year-old Evan Miller, along with a friend, burned the home of Cole Cannon and beat him to death. Miller was transferred from juvenile court to adult court for the capital murder. He was found guilty and sentenced to the mandatory life in prison without the possibility of parole. He filed a motion for a new trial, arguing that sentencing a 14-year-old to life without the possibility of parole constituted cruel and unusual punishment under the Eighth Amendment. The trial court denied the motion, and the appellate court affirmed that decision. The U.S. Supreme Court granted certiorari.

Main Issue

Does the Eighth Amendment's prohibition of cruel and unusual punishment forbid the mandatory sentencing of juveniles to life in prison without the possibility of parole?

Court Holding

Yes. The U.S. Supreme Court reversed and remanded, holding that mandatory sentencing of life in prison without the possibility of parole for juvenile homicide offenders was a violation of the Eighth Amendment because it constituted cruel and unusual punishment.

Court's Reasoning

The court highlighted the difference between children and adults and how that difference must be considered for the purposes of sentencing. Life without parole is a constitutionally and disproportionately different punishment for children. At or near the same time, a similar case was being reviewed (*Jackson v. Hobbs)* in which another 14-year-old was tried as an adult, convicted of murder, and sentenced to life in prison without the possibility of parole, even though he was not the shooter. The Supreme Court decided that both sentences violated the Eighth Amendment's prohibition against cruel and unusual punishment, which bans excessive sanctions. Prior to this case, a judge or jury could not consider mitigating information in crafting a sentence for a particular juvenile based on characteristics of the crime, the offender, or anything else, and the law mandated that they remain in prison until they die.

Quick Summary

In this landmark case, the U.S. Supreme Court ruled that sentencing juvenile homicide offenders under age 18 to life in prison without the possibility of parole violated the Eighth Amendment's ban against cruel and unusual punishment.

Miranda v. Arizona
384 U.S. 436 (1966)
U.S. Supreme Court

Case Facts

On March 13, 1963, Ernesto Miranda was arrested and taken into police custody. He was interrogated by two officers who obtained a written confession. On the top was a paragraph stating the confession was made voluntarily, without threats or promises of immunity and "with full knowledge of my legal rights, understanding any statement I make may be used against me." He was not advised of his right to consult with an attorney or to have an attorney present. Per report, one of the officers read this paragraph to Miranda after he had already confessed orally. At trial, the written confession was admitted into evidence despite defense's objection. He was found guilty of kidnapping and rape and sentenced to 20 to 30 years. The Supreme Court of Arizona, on appeal, affirmed the conviction, holding that Miranda did not specifically request counsel, so his constitutional rights were not violated. The U.S. Supreme Court reversed.

Main Issue

What constitutes proper and sufficient warnings by police to an in-custody suspect prior to interrogation?

Court Holding

- The prosecution may not use statements stemming from questioning initiated by law enforcement officers after a person has been taken into custody or otherwise deprived of his freedom of action in any significant way, unless it demonstrates the use of procedural safeguards effective to secure the Fifth Amendment's privilege against self-incrimination.
- The atmosphere of interrogation is inherently intimidating and works to undermine the privilege against self-incrimination. Unless adequate preventive measures are taken to dispel the compulsion inherent in custodial surroundings, no statement obtained from the defendant can truly be the product of free choice.
- The privilege against self-incrimination guarantees to the individual the "right to remain silent unless he chooses to speak in the unfettered exercise of his own will," during a period of custodial interrogation.
- The person in custody must, prior to interrogation, be clearly informed that he or she has the right to remain silent, and that anything he or she says will be used against them in court; they must be clearly informed that they have the right to consult with a lawyer and to have the lawyer with them during interrogation, and that, if indigent, a lawyer will be appointed to represent them.
- If the individual indicates, prior to or during questioning, that they wish to remain silent, the interrogation must cease; if they want an attorney, the questioning must cease until an attorney is present.
- Where an interrogation is conducted without the presence of an attorney and a statement is taken, a heavy burden rests on the government to demonstrate that the defendant knowingly and intelligently waived the right to counsel.
- The warnings required and the waiver needed are prerequisites to the admissibility of any statement, inculpatory or exculpatory, made by a defendant.

Court's Reasoning

Mr. Miranda was not informed of his right to consult with an attorney or to have one present during the interrogation. His right not to incriminate himself was not protected effectively. Because he signed a statement containing the above clause did not mean he "knowingly and intelligently" waived his right.

Quick Summary

Law enforcement agencies have to protect the constitutional rights of all citizens (Fifth and Sixth Amendments implicated here). When a person is first subjected to police interrogation, "while in custody at the station or otherwise deprived of his freedom of action in any way," these issues come into play. However, any statement given "freely and voluntarily without any compelling influences is admissible."

Montana v. Egelhoff
518 U.S. 37 (1996)
U.S. Supreme Court

Case Facts

Mr. James Egelhoff went camping and met two people with whom he later went out drinking. Police responded to a call of a possible drunk driver and, when they arrived, found the two other men shot to death, a gun on the floor of the car, gun residue on the defendant, and Mr. Egelhoff yelling obscenities in the back seat. His blood alcohol concentration was .36 an hour later, and he was charged with the deliberate killing of both men. In Montana, deliberate homicide requires that the killings were committed "purposely" or "knowingly." Defense argued that, due to his level of intoxication, he was unable to commit the murders, there must have been a fourth person present, and that the defendant was unable to recall the events of the night due to his intoxication. Consistent with Montana statute, the jury was instructed not to consider Mr. Egelhoff's intoxication when deciding if he had the requisite mental state to meet the requirements of the elements. He was convicted and appealed based on a claim of a violation of due process as a result of prohibiting the jury from considering whether his voluntary intoxication negated the knowing and purposeful elements of the crime.

Main Issue

Does the Montana statute that instructs the jury not to consider voluntary intoxication when looking at the mental state of the defendant to meet the elements of "knowingly" and "purposely" violate due process?

Court Holding

No. individual states can determine whether to allow or disallow evidence of voluntary intoxication when considering *mens rea* (intent to commit a crime) for an element of a charged offense.

Court's Reasoning

The U.S. Supreme Court reasoned that there is no absolute right to present relevant evidence. In fact, evidence that is privileged or otherwise inadmissible is restricted, and those restrictions may be overcome when they offend "some principle of justice so rooted in the traditions and conscience of our people as to be ranked as fundamental." To determine what constitutes as fundamental, courts look to historical practice and precedent. The court held that, historically, at common law, the courts did not allow evidence of intoxication as an excuse or justification for an element of the required *mens rea*. The issue of voluntary intoxication is new and has not received enough support to be considered fundamental. Also, the common law rule of deterring people from engaging in irresponsible behavior while intoxicated still exists. The due process clause does not prevent states from crafting their criminal laws in a way that does not allow for the presentation of evidence (e.g., voluntary intoxication) that could negate the mental state required for an element of the crime.

Quick Summary

States may choose to permit or exclude evidence of voluntary intoxication for the purposes of negating a *mens rea* element of an offense without violating the defendant's due process rights.

Montgomery v. Louisiana
136 S. Ct. 718 (2016)
U.S. Supreme Court

Case Facts

Defendant Henry Montgomery was 17 years old in 1963, when he was given a mandatory sentence of life without parole for killing a deputy sheriff. Almost 50 years later, the U.S. Supreme Court held in *Miller v. Alabama* that mandatory life without parole for juvenile homicide offenders violates the Eighth Amendment's prohibition on cruel and unusual punishment. After the Supreme Court issued its decision in *Miller*, Montgomery sought collateral review of his sentence. The trial court denied Montgomery's motion on the ground that *Miller* is not retroactive on collateral review. Montgomery applied for a supervisory writ from the Louisiana Supreme Court, which the court denied on the same ground. The Supreme Court granted cert on the question of retroactivity.[1]

Main Issue

Did *Miller* adopt a new substantive rule that applies retroactively on collateral review to convicted defendants who were sentenced as juveniles to life without parole?

Court Holding

Yes. *Miller* is retroactive in cases on state collateral review.

Court's Reasoning

When a substantive rule of constitutional law controls the outcome of a case, the constitution requires state collateral review courts to give retroactive effect to that rule. Substantive rules include "rules prohibiting a certain category of punishment for a class of defendants because of their status or offense." Here, *Miller*'s holding that the sentence of life without parole is disproportionate for the vast majority of juvenile offenders is a substantive rule of law, because it renders the sentence unconstitutional for "a class of defendants because of their status"—that is, juvenile offenders. As a substantive rule of law, *Miller* is therefore retroactive.

Quick Summary

A defendant who was sentenced to life without parole as a 17-year-old challenged his sentence more than 50 years later, after the Supreme Court held in *Miller v. Alabama* that the sentence of life without parole is disproportionate for the vast majority of juvenile offenders. The Supreme Court held that *Miller* announced a new substantive rule of law, and is therefore retroactive in cases on state collateral review.

Moore v. Texas
137 S.Ct. 1039 (2017)
U.S. Supreme Court

Case Facts

Defendant Moore fatally shot a store clerk during a robbery. He was convicted of capital murder and sentenced to death. Moore challenged his death sentence on the ground that he was intellectually disabled and therefore exempt from execution. A Texas state habeas court made detailed factual findings, relying on current medical diagnostic standards, the generally accepted definition of intellectual disability, and testimony from mental health professionals, and determined that Moore was intellectually disabled under *Atkins v. Virginia* and *Hall v. Florida*. It concluded that Moore's death sentence violated the Eighth

Amendment and recommended that it be vacated. The Texas Court of Criminal Appeals (CCA) declined to adopt the judgment of the habeas court, relying instead on outdated and non-clinical evidentiary factors cited in *Ex parte Briseno* to affirm the sentence. *Briseno* was a 2004 case that adopted the definition and standards for assessing intellectual disability contained in the 1992 edition of the American Association on Mental Retardation manual. In reliance on the *Briseno* factors, the CCA refused to consider deficits in Moore's adaptive functioning that could not be directly tied his intellectual functioning, and weighed examples of Moore's adaptive strengths against his adaptive deficits—both in contravention of prevailing standards in the medical community. The CCA also failed to consider the lower end of the standard-error range of Moore's IQ test, improperly concluding that the test established he was not intellectually disabled. Moore appealed, and the Supreme Court granted review.

Main Issue

In rejecting the habeas court's application of medical guidance in favor of the *Briseno* standards, did the CCA's decision violate the Eight Amendment and Supreme Court precedent?

Court Holding

Yes.

Court's Reasoning

Under *Atkins* and *Hall*, states are given the task of developing appropriate ways to enforce the Eighth Amendment's restriction on executing the intellectually disabled. But this discretion is not unfettered. Rather, under *Hall*, adjudications of intellectual disability should be informed by the views of medical experts. In Moore's case, the CCA erred by rejecting the habeas court's application of medical guidance and instead relying on the outdated and non-medical *Briseno* factors in order to narrow the criteria for whether Moore qualified as intellectually disabled. Because *Briseno* "pervasively infected" the CCA's analysis, the court overruled its decision.

Quick Summary

A defendant appealed his death sentence on the ground he was intellectually disabled. A state habeas court relied on prevailing medical standards and expert medical guidance to determine that the defendant was intellectually disabled, and it recommended to the state court of criminal appeals that his sentence be vacated. The state court of criminal appeals rejected the habeas court's finding, relying instead on factors set forth in *Ex parte Briseno*, which were outdated and unsupported by current standards in the medical community. The Supreme Court held that adjudications of intellectual disability in the death penalty context must be informed by the views of medical experts. Accordingly, the court of criminal appeals' reliance on *Briseno* violated the defendant's Eighth Amendment rights. The Supreme Court reversed the lower court's decision.

Murray v. Giarratano
492 U.S. 1 (1989)
U.S. Supreme Court

Case Facts

Indigent death row inmates in Virginia brought a class action alleging they were entitled to appointed counsel for state post-conviction proceedings. The federal district court granted relief under the Supreme Court's decision in *Bounds v. Smith*, which established that states must furnish adequate law libraries in order to guarantee prisoners' "right of access" to the courts. The district court held that death row inmates were entitled to trained legal assistance—more than the relief provided for in *Bounds*—because of the limited time inmates had to prepare their petitions, the complexity of their cases, and the likelihood that the "shadow of impending execution" would interfere with their ability to do legal work. A divided panel for the Fourth Circuit reversed, but an en banc panel subsequently reheard the case and affirmed. The Supreme Court granted review.

Main Issue

Does the Eighth Amendment or Due Process Clause require a state to appoint counsel for death row inmates to pursue state post-conviction relief?

Court Holding

No.

Court's Reasoning

Nothing in the constitution requires states to provide post-conviction proceedings. They are not part of the criminal process,but are civil actions designed to overturn a presumptively valid criminal judgment. In *Pennsylvania v. Finley*, the Supreme Court held that the constitution did not require states to appoint counsel for indigent prisoners seeking post-conviction relief. Although *Finley* was not a death penalty case, the Court held here that the reasoning still applied—post-conviction relief is a discretionary form of appeal, where the role of an attorney is not as a shield to protect against conviction, but as a sword to upset a prior determination of guilt. Because state collateral proceedings are not constitutionally required and serve a different and more limited purpose than trial or a direct appeal, *Finley* applies to death penalty cases. States are not required to provide appointed counsel to indigent death row inmates to pursue state post-conviction relief.

Quick Summary

Indigent death row inmates brought a class action seeking appointed counsel for state post-conviction proceedings. The Supreme Court held that because states are not required to provide post-conviction proceedings, and because post-conviction proceedings are civil actions with a different and more limited purpose than a trial or direct appeal, states are not required to provide appointed counsel.

North Carolina v. Alford
400 U.S. 25 (1970)
U.S. Supreme Court

Case Facts

In 1963, Mr. Henry Alford was indicted for first degree murder. Under N.C. law, a defendant charged with first degree murder could receive life imprisonment instead of the death penalty if they pled guilty. If, on the other hand, they were found guilty at trial, they would receive the death penalty unless the jury recommended life imprisonment. The penalty for second degree murder was two to 30 years imprisonment. Several witnesses gave statements that strongly indicated Mr. Alford's guilt, and his attorney recommended Mr. Alford plead guilty. The prosecutor agreed to accept a plea of guilty to second degree murder. Before the trial court accepted the guilty plea, the court heard damaging testimony from several witnesses, including a police officer who summarized the state's case. During the hearing, Mr. Alford testified that he had not committed the murder but was pleading guilty because he faced the death penalty if he did not do so. The trial court accepted the guilty plea to second degree murder and sentenced Mr. Alford to 30 years of imprisonment. Mr. Alford sought post-conviction relief. He argued that his plea was invalid because it was a product of fear and coercion because of his fear of the death penalty. The Court of Appeals reversed the trial court's decision on the ground that Mr. Alford's plea was made involuntarily because it was motivated principally by fear of the death penalty. The U.S. Supreme Court heard the case.

Main Issue

Can a defendant plead guilty and accept a sentence even when protesting his innocence?

Court's Holding

The U.S. Supreme Court vacated the Court of Appeals decision, holding that the trial court did not commit a constitutional error by accepting Mr. Alford's guilty plea. A defendant can plead guilty and accept a sentence even when protesting his innocence.

Court's Reasoning

A guilty plea that represents a voluntary and intelligent choice among the alternatives available to a defendant, especially one represented by competent counsel, is not compelled within the Fifth Amendment because it was entered to avoid the possibility of the death penalty. There is no constitutional bar to imposing a prison sentence upon a defendant who is unwilling to admit guilt but is willing to waive trial and accept the sentence. A defendant may voluntarily, knowingly, and understandingly consent to the imposition of a prison sentence even if their guilty plea contains a protestation of innocence, when (as in this case), they intelligently conclude that their interests require a guilty plea and there is strong evidence of guilt.

Quick Summary

A defendant can plead guilty and accept a sentence even when protesting his innocence. Making an "Alford plea" means entering into a plea bargain while asserting innocence.

O'Connor v. Donaldson
422 U.S. 563 (1975)
U.S. Supreme Court

Case Facts

Mr. Kenneth Donaldson, who was a married father of three, went to Florida to visit his parents. His parents observed him to be paranoid and delusional. They petitioned the court for a hearing and, although he did not have an attorney, he was subsequently committed to a Florida state hospital for "care, maintenance, and treatment" of paranoid schizophrenia. At the time, Florida state law allowed for the confinement of "mentally incompetent" persons to prevent self-injury or violence to others, or to ensure proper treatment. He had no history of violence toward self or others and was committed only for treatment. When he arrived at the state hospital, he was housed with dangerous offenders, and there was only one doctor (an obstetrician) for 1,000 patients. Mr. Donaldson was subsequently hospitalized for 15 years against his will. In 1971, he filed a class action suit alleging that he (and other patients) had been intentionally and maliciously deprived of their liberty. Dr. O'Connor, who was the director of the hospital, claimed that he was acting "in good faith" and thus should be immune from any liability. A jury considered both compensatory and punitive damages against Dr. O'Connor and the codefendants and awarded Mr. Donaldson $38,500. As soon as he was released, Mr. Donaldson found a job as a hotel clerk and had no problems working and living on his own. The Court of Appeals affirmed the district court's finding. Confined individuals have a constitutional right to receive treatment that will give them a "reasonable opportunity to be cured or to improve his mental condition." The U.S. Supreme Court granted certiorari given the complexity of the issues.

Main Issue

What are the criteria for the involuntarily commitment of a mentally ill individual?

Court Holding

A state cannot constitutionally confine (*without more*) a non-dangerous mentally ill individual who is capable of surviving safely in freedom by themself or with the help of family members or friends.

Court's Reasoning

Prior to this case, mentally ill individuals could be committed to a psychiatric hospital if they were considered to pose a threat of harm to self or others, or if they would receive treatment for their mental disorder. The court reasoned that just because state law permits the confinement of harmless mentally ill individuals does not itself provide a constitutionally adequate reason for confinement. Even if an individual with mental illness is initially confined in a lawful manner, that confinement must be discontinued as soon as the criteria for commitment are no longer met. Mental illness alone is not a sufficient reason to involuntarily commit an individual if they do not pose a threat of harm to self or others. If such individuals can live freely and safely in the community, either on their own or with the assistance of family or friends, then they have the right to do so. A state cannot confine harmless mentally ill individuals as a way to deal with the general public's own intolerance or animosity regarding mental illness.

Quick Summary

It is unconstitutional to involuntarily commit harmless mentally ill individuals who are not also dangerous. Mental illness alone (i.e., without danger to self or others in addition) is insufficient to warrant involuntary civil commitment.

Panetti v. Quarterman
551 U.S. 930 (2007)
U.S. Supreme Court

Case Facts

In 1992, Scott Panetti went to his estranged wife's home, shot and killed his wife's parents, and took his wife and daughter hostage overnight. In his capital murder trial, Mr. Panetti underwent an evaluation to determine if he was competent to waive counsel. Although he had an extensive history of psychiatric hospitalizations, he was found competent to stand trial and waive counsel. He asserted a not guilty by reason of insanity (NGRI) defense but was convicted and sentenced to death. In 2003, following his set execution date, he raised the issue of competence to be executed for the first time. The judge denied the motion without a hearing, but a stay of execution was ordered to allow a "reasonable period of time to consider the evidence of [Panetti's] current mental state." Two experts found him to be aware of his impending execution and, thus, competent to be executed. He objected to the experts' opinions, requested funds for mental health experts, and requested a hearing on his competency, but the court closed the case, arguing that Mr. Panetti "failed to show, by a preponderance of the evidence, that he is incompetent to be executed." The Court of Appeals stated that competency comprises knowledge that the prisoner is going to be executed and why.

Main Issue

At what point can competency to be executed claims be raised? What is the proper test of competency to be executed?

Court Holding

- It is acceptable for an inmate not to raise a claim of incompetence to be executed prematurely.
- The state court's procedures violated 8th and 14th Amendment rights by failing to hold a final competence hearing or to permit expert evidence.

Court's Reasoning

The Antiterrorism and Effective Death Penalty Act of 1996 (AEDPA) states that the "second of successive" petitions that include new/not previously raised claims should be dismissed. However, there are exceptions to AEDPA. The court noted that under the strict interpretation of AEDPA, petitioners may "forever [lose] their opportunity for any federal review of their unexhausted claims." Competence to be executed claims should be brought forth when the claim is first ripe. Further, such evaluations should have "no less stringent standards" than when a prisoner raises incompetency to stand trial. When there is "substantial" evidence of insanity in death penalty cases, the 8th and 14th Amendments entitle the prisoner to a fair hearing and a chance to submit expert evidence. The court reasoned that the fifth circuit's incompetency standard is too restrictive. A prisoner's awareness of the reason for their impending execution is not the same as their rational understanding for the execution. For example, a delusional prisoner may understand that they are to be executed, but unable to associate the punishment with the criminal act. The court, however, did not attempt to lay down the rules governing competency determinations.

Quick Summary

A *Ford* claim (of competence to be executed) can be raised at any point when it is ripe. There is no set standard for determining competency to be executed, but a simple factual awareness of the impending execution is insufficient.

Parham v. J.R.
442 U.S. 584 (1979)
U.S. Supreme Court

Case Facts

JR, a child who was admitted to a Georgia state psychiatric hospital after multiple failed foster care placements, was one of a number of children who brought suit against James Parham and other Georgia state mental health officials for violating their due process rights by admitting them to state hospitals based on the request of a parent. The minors instituted the class action lawsuit arguing that their 14th Amendment rights were being violated due to Georgia's voluntary admission policies and practices. The lower court agreed with the juveniles and found that the Georgia's statutory practices were unconstitutional because they did not provide for an adversarial-type hearing prior or admission. The case made its way to the U.S. Supreme Court which granted certiorari.

Main Issue

Was Georgia's process for voluntarily admitting children under the age of 18 a violation of their constitutional rights under the due process clause of the 14th Amendment? What process is due a minor whose parents or guardian seek state mental health care for their child?

Court Holding

No. Georgia's process for admitting juveniles into state hospitals is reasonable and affords the proper constitutional safeguards and protections. The minor is entitled to a neutral factfinder (e.g., a mental health professional) to determine whether the admission process was fair and correct and whether the child should be admitted. The commitment must also be reviewed periodically.

Court's Reasoning

A child does have an interest in avoiding unnecessary confinement. Parents also have an interest in seeking treatment for their child and are given wide latitude because they are generally thought to want what is in their child's best interest. There needs to be a balance of *parens patriae* (the notion that authorities protect those who cannot protect themselves) and individual liberties. In Georgia, the parent's application for commitment is only the beginning of the process. A mental health professional then must make an independent determination of the need for commitment. There must be an independent finding that the child meets commitment criteria. The child may be released after five days if no longer mentally ill or meeting commitment criteria. The state has interests in not wasting money or staff time and not making the process so strict and arduous that parents will not seek treatment for their children. As long as a child is appointed a neutral factfinder (not necessarily a judicial official) such as a mental health professional, the child is interviewed, and medical, including mental health, records are reviewed, there does not need to be a formal hearing. The court actually reasoned that a hearing may be contraindicated because it could damage the parent-child relationship as well as a treatment relationship. The child's commitment must also be reviewed periodically.

Quick Summary

Children are entitled to some procedural and due process protections prior to admission to a state psychiatric hospital, including the appointment of a neutral factfinder who conducts an interview, reviews records, and provides periodic review of the necessity of ongoing commitment.

Parker v. State
254 A. 2d 381 (Md. Ct. Spec. App. 1969)
Maryland Court of Special Appeals

Case Facts

Jackie Parker was convicted of murder and sentenced to life in prison despite his attempt to raise insanity at trial. An expert testified that Parker had a chronic brain syndrome/brain damage that by itself did not prevent him from appreciating the nature of his actions or the wrongfulness, but when combined with alcohol produced an acute brain syndrome that rendered him insane at the time of the offense. At the time of the trial, the previous M'Naghten standard for insanity was replaced with a Maryland codified definition (Art 59, s 9a). The judge explained to the jury that when considering the defendant's voluntary intoxication as it related to his mental state at the time of the offense, they should decide whether the accused lacked completely the ability to abstain from taking the first drink and then from continued drinking until he reached a state of intoxication. Only after that initial consideration would his intoxication be deemed involuntary and allowed for consideration along with other elements of mental state at the time of the offense. If the jury found that he was able to avoid taking the first drink and then subsequent drinks and ultimately able to prevent intoxication, then his intoxication was to be considered voluntary and could not constitute insanity. Parker appealed, arguing that the jury should be allowed to consider whether voluntary intoxication triggered a separate and distinct psychosis that was proper for a sanity defense. He argued that if mental state is impacted, it should not matter what caused the insanity, and the symptoms that were present at the time should be the focus, rather than their etiology. The Court of Appeals reversed and remanded due to an error in which the jury was instructed that the burden was on the defendant to prove insanity by a preponderance of the evidence, but then the burden shifts to the prosecution to prove beyond a reasonable doubt that he was sane.

Main Issue

Can voluntary intoxication ever be considered when assessing whether a defendant was insane at the time of an offense even if a brain syndrome was triggered by the intoxication?

Court Holding

Voluntary intoxication can be considered in regard to mental state defenses if it results in an unintended and ongoing mental disorder that persists after the direct and acute effects of the intoxication have worn off.

Court's Reasoning

Courts have historically held that acute voluntary intoxication is not a defense to a crime but that settled insanity, or an ongoing mental disease or defect that persists in the absence of the substance, can be considered for the purpose of establishing insanity. The appellant argued that he does not meet the definition of someone who has "an abnormality manifested only by repeated criminal or otherwise antisocial conduct" (as the Maryland statute specifies), so the sanity statute should include him. The court reasoned, however, that if the intoxication could have been prevented and the crime would not have been committed but for the intoxication, the individual should be responsible. If the intoxication prevented the formation of intent relevant to an element of a specific crime, it is permissible to acquit but a mental state arising from the acute voluntary ingestion of substances should not be permitted for an insanity defense.

Quick Summary

In Maryland, an altered mental state that is brought on by the acute and direct effects of voluntary intoxication is not permissible for a defense of insanity, however, if the effects are long-lasting and permanent (settled), the mental state may be recognized as a mental disease or defect.

Pate v. Robinson
383 U.S. 375 (1966)
U.S. Supreme Court

Case Facts

Mr. Robinson was convicted in 1959 of murdering his common law wife and given a life sentence. He did not demand a hearing for competency; however, his attorneys did bring it up as an issue at trial. Witnesses testified that he had a long history of disturbed and irrational behavior, including being psychiatrically hospitalized and paranoid. The trial judge denied the request for continuance to get a psychiatric examination and convicted him. Illinois Supreme Court affirmed the conviction, saying that no hearing for competency had been requested, and there was insufficient evidence for the judge to order one on his own. The U.S. Court of Appeals reversed, holding that the case was hurried and did not allow fair opportunity to develop the facts on the insanity/competency issues. The Court of Appeals remanded the case back to the district court for a hearing as to the sanity of the respondent at the time of the homicide and whether he was entitled to a hearing regarding his competency. The U.S. Supreme Court granted certiorari.

Main Issue

Does the failure to assess and address competency or sanity is a violation of a defendant's due process rights?

Court Holding

Yes. A defendant has the right to be competent to stand trial. Robinson was entitled to a hearing about his competency; therefore, there was a violation of his 14th amendment rights, based on there being sufficient evidence to raise the issue.

Court's Reasoning

Just because the defendant did not demand a competency or sanity hearing does not mean he waived the right to have one. If a defendant is incompetent, he or she cannot knowingly or intelligently waive the right to the hearing, and convicting an incompetent defendant is a violation of due process. The decision to have a competency hearing should not have been based solely on the defendant's behavior during the trial and the stipulation of an expert's testimony; there should have been a separate hearing.

Quick Summary

1. Just because a defendant does not demand a competency hearing does not mean they waived their rights. The right can only be waived if it is done knowingly and intelligently.
2. A separate hearing is necessary to determine competency or "sanity."
3. It is difficult to retry someone's competency retrospectively; therefore, the defendant must be retried if their due process rights were violated.

Payne v. Tennessee
501 U.S. 808 (1991)
U.S. Supreme Court

Case Facts

Pervis Payne was convicted by a jury on two counts of first-degree murder and one count of assault with intent to commit murder in the first degree. He was sentenced to death for each of the murders and to 30 years in prison for the assault. The victims were a mother, her two-year-old daughter, and her three-year-old son, who all had suffered numerous stab wounds caused by a butcher knife. The son survived, despite his stab wounds. During the sentencing phase, Mr. Payne provided the testimony of several witnesses (his mother, father, girlfriend, and a psychologist), all of whom presented mitigating evidence. The prosecution presented the young boy's maternal grandmother who spoke about how the boy had been affected by the murders. In arguing for the death penalty, the prosecutor noted the way the crime affected the boy and the victims' family. Mr. Payne was sentenced to death and appealed, arguing that the admission of the victim impact testimony violated his Eighth Amendment rights. The Supreme Court of Tennessee affirmed the conviction and sentence. The U.S. Supreme Court granted certiorari.

Main Issue

Does the Eighth Amendment bar the admission of *victim impact evidence* during the penalty phase of a capital trial?

Court Holding

No. The U.S. Supreme Court affirmed the lower court's rulings. The Eighth Amendment does not bar a capital sentencing jury from considering victim impact evidence.

Court's Reasoning

Harm caused by the defendant has long been an important factor in determining punishment. Victim impact evidence is another way of informing the sentencing authority about such harm. If no limits are placed on the mitigating evidence a capital defendant may introduce, aggravating evidence (victim impact) also has a place in sentencing. The sentencer should have access to all available evidence (permissible by the rules of evidence) to craft the appropriate sentence. The court overturned its own prior rulings in similar cases and recognized the principle that the punishment should fit the crime by allowing testimony from those impacted by the offense (i.e., aggravating, not just mitigating, evidence).

Quick Summary

Victim impact evidence in the sentencing phase of a capital case does not necessarily infringe upon Eighth Amendment rights. A sentencer should be allowed to consider aggravating as well as mitigating evidence when determining punishment in a capital case.

Penry v. Lynaugh, Director, Texas Department of Corrections
492 U.S. 302 (1989)
No. 87-6177.
Supreme Court of United States.

Case Facts

Pamela Carpenter was raped, beaten, and stabbed to death with a pair of scissors in her home in Texas in October 1979. Johnny Penry subsequently confessed and was charged with capital murder. At a competency hearing before trial, a clinical psychologist testified that Penry was mentally retarded. IQ testing of Penry over the years revealed scores between 50 and 63, consistent with mild to moderate retardation. Penry's social maturity (i.e., ability to function in the world) was opined to be that of a nine- or ten-year-old. The expert testified that "there's a point at which anyone with [Penry's] IQ is always incompetent, but, you know, this man is more in the borderline range." He was found competent to stand trial. The trial court determined that Penry's confessions to law enforcement were voluntary, and they were introduced into evidence. At trial, Penry raised an insanity defense. A psychiatrist testified that Penry had organic brain damage and moderate retardation, which resulted in poor impulse control and an inability to learn from experience. According to the psychiatrist, Penry's brain disorder made it impossible for him to appreciate the wrongfulness of his conduct at the time of the offense or to conform his conduct to the law.

Penry's mother testified that Penry was unable to learn in school and failed to complete the first grade. Penry's sister testified that when Penry was a child their mother had frequently beaten him on the head with a belt. Penry spent time in multiple state schools and hospitals, until he was 12 and his father removed him from state schools altogether. Penry's aunt subsequently spent more than a year trying to teach Penry how to print his name but was unsuccessful.

In rebuttal, the state introduced the testimony of two psychiatrists who testified that although Penry possessed limited mental ability, he did not have any mental illness or defect at the time of the crime, and he knew the difference between right and wrong and had the potential to conform his conduct to the law. Further, Penry had traits consistent with an antisocial personality, including an inability to learn from experience and a tendency to be impulsive and violate society's norms. A second forensic mental health professional testified essentially the same.

The jury rejected Penry's insanity defense. He was found guilty of capital murder and was sentenced to death. On direct appeal, the Texas Court of Criminal Appeals affirmed his conviction and sentence. The court also held that Penry's mental retardation did not prohibit imposition of the death penalty. Penry then filed a federal habeas corpus petition challenging his death sentence. Among other claims, Penry argued that he was sentenced in violation of the Eighth Amendment because the trial court failed to instruct the jury on how to weigh mitigating factors (such as his mental retardation, arrested emotional development, and abused background) and that it was cruel and unusual punishment to execute a mentally retarded person. The district court denied relief, and Penry appealed to the Court of Appeals for the Fifth Circuit. The Court of Appeals affirmed the district court's judgment. The court stressed, however, that it found considerable merit in Penry's claim. The U.S. Supreme Court granted certiorari.

Main Issues

1. Was Penry was sentenced to death in violation of the Eighth Amendment because the jury was not instructed that it could consider mitigating evidence in imposing its sentence?

2. Did the Eighth Amendment categorically prohibit Penry's execution because he was mentally retarded?

Court Holding

1. The court reversed and required a remand for resentencing to allow the jury to consider mitigating evidence.
2. The court determined that precluding the execution of any mentally retarded person is not supported simply by virtue of mental retardation alone; therefore, the original judgment was affirmed.

Court's Reasoning

1. The court concluded that the jury was not provided with a vehicle for expressing its "reasoned moral response" to mitigating evidence in rendering its sentencing decision.
2. Mental retardation has long been regarded as a factor that may diminish an individual's culpability for a criminal act, including a capital offense. However, the court did not conclude that all mentally retarded people of Penry's ability—by virtue of their mental retardation alone, inevitably lack the cognitive, volitional, and moral capacity to act with the degree of culpability associated with the death penalty. Mentally retarded persons are individuals whose abilities and experiences can vary greatly. So long as sentencers can consider and give effect to mitigating evidence of mental retardation in imposing sentence, an individualized determination whether "death is the appropriate punishment" can be made in each particular case.

Quick Summary

1. Juries should be instructed that mitigating evidence can be taken into account in sentencing.
2. Mental retardation alone is insufficient for culpability associated with the death penalty.

See also *Penry v. Johnson*, Director, Texas Department of Criminal Justice, Institutional Division (523 U.S. 782, 2001). The State of Texas retried Penry in 1990, and he again was found guilty of capital murder and sentenced him to death. However, the trial court again failed to give adequate instructions to the jury regarding consideration of mitigating evidence, the Supreme Court again reversed and remanded the case for further proceedings.

People v. Bieber
835 P. 2d 542 (Colo. Ct. App. 1992)
Colorado Court of Appeals

Case Facts

Armed with rifles and a meat cleaver, long-time substance user Donald Bieber shot a stranger for no apparent reason after hours of odd behavior, including singing the Marine Corps Hymn and God Bless America, and backing the victim's truck up into a fence. He was diagnosed with an amphetamine delusional disorder and ASPD. The amphetamine-induced psychosis, according to expert testimony, can last anywhere from two weeks to a year after the drug is ingested and can result in a defendant's ability to distinguish right from wrong to be impaired. The prosecution and defense stipulated, based on urinalysis results, that he had not ingested amphetamines for at least two days prior to the offense. Evidence showed that he had entered a psychiatric hospital several years before the offense for treatment of mental impairments secondary to long-term drug use whereby the drug-related psychosis cleared rapidly as it did following confinement on the current charges. The jury was instructed that mental disease or defect that impaired the defendant's ability to distinguish right from wrong results in a finding of insanity, but that antisocial behavior and intoxication do not count. He was convicted and appealed that the court erred by not instructing on *settled insanity* (i.e., a fixed or permanent condition arising from substance use). Court of Appeals upheld the conviction, finding no error in failing to instruct on settled insanity.

Main Issue

Is it a violation of due process for a court to refuse to instruct a jury on settled insanity? Does settled insanity qualify as a mental disease or defect for the purposes of an insanity defense?

Court Holding

No and no. It is up to the states to establish if and to what extent they will recognize settled insanity as a defense. Colorado does not recognize settled insanity as a qualifying mental disease or defect for the purposes of a sanity defense.

Court's Reasoning

The General Assembly of Colorado had previously decided that the voluntary use of substances should be reasonably expected to cause impairments in mental, physical, and behavioral functioning, and, therefore, any resulting settled insanity is thought to have been both foreseeable and preventable. Intoxication may be used to negate specific intent of a charged crime but not for general intent crimes. If a defendant voluntarily chooses to use substances knowing, as is common knowledge, that they may result in mental impairments, then that defendant may not later claim the effects as a mental disease or defect.

Quick Summary

States may decide if and to what extent to recognize settled insanity as a defense to a crime. In Colorado, if a defendant knowingly and voluntarily chose to use substances, then they assume the responsibility of the potential resulting mental changes that should be common knowledge and foreseeable. It is not a violation of due process that Colorado does not recognize settled insanity as a qualifying mental disease or defect for the purposes of an insanity defense.

People v. Conrad
385 N.W. 2d 277 (Mi. Ct. App. 1986)
Michigan Court of Appeals

Case Facts

Glenn Conrad was 18 years old when he stabbed his brother to death. He was found guilty but mentally ill and sentenced to life in prison. Prior to the murder, Conrad was a good student and worked at the Police Officer's Association but subsequently dropped out of school and quit his job. He smoked PCP with his cousin, and several days later was found on top of his brother, having stabbed him 45 times. Conrad's cousin reported that the defendant was acting oddly before, during, and after the offense, including claiming he was Christ. He was evaluated for competence and sanity and was deemed incompetent to stand trial after being observed as "grossly psychotic." He was further observed to be lapping up his food like a dog and kicking the walls, and he was hallucinating and disoriented. After six weeks on antipsychotic medication, he stabilized and was found competent to stand trial. Although forensic mental health professionals testified that PCP can cause acute and prolonged psychosis, the court ruled that Conrad could not use the insanity defense because he willingly ingested the drug. On appeal, Conrad argued that trial court erred in preventing him from raising the sanity defense. Michigan Court of Appeals agreed and reversed and remanded.

Main Issue

Can a defendant be acquitted not guilty by reason of insanity (NGRI) for a settled insanity (e.g., a stable, permanent condition that results from substance use) that continues in the time period after voluntary or involuntary intoxication?

Court Holding

Yes. The Michigan Court of Appeals disagreed with the trial court that just because the defendant voluntarily ingested PCP, he foreclosed on the possibility that he was insane at the time of the offense (a time at which he was no longer under the influence of the substance). The Court of Appeals differentiated the acute effects of substance intoxication from the lasting and unanticipated effects of the drug following use.

Court's Reasoning

Just because a defendant voluntarily ingested a drug that caused a psychotic reaction that could not qualify for an insanity defense at the time of intoxication does not mean that if the drug resulted in an ongoing or fixed insanity, it could not be considered for the sanity defense if the crime took place following the acute intoxication. If a drug wears off but the ongoing psychotic effects remain, then psychotic symptoms are psychotic symptoms regardless of their etiology and should be given consideration for a defense of insanity if the crime is committed in the aftermath of the substance intoxication.

Quick Summary

Although the effects of acute voluntary intoxication cannot qualify a defendant for the sanity defense, if the long lasting and persisting effects of the substance result in a settled or fixed insanity, that may be considered as a potential affirmative defense as long as the insanity was settled in nature.

People v. Dong
78 P.2d 1026 (Cal. Ct. App. 1938)
California Court of Appeal

Case Facts

Lim Dum Dong was addicted to cocaine, alcohol, and morphine for ten years prior to the offenses that occurred in 1937, which resulted in charges of assault with a deadly weapon. He admitted that he did shoot the victim, Susie Yamagawa, who was a stranger to him, and subsequently shot himself but claimed he was insane at the time and did not know the nature of the act he was doing. He was evaluated at the state psychiatric hospital, and experts opined that he was suffering from a temporary insanity, which resulted from his substance use. He was observed to have returned to a clear mental state when evaluated three months after the offense. A jury found him sane and guilty. He appealed, arguing that his temporary insanity prevented him from being capable of distinguishing between right and wrong.

Main Issue

Must the insanity that arises out of the voluntary use of substances be settled, or can it still qualify for an affirmative defense if it is the immediate result of the intoxication?

Court Holding

The Court of Appeals affirmed the lower court's denial of a new trial. In order for a defendant's mental state to qualify for an affirmative defense of insanity, the effects of the voluntary intoxication must have subsided completely, and there must either be a settled insanity separate and apart from the acute intoxication or an entirely separate mental illness that is not related to intoxication. Acute effects of voluntary intoxication can only be used to negate a specific intent element of a charged offense.

Court's Reasoning

The court focused on the voluntary nature of the intoxication as well as the immediacy of the effects, which were the direct result of the acute intoxication. The court found that there is no injustice in holding a person accountable for the acts they commit in a state of intoxication when that intoxication is voluntary. If a person brings upon themselves or society wrongful criminal conduct by voluntarily ingesting drugs, his or her conduct should not be excused. The instruction that was given allowed the jury to acquit him if they found that he was unable to know what he was doing or that it was wrong, without even specifying that it was the result of insanity. If the voluntary intoxication leads to a permanent or settled state of insanity and the crime is committed while in that settled state, and the person cannot differentiate between right and wrong as a result, then the resulting mental state should be considered the same as any other mental illness.

Quick Summary

Temporary insanity from the voluntary ingestion of substances cannot be used as an affirmative defense of insanity but may be used to negate a specific intent element of a charged offense. If the resulting effects of chronic substance use are persistent, permanent, or ongoing in the absence of such use, the mental condition may then be properly considered for an insanity defense.

The People of the State of New York v. Hans Schmidt
216 N.Y. 324 (N.Y. 1915)
110 N.E. 945
Court of Appeals of the State of New York

Case Facts

The dismembered body of Anna Aumuller was found in the Hudson River in September 2013. Hans Schmidt was arrested and confessed that he had killed the victim by cutting her throat. He entered an insanity plea. He told the physicians who examined him that he had heard the voice of God instructing him to kill the victim as a sacrifice and atonement. Two examiners, who believed his statement that he was overpowered by the delusion, expressed the opinion that he was insane. Other physicians, however, believed that his delusion was feigned and that his insanity was fabricated. The jury, accepting the latter view, found him guilty of first-degree murder, and he was sentenced to death.

Schmidt made a motion for a new trial on the grounds that his confession of guilt was false and that he hacked the body to pieces only after she had died from a criminally performed abortion. His crime, he was claiming, was manslaughter rather than murder. He said he originally chose the graver offense because he believed that he could feign insanity successfully, and that after, a brief term in an asylum, he would be released back into the community. In contrast, confessing to the abortion would implicate his partners and bring punishment to everyone involved. Instead, confessing to murder and feigning insanity had the potential to permit everyone to go free. He asked that he be given another opportunity to put before a jury the true narrative of the crime.

When his motion for a new trial was denied, Schmidt petitioned the court to reverse the judgment based on error committed in the definition of the degree of insanity that relieves one from responsibility for crime. The rule of the New York statute was that "a person is not excused from criminal liability as an idiot, imbecile, lunatic or insane person, except upon proof that, at the time of committing the alleged criminal act, he was laboring under such a defect of reason as: (1) not to know the nature and quality of the act he was doing; or (2) not to know that the act was wrong" (Penal Law, § 1120). The trial judge defined "wrong" for the jury as meaning "contrary to the law of the state." The jury was instructed that, even if Schmidt believed in good faith that God had appeared to him and commanded the sacrifice of the victim, and this belief was a delusion (i.e., the result of a defect of reason), Schmidt still must adhere to the law if he knew the nature and quality of the act, and knew that it was wrong, in the sense that it was forbidden by the law of the state. The definition of "wrong" was questioned.

Main Issues

1. In terms of knowing whether the illegal act was wrong is the definition of

"wrong" limited to the legal sense of forbidden by the law of the state? Or, would a broader definition (i.e., a moral sense of right and wrong) also apply?
2. Will a motion for a new trial succeed if it is based on the revelation that the defendant feigned mental illness to support an insanity defense in the original trial?

Court Holding

1. The court interpreted "wrong" to include knowledge the act was morally wrong, not only legally wrong.
2. There is no power in any court to grant a new trial upon the grounds that the initial defense was fraudulently based. The court stated that is would not aid the defendant in his effort to gain the benefit of a fraudulent defense.

For these reasons, the judgment of conviction was affirmed.

Court's Reasoning

1. The M'naghten rule includes that a person is not guilty because due to insanity if, because of a mental disorder, the person was unable to know their act was wrong. However, "wrong" was not defined in terms of legal versus moral wrong. The trial court interpreted "wrong" to apply in the legal sense. In contrast, the Court of Appeals did not accept the view that the word, "wrong" in the statutory definition should be interpreted so narrowly. The definition reaffirmed the position that a defendant who knew nothing of the law would still be responsible if they knew the act was wrong, in a moral sense. The court noted that there is no support for the belief that the words right and wrong, when they became limited by M'Naghten's case to the right and wrong of the particular act, lost their meaning as terms of morals, and became terms of pure legality. Thus, the court held that there are times and circumstances in which the word "wrong," as used in the statutory test of responsibility, should not to be limited to legal wrong but also include moral wrong.
2. The court did not attempt to determine how much of Schmidt's second tale was true. The court noted that even if the entire story were true, the courts were powerless to help him. A defendant may not experiment with one defense and then, when it fails, invoke the assistance of the law that he has flouted, to experiment with another defense, in contempt of the law's authority. The court further noted that the only remedy available to a criminal who finds himself stuck in such a trap of his own design is to appeal to the clemency of the governor. In response to Schmidt's confession that his insanity defense was fabricated, the court noted the fundamental principle no person shall be permitted to profit from their own wrong.

The appeals court also noted that it was of no importance at that time whether the trial judge charged the jury correctly upon the question of insanity, because Schmidt conceded that he was sane, and that everything which he previously said to the contrary was a fraud upon the court. He conceded that (1) the issue of his sanity was correctly determined by the jury; (2) even if there were error in the definition of insanity, no injustice has resulted; and (3) his position was that, having fabricated a defense of insanity to deceive the trial court, it became the duty of the appeals court to give him a new trial because his fabricated defense was unsuccessful. The appeals court refused to do so.

The court noted that cases will continue arise in which criminals, like Schmidt, will take shelter behind the position that their crime was ordained by God. The court was confident in leaving such fabrications, which are not the product of mental disease, to the common sense of juries.

Quick Summary

1. A person may be found not guilty because of insanity if, because of a mental disorder, they were not able to know her act was wrong, *morally or legally*.
2. A convicted criminal who is found to have feigned insanity as an initial defense cannot, after failing with that defense, have a new trial based on a different defense.

People v. Kelly
516 P. 2d 875 (Cal. 1973)
California Supreme Court

Case Facts

Valerie Kelly was charged with multiple counts of assault with a deadly weapon with intent to commit murder for the stabbing of her mother. She pled not guilty and not guilty by reason of insanity to the charges. She was found sane and guilty. She argued in her appeal that she had used mescaline and LSD 50 to 100 times in the months leading up to the offense and that the drug use had resulted in an insanity that prevented her from knowing that her actions were wrong. She further argued that the trial court failed to consider the insanity defense given the voluntary nature of her substance use because the resulting insanity was not permanent. The Supreme Court of California reversed the trial court's decision and remanded the case for a new trial.

Main Issue

What constitutes settled insanity as a result of substance use?

Court Holding

The court made it clear that while the acute effects of substance intoxication are not a defense to a crime, the ongoing, settled effects of the substance use is an appropriate consideration for a sanity defense.

Court's Reasoning

Insanity need not be permanent to establish a defense. Whether the settled insanity lasts a few hours, months, or years, as long as it is not attributable to the direct result of acute intoxication (i.e., the direct effects of ingestion are over), it is the same insanity as if it were due to another cause. The court explained that the defendant's psychosis was not limited to periods of intoxication but continued in the absence of the drugs. If the evidence shows that her mental state prevented her from knowing that her actions were wrong, as psychiatrists explained in this defendant's case, there is a legitimate defense of insanity.

Quick Summary

This case clarified that settled insanity from chronic and ongoing substance use does not have to result in permanent insanity. As long as the insanity (symptoms of serious mental illness) remains after the effects of the substance have fully worn off, it can be recognized as a mental illness like any other and used for the purposes of establishing a defense, even if it remits after even a short period of time.

People v. Sanchez
63 Cal.4th 665 (2016)
204 Cal.Rptr.3d 102
374 P.3d 320
No. S216681.
Supreme Court of California

Case Facts

In October 2011, two police officers made eye contact with Marcos Sanchez, who was standing nearby. He reached into an electrical box with one hand, then ran upstairs into an apartment while holding his other hand near his waistband. When the police were informed that Sanchez did not live in the apartment, they entered and apprehended him. A loaded gun and a plastic baggie were found nearby. The baggie contained 14 bindles of heroin and four baggies of methamphetamine, all packaged for sale. Sanchez was charged with possession of a firearm by a felon, possession of drugs while armed with a loaded firearm, active participation in a street gang, and commission of a felony for the benefit of the gang.

A police detective who had never met Sanchez testified for the prosecution as a gang expert and on specific aspects of Sanchez's legal history. The detective was not present when during any of Sanchez's police contacts. Stow's knowledge of Sanchez was derived from police reports and information on a field identification card. The jury convicted Sanchez as charged. The Court of Appeal reversed Sanchez's conviction for active gang participation but otherwise affirmed. The Supreme Court of California granted Sanchez's petition for review.

Sanchez argued that the expert's description of his past contacts with police was offered for its truth and constituted testimonial hearsay. He contended that admission of the testimony violated the federal confrontation clause because the declarants were not unavailable, and he had not been given the opportunity to cross-examine them. The Attorney General responded that the statements upon which the gang expert based his opinions were not admitted for their truth and, even if they had been, most of the statements were not testimonial.

Main Issue

Are facts an expert relates as the basis for an opinion admitted for their truth? If so, would they constitute hearsay?

Court Holding

Yes. An expert's testimony regarding the basis for an opinion *must* be considered for its truth by the jury. The findings on the street gang enhancements were reversed, but the judgment of conviction was otherwise affirmed, and the matter was remanded to the Court of Appeal.

Court's Reasoning

The admission of expert testimony is governed not only by state evidence law but also by the Sixth Amendment's confrontation clause, which provides that, "in all criminal prosecutions, the accused shall enjoy the right … to be confronted with the witnesses against him." Hearsay, which is an out-of-court statement offered for the truth of its content, may deny a defendant of that right. Documents such as letters, reports, and memoranda are often considered hearsay because they are prepared by a person outside of the courtroom and are usually offered to prove the truth of the information they contain. Documents may contain multiple levels of hearsay. The Supreme Court of California noted, for example, that an emergency room report may contain the observations of the writer, as well as statements made by the patient. If offered for its truth, the report itself is a hearsay statement made by the person who wrote it. Statements of others, related by the report writer, are a second level of hearsay. Multiple hearsay may not be admitted unless there is an exception for each level. The court noted, in the example of the emergency room document, the report itself may be a business record, while the patient's statement may qualify as a statement of the patient's existing mental or physical state.

Whereas lay witnesses can testify only about matters within their personal knowledge, expert witnesses are given greater latitude. "A person is qualified to testify as an expert if he has special knowledge, skill, experience, training, or education sufficient to qualify him as an expert on the subject to which his testimony relates" (Evid. Code, § 720, subd. (a)). In addition to matters within their own personal knowledge, experts may relate information acquired through their training and experience, even though that information may have been derived from conversations with others, lectures, study of learned treatises, and so forth.

The court noted that a jury is not required to accept an expert's opinion. The final resolution of the facts at issue resides solely with the jury. If an essential fact is not found proven, the jury may reject the opinion as lacking foundation. Even if all the necessary facts are found proven, the jury is free to reject the expert's opinion about them as unsound, based on faulty reasoning or analysis, or based on information the jury finds unreliable. The jury may also reject an opinion because it finds the expert lacks credibility as a witness.

An expert's testimony concerning their general knowledge, even if technically hearsay, has not been subject to exclusion on hearsay grounds. By contrast, an expert has traditionally been precluded from relating *case-specific* facts about which the expert has no independent knowledge. There are exceptions to the general rule barring disclosure of, and reliance on, otherwise inadmissible case-specific hearsay; medical diagnoses are one such exception because physicians often rely on patients' hearsay descriptions of their symptoms to form diagnoses.

In support of their opinion, an expert can explain to the jury the "matter" upon which he relied, even if that matter would ordinarily be inadmissible. When that matter is hearsay, there is a question as to how much substantive detail may be given by the expert and how the jury may consider the evidence in evaluating the expert's opinion.

An expert may *rely* on hearsay in forming an opinion, and may tell the jury *in general terms* that they did so, because the jury must independently evaluate the probative value of an expert's testimony. What an expert *cannot* do is relate as true case-specific facts asserted in hearsay statements, unless they are independently proven by competent evidence or are covered by a hearsay exception.

When any expert relates to the jury case-specific out-of-court statements, and treats the content of those statements as true and accurate to support the expert's opinion, the statements are hearsay. It cannot logically be maintained that the statements are not being admitted for their truth. If the case is one in which a prosecution expert seeks to relate *testimonial* hearsay, there is a confrontation clause violation unless (1) there is a showing of unavailability and (2) the defendant had a prior opportunity for cross-examination, or forfeited that right by wrongdoing.

Quick Summary

An expert's testimony regarding the basis for an opinion *must* be considered for its truth by the jury. Case-specific statements related by an expert are hearsay and may not be presented as true statements of fact without the requisite independent proof.

People v. Patterson
347 N.E.2d 898 (N.Y. 1976)
New York Court of Appeals

Case Facts

Gordon Patterson and his wife had an unstable relationship. When she filed for divorce and began dating another man, Mr. Patterson shot the man twice, killing him. He was charged with second degree murder. Defense raised extreme emotional disturbance (EED) as an affirmative defense. They explained to the jury that the elements of the crime as charged required a finding that the defendant acted intentionally, but that because of his EED, Mr. Patterson should be found guilty of manslaughter, if at all. The jury was further instructed that the burden was on the defendant to prove EED by a preponderance of the evidence and that EED was a viable defense to reduce the murder to manslaughter, rather than exoneration. Patterson was convicted, and he appealed, arguing that placing the burden on him to prove EED was a violation of his due process rights. Patterson argued that another case, *Mullaney v. Wilbur 421 US 684,* that was decided by the Supreme Court at the same time, governed his case too. In that case, the court ruled that the burden should remain on the prosecution to show that it was not a heat of passion crime rather than placing the burden on the defense to prove that it was.

Main Issue

Is it a violation of due process to place the burden on the defendant to show EED at the time of the alleged offense?

Court Holding

No. The homicide laws in New York make it permissible to place the burden on the defendant. In New York, the prosecution must prove beyond a reasonable doubt that the defendant caused the death of another person with intent and that it was their "conscious objective" to kill the person. EED can be considered regarding intent. The prosecution must still prove intent beyond a reasonable doubt, so it is not a violation of due process to place a burden on the defense to show EED by a preponderance.

Court's Reasoning

The New York Court of Appeals argued that the homicide laws in Maine (where *Mullaney* was decided) are different from in New York. The court also noted that Mullaney was not decided until after this court ruled on Mr. Patterson's appeal. The court claimed that a strict reading of New York's state law finds it permissible for a defendant to be found guilty of manslaughter rather than murder if an affirmative defense of EED is successful, but the burden is on the defendant.

Quick Summary

New York's law allowing a defendant to be convicted of the lesser charge of manslaughter instead of murder because of EED is permissible and placing the burden on the defendant to prove EED by a preponderance is not a violation of due process. The burden is still on the prosecution to prove every element of the murder charge beyond a reasonable doubt.

People v. Saille
820 P.2d 588 (Cal. 1991)
California Supreme Court

Case Facts

Mr. Manuel Saille, after a day of heavy drinking, returned to the bar he had previously been asked to leave (due to his level of intoxication) with a gun. He shot and killed a patron and wounded a security guard at the bar. There was lay testimony at trial that the defendant was very drunk at the time of the offense. Additionally, a psychologist testified about the effects of alcohol intoxication, including on the ability to form intent. The court provided instructions to the jury that voluntary intoxication could negate specific intent to kill, but Mr. Saille appealed following his first-degree murder and attempted murder conviction, arguing that the instructions did not provide the jury with enough information about the ways that voluntary intoxication may reduce the ability to form malice, reducing murder to manslaughter. Saille also argued that the court should have, sua sponte (i.e., on its own), instructed the jury that it could consider voluntary intoxication when determining whether the killing was premeditated. His appeal focused on the argument that a heavily intoxicated person might be able to form intent to kill but not the malice required for murder, and that if a crime requires a particular mental state, the defendant must be permitted to offer evidence that negates the mental state. The Court of Appeals affirmed the lower court's decision, and the Supreme Court of California granted review.

Main Issue

In California, can voluntary intoxication be used to show that the defendant did not form specific intent to kill?

Court Holding

Yes. Voluntary intoxication can be used to reduce first degree murder to involuntary manslaughter or to acquit entirely if the defense can show that it prevented the defendant from forming the specific intent to commit murder. A diminished capacity defense that would reduce murder to voluntary manslaughter, however, is not available. A defendant may introduce evidence of voluntary intoxication to negate the specific intent to kill, which would result in a finding of involuntary manslaughter or acquittal.

Court's Reasoning

California code allows for a finding of involuntary manslaughter instead of murder if the defendant can prove the inability to form the specific intent for premeditated murder as a result of voluntary intoxication. The defendant was permitted to show that voluntary intoxication impaired his ability to form the requisite intent to kill. The lower courts did not err in the instructions provided to the jury. The instructions provided did inform the jury that a defendant may not be able to form the requisite intent for murder as a result of mental disease or intoxication.

Quick Summary

A defendant may introduce evidence of intoxication to show the inability to form the specific intent for murder, thereby resulting in a conviction for involuntary manslaughter or an acquittal.

People v. Toner
187 N.W. 386 (Mich. 1922)
Michigan Supreme Court

Case Facts

J. Glenn Toner was convicted of murdering his neighbor. Defense argued that he was experiencing delirium tremens (DTs), which is a period of confusion and altered mental state as a result of withdrawal from excessive use of alcohol. The defendant had experienced DTs many times before due to his alcohol addiction, but defense argued that he was not responsible for the crime because in that intoxicated state he could not distinguish between right and wrong. Defense asked that the jury be instructed that if they found that Toner was in a confused mental state as a result of DTs, then he could be excused from the murder. The court denied this request, and the jury was instructed that if Toner knew the drinking would lead to the mental changes (i.e., DTs), he was to be held responsible; only if they found that he did not know DTs would be a reasonable possibility of his drinking could they find him lacking in criminal responsibility. The defendant appealed his conviction, arguing that he in fact was not intoxicated at the time and that DTs result precisely from the opposite—withdrawal from, or the absence of, alcohol use. The court noted the pieces of evidence that suggested that he was in a state of intoxication, rather than DTs, at the time of the offense, implicating acute voluntary intoxication rather than the absence of it. Toner further argued that the symptoms present at the time of the offense matter, and that the trier of fact should look to the immediate, rather than remote, causes of those symptoms as cited in (*United States v. Drew, 1828*). The jury convicted, and the State Supreme Court affirmed.

Main Issue

Can a defendant who is in a withdrawal state of delirium tremens from excessive alcohol use successfully raise an insanity defense for a crime committed while in that state?

Court Holding

Yes, delirium tremens can result in a finding of not guilty by reason of insanity (but the defendant in this case was found not to be in this mental state).

Court's Reasoning

The State Supreme Court agreed with the appellate court that prior case law (*United States v. Drew, 1828)* had established that a crime committed while in a state of confusion or psychosis that results not from the acute effects of a substance but during the absence/withdrawal of it can warrant a defense of insanity. However, the court cited evidence that came out at trial establishing that the appellant committed the crime while in a state of intoxication, not DTs, and thus was disqualified from that defense. The court also focused on the defendant's knowledge of his susceptibility and proneness to that altered mental state because he had experienced it multiple times before. If he knew that the "mental derangement" would result, he should be assumed to have intended the derangement and the effects of it. If he was ignorant as to any insanity that would result, and the altered state did not occur in the period of time during acute intoxication, insanity could be raised as a defense.

Quick Summary

This case reaffirmed that a defendant may utilize the insanity defense for a crime committed in a psychotic or grossly impaired mental state that arises in the aftermath of intoxication (i.e., delirium tremens) but not while acutely intoxicated. It also placed an emphasis on the defendant's knowledge of the likelihood of mental state changes following intoxication based on prior experience.

Porreca v. State
433 A.2d 1204 (Md. Ct. Spec. App. 1981)
Maryland Court of Special Appeals

Case Facts

Michael Porreca was convicted of attempted murder and sentenced to 20 years confinement. He appealed, claiming that the trial court failed to consider his mental state of insanity as a result of PCP intoxication. He had randomly attacked, beaten, and stabbed his roommate, and, when police found him, he was naked and unconscious on the bed. When he came to, he told police that he was Satan, that the victim had the devil inside of her, and that she wanted to kill him. At trial, a psychiatrist testified that Porreca lacked capacity to appreciate the criminality of his conduct or to conform his conduct to the requirements of the law as a result of his longtime PCP use. He also testified that the psychotic symptoms pre- and post-dated not only the offense but also the instant intoxication. According to the expert testimony, the symptoms abated with prolonged abstinence, and he would not have committed the offense if he had not been using PCP. The trial court judge ruled that the psychiatrist's testimony was insufficient to raise sanity because the psychosis was the result of acute intoxication. The appellate court reversed and remanded.

Main Issue

When can insanity that is produced as a result of substance use be legitimately raised as an affirmative defense?

Court Holding

If the chronic use of a substance results in a settled and fixed insanity, that may warrant an affirmative defense to a crime committed as a result of the persistent, rather than acute, symptoms.

Court's Reasoning

The court explained that the psychiatrist's testimony indicated that although the effects of the drug wore off, the psychosis experienced by the defendant remained for months at a time, even in the absence of the intoxicant in the system. The psychosis-inducing effects of the drug persisted for months following the direct influence of it, which made it a settled, even if not a permanent, insanity. The trial court erred in not permitting the question of sanity to be raised, given the testimony that there clearly was ongoing psychotic disturbance after the acute intoxication wore off.

Quick Summary

It is inappropriate to fail to consider the question of insanity when a substance caused the mental disease/insanity, even once the acute and direct effects of the substance have remitted. Put another way, there may be a legitimate defense of insanity if the symptoms of psychosis persisted after the acute effects of intoxication subsided. Although it is not permissible to use a substance and get away with an offense, if the chronic use of a substance results in settled insanity, such information should be considered when assessing criminal responsibility.

Powell v. Texas
392 U.S. 514 (1968)
U.S. Supreme Court

Case Facts

Texas Penal Code addressing public drunkenness states, "Whoever shall get drunk or be found in a state of intoxication in any public place … shall be fined." Leroy Powell was arrested under this code, found guilty, and ordered to pay a fine. He appealed and argued that he had a "disease of chronic alcoholism," and to criminalize his alcoholism would be in violation of the 8th and 14th Amendments. The trial judge made several "findings of fact" (e.g., alcoholism destroys one's will to resist consumption; an alcoholic's public appearance is a compulsive symptom of the disease; Powell has the disease of alcoholism), but found that alcoholism is not a proper defense for the charges. Powell was found guilty and fined. Under Texas law, Powell had no additional right to appeal. Thus, he appealed in the U.S. Supreme Court. The court focused, in part, on Powell's loss of control and inability to abstain.

Main Issue

Is the Texas court criminalizing alcoholism, and if so, is that a violation of the 8th and 14th amendments?

Court Holding

Alcoholism, in and of itself, is not grounds for arrest and punishment by law. Illegal behaviors that occur while under the influence of alcohol are considered criminal and therefore punishable. Therefore, the criminalization of public intoxication does not violate the 8th and 14th Amendments.

Court's Reasoning

There are debates among medical professionals regarding the extent to which alcoholism can be considered a "disease." There is also no clear distinction between a "compulsion (i.e., a craving to off-set symptoms of withdrawal)" and an "impulse (i.e., voluntary, does not involve a lack of control)." The court cited *Robinson v. California,* which noted that it is cruel and unusual to criminalize drug addiction. The court noted that Powell "was convicted, not for being a chronic alcoholic, but for being in public while drunk on a particular occasion." The Court added that it would be "obnoxious" to punish someone for their mere propensity to drink. But to argue that "compulsions" are "symptomatic" of a "disease" and therefore should not be criminalized is beyond the capacity of the court to make decisions of mens rea. Thus, it is impossible to conclude if "chronic alcoholics … suffer from such an irresistible compulsion to drink and to get drunk in public that they are utterly unable to control their performance of either or both of these acts and thus cannot be deterred at all from public intoxication."

Quick Summary

Criminalizing illegal behaviors that occur when someone is an alcoholic is different from arguing that that it is criminal to be an alcoholic. As such, it is not in violation of the 8th and 14th Amendments. It is not illegal to be an alcoholic, but being an alcoholic is not a defense for engaging in illegal activities.

R v. Arnold
16 How. St. Tr. 695 (1724)
United Kingdom

Case Facts

Mr. Edward Arnold was charged with attempting to murder Lord Onslow in 1724 in England. Mr. Arnold had a delusion that Onslow had bewitched him and was using imps to torture him, causing all his problems. At the trial, there was no question that he shot the victim. The question focused on by the court was the maliciousness of the act. The judge instructed the jury that the question was not just whether Mr. Arnold shot Lord Onslow, but whether he did so maliciously. Arnold testified at trial that "I can't be easy. He plagues me day and night. I can't eat or drink. If I eat anything it comes out of my body. I am as if they pumped the breath out of my body." The prosecution focused on the witnesses who testified that they tried to get Mr. Arnold to change and that if the defendant had truly been incapable of thoughtful behavior, those people would not have attempted to have reasoned discussions with him. The judge instructed the jury that not to be culpable, a defendant had to be deprived of understanding and memory and not know what they are doing, like a wild beast, a brute, an infant, or a madman. With the standard explained this way, the jury convicted Mr. Arnold. He was later sentenced to life in prison rather than death, which was not uncommon prior to the establishment of an official plea of insanity. This was the early court's way of recognizing insanity, albeit post-conviction.

Main Issue

How should courts recognize insanity and what should be the proper adjudicative test?

Court Holding

Judge Tracy, the trial judge in this case, articulated that for a defendant to be considered lacking in culpability, they must have no ability to know what they are doing, no memory, no understanding, nothing more sophisticated than that of a wild beast. This very early definition of insanity was the so-called Wild Beast Test, which proposed strict and imprecise criteria for a defendant to be found lacking in criminal responsibility.

Court's Reasoning

The court offered no consideration of the delusions held by Mr. Arnold in terms of his responsibility and instead focused on whether he could act purposefully. The court did not recognize the role that the defendant's delusions played in his choices and behavior and instead focused on whether he could in fact conduct purposeful choices and behavior and was not functioning merely as a farm animal would, absent cognition.

Quick Summary

In this early case addressing insanity, the court instructed the jury that a defendant would not be culpable only if they did not know what they were doing, were unable to distinguish good from evil, and unable to understand what they did. This case led to the so-called Wild Beast Test, equating a person lacking in criminal culpability to a beast.

R v. M'Naghten
8 Eng. Rep. 718 (H.L. 1843)
United Kingdom House of Lords

Case Facts

On January 20, 1843, Daniel M'Naghten shot and killed Edward Drummond. M'Naghten had Schizophrenia and believed he was killing Sir Robert Peel. M'Naghten raised an insanity defense and was found not guilty by reason of insanity (NGRI). Following public outrage following the acquittal, Queen Victoria requested that the House of Lords examine the insanity defense. The House of Lords requested the help of the common law courts, resulting in this decision.

Main Issues

1. What is the law regarding the insanity defense?
2. Can a medical expert give an opinion regarding insanity?

Court Holding

There should be a presumption of sanity. There should be clearly defined criteria for a defense of insanity. The criteria should focus on the defendant's ability to know what they are doing and to know that what they are doing is wrong. The nature of the delusion must be considered for the defense to be viable.

Court's Reasoning

1. The jury should be told that in "all cases every man is to be presumed sane and … to establish a defence on the ground of insanity, it must be clearly proved that, at the time of committing the act, the party accused as labouring under such a defect of reason, from disease of the mind, as not to know the nature and quality of the act he was doing; or, if he did know it, that he did not know he was doing what was wrong." However, the defendant need not have actual knowledge of the law; it is enough that the act was against the law at the time, and the individual knew that the act was one that they should not do. Whether the person should be excused from punishment depends upon the nature of their delusion. For example, the individual would be excused if assuming their delusion were true would create a valid self-defense argument (e.g., the defendant believes a person is about to kill them and kills that person in self-defense). In such instances, the individual should be excused from culpability.

2. An expert can testify with regard to matters involving science but may not testify regarding the truth of the facts, which is the province of the jury.

Quick Summary

The M'Naghten Test, as it became known, defines insanity as the accused laboring under such a defect of reason, from disease of the mind, as not to know the nature and quality of the act he was doing; or, if he did know it, that he did not know he was doing what was wrong. Experts should testify only regarding matters within their area of expertise and should avoid commenting on legal/moral matters.

Ring v. Arizona
536 U.S. 584 (2002)
U.S. Supreme Court

Case Facts

In 1994, a Wells Fargo armored van stopped at a department store, and a courier left the van to pick up money inside the store. When he returned, the van and its driver were gone. Later that day, sheriff's deputies found the van in a distant parking lot. Inside, they found the driver, dead from a gunshot wound to the head, and more than $800,000 in cash and checks missing from the van. Based on an informant's tip, law enforcement investigated Timothy Ring and two other suspects. A search of Ring's residence yielded a duffel bag with more than $270,000 in cash. The state charged Ring with premeditated murder. The jury deadlocked on that charge, but convicted Ring of the lesser charge of first-degree felony murder, acknowledging its uncertainty about the roles of the three suspects in the crime. Under Arizona law, the maximum punishment Ring faced was life imprisonment, unless further findings were made to support the death penalty. To sentence a defendant to death for first-degree murder, Arizona law directed the trial judge to conduct a separate sentencing hearing and make factual findings as to the presence or absence of aggravating and mitigating factors. In Ring's case, the judge concluded that Ring shot the driver of the armored van and that he was a major participant in the robbery—findings the jury had not made. The judge found that these facts constituted aggravating factors and sentenced Ring to death.

Main Issue

Does the Sixth Amendment permit a judge to find aggravating factors necessary for imposition of the death penalty, or must aggravating factors be found by a jury?

Court Holding

The Sixth Amendment requires that aggravating factors be found by a jury.

Court's Reasoning

In *Walton v. Arizona*, 497 U.S. 639 (1990), the Supreme Court held that a judge could find additional facts in a death penalty case, so long as they were "sentencing considerations" and not "elements of the offense of capital murder." Ten years later, in *Apprendi v. New Jersey*, 530 U.S. 466 (2000), the court held that the Sixth Amendment does not permit a defendant to be exposed to a penalty exceeding the maximum he would receive if punished according to the facts reflected in the jury verdict alone. This is the case even if a state characterizes the additional findings made by a judge as "sentencing factors." In *Ring*, the court recognized that *Walton* and *Apprendi* were in conflict. It overruled *Walton*, and held that capital defendants are entitled to a jury determination on any fact on which the legislature conditions an increase in their maximum punishment. Here, based solely on the jury's verdict of first-degree felony murder, the maximum punishment Ring could have received was life imprisonment. Because Arizona's aggravating factors operate as the functional equivalent of an element of a greater offense, exposing a defendant to a higher penalty, the Sixth Amendment requires they be found by a jury.

Quick Summary

Defendant was convicted of first-degree felony murder, which carried a maximum penalty of life imprisonment under Arizona law. Under the state's capital sentencing scheme, the trial judge found aggravating factors and sentenced the defendant to death. The Supreme Court held that Arizona's sentencing scheme was unconstitutional, and that the Sixth Amendment requires aggravating factors to be found by a jury, not a judge.

Riggins v. Nevada
504 U.S. 127 (1992)
U.S. Supreme Court

Case Facts

In November of 1987, David Riggins was arrested for murder and robbery. Riggins was evaluated for competency, found competent to stand trial, and pled not guilty by reason of insanity (NGRI). While awaiting trial, Mr. Riggins complained of psychiatric symptoms, including psychosis, and was administered the medication Mellaril to treat it. The medication was gradually increased. Later, Mr. Riggins made a motion to have his medications stopped during trial because 1) the administration of these drugs infringed upon his freedom, and 2) the way the jury saw him during trial while stable on his medications would deny him due process of law. The motion was denied. Mr. Riggins was convicted and sentenced to death.

Main Issue

Did the forced administration of antipsychotic medication during trial violate the due process rights guaranteed by the 6th and 14th Amendments?

Court Holding

Yes, the U.S. Supreme Court ruled that the forced administration of medication during trial does violate the 6th and 14th Amendments.

Court's Reasoning

The U.S. Supreme Court held that the forcible administration of drugs is a substantial interference with a person's liberty, and an individual's interest in avoiding this administration is protected under the 14th Amendment's Due Process Clause. There must be an overriding justification and a finding of medical appropriateness to forcibly medicate. Also, the precise consequences of taking Mr. Riggins off of his medications could not be determined from the existing record. The court reasoned that Riggins' defense was harmed by the administration of Mellaril. Simply allowing him to present expert testimony about the effects of Mellaril was not enough because the medication may also have affected his testimony's content, his ability to follow the proceedings, or the substance of his communication with counsel.

Quick Summary

Involuntary administration of antipsychotic medication without the state establishing the need for the medication and its medical appropriateness is a violation of due process.

Rodriguez v. Wal-Mart Stores, Inc.
203 A.3d 114 (N.J. 2019)
New Jersey Supreme Court

Case Facts

In this personal injury case, plaintiff Alexandra Rodriguez was struck by a clothing display rack that fell on her while she shopped at Walmart. She sued Walmart for negligence and, at the trial, doctors testified to her medical ailments that caused her pain (despite her pre-existing conditions). When asked if her history of "psychiatric family issues" could be causing her pain, the physicians testified that her psychiatric issues had nothing to do with her pain condition. Walmart's expert, a neurologist, testified that not only could he find no evidence of anything objectively wrong with her, he claimed that her complaints did not make sense medically. The court permitted him to testify about symptom magnification and somatization. The jury determined that the plaintiff had not proven by a preponderance of the evidence that Walmart was negligent. The appellate court reversed and remanded for a new trial, citing that expert witnesses cannot testify about malingering because it is synonymous with testimony about credibility or believability, and is not permitted in a civil jury trial in New Jersey. The appellate court further opined that the expert who offered the symptom magnification testimony was not qualified to do so.

Main Issue

Is expert testimony about "symptom magnification" and malingering permitted in a civil trial in New Jersey or impermissible because is serves as lie detector testimony or otherwise impugns witness credibility?

Court Holding

The Supreme Court of New Jersey heard the case and reversed. The court found that such decisions must be made on a case-by-case basis and that the trial court did not err by allowing this type of testimony.

Court's Reasoning

The court reasoned that according to New Jersey Rule of Evidence 403, testimony is to be kept out only when its probative value is so substantially outweighed by its inflammatory potential that it would confuse the jurors to the point they could no longer fairly and reasonably consider the case. It further explained that this door was opened by the plaintiff when her own experts testified about her mental health and somatization. While the court did take note of the potential for negative impact on credibility assessment when an expert testifies about malingering (although the term malingering was not used in this case), it is admissible if it is carefully scrutinized and relevant. In this case, evidence of the plaintiff's past medical history, including psychiatric history, was relevant because it was logically related to the pre-existing injury and lack of medical evidence to support her claims.

Quick Summary

In this personal injury case, the New Jersey Supreme Court permitted expert testimony regarding "symptom magnification" and somatization and held that it is up to trial courts to determine the admissibility and relevance of such testimony on a case-by-case basis.

Rompilla v. Beard
545 U.S. 374 (2005)
U.S. Supreme Court

Case Facts

Defendant Rompilla was convicted of murder and related offenses, after fatally stabbing a bar owner and setting his body on fire. The Commonwealth of Pennsylvania sought the death penalty. At sentencing, the Commonwealth sought to prove that Rompilla had a significant history of violent felony convictions. To that end, it notified Rompilla of its intent to introduce a prior conviction for rape and assault, and a transcript of the victim's testimony. Rompilla's counsel failed to examine the case file for the prior conviction. Instead, Rompilla presented a mitigation case based on witnesses who testified that Rompilla was innocent or could be rehabilitated. The jury was unpersuaded, and sentenced Rompilla to death. Rompilla sought post-conviction and *habeas* relief, arguing ineffective assistance of counsel. He claimed that trial counsel failed to present significant mitigating evidence about his childhood, mental capacity and health, and alcoholism. The post-conviction court denied relief, and the Supreme Court of Pennsylvania affirmed. The federal district court granted relief on Rompilla's *habeas* claim, finding that Rompilla's counsel had failed to investigate "pretty obvious signs" that Rompilla had a troubled childhood, mental illness, and alcoholism, and had unjustifiably relied on Rompilla's own unexceptional description of his background. A divided panel of the Third Circuit reversed, holding that counsel were justified in failing to hunt through Rompilla's school, medical, police, and prison records, when they had no reason to believe such a search would be fruitful. The Supreme Court granted review and reversed.

Main Issue

Under *Strickland v. Washington*, must counsel make reasonable efforts to obtain and review material that they know the prosecution will rely on as evidence of aggravation at sentencing?

Court Holding

Yes.

Court's Reasoning

The court narrowed the issue before it, holding that Rompilla's claim that trial counsel was obligated to follow up on lines of inquiry regarding his schooling, incarcerations, and alcohol history was open to debate, but the dispositive issue was counsel's failure to examine the court file on Rompilla's prior conviction for rape and assault. In presenting its case on aggravation, the prosecutor twice gave Rompilla's counsel notice that it intended to introduce evidence of this conviction. Counsel's failure to review the file was unreasonable under *Strickland*, and violated American Bar Association standards governing counsel's duty to investigate "information in the possession of the prosecution." Rompilla was prejudiced by this failure, because the file contained a wealth of mitigation information, including that Rompilla was abused and neglected as a child, and suffered from fetal alcohol syndrome, mental retardation, brain damage, and symptoms of Schizophrenia. This evidence "might well have" influenced the jury on Rompilla's culpability and resulted in a different sentencing outcome.

Quick Summary

The court vacated a defendant's death sentence based on ineffective assistance of counsel, where defense counsel failed to review the case file for a prior conviction, even after the Commonwealth gave notice of intent to present the conviction to the jury as an aggravating factor. Had counsel reviewed the file, they would have discovered a number of mitigating factors that may have led the jury to impose a lesser sentence.

Roper v. Simmons
543 U.S. 551 (2005)
U.S. Supreme Court

Case Facts

In 1993, 17-year-old Christopher Simmons plotted with a friend, broke into a woman's house, tied her up, and threw her off a bridge. He discussed the murder with friends beforehand, subsequently bragged about it, and ultimately confessed to police. He was tried after turning 18, found guilty, and sentenced to death. He appealed, but the trial court denied a motion for postconviction relief. The Missouri Supreme Court affirmed. In 2002, the U.S. Supreme Court held in *Atkins v. Virginia* that the 8th and 14th Amendments prohibited the execution of the intellectually disabled. Simmons filed a new petition, arguing that the reasoning behind *Atkins* also barred the execution of those who committed capital crimes when under the age of 18. The Supreme Court of Missouri agreed and set aside the death sentence and resentenced him to life imprisonment without parole. The U.S. Supreme Court granted certiorari.

Main Issue

Does the Constitution prohibit the execution of individuals who committed a capital crime when they were under the age of 18 years?

Court Holding

Yes, the 8th and 14th Amendments of the Constitution prohibit the execution of those who were under 18 when they committed a capital crime. The U.S. Supreme Court affirmed the state Supreme Court's decision.

Court's Reasoning

Despite the decision in *Stanford v. Kentucky,* which rejected the proposition that the Constitution prohibited the execution of 16- and 17-year-olds, the court focused on the necessity of referring to "the evolving standards of decency that mark the progress of a maturing society," and opined that times had changed since *Stanford*. Many states had banned juvenile execution, and it was rarely practiced in the states where it was not prohibited. The court looked at the paralleling cases of *Atkins v. Virginia* and *Penry v. Lynaugh* to make decisions and support its reasoning in this case (*Atkins* overturned the decisions made in *Penry*, which said execution of persons with intellectual disabilities was not prohibited by the Constitution). *Atkins* stated that persons with intellectual disabilities were "categorically less culpable than the average criminal," and *Roper* concluded the same was true for juveniles. The court focused on three primary differences between adults and juveniles (i.e., impulsivity, peer and environmental influences, and less well-formed character that can change for the better with time). As a result, juveniles cannot be held to the same standards as adults. Finally, the court decided to draw the line at 18 because that is where society defines adulthood.

Quick Summary

The constitution prohibits the execution of individuals under the age of 18. "Evolving standards of decency" and new research can influence how the constitution is interpreted in a maturing society.

Schlagenhauf v. Holder
379 U.S. 104 (1964)
U.S. Supreme Court

Case Facts

Defendant Schlagenhauf was the driver of a bus that collided with a tractor-trailer. The passengers of the bus sued Schlagenhauf, as well as the driver of the tractor-trailer and the owners of both vehicles, for personal injury damages arising from the defendants' negligence. The owners of the tractor-trailer alleged that Schlagenhauf was "not mentally or physically capable" of driving a bus at the time of the accident, and sought to compel him to undergo four mental and physical examinations under Federal Rule of Civil Procedure

35(a). Rule 35(a) provides that in an action where the mental or physical condition of a party is "in controversy," the court may order a party to undergo an examination. The order may be made only on a motion for good cause. Here, the moving parties alleged that good cause supported the requested examinations because Schlagenhauf saw the tractor-trailer's rear lights 10 to 15 seconds before the accident but did not reduce his speed, an eyewitness also saw the tractor-trailer's lights from a distance of half a mile, and Schlagenhauf had been involved in a prior rear-end collision. The district court granted the motion and ordered Schlagenhauf to submit to the examinations. Schlagenhauf applied for a writ of mandamus in the Court of Appeals to prohibit the examinations, which was denied. The Supreme Court granted review.

Main Issue

Under Rule 35, was the mental or physical condition of the defendant "in controversy," and was there good cause to order him to undergo physical and mental examinations, where he was generally charged with negligence in a rear-end collision?

Court Holding

No.

Court's Reasoning

Under Rule 35, a party seeking to compel another party to undergo a physical or mental examination must make an affirmative showing that the party's physical or mental condition is in controversy, and that there is good cause for the examinations requested. Here, Schlagenhauf did not assert his own mental or physical condition in support of, or in defense of, any claim. Thus, it was the obligation of the owners of the tractor-trailer to make a sufficient showing that Schlagenhauf's mental and physical condition were in controversy, and that there was good cause to order an examination. They failed to do so, as there was nothing in the pleadings or the movants' affidavits to show that Schlagenhauf was suffering from a mental or neurological illness warranting wide-ranging psychiatric or neurological examination. Rule 35 prohibits a trial court from ordering sweeping examinations of a party who has not put his own mental or physical condition in issue, merely where the person has been involved in an accident and a general charge of negligence is lodged.

Quick Summary

Under FRCP 35, a court may order a party to undergo a physical or mental examination only where the party's physical or mental condition is in controversy, and there is good cause to order the examination. The defendant in this case was the driver of a bus that was involved in a rear-end collision, who was sued by the passengers for negligence. His codefendants sought to compel him to undergo four mental and physical examinations. The court held that neither the driver's mental nor physical condition was "in controversy" and the trial court's order compelling the examinations was unsupported by good cause.

Seiling v. Eyman
478 F.2d. 211 (9th Cir. 1973)
Ninth Circuit Court of Appeals

Case Facts

Gilbert Seiling was charged with multiple counts of assault with intent to commit murder. Defense requested a competency hearing. Two mental health professionals evaluated him and provided conflicting opinions. A third was appointed, and Mr. Seiling was found competent to stand trial. He pled guilty to some of the charges, and others were dismissed as part of a plea bargain. He was convicted and sentenced. He appealed, arguing that while he had been deemed competent to stand trial, he was incompetent to plead guilty. His conviction was reversed and remanded back to district court with guidance that it be reviewed specifically for competence to plead guilty.

Main Issue

Should there be a separate assessment of a defendant's competency to plead guilty beyond the assessment of competence to stand trial?

Court Holding

The Ninth Circuit Court of Appeals decided in this case that pleading guilty required a higher standard of competence than competence to stand trial. The standard adopted by the Court was whether the defendant had the capacity to make a "reasoned choice."

Court's Reasoning

The Seiling court reasoned that once the defendant's competency was placed at issue, "the trial court must look further than to the usual 'objective' criteria in determining the adequacy of a constitutional waiver." The Court further stated, "A defendant is not competent to plead guilty if a mental illness has substantially impaired his ability to make a reasoned choice among the alternatives presented to him and to understand the nature and consequences of his plea."

Quick Summary

In this case, the court placed a higher standard on a defendant's competence to plead guilty than was required for competence to stand trial. Competence to plead guilty required the defendant to have the capacity to make a "reasoned choice" about how to plead.

Sell v. United States
539 U.S. 166 (2003)
U.S. Supreme Court

Case Facts

Charles Sell was a dentist with a long history of psychotic mental illness. In 1997, he was charged with submitting fictitious insurance claims for payment. A Federal judge ordered a psychiatric examination in which Mr. Sell was deemed competent to stand trial (CST), but his bail was revoked due to his behavior. At a revocation hearing he was, according to the judge, "totally out of control ... screaming and shouting" and "spitting in the judge's face." Trial was scheduled, and Mr. Sell requested a CST evaluation. The judge sent him to the US Medical Center for Federal Prisoners where he was found incompetent and hospitalized. The hospital staff recommended that he take antipsychotic medication, but he refused. The staff sought permission to medicate him against his will. A reviewing psychiatrist authorized involuntary medication because Mr. Sell was mentally ill and dangerous and so that he would become competent for trial. Mr. Sell appealed, and the Appeals Court said that the government had not proven that Mr. Sell was a danger to self/others or gravely disabled (see *Harper* below), but that medications could be involuntarily administered to restore him to competency nonetheless. The U.S. Supreme Court granted certiorari to consider this issue of forced medications to restore competency.

Main Issue

Does the Constitution permit the administration of antipsychotic medications solely in order to render a criminal defendant competent to stand trial?

Court Holding

The U.S. Supreme Court held that the constitution does allow the government to involuntarily administer antipsychotic drugs to render a defendant CST, in limited circumstances:

1. "A court must find that important governmental interests (e.g., the adjudication of guilt or innocence vs refusal to take medication resulting in a long hospital commitment) are at stake."

2. "The court must conclude that involuntary medication will significantly further" those interests.
3. "The court must conclude that involuntary medication is necessary to further those interests" and that less intrusive methods of treatment are not likely to achieve the same results.
4. "The court must conclude that administration of the drugs is medically appropriate (in the patient's best interest in light of his medical condition)."

These criteria may not have to be considered if alternative criteria (i.e., dangerousness) are met or if *Harper* criteria (see *Washington v. Harper 494 US 210)* are met first.

Court's Reasoning

The U.S. Supreme Court referred to *Harper* in which the court authorized involuntary medication for inmates who are gravely disabled or are a danger to self/others. The *Harper* court held there was a justified balance between the inmate's liberty and the state's interests. The court reasoned that because Mr. Sell was not dangerous, the Court of Appeals erred in approving forced medication solely to restore competence because it did not consider the above criteria.

Quick Summary

The government may involuntarily administer medications to render a defendant competent to stand trial under limited circumstances.

Singleton v. Norris
319 F.3d 1018 (2003)
No. 00-1492
U.S. Court of Appeals, Eighth Circuit

Case Facts

Mary Lou York was murdered on June 1, 1979, while working in the grocery store she owned. The State of Arkansas convicted Charles Singleton, age 20, of capital felony murder and aggravated robbery. He received a sentence of death for the murder and a sentence of life imprisonment for the robbery.

Singleton petitioned the district court for a stay of execution and writ of habeas corpus, claiming, among other things, that he was incompetent and therefore ineligible for execution. The district court upheld the conviction but reversed the death sentence. On appeal, the U.S. Court of Appeals affirmed the conviction but reversed the order vacating the death sentence.

In December 1992, Singleton filed an action in state court claiming that he could not be executed because he was incompetent. He requested that his treatment with antipsychotic medications be terminated and that a competency examination be held after the effects of the medications had subsided. The trial court denied his motion, and the Arkansas Supreme Court affirmed. Upon appeal, Singleton conceded that he was competent because of the antipsychotic medication he was taking voluntarily.

In 1997, the state placed Singleton on a *Harper* (*Washington et al. v. Harper*; 494 U.S. 210, 1990) involuntary medication regimen after a medication review panel determined that he posed a danger to himself and others. After the medication took effect, Singleton's psychotic symptoms abated. In January 2000, the state scheduled his execution for March 1, 2000. In February 2000, Singleton filed a petition for habeas corpus, arguing that the state could not constitutionally restore his *Ford* competency through use of forced medication and then execute him. The district court denied the petition, finding no evidence that the actions and decisions of the medical personnel involved were motivated by the desire to make Singleton competent so that he could be executed. Singleton appealed to the U.S. Court of Appeals and was granted a stay of execution.

That court also ordered a limited remand in March 2000 to answer two remaining questions of fact. First, was Singleton *Ford*-competent prior to the implementation of the *Harper* mandatory medication order in 1997? The district court found that Singleton was not *Ford*-competent at the time the involuntary medication regime began in 1997. Second, would Singleton regress into psychosis and become *Ford*-incompetent if he stopped taking the medication? The district court found that Singleton would regress into psychosis without medication, but could not say with certainty when psychotic symptoms would resume and whether he would become *Ford*-incompetent. Although the district court did not make a specific finding as to Singleton's present competence, Singleton did not argue that under medication he is unaware of his punishment and why he is to be punished.

Main Issue

Does a state violate the 8th or 14th Amendments by executing an inmate who has regained competency through appropriate medical care, even when that care is provided against the inmate's wishes (e.g., forced medication)?

Court Holding

No. A state does not violate the 8th or 14th Amendments by executing an inmate who regained competency through appropriate medical care.

Court's Reasoning

When a state is under an obligation to administer antipsychotic medication for treatment purposes, any additional motive or effect is irrelevant. *Ford* prohibits only the execution of an inmate who is unaware of the punishment they will receive and why they will receive it. A state does not violate the Eighth Amendment when it executes an inmate who became incompetent during his long stay on death row but subsequently regained competency through appropriate medical care, even when the care is administered against the inmate's wishes.

Quick Summary

A state will not violate the 8th or 14th Amendments by executing an inmate whose competency was restored and maintained through appropriate, including forced.

> ***Spano v. New York***
> **360 U.S. 315 (1959)**
> **No. 582.**
> **U.S. Supreme Court.**

Case Facts

Vincent Joseph Spano, born in Italy, was 25 years old 1957 when he shot and killed another man. On that day, while drinking in a bar, a former professional boxer took some of Spano's money from the bar. Spano followed him out of the bar to recover the money, and a fight ensued. The former boxer knocked Spano down and then kicking him in the head multiple times. Shock from the force of these blows caused Spano to vomit. After the bartender applied some ice to his head, Spano went to his apartment, got a gun, and walked to a candy store where the other man often spent time and shot and killed the man. Spano was arrested and charged with first-degree murder. His attorney cautioned him to answer no questions, and left him in the custody of the officers. Spano was promptly questioned. The questioning was both persistent and continuous. Spano steadfastly refused to answer; however, ultimately, a confession was obtained. At the trial, the confession was introduced in evidence over appropriate objections. The jury was instructed that it could rely on it only if it was found to be voluntary. The jury returned a guilty verdict, and Spano was sentenced to death. The New York Court of Appeals affirmed the conviction. The U.S. Supreme Court granted certiorari to resolve the problem presented under the 14th Amendment. Spano argued that, following indictment, no confession obtained in the absence of counsel can be used without violating the 14th Amendment.

Main Issue

Can the confession of a person already indicted for murder, obtained without the presence of counsel, be used in court without violating his or her 14th Amendment rights?

Court Holding

No. The U.S. Supreme Court found use of the confession obtained in this case inconsistent with the 14th Amendment and thus determined that the confession was inadmissible.

Court's Reasoning

This is one of numerous cases presenting the question of whether a confession was properly admitted into evidence under the 14th Amendment. As in all such cases, the court was required to resolve a conflict between two fundamental interests of society; its interest in prompt and efficient law enforcement, and its interest in preventing the rights of its individual members from being abridged by unconstitutional methods of law enforcement.

The court determined that the abhorrence of society to the use of involuntary confessions does not turn alone on the inherent untrust-worthiness of the confessions. It also turns on the deep-rooted feeling that the police must obey the law while enforcing the law; that in the end, life and liberty can be as much endangered from illegal methods used to convict suspects as from the actual criminals themselves. The court's judgment was that Spano's conviction could not stand.

The court emphasized that this was not a case where the police were questioning a suspect in the course of investigating an unsolved crime. Rather, when Spano surrendered to the New York authorities, he was already under indictment for first degree murder.

Under the U.S. system of justice, an indictment is supposed to be followed by an arraignment and a trial. At every stage in those proceedings, the accused has an absolute right to a lawyer's assistance.

Quick Summary

Confessions obtained from persons under indictment for a crime, without the presence of their attorney, if requested, are inadmissible.

Stanford v. Kentucky
492 U.S. 361 (1989)
U.S. Supreme Court

Case Facts

Kevin Stanford robbed, raped, and killed 20-year-old Barbel Poore by shooting her in the face in 1981 when he was 17 years and four months of age. He was tried as an adult, convicted, and sentenced to death and 45 years. He appealed, arguing that he had a right to treatment as a juvenile, but the Kentucky Supreme Court indicated that there was no appropriate treatment for him and that the jury had been able to consider his age during their sentencing. The lower court's sentence was upheld. The U.S. Supreme Court granted certiorari.

Main Issue

While *Thompson v. Oklahoma* (decided the year prior to this case) set the precedent that juveniles under 16 years of age could not be sentenced to death, what about juveniles older than 16?

Court Holding

The Kentucky Supreme Court affirmed the lower court's decision that a death sentence was constitutional as long as the juvenile was older than 16 years. The U.S. Supreme Court agreed, and the sentence remained.

Court's Reasoning

The court reasoned that while the states agree that a person under 16 should not be sentenced to death, states are less uniform in their practices for those above age 16. It also reasoned that the court is not composed of philosophers to decide at which precise age a death sentence is permissible and that the process of evaluating whether a particular juvenile defendant is appropriate for waiver to adult court considers an individualized approach to sentencing options. The court also indicated that age is a factor the jury can consider in mitigation when crafting a sentence.

Quick Summary

The U.S. Supreme Court affirmed the death sentence of a 17-year-old, holding that age is a matter in mitigation for the jury to consider at sentencing and that the process of waiver to adult court also considers the individual factors present that might prevent such transfer and sentencing. It is not a violation of the eighth amendment to sentence a juvenile over age 16 to death.

State v. Alberico
861 P.2d 192 (N.M. 1993)
New Mexico Supreme Court

Case Facts

In one case, Ralph Alberico was convicted of criminal sexual penetration and kidnapping. In a separate but similar case, Richard Marquez was also convicted of criminal sexual penetration. Both trial court convictions were overturned by the New Mexico Court of appeals, on the basis that the trial court should not have admitted expert testimony "to the effect that the alleged victim suffered from post traumatic stress disorder (PTSD) consistent with sexual abuse." This prompted the state to appeal these two decisions with writs of certiorari to the New Mexico Supreme Court. The New Mexico Supreme Court accepted both cases as one, given the similarities between the two cases.

Main Issues

The New Mexico Supreme Court wrote: "In this opinion, we address the subject of the admissibility of expert opinion testimony regarding alleged victims of sexual abuse who suffer from post traumatic stress disorder. As a necessary sub-issue, we must also discuss in general the admissibility of scientific evidence by way of expert opinion testimony under our Rules of Evidence."

In other words, there are two main issues in this case:

1. Can mental health professionals (forensic psychologists in this particular decision) offer expert testimony on the presence of posttraumatic stress disorder (PTSD) *that is consistent with* sexual abuse?
2. What is the appropriate standard for admitting expert testimony in the state of New Mexico?

Court Holding

The New Mexico Supreme Court held that forensic mental health professionals who qualify as experts *can* opine on the presence of PTSD, including PTSD that is consistent with sexual abuse.

The Court also held that the *Frye* test of general acceptance is no longer the appropriate standard for admission of expert testimony. Instead, it is Rule 702 from the New Mexico Rules of Evidence that should be used as the filter for expert testimony.

Court's Reasoning

With regard to mental health professionals being allowed to opine on the presence of PTSD, including PTSD that is consistent with sexual abuse, the New Mexico Supreme Court emphasized that PTSD is a diagnosis recognized in the *Diagnostic and Statistical Manual* (*DSM*). Notably, the Court did *not* recognize Rape Trauma Syndrome as a scientific diagnosis because it, in contrast to PTSD, was not included in the *DSM*:

> We hold that expert testimony concerning RTS is inadmissible mainly because it is not part of the specialized manual DSM III-R like PTSD is, even though there is evidence in the record that RTS is generally accepted by psychologists just like PTSD is.

With regard to abandoning the *Frye* test, in favor of Rule 702, the New Mexico Supreme Court noted that the U.S. Supreme Court had recently done the same thing, citing *Daubert* v. *Merrill Dow Pharmaceuticals* (1993). In other words, this decision represents an alignment between the New Mexico Supreme Court and the U.S. Supreme Court with respect to admitting expert testimony.

Quick Summary

Forensic mental health experts *can* offer expert opinions about the presence of PTSD that is consistent with sexual abuse. Doing so does not usurp the decision-making ability of the jury on the basis that the jury will be unduly swayed by the expert's opinion. In contrast, rape trauma syndrome is *not* recognized as a scientifically supported diagnosis, because it is not included in the DSM.

Rule 702 of the New Mexico Rules of Evidence, not the general-acceptance/*Frye* test, is the appropriate standard for admitting expert testimony in the state of New Mexico. Accordingly, this decision reinforces—in the state of New Mexico—the message conveyed in the *Daubert* decision and the standard set forth in Rule 702 from the Federal Rules of Evidence. Namely, expert testimony in New Mexico can be admitted under the following circumstances:

> If scientific, technical or other specialized knowledge will assist the trier of fact to understand the evidence or to determine a fact in issue, a witness qualified as an expert by knowledge, skill, experience, training, or education may testify thereto in the form of an opinion or otherwise. (Rule 702).

State v. Andring
342 N.W.2d 128 (Minn. 1984)
Minnesota Supreme Court

Case Facts

David Andring was charged with criminal sexual conduct and was released on bond. He entered the Crisis Intervention Unit of a local medical center and was diagnosed with alcoholism and depression. He was told that the information he shared in therapy was confidential, so he told the intake nurse, his individual therapist, and his group therapist details about the sexual conduct. The state then sought to access those statements for use in trial. The trial court denied the discovery of statements made during intake and individual therapy but allowed the discovery of statements made in group therapy. The defendant argued that all the statements were protected under the Comprehensive Alcohol Abuse and Alcoholism Prevention, Treatment, and Rehabilitation Act Amendments of 1974, which provides for "confidentiality of the records of patient identity, diagnosis, prognosis or treatment." But the Minnesota Maltreatment of Minors Reporting Act (which came from the

Federal Child Abuse Prevention Act) said that the doctor-patient privilege cannot be used when it comes to cases of child maltreatment and that doctors are required to report child abuse. The lower court asked the Supreme Court of Minnesota if group therapy is confidential and privileged.

Main Issue

What information in a doctor-patient relationship is not privileged when it comes to child abuse reporting? Are statements made in group therapy to be treated as privileged just as intake or individual sessions?

Court Holding

1. Limited information is required by a mental health professional for disclosure to authorities when child abuse is alleged, such as the identity of the child; the parent, guardian, or other person responsible for care; the nature and extent of the child's injuries; and the name and address of the reporter, but it is not necessary to release the patient's entire record that has other confidential and protected information.
2. Statements made in group therapy are privileged and cannot be released.

Court's Reasoning

Just because child abuse is alleged, the doctor-patient relationship cannot be totally disregarded. The purpose of child abuse reporting laws is to protect children, not punish those who maltreat them (in fact, one of the goals of the reporting laws is for the abuser to get treatment). Therefore, the medical privilege is negated only to the extent necessary to obtain specific and limited information (listed above). Treatment in group settings works largely because the patients feel that what they share is safe and protected.

Quick Summary

Therapy groups are to be considered confidential and privileged, and only certain limited information shared during an intake session, individual therapy, or group therapy (listed earlier) can be disclosed in a child abuse investigation.

State v. Cantrell
179 P.3d 1214 (N.M. 2008)
New Mexico Supreme Court

Case Facts

"On October 1, 2003, the Grant County Sheriff's Office received information that Defendant, Dawna Cantrell, killed her husband, Gentry Cantrell, by stabbing him with a knife; that she did so in self-defense; and that the knife was in a drawer in Defendant's van. Defendant was arrested and charged with an open count of murder and two counts of tampering with evidence."

Defense-retained forensic neuropsychologist, Dr. Eric Westfried, and state-retained forensic psychologist, Dr. Edward Siegel, both concluded that Ms. Cantrell "suffer[ed] from a persecutory delusional disorder that causes her to believe that there is a conspiracy against her ... [and] that this delusional disorder makes it difficult for Defendant to assist her attorney in her defense." Based on the opinions of these two mental health experts, "the parties stipulated that Defendant understood the nature and significance of the criminal proceedings against her and had a factual understanding of the criminal charges, meeting the first two criteria for trial competency ... [but] that because Defendant was unable to assist her counsel in her defense, she was legally incompetent to stand trial under the third criterion for trial competency."

The Court then ordered Ms. Cantrell to undergo a "dangerousness" evaluation (i.e., a violence risk assessment), which Dr. Siegel conducted. Dr. Siegel concluded that Ms. Cantrell was not dangerous, prompting the trial court to appoint "a new forensic evaluator, Dr. Gerald Fredman, to re-evaluate Defendant's competency to stand trial." Dr. Fredman opined that Ms. Cantrell was likely to be incompetent, but that she would likely attain competence if treated with antipsychotic medication. Based on Dr. Fredman's new input, "the State filed a motion asking the court to order Defendant to submit to a psychiatric examination for the purpose of prescribing anti-psychotic medication and treating Defendant to trial competency." The trial court used the standard established in the U.S. Supreme Court decision, *Sell v. United States* (2003), to justify an order that Ms. Cantrell be treated to a state of competency with psychotropic medication. An appeal was initiated by the defense, which is how the case went to the New Mexico Supreme Court.

Main Issue

In the state of New Mexico, can a defendant be ordered to submit to involuntary psychotropic drug treatment "for the sole purpose of establishing Defendant's competency to stand trial"? Or is this a violation of the defendant's due process rights?

Court Holding

The district court's order for involuntary drug treatment of defendant Cantrell was affirmed, thereby aligning the criminal laws in the state of New Mexico with the U.S. Supreme Court's decision in *Sell v. United States* (2003). In other words, a criminal defendant in the state of New Mexico *can* be medicated against their will for the purpose of establishing their adjudicative competence.

Court's Reasoning

By and large, the New Mexico Supreme Court relied on the so-called Sell factors, already established in *Sell v. United States* (2003):

> There is an important governmental interest in bringing the defendant to trial.
>
> Administration of antipsychotic medication will substantially render the defendant competent to stand trial and is substantially unlikely to have side effects which will interfere significantly with the defendant's ability to assist counsel in conducting a defense.
>
> The defendant has participated in out-patient therapy for over a year and this or any other alternative, less intrusive treatments are unlikely to achieve substantially the same results;
>
> Administration of antipsychotic medication is medically appropriate and in the patient's best medical interest in light of her medical condition.

Quick Summary

Defendant Cantrell was found to be suffering from a delusion that prevented her from attaining competence to stand trial. At the suggestion of a forensic psychiatrist, the district court ordered Cantrell to take antipsychotic medication, in an attempt to make her competent. The district court's order for involuntary drug treatment of Cantrell was affirmed by the New Mexico Supreme Court, aligning the decision with *Sell v. United States* (2003, U.S. Supreme Court), which established the Sell factors (e.g., an important governmental interest exists to try the defendant in court, the medication will likely work and not likely harm the defendant, less-restrictive treatments will not likely work, and the medication is medically appropriate).

State v. Chavez
174 P.3d 988 (N.M. 2007)
New Mexico Supreme Court

Case Facts

Elias Chavez was indicted "on two open counts of murder, alternatively charged as felony murder; attempted first degree murder; aggravated stalking; two counts of child abuse; and tampering with evidence." He was found incompetent to stand trial and ordered to undergo competency restoration. Less than a year later, the state moved to have Chavez criminally committed "for the period of time equal to the maximum sentence for the offenses with which he [was] charged." Following statute, the district court conducted a competency hearing to redetermine Chavez's adjudicative competence. This resulted in a finding of competence "by a preponderance of the evidence standard but not by a clear and convincing evidence standard." In other words, just over 50% of the evidence pointed toward competence, but the higher hurdle of clear and convincing evidence was *not* met, meaning that a larger percentage of the evidence (approximately 75% or more) did *not* support competence. Had the clear-and-convincing evidence standard been applied, Chavez would not have been found competent.

Because "The district court noted uncertainty with respect to the state of the law regarding the requisite standard of proof for a redetermination of competency," it decided Chavez' competence using the clear-and-convincing-evidence standard, not preponderance of the evidence. Hence, the district court found Chavez incompetent. The state, not liking this decision, appealed to the New Mexico Supreme Court.

Main Issue

"The sole issue before us is the proper standard of proof for a redetermination of competency, following a prior determination that a defendant is incompetent to stand trial." In other words, how much of the evidence is required to determine that a defendant is *in*competent to stand trial? A preponderance of the evidence? Or clear and convincing evidence?

Court Holding

The appropriate standard of proof for deciding *in*competence in the state of New Mexico is preponderance of the evidence, not clear and convincing evidence. Hence, only slightly more than 50% of the evidence must point toward incompetence for the defendant to be found incompetent. If as little as 50.1% of the evidence points toward incompetence, the defendant will be found incompetent. If more of the evidence points toward incompetence (e.g., 60%, 70%, or even 90%), that is not a problem. But this higher standard of proof is not required in the state of New Mexico. The New Mexico Supreme Court wrote as follows:

> We reaffirm the longstanding rule, established by our case law, that a criminal defendant initially bears the burden of proving by a preponderance of the evidence that he or she is incompetent to stand trial, whereupon the burden shifts to the State to prove by the same standard, *a preponderance of the evidence,* that the defendant is competent to stand trial.

Court's Reasoning

The New Mexico Supreme Court relied on established precedent to make the decision:

> Our case law, decided under these provisions, has established clear rules … it is well established that the defendant in a criminal case bears the initial

burden of proving his or her incompetence by a preponderance of the evidence standard. It has also been long held that, once there is a finding of incompetence, the burden shifts to the State on the redetermination of competency "to overcome a presumption of incompetency by *a preponderance of the evidence.*"

Quick Summary

Elias Chavez was indicted on murder charges, aggravated stalking, child abuse, and tampering with evidence and was found incompetent to stand trial using the preponderance-of-the-evidence burden of proof. Soon thereafter, the State moved for a criminal commitment, but statute required another competence-to-stand trial determination. It was determined that a preponderance of the evidence supported competence, but that Chavez would not be found competent, if the higher, clear-and-convincing-evidence standard were used. The district court opted for the clear-and-convincing-evidence standard and concluded that Chavez was incompetent. So the State appealed and the New Mexico Supreme Court concluded that the preponderance-of-the-evidence standard for *in*competence is the appropriate standard in the state of New Mexico.

This case also emphasizes that the defendant *initially* bears the burden of proving their incompetence, by a preponderance of the evidence. However, this burden (still by a preponderance of the evidence) shifts to the State if the defendant has already been found incompetent to stand trial.

Curiously, *Cooper v. Oklahoma* (1996, U.S. Supreme Court) was not cited in *State v. Chavez*. This is interesting because in *Cooper v. Oklahoma*, the U.S. Supreme Court said that preponderance-of-the-evidence is the appropriate standard for adjudicative competence.

State v. Crenshaw
98 Wn.2d 789 (1983)
659 P.2d 488
No. 47498-2.
The Supreme Court of Washington, En Banc.

Case Facts

Rodney Crenshaw and his wife were on their honeymoon in Canada when Crenshaw became involved in a brawl and was then deported. He got a motel room in Washington and waited for his wife to join him. When she arrived two days later, he suspected that she had been unfaithful. He took her to the motel room and beat her until she was unconscious. He then went to a store, stole a knife, returned, and stabbed his wife 24 times, killing her. He then left to get an axe, returned to the motel room, and decapitated his wife. He then proceeded to conceal his actions by placing her body in a blanket and her head in a pillowcase, and putting both in his wife's car. Next, he cleaned the room of blood and fingerprints. Before leaving, he spoke to the motel manager about a phone bill and chatted with him while having a beer.

Crenshaw left the motel and drove to a remote area where he hid the two parts of his wife's body in thick brush. He then drove additional hundreds of miles from the scene. On the way, he picked up two hitchhikers, told them of his crime, and had them help dispose of his wife's car in a river. The hitchhikers informed the police, and Crenshaw was apprehended, voluntarily confessing to the crime. His plea of not guilty by reason of insanity was a major issue during the trial. He testified that he was of the Moscovite religious faith, and consistent with that religion, it would have been improper for him not to kill his wife if she committed adultery. Although Crenshaw also had a history of psychiatric problems, for which he had been hospitalized, the jury rejected his insanity defense and found him guilty of murder in the first degree.

Crenshaw appealed his conviction. After the Court of Appeals affirmed the trial court, Crenshaw raised the same issues before the Supreme Court of Washington. The propriety of the insanity defense instruction, which explained the right-wrong standard in the *M'Naghten* test in terms of "legal" right and wrong, was a focus of the appeal. Crenshaw contended that the trial court erred in defining "right and wrong" as legal, rather than moral, right and wrong.

Main Issue

Is the *M'Naghten* test specific to "legal" right and wrong, or does it also include "moral" right and wrong?

Court Holding

The state Supreme Court held that the instruction to the jury regarding right and wrong was sufficient; that legal wrong includes more wrong.

Court's Reasoning

The state Supreme Court upheld the prior finding on three grounds: (1) *M'Naghten* supported the "legal" wrong definition; (2) "moral" wrong and "legal" wrong are synonymous; therefore, the "legal" wrong definition did not alter the meaning of the test, and, (3) because Crenshaw did not prove other elements of his insanity defense, any error in the definition of wrong was harmless.

Society's morals and legal wrongs are interchangeable concepts in the context of this case. Crenshaw's crime was clearly contrary to society's morals and the law. Therefore, by defining wrong in terms of legal wrong, the trial court did not alter the meaning of the *M'Naghten* test.

Quick Summary

Defining *wrong* in terms of legal wrong (versus moral wrong) is consistent with the meaning of the *M'Naghten* test.

State v. Flores
124 P.3d 1175 (N.M. Ct. App. 2005)
New Mexico Court of Appeals

Case Facts

Despite multiple evaluations from both sides, and lengthy legal proceedings, murder defendant Ruben Flores, also later charged with assaulting a guard while incarcerated, was ultimately found competent to stand trial. He appealed this decision to the Court of Appeals of New Mexico.

Main Issues

In concluding that Mr. Flores was incompetent to proceed, did the district court err by "(1) refusing to make a contemporaneous determination of Defendant's present ability to intelligently assist his attorney, (2) blindly relying on the prior competency ruling without independently analyzing the past and present evidence of Defendant's competency, (3) not allowing Defendant to present the issue of his present competency to the jury, and (4) giving a confusing excessive force instruction to the jury"?

Court Holding

The Court of Appeals of New Mexico held that the district court did not err by determining that defendant Flores was incompetent and that the matter did not need to be heard before a jury.

Court's Reasoning

One of the judges found the opinions of experts for the state to be more credible than the opinions of the experts presented by the defense: "As stated earlier in this opinion, Judge Gallini found the LVMC experts to be more credible than Defendant's experts."

While testimony by mental health experts "is not required to support a contention of incompetency," this court was not sufficiently moved by the testimony of Mr. Flores' own attorney, who said that her client was deteriorating as a result of solitary confinement and that the court needed to factor this into its determination of Flores' competence. In support of this position, the court wrote: "In New Mexico law, something more than counsel's unsubstantiated assertions and opinion regarding a defendant's competency is required to pass the reasonable doubt and good cause tests." In other words, considerably more information than the testimony of defense counsel is needed to influence the court as to a defendant's incompetence.

The court acknowledged that much time had lapsed between evaluations—"The length of time from the evaluations of Defendant and also from Defendant's second competency hearing, and Defendant's possible deterioration over time, present a somewhat troubling history"—but ultimately reasoned that it is the job of the defense counsel to initiate updated competency evaluations, as opposed to testifying based on their own observations of their client.

With regard to Mr. Flores' claim that a jury should have determined his competence, not the district court judge, the New Mexico Court of Appeals reasoned that this only holds if there is "reasonable doubt" as to the defendant's adjudicative competence. Because there was no reasonable doubt in this case, this court found no merit in this argument.

Finally, the court reasoned that the district court used appropriate jury instructions, because the instructions included all the necessary elements.

Quick Summary

After being found incompetent by a district court, murder defendant Flores appealed based on testimony from his attorney. He asserted that his attorney's testimony alone was adequate to raise "reasonable doubt" as to his competence. He also asserted that his competence should be determined by a jury, not the district court judge, and that the judge gave confusing jury instructions during his trial. The New Mexico Court of Appeals disagreed and supported its position largely on the basis that defense counsel failed to demonstrate "reasonable doubt" as to her client's competence. Had she presented new, compelling evidence—that is, not just her opinion—the Court may have been persuaded to reconsider Mr. Flores' competence.

State v. Hamann
285 N.W.2d 180 (1979)
No. 61812.
Supreme Court of Iowa

Case Facts

John Hamann shot and killed Richard Slattery at Slattery's office. Hamann's father and Slattery worked together and apparently were rivals for leadership of their department. The trial centered on Hamann's insanity defense, with both sides introducing expert psychiatric testimony. Hamann's psychiatric witness testified that Hamann's ability to know right from wrong was impaired by a delusion that his father's life was endangered by a malicious adversary, that Hamann was the only one who could enforce justice, and that, after he killed Slattery, society would "understand that a great injustice had been righted."

Another psychiatric expert for the defense testified that, although Hamann knew his act was criminal, his psychiatric illness led him to believe he was doing right by shooting Slattery. In contrast, the expert for the state testified that Hamann believed society would be better off without Slattery but that his belief was an opinion, not a delusion. Hamann moved for directed verdict on the ground that the evidence established he was insane within the *M'Naghten* rule. The motion was overruled, and Hamann was found guilty of first-degree murder. He appealed. He requested that the court overrule the *M'Naghten* rule, and he challenged the trial court's interpretation of "right" and "wrong" under the *M'Naghten* rule.

Main Issues

1. Should the Supreme Court of Iowa overrule the *M'Naghten* common law doctrine and instead adopt the standard recommended by the American Law Institute's model penal code?
2. Does the *M'Naghten* rule refer to right and wrong in a moral sense or only in the legal sense?

Court Holding

1. The Supreme Court of Iowa declined to overrule the *M'Naghten* rule.
2. The court held that the words "right" and "wrong" under the *M'Naghten* rule refer to legal right or wrong. Thus, Hamann's contention to the contrary was without merit.

Court's Reasoning

1. The court had been asked multiple times to overrule the *M'Naghten* rule, and it consistently refused to do so. The *M'Naghten* rule is codified.
2. Hamann argued that the trial court should have instructed that "right" or "wrong," as used in the *M'Naghten* rule refers to right and wrong in a moral sense rather than a legal sense. The *M'Naghten* case itself does not answer the question, and cases from other states are divided on the issue. The Supreme Court of Iowa took the position that the words "right" or "wrong" under the *M'Naghten* rule should be understood in their legal, rather than moral, sense. The court acknowledged that the view to which it subscribed was sometimes referred to as the minority view on this question.

The court noted that in this world of revolutionary and often violent change, it is futile to pretend that our society maintains a consensus on moral questions beyond what it writes into its laws. The court found only 14 Anglo-American jurisdictions, involving 16 cases, which considered this question. Eight jurisdictions hold that right or wrong in the *M'Naghten* rule refers to moral right or wrong, whereas six jurisdictions hold that the term involves the force of law. The court also noted that the so-called majority rule calls for application of what seemed to it an amorphous and shifting standard and that the courts can only pretend to possess knowledge on general mores. The court went on to note that only a part of a society's moral standards becomes so fixed and agreed upon as to become law and that until a moral standard becomes law, it is an unreliable test for sanity. The court was of the belief that it is a more accurate measure of mental health to test a defendant's ability to understand what society has established as law.

Regarding Hamann specifically, the court noted that he was in a poor position to request that the court adopt his interpretation of the *M'Naghten* rule because the authorities he cited would not be helpful to him. The states that believe the right or wrong test should be conducted with a view to moral right or wrong reject a subjective test; that is, the test in those jurisdictions is conducted in accordance with society's general mores and not in accordance with an accused's personal views on morality. However, Hamann's insanity defense was subjective rather than being based on the mores of society generally. The court also noted that impossible uncertainty over so-called general mores renders the appreciation of morality a tool unfit for the task of measuring sanity.

Quick Summary

1. The *M'Naghten* rule is codified in Iowa and will not be overruled.
2. There is no practical distinction between moral and legal right or wrong in a murder case. Under any rational legal system, ever devised murder would be prohibited. And under any rational moral system, ever imagined murder would be reprehensible.

State v. Garcia
998 P.2d 186 (N.M. Ct. App. 2000)
New Mexico Court of Appeals

Case Facts

Mr. Arthur Garcia was determined incompetent to stand trial by a district court, based on a forensic psychological assessment by forensic psychologist, Dr. Susan Cave. The State requested that another expert of their choosing reevaluate Mr. Garcia, on the basis that they would not have selected Dr. Cave as their expert: "We would like to have a separate person or group of people evaluate the defendant other than Dr. Cave. If given the choice, we would not choose Dr. Cave to have the defendant evaluated." The district court denied this particular request by the State, but approved a separate evaluation on Mr. Garcia's "potential dangerousness." The district court ultimately determined that Mr. Garcia was incompetent and not dangerous and so his charges were dismissed without prejudice. The State appealed.

Main Issues

1. Did the district court abuse its discretion by finding the defendant incompetent to stand trial?
2. Did the district court err by not allowing the State to have its own expert conduct a second competency evaluation?

Court Holding

1. No.
2. No.

Court's Reasoning

1. With regard to the district court abusing its discretion by finding Mr. Garcia incompetent, the New Mexico Court of Appeals reasoned that the district court had done its job appropriately and that it had adequate grounds to conclude that the defendant was incompetent:

   > It is beyond dispute that the district court acts within its authority as fact finder by weighing and drawing its own conclusions from the evidence presented … the district court did not abuse its discretion in concluding that Defendant was incompetent to stand trial.

2. With regard to the State not being allowed to have its own expert evaluate the defendant, the court reasoned as follows:

   > There is no explicit provision, in either rule or statute, that allows the district court to order more than one mental evaluation of a criminal defendant insofar as his or her competency to stand trial. However, there is also no prohibition.

The Court went on:

> We conclude that Rule 5-602(C) NMRA 1999 provides an appropriate procedure for any request, be it initial or subsequent, for court-ordered mental evaluations of a criminal defendant … [which] provides: "Upon motion and upon good cause shown, the court shall order a mental examination of the defendant before making any determination of competency under this rule." As such, it does not specify who can move for an evaluation. Cf. Rule 5-602(B)(1)

In other words, if there is "good cause" for a second evaluation, the district court may approve a state-initiated second evaluation. But in this case, such "good cause" was not demonstrated by the state.

Quick Summary

After being found incompetent to stand trial by the court-appointed forensic mental health expert, the State appealed on the basis that the district court had abused its discretion by finding the defendant incompetent and that it erred by not granting the State the opportunity to have its own expert evaluation the defendant for competence. The New Mexico Court of Appeals affirmed the district court's decisions (1) on the basis that the district court made the incompetence determination based on quality information (e.g., a forensic assessment that included full-battery IQ testing, a competency interview, and review of collateral records) and (2) on the basis that the State did not demonstrate "good cause" for a second evaluation.

State v. Gardner
509 P.2d 871 (N.M. 1973)
New Mexico Supreme Court

Case Facts

After a domestic disagreement, defendant Gardner purchased a handgun and ammunition and went to the apartment where her husband was staying with a friend. When the husband told Gardner he planned to leave her and get a divorce, she shot him twice, killing him. Gardner admitted at trial that she had shot her husband, but pleaded not guilty by reason of insanity. The state presented no evidence of sanity. Gardner presented the testimony of two psychiatrists, both of whom testified that because of a "disease of the mind," Gardner was "incapable of preventing herself from committing" the murder. The two psychiatrists reached different diagnoses for Gardner's mental condition, and provided different views as to whether she knew the difference between right and wrong. The trial court put the question of Gardner's sanity to the jury, which convicted her of first-degree murder. Gardner appealed, arguing that because the state presented no evidence of sanity, the trial court should have ruled that Gardner had proven her defense as a matter of law. Accordingly, the question of sanity should not have been submitted to the jury.

Main Issue

Where a defendant presents evidence in support of a defense of not guilty by reason of insanity, and the state presents no evidence of sanity, should a court rule on the defense as a matter of law, or submit the question of sanity to the jury?

Court Holding

The defense should be submitted to the jury.

Court's Reasoning

Under New Mexico law, sanity is presumed to exist, even without evidence of its existence. When a defendant offers evidence that tends to show she was insane at the time of the alleged offense, it is the duty of the jury to determine the issue of sanity from the evidence. If the jury disbelieves the defendant's evidence, the presumption of sanity stands.[2]

Quick Summary

Under New Mexico law, the state enjoys a presumption of sanity. Where a defendant proffers evidence in support of a defense of not guilty by reason of insanity, the presumption of sanity is not automatically rebutted – rather, a jury decides the issue. This is the case even if the state presents no affirmative evidence of sanity.

State v. Gutierrez
355 P.3d 93 (N.M. Ct. App. 2015)
New Mexico Court of Appeals

Case Facts

Defendant Johnny Gutierrez "was indicted in 2005 on twenty-three charges related to an incident in Las Cruces, wherein he and two other men trapped four adults and two children in a trailer and threatened them with firearms for several hours." Forensic psychologist, Dr. Janette Castillo, measured Gutierrez' IQ to be 62 and, ultimately, Gutierrez was found by Judge Driggers to be incompetent and dangerous. Gutierrez was then committed to the New Mexico Behavioral Health Institute (NMBHI) in Las Vegas, New Mexico, for competency restoration, under NMSA § 31-9-1.2. At a 90-day review hearing, Judge Driggers determined that Gutierrez was still incompetent to stand trial and dangerous, and unlikely to ever become competent. Because of the low IQ, Judge Driggers granted the motion to determine if Gutierrez had "mental retardation," as defined under NMSA § 31-9-1.6, and the case was reassigned to Judge Lisa Schultz. At the 1.6 hearing, "Judge Schultz on her own motion, and without notice to the parties, took up the issue of competency once again and found that Defendant was competent to stand trial 'beyond a reasonable doubt.'"

Main Issue

Can a district court judge in the state of New Mexico use a 1.6 hearing (i.e., a hearing for determining if a defendant satisfies the legal definition of "mental retardation" in New Mexico) to determine a defendant's competence?

Court Holding

No.

Court's Reasoning

The defendant's demeanor in court alone cannot be relied upon by a district court judge to conclude that the defendant is competent. Such actions violate due process rights:

> The United States Supreme Court has held specifically that a state court violates a defendant's due process rights when it fails to inquire into competency after the defendant presents enough evidence to entitle him to a hearing on the issue. Such a hearing cannot be dispensed with based on factors like the defendant's demeanor before the court but is, rather, a procedural right. As such, it requires adequate notice, an adversarial hearing before an independent decision-maker, and a written statement from the fact finder clarifying the evidence relied upon and reasons for the decision.

Moreover, the New Mexico Court of Appeals emphasized that determination of competence, or incompetence, requires an evaluation by "a qualified professional, such as a psychologist or psychiatrist, whom the district court recognizes as an expert" (see NMSA § 31-9-1.1).

Because the defendant had already been found incompetent, the burden of proving his competence shifted to the State. By turning the 1.6 hearing into a competence hearing, Judge Schultz "effectively required defendant to re-prove his incompetence … this was fundamental error."

Quick Summary

An adult criminal defendant with an IQ of 62 was found incompetent by a district court judge, following two competency evaluations by qualified mental health professionals. A 1.6 hearing was then ordered by the judge, to determine if the defendant was "mentally retarded," as defined under New Mexico law. At the 1.6 hearing, a different judge independently—and without prior notice to the defendant or the prosecution—concluded that the defendant was competent to stand trial, based on his demeanor in court:

Judge Schultz stated that it would "shock the conscience" if she did not revisit the earlier competency ruling and limited herself to considering only whether Defendant had mental retardation. In her opinion, Defendant was "clearly competent."

The New Mexico Court of Appeals disagreed with Judge Schultz, reversed her decision, and remanded the case. In so doing, it was established that a district court judge *cannot* independently determine that a defendant is competent at a 1.6 hearing, without initiating due process rights, including the right to a forensic evaluation from a qualified mental health professional (e.g., a forensic psychologist or forensic psychiatrist).

State v. Hartfield
388 S.E.2d 802 (S.C. 1990)
South Carolina Supreme Court

Case Facts

Dan Hartfield was convicted of marijuana trafficking and possession of cocaine. He had previously been hospitalized for examination of his competency to stand trial. At his competency hearing, a psychologist testified that Hartfield had a brain syndrome that produced psychosis as a result of his long-term drug use and was always insane and delusional at baseline. The expert testified that immediately following the offense, Hartfield was as "Crazy as a Billy goat" and committed to the state psychiatric hospital. Nonetheless, Hartfield was found competent to proceed to trial. The defense indicated their intent to raise an insanity defense or seek a finding of guilty but mentally ill, but the court ruled that those options were not available given that his conditions were the result of voluntary intoxication. He was convicted and appealed, arguing that the trial court erred by preventing him from presenting a sanity defense or having the option of a guilty but mentally ill finding.

Main Issue

Is settled insanity as a result of the use of substances recognized as a qualifying mental disease or defect for either a finding of not guilty by reason of insanity or guilty but mentally ill in South Carolina?

Court Holding

Yes. Permanent insanity, even if caused by voluntary intoxication, is a legitimate mental disease or defect that can be used in either an affirmative defense of insanity or a finding of guilty but mentally ill. The Supreme Court of South Carolina reversed and remanded for a new trial.

Court's Reasoning

In South Carolina, voluntary intoxication is not an excuse for criminal conduct. A settled insanity, however, in which sufficient and qualifying symptoms remain after the effects of the substance have worn off, is a permissible mental disease or defect for the purposes of potentially impairing a defendant's capacity to distinguish right from wrong or to be unable to conform their conduct to the requirements of the law even if they were able to distinguish that the behavior was wrong (resulting in a finding of guilty but mentally ill in South Carolina). Mr. Hartfield had presented evidence that his use of substances had resulted in permanent mental illness and was thus entitled to present an insanity or guilty but mentally ill defense based on the statutory definition of insanity in the South Carolina statute.

Quick Summary

In South Carolina, although the acute effects of voluntary intoxication do not provide an excuse for criminal conduct, a settled insanity that results in a permanent mental illness as a result of that substance use is a qualifying condition for the purposes of either an affirmative sanity defense or a finding of guilty but mentally ill. The trial court erred by not recognizing the difference between direct effects of intoxication and a settled insanity that persists in the absence of the substance.

State v. Jacob F.
446 P.3d 1237 (N.M. Ct. App. 2019)
New Mexico Court of Appeals

Case Facts

Defendant Jacob F. was arrested after he allegedly tried to harm his mother with garden shears. He was found both incompetent to proceed and "dangerous," as legally defined in the state of New Mexico under NMSA § 31-9-1.2.D (i.e., "dangerous" means that, if released, the defendant presents a serious threat of inflicting great bodily harm on another or of violating Section 30-9-11 or 30-9-13 NMSA 1978"). Because Jacob F. was found both incompetent *and* dangerous, he moved for a "1.6 hearing," to determine if—by a preponderance of the evidence—he was "mentally retarded," as legally defined in the state of New Mexico under NMSA § 31-9-1.6:

> As used in this section, "mental retardation" means significantly subaverage general intellectual functioning existing concurrently with deficits in adaptive behavior. An intelligence quotient of seventy or below on a reliably administered intelligence quotient test shall be presumptive evidence of mental retardation.

The motion for a 1.6 hearing was initiated because those found incompetent, dangerous, and "mentally retarded" in the state of New Mexico are only subject to civil commitment, not criminal prosecution or criminal commitment. However, the district court did *not* find Jacob F. to be "mentally retarded," on the basis that the two IQ test scores (67 and 68) were not reliable, because Jacob F. was experiencing symptoms of psychosis when tested. In making this determination, the district court emphasized that the IQ tests had not been "reliably administered," as called for under NMSA § 31-9-1.6. Jacob F. appealed this decision to the New Mexico Court of Appeals, asserting that his IQ was low enough to be designated as "mentally retarded" and, as a result, subject only to civil commitment.

Main Issues

1. Did Jacob F. fail to establish "based on a reliably administered IQ test … that his IQ was at or below seventy?" In other words, were the two IQs of 67 and 68 a result of "reliably administered" IQ tests? Or did psychosis make the administrations unreliable?
2. Did Jacob F. fail "to establish by a preponderance of the evidence that [he] was mentally retard[ed] as defined by [Section] 31-9-1.6(E)."?

Court Holding

1. The New Mexico Court of Appeals reversed the district court's decision that Jacob F. (1) failed to establish that his IQ was below 70 and (2) failed to establish by a preponderance of the evidence that he was "mentally retarded" under 31-9-1.6(E). In other words, the appeals court held that the presence of psychosis during testing did *not* make the IQ test administration unreliable.
2. No. The court held that Jacob F. did not bear the burden of proving by a preponderance of the evidence that he had "mental retardation" because that burden was on the State, not on him.

Court's Reasoning

In the state of New Mexico, an IQ of 70 or lower on a "reliably administered" IQ test is considered "presumptive evidence of mental retardation." Once this is established, the State has the burden of proving by a preponderance of the evidence that the defendant does *not* have "mental retardation." The New Mexico Court of Appeals in this case reasoned that the IQs of 67 and 68 had in fact been reliably administered, despite Jacob F. experiencing psychosis during the testing.

> Having considered the language of the statute and the testimony of the doctors, we agree with Defendant that the legislative requirement of a

> "reliably administered" IQ test is directed at the manner in which the test is given to the subject, rather than the accuracy of the results reached.

This Court also emphasized what needs to occur at the two stages of a 1.6 hearing. First is the presumptive stage, which only requires that the IQ test be administered in a reliable manner:

> Obviously, a "reliably administered" test is more likely to yield an accurate result than a test that is not "reliably administered." Nonetheless, at the "presumption" stage of the mental retardation analysis, the Legislature has made clear that nothing more is required than that the test be "reliably administered."

At the second stage of a 1.6 hearing, assuming an IQ of 70 or lower has been established in the first stage, the burden of proving that the defendant does *not* have "mental retardation" falls on the State. Accordingly, the New Mexico Court of Appeals reasoned that it was not Jacob F.'s burden to prove that he had "mental retardation" at the second stage of the 1.6 hearing. Rather, that burden was on the state, since Jacob F. had already demonstrated presumptive evidence of mental retardation through the two IQs below 70s, administered by two separate psychologists.

Quick Summary

After being found both incompetent to stand trial and legally "dangerous," defendant Jacob F. moved for a 1.6 hearing, to see if he was also "mentally retarded," as legally defined in the state of New Mexico. His motion for a 1.6 hearing was made in an attempt to avoid subsequent criminal prosecution or criminal commitment, and instead only be subject to civil commitment. Despite IQs of 67 and 68, from two different psychologists, the district court judge found Jacob F. to *not* be "mentally retarded" because he felt the IQ tests had not been reliably administered, on the basis that Jacob F. was experiencing symptoms of psychosis while being tested. The New Mexico Court of Appeals reversed the decision on the basis that having mental illness during IQ testing does not mean the test was administered unreliably. Moreover, the appeals court emphasized that it was never Jacob F.'s responsibility to prove he had "mental retardation" by a preponderance of the evidence because that burden was on the State, in the second stage of the 1.6 hearing. The first stage of the 1.6 hearing, in contrast, was to demonstrate presumptive evidence of "mental retardation" with an IQ of 70 or below, which Jacob F. had already done since the two IQ tests were in fact administered reliably.

State v. Javier M.
33 P.3d 1 (N.M. 2001)
New Mexico Supreme Court

Case Facts

Fifteen-year-old Javier M. was charged with minor in possession of alcoholic beverages. After making incriminating statements to a police officer "while he was detained and not free to leave," he was eventually "found to be a delinquent ... and committed to a youth facility for one year." Javier M. appealed the case on the basis that "the officer did not advise him of his basic rights pursuant to Section 32A-2-14(C) of the Children's Code," which is as follows:

> No person subject to the provisions of the Delinquency Act who is alleged or suspected of being a delinquent child shall be interrogated or questioned without first advising the child of the child's constitutional rights and securing a knowing, intelligent and voluntary waiver.

Main Issue

Does § 32A-2-14 from the New Mexico Children's Code provide "children with broader rights than those granted [to adults] by *Miranda v. Arizona*"?

Court Holding

Yes. Because Javier M. was not advised of his right to remain silent, the New Mexico Supreme Court held that his incriminating statements were "inadmissible and should not have been used to support the Children's Court's finding of delinquency." Accordingly, the New Mexico Supreme Court reversed the decision of the lower court.

Court's Reasoning

The court reasoned that § 32A-2-14 from the New Mexico Children's Code expresses "a legislative intent to expand the rights of children beyond those embodied in *Miranda* jurisprudence." This expansion of rights is evident in the following:

> 32A-2-14.E. In determining whether the child knowingly, intelligently and voluntarily waived the child's rights, the court shall consider the following factors:
>
> 1. The age and education of the respondent.
> 2. Whether the respondent is in custody.

3. The manner in which the respondent was advised of the respondent's rights.
4. the length of questioning and circumstances under which the respondent was questioned.
5. The condition of the quarters where the respondent was being kept at the time of being questioned.
6. The time of day and the treatment of the respondent at the time of being questioned.
7. The mental and physical condition of the respondent at the time of being questioned.
8. Whether the respondent had the counsel of an attorney, friends or relatives at the time of being questioned.

> 32A-2-14.E. Notwithstanding any other provision to the contrary, no confessions, statements or admissions may be introduced against a child under the age of 13 years on the allegations of the petition. There is a rebuttable presumption that any confessions, statements, or admissions made by a child 13 or 14 years old to a person in a position of authority are inadmissible.

Accordingly, this court—through its interpretation of what the state Legislature intended in the Children's Code—concluded the following:

> A child need not be under custodial interrogation in order to trigger the protections of the statute. Instead, [this court found] that the protections are triggered when a child is subject to an investigatory detention. Therefore, Section 32A-2-14 requires that, prior to questioning, a child who is detained or seized and suspected of wrongdoing must be advised that he or she has the right to remain silent and that anything said can be used in court. If a child is not advised of the right to remain silent and warned of the consequence of waiving that right, any statement or confession obtained as a result of the detention or seizure is inadmissible in any delinquency proceeding.

Quick Summary

A 15-year-old was charged with possession of alcohol after making incriminating statements to a police officer at a party. However, because the police officer did not advise the teen of his basic rights, as required under the New Mexico Children's Code, the case was successfully appealed. Children in the state of New Mexico have even more rights than are afforded to adults under the *Miranda* decision. Moreover, confessions made to persons of authority from children age 13 or 14 may not be introduced, since this age range is considered borderline. And confessions from children under the age of 13 years may not be introduced as evidence.

State v. Linares
393 P.3d 691 (N.M. 2017)
New Mexico Supreme Court

Case Facts

Two teenagers in foster care, Desiree Linares and Alexis Shields, suffocated their foster mother to death in her sleep as a part of a plan to escape from foster care. After being caught by authorities, Linares was charged with first-degree murder, among other charges. The case was repeatedly delayed, largely due to plea negotiations, but ultimately the State opted to not pursue adult sanctions and to instead have Linares committed to the care of Children, Youth, and Family Department (CYFD) until age 21 years.

The Court ordered forensic psychologist, Dr. Susan Cave, to conduct "a predispositional diagnostic evaluation," which led Dr. Cave to conclude that Linares' IQ was 68 and that she was "mildly mentally retarded." Despite the low IQ and mental retardation diagnosis, Dr. Cave concluded that Linares was nonetheless competent to proceed, although "minimally" so. A change-of-plea hearing then took place, after which Linares withdrew her original plea of guilty in exchange for commitment to the care of CYFD until the age of 21. Instead, she pled not guilty, which could potentially result in an adult sentence if found guilty. But then the district court ordered that the trial be vacated on the basis that Linares might not be competent to stand trial.

In response, "The State filed a motion to compel an independent evaluation of Linares's alleged mental retardation on the grounds that Dr. Cave's … report contained problematic internal inconsistencies. The State emphasized that Dr. Cave's conclusion that Linares is mentally retarded, and thus, incompetent, could not be reconciled with Dr. Cave's conclusion that Linares was competent to enter into a plea. The State also emphasized that Dr. Cave [later] submitted an additional report … in which she withdrew her initial conclusion that Linares was ever competent. This subsequent report, the State argued, was further evidence that Dr. Cave's conclusions were suspect." So a hearing took place regarding the State's motion for an independent evaluation of Linares.

"At that hearing, the State called Dr. Noah Kaufman, a neuropsychologist, as a witness and elicited testimony from him that called into question both the methodology underlying Dr. Cave's assessment of Linares's IQ and Dr. Cave's determination that Linares is mildly mentally retarded." Dr. Kaufman emphasized that Linares's IQ had been measured with an abbreviated-battery IQ test—not a full-battery IQ test—and that Dr. Cave had used her own, unpublished and un-peer-reviewed competence test. "At the end of the hearing, the Court agreed that the State's concerns about the reliability of Dr. Cave's evaluation were legitimate and further concluded that the State should have an opportunity to perform an independent assessment of Linares's mental faculties."

However, Dr. Kaufman refused to conduct the independent evaluation himself because the Court had granted "defense counsel's request that Dr. Cave be permitted to [sit in on] the State's independent evaluation." Although "the Court made clear … that Dr. Cave could not participate or interfere with the State's evaluation in any way," Dr. Kaufman "insisted that the rules of professional conduct governing [neuropsychologists] precluded him from conducting a neuropsychological examination where a third-party observer would be present … The district court was unpersuaded and affirmed its earlier ruling that Dr. Cave could attend and observe the independent evaluation … The State stood firm and indicated that it would not conduct the evaluation if Dr. Cave would be present."

Ultimately a hearing took place to ascertain whether Linares was mentally retarded. At this hearing, Dr. Cave testified that Linares's IQ was 68 and that she was mentally retarded "as that term is defined in Section 31-9-1.6(E)." At this hearing, the "state called yet another psychologist, Dr. Edward Siegel, as a witness. Like Dr. Kaufman, Dr. Siegel attempted to discredit and undermine Dr. Cave's conclusions by highlighting the alleged inadequacies of her evaluation methods and by pointing out several inconsistencies throughout her reports."

Despite this testimony, the district court concluded that Linares's IQ was in fact 68—despite the fact that abbreviated-battery IQ testing had been relied upon to make the diagnosis—and Linares was also found to be incompetent to stand trial, in contrast to Dr. Cave's initial conclusion of competence and despite the fact that Dr. Cave's competency test was unpublished, had not been peer-reviewed, and had never been studied to establish an error rate. Linares was then ordered "to remain in the custody of the Lincoln County Detention Center pending commencement of civil commitment proceedings."

During the civil commitment proceedings, Linares was found to be a danger to herself and others and was civilly committed "for a period of habilitation." The State then filed a direct appeal, contending the following: "that the district court abused its discretion" by denying the State's request to have an independent forensic evaluation without a third-party observer (i.e., Dr. Cave) in the room; "that the district court abused its discretion in concluding that Linares [was] incompetent to stand trial;" and "that the [civil commitment] procedural requirements of Section 31-9-1.6(B) and (C) … were not followed."

Main Issues

1. Did the district court abuse its discretion by effectively denying the State an opportunity for its own independent forensic *neuropsychological* evaluation "by permitting the court-appointed psychologist [not a neuropsychologist] to attend the second, independent [neuropsychological] evaluation"?
2. Did the district court abuse its discretion by concluding that the defendant was incompetent to proceed based, in part, on a diagnosis of "mental retardation"?

3. Did the district court fail to follow Section 31-9-1.6(B) and (C), which requires the district court in New Mexico to order a violence risk assessment before civilly committing a defendant found incompetent to proceed?
4. What is the correct definition of adjudicative competence in the state of New Mexico?

Court Holding

The New Mexico Supreme Court found no error in the proceedings and affirmed the district court's rulings. In other words, this court ruled as follows:

1. A non-neuropsychologist *can* sit in on a forensic neuropsychological evaluation by a forensic neuropsychologist in the state of New Mexico, in contrast to positions taken by neuropsychological organizations and research showing that third-parties can affect test performances. (see Chapter 2 of this book for discussion of this topic).
2. A diagnosis of mental retardation *can* be used, in part, to support a finding of adjudicative incompetence.
3. The district court did not err because defendant Linares' potential to engage in dangerous behavior had in fact already been addressed twice.

With regard to the correct definition of adjudicative competence in the state of New Mexico, the *Linares* case is now cited to support the following definition:

> A person is competent to stand trial when he or she has "sufficient present ability to consult with his lawyer with a reasonable degree of rational understanding[,]" "a rational as well as factual understanding of the proceedings against him[,]" and "the capacity to assist in his own defense and to comprehend the reasons for punishment."

Before *Linares*, adjudicative competence had been defined somewhat differently, with *State v. Rotherham* (1996) as the source of the definition.

Court's Reasoning

Regarding the issue of allowing a third-party to sit in during a forensic neuropsychological evaluation, the New Mexico Supreme Court reasoned that having a non-psychologist sit in on a forensic neuropsychological evaluation by a forensic neuropsychologist would "ensure that the proceedings were expedited" and that "if Dr. Cave was satisfied with the procedures used during the independent [neuropsychological] evaluation, there would be no need for any further evaluations and no further delays." This reasoning, however, does not comport with the positions taken by neuropsychological organizations, or research on third-party participants during neuropsychological evaluations.

Regarding the assertion by the State that the district court had abused its discretion by relying on a diagnosis of "mental retardation" to, in part, support a finding of adjudicative incompetence, the New Mexico Supreme Court reasoned that the decision was not *exclusively* based on the presence of "mental retardation" and that other evidence was relied upon to conclude that Linares was incompetent:

> At first blush, the court appears to have done precisely what is impermissible: conclude that Linares is incompetent *solely because* she is mentally retarded. Careful review of the testimony proffered at Linares's September 11, 2014, hearing on mental retardation reveals that this is not so … Dr. Cave reported that Linares performed very poorly on a portion of one test that focuses on "understanding case events." When asked what function a jury serves, Linares replied that the jury was there to "give answers for the other side." When asked what role the prosecutor played at trial, Linares replied that the prosecutor was there to tell her (Linares's) side of the story. Dr. Cave also expressed doubt that Linares would be able to assist defense counsel as Linares could not recall critical events associated with her case. Crucially, Dr. Cave stated that Linares exhibited no signs of malingering.

With regard to concern that the district court failed to order a "dangerousness evaluation" to assess Linares' risk to harm herself or others, the New Mexico Supreme Court reasoned that Linares' dangerousness had, in fact, been addressed twice:

> The State's contention that the "trial court" erred in some respect by initiating civil commitment proceedings without first obtaining the requisite dangerousness evaluation from the DOH is unavailing. When the Thirteenth Judicial District Court committed Linares to the DOH on February 12, 2015, it did so only after the DOH evaluated Linares and concluded that she was a danger to herself and others and after the court presiding over the initial proceedings—the Twelfth Judicial District Court—found that Linares was a danger to others.

Quick Summary

As a part of plan to escape from foster care, teenager Desiree Linares helped suffocate her foster mother, resulting in the death of the foster mother. Linares' *estimated* IQ was found to be 68 using an abbreviated-battery IQ test, which led psychologist, Dr. Susan Cave, to conclude that Linares was "mildly mentally retarded," but nonetheless competent to proceed. Dr. Cave later changed her mind about Linares' competence, prompting the State to question her methods.

A neuropsychologist, Dr. Noah Kaufman, was hired by the State to testify about Dr. Cave's methods, which included abbreviated-battery IQ testing and an unpublished competency test she had developed, but which had never been peer-reviewed or published. The district court agreed that Dr. Cave's methods were suspect and approved another evaluation, which Dr. Kaufman refused to conduct, in part, because the court was requiring that Dr. Cave, a non-neuropsychologist, sit in on the evaluation to make sure it was conducted appropriately. Eventually, Linares was found incompetent to stand trial, "mentally retarded" as defined in Section 31-9-1.6(E), and dangerous, so she was civilly committed. The State appealed, contending that (1) Dr. Cave should not have been allowed to sit in on the forensic neuropsychological evaluation, (2) the district court found Linares incompetent because of the "mental retardation" diagnosis; and (3) the district court failed to order a risk assessment before the civil commitment. The New Mexico Supreme Court found no error at the district-court level and affirmed all three of the district court's rulings.

This case is also now cited as containing the appropriate definition of adjudicative competence in the state of New Mexico:

> A person is competent to stand trial when he or she has "sufficient present ability to consult with his lawyer with a reasonable degree of rational understanding[,]" "a rational as well as factual understanding of the proceedings against him[,]" and "the capacity to assist in his own defense and to comprehend the reasons for punishment."

State v. Lucas
794 P.2d 1201 (N.M. Ct. App. 1990)
New Mexico Court of Appeals

Case Facts

A defendant with "borderline intelligence" was ordered to undergo a forensic competence-to-stand-trial evaluation, but the evaluation was delayed. Eventually the defendant was found to be competent, despite his attorney saying that "things needed to be explained slowly to the defendant," and he pled guilty. Later, however, the defendant "moved to dismiss the charges under Rule 5-604" (timeliness) and then "he moved to withdraw his plea based on his incompetency." The defendant's competence was again assessed, but he was found competent, so he signed a plea agreement. However, he later appealed.

Main Issues

1. Did the trial court err in refusing to dismiss the charges under Rule 5-604(B)(7), which pertains to the timeliness of court filings ("the trial of a criminal case must commence within six months of the latest of several events")?

2. Is there a higher standard of competency to enter a guilty plea, as compared to what is required of the defendant who is competent to stand trial?

Court Holding

1. No.
2. No.

Court's Reasoning

1. The New Mexico Court of Appeals reasoned that "the time during which a plea agreement is being assessed suspends the proceedings with regard to Rule 5-604." In other words, because there was an ongoing plea-deal process, it reset the clock on timeliness of the proceedings, thereby making it so the defendant's case was *not* stagnating in the courts.
2. The New Mexico Court of Appeals equated competence to stand trial with competence to accept a plea deal by saying that each form of competence requires the same amount of mental wherewithal of the defendant: "we are not persuaded the standard to determine competency [to accept a plea deal] should differ from that to stand trial."

Quick Summary

A defendant with "borderline intelligence" for whom "things needed to be explained slowly," was ultimately found competent to stand trial, after some delays related to ongoing plea bargaining. Because of the delays, and because he asserted that competence to make a plea deal requires more than adjudicative competence, the defendant appealed. But the New Mexico Court of Appeals affirmed the lower court's ruling, thereby *not* agreeing with the defendant.

State v. Montoya
238 P.3d 369 (N.M. Ct. App. 2010)
New Mexico Court of Appeals

Case Facts

Mr. Daniel Montoya was charged with unlawful taking of a motor vehicle and ultimately convicted in a jury trial. However, before, during, and after the jury trial, Mr. Montoya's attorney tried to raise the issue of Mr. Montoya's adjudicative competence. However, the district court judge did not allow this, instead "cut[ting] counsel off mid-sentence stating 'I don't want to hear that crap.'" The judge eventually did allow defense counsel to raise the issue of competence, but only *after* Mr. Montoya had been convicted. Mr. Montoya appealed both his conviction and sentence, on the basis that he was not competent to stand trial during the proceedings.

Main Issues

1. Did the district court err by not allowing the defense counsel to raise the issue of adjudicative competence until after the defendant had been convicted?
2. Did the district court err by proceeding with sentencing the defendant, after finding the defendant incompetent to stand trial?

Court Holding

1. Yes.
2. Yes.

Court's Reasoning

The New Mexico Court of Appeals reasoned that the district court's actions denied Mr. Montoya his right to due process, as conveyed in Rule 5-602(B)(1)—for example, "the issue of the defendant's competency to stand trial may be raised … at any stage of the proceedings"—and as conveyed in NMSA Section 31-9-1—namely—"[w]henever it appears that there is a question as to the defendant's competency to proceed in a criminal case, any further proceedings in the cause shall be suspended until the issue is determined." The Court also reasoned that once competence has been raised by a party, it becomes the judge's responsibility to determine if there is adequate evidence, using a reasonable-doubt standard, as to the defendant's adjudicative competence (see Rule 5-602(B)(2)). If there is a reasonable doubt as to the defendant's competence, then the issue must be explored before any further proceedings take place. The New Mexico Court of Appeals reasoned: "A district court does not possess the discretion to ignore the issue once it has been raised," which is what the judge in this case did. The Court also made the distinction between (a) taking up the issue of competence and then rejecting it because of a lack of reasonable doubt about a defendant's competence versus (b) flat out rejection of defense counsel's attempt to raise the issue of competence. This court reasoned that the former is acceptable and in accord with other cases like the U.S. Supreme Court decision in *Drope v. Missouri* (1975), whereas the latter is not.

Quick Summary

Defense counsel tried to raise the issue of his client's adjudicative incompetence before, during, *and* after a jury trial, in which his client was found guilty of unlawful taking of a motor vehicle. But the judge rudely blocked these efforts, "cut[ting] counsel off mid-sentence stating 'I don't want to hear that crap.'" The New Mexico Court of Appeals vacated the defendant's conviction and sentence because the district court judge did not afford the defendant his right to due process, which includes having competence to stand trial explored if there is reason to doubt it.

State v. Perry
610 So. 2d 746 (La. 1992)
Louisiana Supreme Court

Case Facts

Michael Perry was convicted and sentenced to death for the murder of his father, mother, nephew, and two cousins. He had been diagnosed with Schizophrenia as a teenager and received inpatient psychiatric treatment several times. He had continued to live with his parents due to his psychiatric illness, and they had called for his hospitalization on more than one occasion. He escaped from the hospital and was made to live in a shed behind his parents' house due to his aggressive behavior. During his trial, competency to proceed was raised, resulting in an evaluation and treatment, and he was determined to be competent 18 months later. After the trial, he appealed, but the conviction and death sentence were affirmed. The Court of Appeals did, however, raise the issue of his competency to be executed. A sanity commission was convened, and experts testified that without medication he was not competent for execution. The court ordered the state to maintain him on his medication, even if it required forcible administration. The Supreme Court of Louisiana granted certiorari.

Main Issue

Is it constitutional for the state to forcibly medicate an inmate to carry out a death sentence?

Court Holding

No, the state cannot constitutionally forcibly medicate an inmate to ensure competence for execution.

Court's Reasoning

The court reasoned that historically the execution of the mentally ill has been prohibited because the purposes of punishment (e.g., retribution, deterrence) are not furthered. The court also distinguished the current case from *Washington v. Harper 1990* on three bases:

1. Forcing a prisoner to take medication in order to make them competent for execution is contrary to the principles of the medical profession and does not contribute to medical treatment.

2. The factors present in *Harper*, requiring the state to show that the treatment is in the inmate's best medical interest and the state's interest of prison safety, are not present here.
3. *Harper* implies that forcing medication cannot be used as a form of punishment.

The court cited two bases for determining that medicating to execute is unconstitutional: Due Process and Cruel and Unusual Punishment. The court similarly dismissed the argument that the treatment is in the inmate's medical best interest. The court also discussed the inmate's interest in avoiding the numerous potential side effects. Further, involving physicians in such medication decisions violates their role as "beneficent." Weighing these interests, the court determined that the state's interests do not overcome the inmate's rights. Medicating to execute is cruel and unusual punishment because it is degrading the dignity of human beings, arbitrarily inflicted ("no insane offender has been executed in the civilized world for centuries"), unacceptable to contemporary society (standards of decency), and excessive (i.e., failing to serve a penal purpose more effectively than a less severe punishment) and does not further goals of punishment.

Quick Summary

In Louisiana, inmates may not be forcibly medicated in order to carry out their execution.

State v. Rivas
398 P.3d 299 (N.M. 2017)
New Mexico Supreme Court

Case Facts

Fifteen-year-old Juan Rivas brutally stabbed an 83-year-old woman to death, after breaking into her home. Soon thereafter he was located in his neighborhood by police, who requested that Rivas follow them to the police station for a custodial interrogation, which Rivas and his parents agreed to. In the interrogation room, the officer Mirandized Rivas, never deviating from the required protocol. Rivas then confessed to the murder without any accomplices. He also confessed to stealing jewelry and other items from the victim, and then produced from his pocket a ring he had stolen from her. Subsequently, the state filed a delinquency petition in Children's Court, charging Rivas with the following: first-degree murder, aggravated burglary, unlawful taking of a motor vehicle, and tampering with evidence. Soon thereafter, Rivas was appointed a public defender. The State later filed a notice of its intent to pursue an adult sentence. While in the juvenile detention center, Rivas met again with detectives, at the request of Rivas' father. During this second meeting with detectives, Rivas changed his story to implicate an accomplice, in an attempt to shift culpability onto the accomplice. Before eliciting this second confession, detectives again adhered to protocol by properly Mirandizing Rivas using the same standard juvenile advice form of rights and obtaining a waiver of rights from Rivas. Because the detectives obtained a waiver of rights from Rivas, they did not contact his public defender before the meeting, on the basis that Rivas had knowingly, intelligently, and voluntarily waived his Fifth and Sixth Amendment rights. Rivas' attorney later "contended the interview had violated Defendant's federal and state constitutional rights to counsel, as well as his statutory right to counsel provided by the Children's Code." Rivas' attorney moved to suppress the second confession, but not the first. In response, the State asserted that the motion to suppress was last-minute and did not violate Rivas' rights because the waiver of rights was made knowingly, intelligently, and voluntarily. The district court denied the motion made by Rivas' attorney and the trial proceeded. Rivas was found guilty on all four charges and sentenced to life in prison. Rivas appealed directly to the New Mexico Supreme Court, contending (1) that his attorney should have moved to suppress statements he made in his first detective interview and (2) that the district court should have suppressed his statements from the second detective interview.

Main Issues

1. Was it ineffective assistance of counsel for a defense attorney to *not* move to suppress statements made during a custodial interview conducted by a detective who followed proper Miranda protocol for a 15-year-old in the state of New Mexico?
2. Did the district court err by not suppressing statements made by a 15-year-old defendant in a second custodial interview, also conducted with proper Miranda protocol, but without the presence of the defendant's attorney, even though the defendant did not request to have his attorney present?

Court Holding

1. No. The New Mexico Supreme Court concluded that Rivas did not establish "a prima facie case that his counsel was ineffective for failing to move to suppress statements [Rivas] made in his [first] interview with [detectives]." So the first confession held because the police officer properly notified Rivas of his rights.
2. Yes. The New Mexico Supreme Court found that the district court had erred "in admitting statements from [Rivas' second] interview … But that [the] error was harmless because there was no reasonable possibility [the second] admission contributed to [Rivas'] convictions." In other words, the conviction was properly carried out on the basis of information elicited from the first interview, so the Supreme Court of New Mexico affirmed the convictions and life sentence from the district court.

Court's Reasoning

Because Rivas was 15-years-old, the New Mexico Supreme Court reasoned that he was capable of knowingly, intelligently, and voluntarily waiving his Fifth and Sixth Amendment rights, as is the standard for adults. Had Rivas been younger, however, his statements likely would not have been admissible, even if a waiver of rights had been elicited by detectives:

> Statements made by young children, for example, are without exception inadmissible at trial, regardless of any waiver made; statements made by children thirteen and 14 years old are presumptively inadmissible, regardless of any waiver made; and for children fifteen and older, any waiver of rights is subject to specific statutory inquiry before it may be found knowingly, intelligently, and voluntarily made.

Also, the Court was impressed with the cordial manner in which the detective interviewed Rivas and found nothing in the records, as a part of its totality-of-the-circumstances analysis, to indicate that Rivas was not able to knowingly, intelligently, and voluntarily waive his Fifth and Sixth Amendment rights.

That said, the Court also recognized that the Children's Code in New Mexico requires more when waivers are sought from "juveniles":

> For waivers made by juveniles, the Children's Code further sharpens the focus of the analysis ... Section 32A-2-14(E) directs courts to consider various factors in making validity determinations for juveniles. Those factors include the child's age and education; custodial status; the manner in which the rights have been advised; the length and circumstances of questioning; the condition of the quarters in which questioning occurs; the time of day and treatment of the child during questioning; the mental and physical condition of the child at the time of questioning; and whether the child had the counsel of an attorney, friend, or relative at the time of questioning.

Because Rivas had been appointed counsel at the time of the *second* interview, but the detectives did not notify Rivas' counsel, the Court reasoned that this second confession should have been suppressed: "As the parties recognize, however, the August 6 interview, coming as it did after ... Defendant had been appointed counsel, calls for a separate analysis." Moreover, the Court reasoned that defendants have a right to counsel during all stages of legal proceedings, once the criminal proceedings are initiated:

> Once the adversary judicial process has been initiated as it was with the August 2 filing of the petition here, the Sixth Amendment to the United States Constitution and Article II, Section 14 of the New Mexico

Constitution guarantee defendants the right to have counsel present at all critical stages of criminal proceedings.

Quick Summary

A 15-year-old juvenile, Juan Rivas, stabbed an 83-year-old woman to death in her home. After being properly Mirandized, he confessed to the murder. He was then appointed counsel and, in a second detective interview *without* his legal counsel, he confessed again, but attempted to shift some of the blame to an accomplice. His attorney moved to suppress the second confession, but not the first. After being convicted and sentenced to life in prison, Rivas appealed the case, (1) claiming ineffective assistance of counsel for not moving to suppress the first confession as well as the second and (2) on the basis that the district court erred by not suppressing his statements from the second interview. The New Mexico Supreme Court held that there was nothing wrong with the first confession, so his attorney was not deemed ineffective for not moving to suppress it. In contrast, the New Mexico Supreme Court held that the district court *did* err by not suppressing Rivas' statements during the second interview because Rivas should have had his attorney present, since the confession represented a critical stage of the criminal proceedings and Rivas had legal counsel at that point.

State v. Rotherham
923 P.2d 1131 (N.M. 1996)
New Mexico Supreme Court

Case Facts

This is a consolidated case[3] challenging the constitutionality of provisions of the New Mexico Mental Illness and Competency Code (NMMIC) that govern procedures for criminal defendants who are incompetent to stand trial. Each defendant was indicted of at least one serious and violent crime, found to be incompetent and dangerous, and committed to treatment under the NMMIC. Defendants challenged their commitment on the grounds that the NMMIC: (1) violated their equal protection rights by treating them differently from persons civilly committed under the Mental Health and Developmental Disabilities Code (MHDDC) (defendants claimed the commitment criteria under the NMMIC are less stringent, and the release criteria more stringent, than under the MHDDC, they are denied treatment consistent with legitimate treatment objectives, and their confinement is inconsistent with the "least drastic means" principle); (2) violated their substantive due process rights because there is no substantial probability they will become competent in the foreseeable future, and they are held beyond a "reasonable period of time," in contravention of *Jackson v. Indiana*; and (3) violated their procedural due process rights because commitment under the NMMIC requires only clear and convincing evidence rather than proof beyond a reasonable doubt, and because defendants are precluded from raising an insanity defense.

Main Issue

Do the NMMIC's provisions violate defendants' constitutional rights?

Court Holding

No. The NMMIC is constitutional.

Court's Reasoning

With regard to *equal protection*, the court rejected the argument that the NMMIC's commitment criteria are less stringent because they require only incompetence and not mental illness. The government may detain "dangerous defendants who become incompetent to stand trial" without a specific mental illness. The court also held that the NMMIC's release criteria are constitutional because, like the MHDCC, they provide periodic reviews of competence and treatment, and the NMMIC provides for the same treatment rendered under the MHDCC. As to confinement, the court held both the NMMIC and MHDCC restrict physical movement for dangerous offenders. With regard to *substantive due process*, the court held the NMMIC is consistent with *Jackson*, because it provides for hearings to monitor a defendant's competence and treatment, and thus prevents the state from indefinitely confining an incompetent defendant. With regard to *procedural due process*, the court held that the NMMIC's lower burden of proof reflects its regulatory purpose, as distinguished from the punitive purpose of criminal prosecution. According to the court, the clear and convincing standard strikes a balance between avoiding an erroneous deprivation of liberty, and the state's interest in treating the defendant and protecting society. The court also held that because commitment proceedings are not focused on culpability, state of mind at the time of the crime is irrelevant, and the insanity defense does not apply.

Quick Summary

Defendants challenged the constitutionality of the NMMIC's provisions governing defendants who are incompetent to stand trial. The court held the NMMIC contains adequate procedural protections, including court monitoring of a defendant's competence and treatment, consistent with *Jackson v. Indiana* and the constitution's guarantees of equal protection and due process. Incidentally, this case is often cited as the source of a commonly used legal definition of adjudicative competence applied in the state of New Mexico, which is as follows: To be considered competent, a defendant must (1) understand the nature and significance of the proceedings,

(2) have a factual understanding of the charges, and (3) be able to assist in his own defense.

State v. Santillanes
580 P.2d 489 (N.M. Ct. App. 1978)
New Mexico Court of Appeals

Case Facts

The defendant was found incompetent to stand trial and was ordered to be civilly committed to the state hospital. However, he moved for a dismissal of his charges on the basis that he was incompetent.

Main Issues

1. If a defendant is found incompetent to stand trial, are the charges then dropped?
2. Is "beyond a reasonable doubt" the burden of proof for competence in New Mexico?
3. Does the State have the burden of proving competence to stand trial in New Mexico?

Court Holding

1. No.
2. No.
3. Not when the issue is first raised.

Court's Reasoning

1. The New Mexico Court of Appeals held that the "determination … that defendant was incompetent to stand trial was not conclusive that defendant would continue to be incompetent to stand trial." In other words, this court recognized that a defendant might be found incompetent to proceed at one point in time, but that their competence might change in the future.
2. The correct burden of proof for adjudicative competence in New Mexico is preponderance of the evidence, not beyond a reasonable doubt.
3. The New Mexico Court of Appeals held: "When a defendant advances the contention that he is incompetent to stand trial, he has the burden of proving his claim by a preponderance of the evidence." However, if a defendant has been found incompetent already, and the issue is being redetermined, then the state has the burden of rebutting the original finding of incompetence, still by a preponderance of the evidence. Requiring the defendant to again prove their incompetence is unfair to the defendant:

> To require defendant to prove his incompetency a second time while the first determination of incompetency remains in effect, is fundamentally unfair because it would deprive defendant of the prior judicial determination.

Quick Summary

A defendant was found incompetent to stand trial, so he contended that his charges should be dropped. But it was held that his competence might change in the future, requiring a redetermination of his competence. In making its decision, the New Mexico Court of Appeals clarified that the correct burden of proof for proving adjudicative incompetence in New Mexico is preponderance of the evidence and that the burden is on the defendant to make this argument initially, but that the burden shifts to the State if the defendant comes up for redetermination of competence, after being found incompetent.

State v. Serna
429 P.3d 1283 (N.M. 2018)
New Mexico Court of Appeals

Case Facts

Ernest Serna allegedly shot a female victim to death in the parking lot of a restaurant. Shortly after this incident, Mr. Serna was apprehended by Sandoval Country Deputy Sheriff, Sal Tortorici, who engaged Mr. Serna in "casual conversation for several minutes while Deputy Tortorici had his lapel camera turned on." Then, after about six minutes, Deputy Tortorici Mirandized Ms. Serna from memory, instead of reading from a card:

> You have the right to remain silent. Anything you say can and will be used against you in a court of law. You have the right to an attorney during any and all questionings. If you can't afford an attorney, one will be provided for you.

After being driven to the police station, Mr. Serna was again Mirandized, but this time from "a department-issued card":

> You have the right to remain silent. Anything you say can and will be used against you in a court of law. You have the right to talk to a lawyer and you have the right to have him present with you while being questioned. If you cannot afford a lawyer, one will be appointed to you before any questionings. If you decide at any time you want to exercise these rights and not answer any questions, you may do so.

Deputy Tortorici then interrogated Mr. Serna about the events from the restaurant parking lot, during which Mr. Serna "asked if he was being recorded and what it would take to get an attorney." Mr. Serna also "expressed that he was previously unaware he could have an attorney and that he may not have been listening to the first Miranda warning." Mr. Serna also then said he wished to be "left alone." However, he was "charged with an open count of murder (firearm enhancement), tampering with evidence, and aggravated stalking." In response, Mr. Serna filed a motion to have his confession suppressed on the basis "that the first Miranda warning given by Deputy Tortorici was inadequate." The district court did not grant this motion to suppress, finding the initial Miranda warning satisfactory. As a result, the case went to the New Mexico Court of Appeals.

Main Issue

Does a Miranda warning given by an arresting officer in the state of New Mexico need to include *all* elements contained on the department-issued Miranda-warning card? Stated another way, can an arresting officer leave out any of the elements contained in the following Miranda warning?

> You have the right to remain silent. Anything you say can and will be used against you in a court of law. You have the right to talk to a lawyer and you have the right to have him present with you while being questioned. If you cannot afford a lawyer, one will be appointed to you before any questionings. If you decide at any time you want to exercise these rights and not answer any questions, you may do so.

Court Holding

The New Mexico Court of Appeals reversed the district court's order denying the defendant's motion to suppress the confession. In so doing, this court clearly articulated that no elements from the department-issue Miranda warning card can be excluded during a Miranda warning: "We conclude that the *Miranda* warnings given to Defendant by the arresting deputy did not sufficiently convey Defendant's full rights under *Miranda*."

Court's Reasoning

The New Mexico Court of Appeals emphasized the difference between a Miranda warning given from memory versus one read directly from a department-issue card:

> We would be remiss if we did not point out the contrast in language between the first Miranda warning, given from memory, and the second Miranda warning, given from a department-issued card. Not only does the second Miranda warning advise Defendant of his "right to talk to a lawyer and … the right to have him present with [him] while being questioned" but also that "[i]f [he] cannot afford a lawyer, one will be

> appointed to [him] before any questionings." In delivering the first Miranda warning from memory, and not from his department-issued card, Deputy Tortorici risked that he would fail to adequately convey Defendant's rights, and that is precisely what happened.

Also, this court emphasized the importance of informing a defendant of their right to counsel *before* police questioning even starts:

> The warning given to Defendant indicated that he had a right to an attorney "during any and all questioning." The use of the word "during" is pivotal. "During" is a preposition and is defined as "throughout the duration of." … Even viewing this language in a manner extending the utmost latitude to the law enforcement officer—and bringing common sense to bear—we still cannot see how "during" could be understood to apply backwards to also mean prior or before … In this case, where the balance of the warnings contain no "before questioning" language—or any other language, for that matter—by which we could infer that the full right to counsel was adequately conveyed, there is simply no way to reasonably read the warnings given by Deputy Tortorici as conveying to Defendant that he had a right to an attorney prior to questioning …. In sum, by implying that the right to counsel would be effective only during the interrogation, the warnings given by Deputy Tortorici to Defendant placed a misleading temporal limitation on the full right to counsel under Miranda.

Quick Summary

Deputy Tortorici's initial, from-memory Miranda warning left out key information related to (1) the right to counsel before formal questioning starts and (2) the right to exercise Miranda rights "at any time" before, or after, the formal questioning commences. As a result, the New Mexico Court of Appeals reversed the district court's order denying a motion to suppress the confession. This case emphasizes that even small deviations from department-issue Miranda-warning cards can deprive defendants of constitutional rights.

State v. Spriggs-Gore
64 P.3d 506 (N.M. Ct. App. 2003)
New Mexico Court of Appeals

Case Facts

The defendant was a 73-year-old woman "with a very long history of mental illness, who was recently also diagnosed with dementia." Other diagnoses in her history included the following: "a delusional disorder, persecutory type"; "paranoid personality disorder"; "borderline intellectual functioning"; and "schizophrenia with overtly psychotic symptoms." After being suspected of murdering her husband, the unmedicated defendant was Mirandized twice, soon after which she made inculpatory statements during a 5 ½-hour, tape-recorded interview. The defendant was later found incompetent to stand trial, unlikely to be restorable to a state of competence, but also dangerous. Hence, pursuant to NMSA Section 31-9-1.5, the court determined that there was clear and convincing evidence that she was guilty of second-degree murder, which had a maximum sentence of 15 years. Correspondingly, "The trial court ordered that the Defendant be detained by the Department of Health, Las Vegas Medical Center, in a secure, locked facility for a period of 15 years." At the "1.5 hearing," the trial court denied the defendant's motion to suppress her inculpatory statements during the 5 ½-hour interview, on the basis that "she was incapable of a knowing and intelligent waiver" of her Fifth and Sixth Amendment rights, which the defendant appealed. As a part of the appeal, the defendant also asserted that the procedural process in Section 31-9-1.5 is a violation of her constitutional right to due process.

Main Issues

1. Was "a 73-year-old woman with a very long history of mental illness, who was recently also diagnosed with dementia … incapable of a knowing and intelligent waiver" of her Miranda rights?
2. Is the procedural process involving "being held in a secure, locked facility for 15 years" (see NMSA § 31-9-1.5) a violation of the defendant's constitutional rights? More specifically, can a judge order a defendant to a secure, locked facility? Or must this consequential decision be made by a jury?

Court Holding

1. Regarding the first issue, the New Mexico Court of Appeals reversed and remanded, on the basis that the defendant was not competent to knowingly and intelligently waive her Fifth and Sixth Amendment rights.
2. Regarding the second issue, the New Mexico Court of Appeals held that the procedures of NMSA § 31-9-1.5 do *not* violate the defendant's constitutional rights.

Court's Reasoning

1. Regarding the first issue, the New Mexico Court of Appeals reasoned, "In order for a defendant's waiver of *Miranda* rights to be constitutionally valid, the waiver must be voluntarily, knowingly, and intelligently made." It also emphasized that "the State bears the burden of showing, by a preponderance of the evidence, that Defendant's waiver was voluntary, knowing, and intelligent." It further reasoned, "Courts indulge in every reasonable presumption against the waiver of a constitutional right." Because the

defendant in this case was limited by both mental illness (e.g., "schizophrenia") and neurocognitive dysfunction (e.g., "dementia" and "borderline intellectual functioning"), the totality-of-the-circumstances analysis led to the conclusion by the court that the defendant was not capable of both knowingly and intelligently waiving her Fifth and Sixth Amendment rights:

> The testimony of three experts who had evaluated the Defendant suggests that, unmedicated, Defendant's deficits in memory, reasoning, and ability to converse for an extended period are severely restricted. Both the neuropsychologist and the psychiatrist agreed that Defendant suffered from dementia, which has no cure, as well as various forms of psychosis.

Part of the New Mexico Court of Appeals' reasoning hinged on the fact that the defendant was found incompetent to stand trial "at a time when she was in an optimal treatment setting and taking five medications, and that she was far less competent on the date of offense and could not possibly have made a knowing and intelligent waiver of her rights on that day."

2. Regarding the second issue, NMSA Section 31-9-1.5(D)(1), (2) requires that "a defendant can be ordered held in a secure, locked facility for a period of time equal to a maximum sentence that could have been imposed had the defendant been convicted in a criminal proceeding, if a judge finds by clear and convincing evidence that an incompetent, dangerous defendant has committed the crime in question." Additionally, "If the judge does not find the incompetent defendant either dangerous or, by clear and convincing evidence, that defendant has committed the crime, then the judge must dismiss the criminal case without prejudice pursuant to Section 31-9-1.5(B), (C)." These are criminal commitment laws. In contrast, the defendant unsuccessfully argued that criminal prosecution case law from the U.S. Supreme Court (e.g., *Ring v. Arizona*, 2002) was binding to criminal commitment statutes in New Mexico. Because of the difference between a criminal commitment and a criminal prosecution proceeding, the case law cited by the defendant was not interpreted as binding (see Chapter 4 of this book for discussion of binding versus persuasive authority). Hence, this was the basis for not seeing the criminal commitment laws in the state of New Mexico as unconstitutional.

Quick Summary

A 73-year-old woman with mental illness (e.g., schizophrenia) and neurocognitive dysfunction (e.g., a dementia diagnosis) was charged with murdering her husband. After being stabilized with multiple medications, she was still found incompetent to stand trial, which was later used as justification to suppress inculpatory statements made after she was Mirandized twice. The New Mexico Court of Appeals held that she was not able to knowingly and intelligently waive her Fifth and Sixth Amendment rights. In contrast, this court did not agree with the defendant's argument that the criminal commitment statutes in New Mexico are discordant with U.S. Supreme Court decisions that require a jury—not a judge—to make sentencing decisions. The New Mexico Court of Appeals, in support of its position, reasoned that a criminal commitment proceeding is different from a criminal prosecution proceeding, particularly one involving a death sentence.

State v. Stock
147 P.3d 885 (N.M. Ct. App. 2006)
New Mexico Court of Appeals

Case Facts

Among other charges, Paul Stock was indicted for criminal sexual penetration of a minor on August 17th, 2000. He was promptly arraigned on September 25th, 2000 and a trial date was set for March 6th, 2001. Then, on February 19th, 2001, Mr. Stock's public defender asked for an extension, which was granted by the district court. Mr. Stock's adjudicative competence was then raised and a report, documenting competence, was issued by the forensic evaluator on August 29th, 2001. During a status conference on May 6th, 2002, defense counsel requested a second competence evaluation, which was granted by the court. Approximately 1 ½ years went by without any progress made on the case, during which time Mr. Stock remained incarcerated. During another status conference on October 9th, 2002, it was learned that the second competency evaluation had led to equivocal findings about competence, so a third competency evaluation was ordered by the court, but the defendant was deemed competent on December 4th, 2003. However, the court then ordered a fourth competency evaluation on December 8th, 2003. Three more status hearings were held by the court in February of 2004, during which time the fourth competency evaluation had not been completed. At this point, the district court ruled that Mr. Stock's right to a speedy trial had been violated, so the court dismissed all charges and ordered Mr. Stock's release from custody. The State appealed this decision to the New Mexico Court of Appeals.

Main Issue

The New Mexico Court of Appeals wrote: "This case raises the difficult question of whether a defendant's constitutional right to a speedy trial is violated when he is incarcerated and awaiting trial for more than three years, but the delay is in part attributable to the neglect of his overworked public defenders." In other words, can criminal charges be dismissed and a defendant released from custody if their speedy-trial rights are violated by overworked attorneys with inadequate resources?

Court Holding

The Court of Appeals of New Mexico affirmed the decision from the district court to dismiss all criminal charges and release the defendant from custody, on the basis that his right to a speedy trial had been violated by overworked attorneys, operating with limited resources.

Court's Reasoning

Because the defendant "was found to have the intellectual functioning of a 12-year-old," the New Mexico Court of Appeals was concerned about his capacity to agree to all of the continuances. Similarly, the defendant was often not transported to the court hearings, preventing him from objecting to the delays in his case. In short, the Court concluded that all of the delays ultimately violated Mr. Stock's speedy-trial rights, as "protected by the Sixth Amendment, made applicable to the states through the 14th Amendment, and Article II, Section 14 of our state constitution."

In arriving at this decision, the Court also emphasized that both the public defenders and prosecutors in the state of New Mexico are overworked and under-resourced, which is the reason why Mr. Stock's speedy-trial rights were violated:

> The Court found that, while all of the public defenders who worked on Defendant's case were competent and ethical, it was "humanly impossible for lawyers to practice law under the conditions that we're asking them to practice law." The Court stated that the case showed "the need for the legislature, and the governor, and the people of this state to wake up and start properly funding not only the public defenders' office but also the district attorneys' offices," because otherwise courts would have to continue dismissing cases that were not timely prosecuted.

Quick Summary

An adult criminal defendant with limited intellectual functioning was indicated for criminal sexual penetration of a minor, but the case stagnated for several years as a result of overworked attorneys, in an under-funded criminal justice system. This ultimately led the district court to dismiss all charges on the basis that the defendant's right to a speedy trial had been violated. The New Mexico Court of Appeals affirmed the district court's decision, thereby reinforcing the importance of speedy-trial rights, while also calling attention to the dearth of resources within the criminal justice system in the state of New Mexico.

State v. Trujillo
206 P.3d 125 (N.M. 2009)
New Mexico Supreme Court

Case Facts

Defendant Daniel Trujillo was accused of first-degree murder. Trujillo was known to have suffered brain damage as a result of "self-inflicted carbon monoxide poisoning that occurred over 20 years ago when Defendant was twenty-six years old." This left him with an IQ in the 50s to 60s. After a competency evaluation by forensic neuropsychologist, Dr. Eric Westfried, both sides agreed that Mr. Trujillo was incompetent to proceed. A hearing was then held to determine if Mr. Trujillo had "mental retardation," as defined in NMSA § 31-9-1.6. Forensic psychologist, Dr. Renee Wilkins agreed with Dr. Westfried about Mr. Trujillo's adjudicative incompetence, but found that Mr. Trujillo was legally dangerous, as defined under NMSA § 31-9-1.2.D. Dr. Wilkins, using the DSM-IV-TR definition of "mental retardation," concluded that Mr. Trujillo did not meet diagnostic criteria for this *neurodevelopmental* disorder. Instead, she diagnosed Mr. Trujillo with dementia, since the brain damage was a result of an unsuccessful suicide attempt, after the cutoff-age of 18 years.

Despite the diagnosis of dementia, as opposed to "mental retardation," the district court still held that Mr. Trujillo "had mental retardation per the definition in Section 31-9-1.6(E)." The court also concluded that Mr. Trujillo could not be civilly committed, but that he could be criminally committed, pursuant to Section 31-9-1 to -1.5; § 31-9-1.6(C) of the New Mexico Mental Illness and Competency Code (NMMICC).

Before going to the New Mexico Supreme Court, the case went to the New Mexico Court of Appeals, where part of the district court's decision was affirmed and part was reversed: "It upheld the district court's determination that Defendant has mental retardation. However, in a split opinion, it reversed the district court's order allowing Defendant to be criminally committed under the NMMIC." The Court of Appeals also held that Mr. Trujillo could be referred to the district attorney for legal proceedings to see if he was eligible to civil commitment, under Section 43-1-1(E) of the Mental Health and Developmental Disabilities Code. The case then went to the New Mexico Supreme Court.

Main Issues

1. Is the definition of "mental retardation" in NMSA § 31-9-1.6 equivalent to the definition of "mental retardation" in the *Diagnostic and Statistical Manual of Mental Disorders-IV-TR* (*DSM-IV-TR*)?
2. If a defendant *not* charged with first-degree murder, first-degree criminal sexual penetration, criminal sexual contact of a minor, or arson who is also

(1) legally "mentally retarded" (i.e., under NMSA § 31-9-1.6), (2) legally dangerous (i.e., under NMSA § 31-9-1.2.D), (3) incompetent to stand trial, and (4) "without substantial probability of gaining competence," can they be *criminally* (not civilly) committed?

Court Holding

1. No. The definition of "mental retardation" in NMSA § 31-9-1.6 differs from the definition in DSM-IV-TR: "We hold that the New Mexico definition of mental retardation in Section 31-9-1.6 is not equivalent to that of the DSM in that it does not contain an age of onset requirement."
2. No: "We hold that Section 31-9-1.6 mandates that defendants with mental retardation who are dangerous, incompetent, and without a substantial probability of gaining competence may not be criminally committed, though they may be civilly committed at the discretion of the district court and the district attorney ... We therefore affirm the Court of Appeals."

Court's Reasoning

1. In the state of New Mexico, "mental retardation" is defined under Section 31-9-1.6(E) as "significantly subaverage general intellectual functioning existing concurrently with deficits in adaptive behavior." While this legal definition is *similar* to DSM-IV-TR, it excludes the requirement that the intellectual deficits arise before age 18 years. The New Mexico Supreme Court reasoned that the state legislature knew this and intentionally excluded the age requirement, thereby making it easier to be legally "mentally retarded." This court further reasoned that the state legislature likely did this because what matters is not *when* the intellectual deficits arose, but that they arose in the first place: "The Legislature's decision to exclude the age of onset factor is logical given that what is legally relevant are the symptoms probative of culpability at the time of the alleged crime and coherence at the time of trial, not the age at which those symptoms started to affect the individual."
2. With regard to the criminal (not civil) commitment of a defendant *not* charged with first-degree murder, first-degree criminal sexual penetration, criminal sexual contact of a minor, or arson, but who has "mental retardation," is dangerous, and is incompetent to stand trial without the likelihood of becoming competent, the New Mexico Supreme Court reasoned that criminal commitment of these defendants is inappropriate because it does not pass the common-sense test: "Though we begin our inquiry into legislative intent with the plain meaning of the language, such plain meaning does not trump common sense." In other words, this court reasoned that it makes no sense to criminally commit this subset of defendants and that a civil commitment for these

defendants is the most logical outcome. Notably, this decision does not hold for defendants charged with first-degree murder, first-degree criminal sexual penetration, criminal sexual contact of a minor, or arson. If these are the charges, criminal commitment remains on the table.

Quick Summary

An adult defendant with an IQ in the 50s or 60s, as a result of a failed suicide attempt in his 20s, was found incompetent to stand trial, unlikely to become competent, but legally dangerous. Because his low IQ was a result of brain damage suffered past the age of 18 years, it was argued that he did not also satisfy the legal definition of "mental retardation." But the New Mexico Supreme Court held that the legal definition of "mental retardation" does *not* require that the intellectual deficits start before age 18 years, as required in the *DSM-IV-TR*. Hence, this defendant was found to have legal "mental retardation," even though his drop in IQ occurred in his 20s, after a failed suicide attempt. This court also held that defendants *not* charged with first-degree murder, first-degree criminal sexual penetration, criminal sexual contact of a minor, or arson, but who (1) have legal "mental retardation," (2) are deemed legally dangerous, (3) are incompetent to stand trial, and (4) are without any chance of becoming competent, *cannot* be criminally committed. Instead, they must be subject to civil commitment. Hence, the defendant in this particular case—because he was charged with first-degree murder—was subject to criminal commitment.

State v. Werner
796 P.2d 610 (N.M. Ct. App. 1990)
New Mexico Court of Appeals

Case Facts

The defendant in this case was charged with attempted armed robbery and aggravated battery. Soon thereafter, he was found incompetent to stand trial and ordered to be treated to a state of competence at the Forensic Division of the New Mexico State Hospital in Las Vegas, New Mexico. It was then concluded that the defendant was not likely to ever become competent to stand trial, but that he was legally dangerous (see NMSA Section 31-9-1.2). Because the defendant was incompetent, unlikely to ever become competent, and dangerous, a "1.5 hearing" took place under NMSA Section 31-9-1.5(A), where it would be determined, based on clear and convincing evidence, if the defendant had committed the crimes. If not found guilty, the charges would be dismissed *without prejudice* (i.e., charges could be brought later). But if found guilty, the defendant would be criminally (not civilly) committed to the Department of Health in a locked and secure psychiatric facility. At this "1.5 hearing," the "defendant filed a notice of intent to claim not guilty by reason of insanity and inability to form a specific intent," and so the case went to the New Mexico Court of Appeals via *interlocutory appeal* (i.e., only part of the case was appealed, while other parts of the case continued on).

Main Issue

"The dispositive issue here is whether the defenses of insanity and inability to form a specific intent are available to a defendant in a hearing conducted pursuant to NMSA 1978, Section 31-9-1.5(A)." In other words, a "1.5 hearing" is a criminal commitment hearing, not to be confused with a criminal prosecution hearing, in which the burden of proof is "beyond a reasonable doubt" and incarceration in a jail or prison is frequently the outcome. With criminal commitment, the burden of proof is "clear and convincing evidence" and the defendant is held by the department of health in a secure, locked facility, not a jail or prison. With this in mind, the issue presented in this case was whether a defendant can assert a mental state defense (i.e., insanity or diminished capacity/*mens rea*/specific intent).

Court Holding

"We hold the foregoing defenses are not available in a hearing conducted pursuant to Section 31-9-1.5. Accordingly, we affirm the trial court's ruling on this issue and remand this case for further proceedings." In other words, a defendant in a criminal commitment hearing (i.e., a "1.5 hearing") cannot plead insanity or assert that they were unable to form specific intent at the time of the offense. These legal defenses are for criminal prosecution proceedings, not criminal commitment proceedings, which require—among other things—that the defendant is incompetent to ever stand trial.

Court's Reasoning

Defendants at a "1.5 hearing" have already been found incompetent, unlikely to ever become competent, *and* dangerous. Accordingly, they are not adjudicated through a typical criminal prosecution process. Instead, they can be criminally committed, which requires being found guilty by "clear and convincing evidence" and then sentenced to a locked psychiatric facility for up to the maximum amount of time they would have been sent to prison. In rendering this decision, the New Mexico Court of Appeals reasoned that the state legislature did not intend for this subset of "dangerous mentally disturbed persons" to have the insanity defense or a diminished capacity/*mens rea*/specific intent defense as an option in a criminal commitment hearing.

Quick Summary

A defendant charged with attempted armed robbery and aggravated battery was subsequently found incompetent to ever stand trial, but also dangerous. So a criminal commitment hearing was initiated, which involves a clear-and-convincing-evidence burden of proof, as opposed to the beyond-a-reasonable-doubt standard used in criminal prosecution proceedings. At the criminal commitment hearing, the defendant "filed notice of intent to claim not guilty by reason of insanity and inability to form a specific intent." But the New Mexico Court of Appeals held that such a defense is not available at a criminal commitment hearing.

Thompson v. Oklahoma
487 U.S. 815 (1988)
U.S. Supreme Court

Case Facts

William Thompson was a 15-year-old juvenile who committed numerous and repeated offenses. He was accused of murdering a man who had allegedly been beating both he and his sister. He underwent a psychological evaluation and was determined to be eligible to be tried as an adult. He was convicted and sentenced to death. His attorneys appealed, arguing that it was a violation of the eighth amendment, cruel and unusual punishment, to execute a juvenile. The appellate court affirmed the lower court's decision, and the U.S. Supreme Court then agreed to hear the case.

Main Issue

Is it a violation of the eighth amendment, cruel and unusual punishment, to sentence a 15-year-old juvenile to death?

Court Holding

Yes. The U.S. Supreme Court held that it is unconstitutional to execute a juvenile, defined as under 16 years of age.

Court's Reasoning

The court indicated that executing a juvenile under the age of 16 would violate the "evolving standards of decency that mark the progress of a maturing society." The state's ruling was reversed, and the case was remanded; Thompson was sentence to life in prison.

Quick Summary

In this case, the U.S. Supreme Court held that it is unconstitutional to sentence a juvenile (under 16) to death.

United States v. Alvarez
519 F.2d 1036 (3d Cir. 1975)
Third Circuit Court of Appeals

Case Facts

Defendant Martinez was convicted and sentenced to 25 years imprisonment for kidnapping and conspiracy to kidnap. Prior to trial, he raised the issue of his competence to stand trial, and the trial court found him to be competent. At trial, Martinez relied on an insanity defense. He presented expert testimony that established he lacked substantial capacity at the time of the kidnapping, due to mental disease or defect, to conform his conduct to the requirements of the law.[4] The government called three psychiatrists in opposition. One of these, Flicker, was the psychiatrist who had been appointed to conduct Martinez's competency evaluation. Over objection, the trial court allowed Flicker to testify as to Martinez's sanity, based on disclosures he had made during the competency evaluation. A second psychiatrist, Sadoff, had been retained by Martinez but determined that he did not meet the legal test for insanity. Although Martinez did not call Sadoff as a witness, the government subpoenaed him. Over objection, the trial court allowed Sadoff to testify in the government's case. Martinez appealed his conviction on the ground that the trial court erred in admitting the testimony of Flicker and Sadoff.

Main Issue

1. When an expert is appointed to conduct a competency evaluation under 18 U.S.C. § 4244, may that expert use statements the defendant makes during the evaluation to testify against him at trial?
2. If a defendant consults an expert but does not present him as a witness, may the government call the expert as a witness in its own case?

Court Holding

No, on both issues.

Court's Reasoning

With regard to the first issue, the court analyzed the language, history, and purpose of section 4244, and noted the explicit language that "no statement made [during the competency evaluation] shall be admitted in evidence against the accused on the issue of guilt in any criminal proceeding." It also found that Martinez was not informed and did not consent to the use of the competency examination for a dual purpose. The court thus held that when a psychiatrist is appointed to evaluate competency under the statute, they may only testify at a hearing for that purpose. With regard to the second issue, the court analyzed Sadoff's testimony under the Sixth Amendment. It held that the effective assistance of counsel in preparing for an insanity defense requires that a defendant communicate with a psychiatric expert. If the defendant does not call the expert, the same privilege applies with respect to his communications with the expert that applies to his communications with his attorney. Defendants need not run the risk that an expert his counsel hires to advise him as to the defendant's mental condition will be "forced to be an involuntary government witness."

Quick Summary

Defendant successfully appealed his conviction on the ground the trial court erred in admitting the testimony of two experts against him. The court held that (1) a psychiatrist who was appointed to evaluate defendant's competence could not testify against him at trial, and (2) the government could not call as a witness an expert who evaluated the defendant's mental condition but who did not testify on the defendant's behalf.

United States v. Barnette
211 F.3d 803 (4th Cir. 2000)
Fourth Circuit Court of Appeals

Case Facts

Defendant Barnette was convicted of capital murder after shooting and killing his ex-girlfriend, and carjacking and killing a second victim. Following the jury's recommendation, the trial court sentenced him to death. On appeal, Barnette made two arguments concerning the psychiatric expert testimony presented at sentencing. First, he argued the trial court abused its discretion by admitting expert testimony pertaining to the Psychopathy Checklist Revised (PCL-R). According to Barnette, the PCL-R is unreliable because it has not been standardized as to black inmates or the post-middle-age population. Second, he argued that the trial court erred by refusing to allow him to present expert testimony to rebut the government expert's diagnosis of him as a psychopath. Barnette had presented his own expert during mitigation, who had opined as to Barnette's mental health diagnoses and assessment of future risk of dangerousness. In rebuttal, the government's expert testified at length that Barnette was a psychopath, and opined that he would be a future danger if placed in prison for life. Barnette sought to present further expert testimony in surrebuttal, but the trial court denied his request.

Main Issue

1. Did the trial court abuse its discretion by admitting expert testimony regarding the PCL-R?
2. Did the trial court err by refusing to allow Barnette to offer expert testimony on surrebuttal?

Court Holding

No, as to the first issue. Yes, as to the second.

Court's Reasoning

With regard to the admissibility of the PCL-R and related testimony, the court applied the *Daubert* standard. It noted that the court considered Barnette's objections to the test, but applied its discretion to admit the evidence. On the record before it, the court could not find that this decision was a clear error of judgment under *Daubert*. With regard to the trial court's refusal to permit Barnette's expert to testify in surrebuttal, the court noted that surrebuttal evidence is admissible to respond to any new matter brought up on rebuttal. Because the issue of psychopathy was not raised until the government's expert testified in rebuttal to Barnette's mitigation expert, Barnette was entitled to present his expert in surrebuttal. The fact that Barnette's attorney was able to cross-examine the government's expert was insufficient to overcome the effect of the government expert's testimony, because "questions from an attorney are not nearly so effective as the testimony of a qualified expert witness." This is especially so when the subject is "the highly technical and specialized subject of the condition of a man's mind." The Court held that the trial court had erred, and that the error was not harmless, because it left the jury with the "unrebutted expert opinion that Barnette was a psychopath who felt no remorse or guilt, and that he resembled a fake bowl of fruit." The Court vacated Barnette's sentence and remanded for a new sentencing proceeding.

Quick Summary

A defendant who was sentenced to death for capital murder appealed on the grounds that the trial court (1) abused its discretion in admitting the PCL-R under *Daubert*, and (2) erred by refusing to allow his expert to testify in surrebuttal as to the government expert's testimony regarding psychopathy. The Fourth Circuit held that the trial court heard the defendant's evidence and objections that the PCL-R was not standardized to black and post-middle-aged populations, and did not commit any clear error of judgment. The court also held that the trial court committed prejudicial error in refusing to allow the defendant to rebut the government expert's diagnosis of psychopathy. It vacated the sentence and remanded for a new sentencing proceeding.

United States v. Batista
483 F.3d 193 (3d Cir. 2007)
Third Circuit Court of Appeals

Case Facts

Defendant Batista pleaded guilty to conspiracy to distribute crack cocaine, and was sentenced to a 188-month term of imprisonment. In determining his sentence, the trial court granted a two-level enhancement for obstruction of justice, on the ground that Batista had feigned mental illness in an effort to avoid trial. Prior to trial, Batista requested an evaluation to determine whether he was competent to stand trial. Over the course of two years, Batista was evaluated by mental health experts on at least five occasions. Four of the five experts concluded that Batista was faking or exaggerating psychiatric symptoms in order to avoid going to trial. In addition, the government presented testimony from an investigating agent, who stated that a co-conspirator told him that Batista planned to feign mental illness and stop taking his medication to increase his chances of being found incompetent. Batista appealed his sentence.

Main Issue

Is feigning mental illness an appropriate basis for an obstruction of justice enhancement under the federal Sentencing Guidelines?

Court Holding

Yes.

Court's Reasoning

Under the federal Sentencing Guidelines, a district court may enhance a defendant's base offense level by two levels if it determines that the defendant "willfully obstructed or impeded, or attempted to obstruct or impede, the administration of justice with respect to the investigation, prosecution, or sentencing of the instant offense of conviction." The court noted that several other circuits had found that a defendant's feigning of mental illness is sufficient grounds for the imposition of the obstruction of justice enhancement. It also found that in Batista's case, Batista's feigned mental illness required substantial expenditures of government resources and the district court's time. It rejected Batista's argument that allowing the enhancement would chill a defendant's ability to not stand trial if he is mentally incompetent. The court found it unlikely that a district court would apply an obstruction enhancement as a matter of course, when a defendant requested a competency hearing but was later found competent to stand trial.

Quick Summary

A defendant appealed his sentence, after the district court granted a two-level enhancement for obstruction of justice, based on the defendant's feigning of mental illness to avoid trial. The Court of Appeals held that malingering psychiatric symptoms was an appropriate basis for an obstruction of justice enhancement, and affirmed the sentence.

United States v. Beckford
962 F. Supp. 748 (E.D. Va. 1997)
United States District Court for the Eastern District of Virginia

Case Facts

Defendant Beckford and three codefendants were charged in federal court with intentional murder in furtherance of a Continuing Criminal Enterprise under 21 U.S.C. § 848(e). The government notified each defendant that it intended to seek the death penalty in the event of a conviction. The government also filed a motion asking the district court to order that each defendant who intended to introduce evidence of his mental health or capacity at the guilt *or penalty* phase provide pretrial notice of his intent to do so, submit to examination by an expert of the government's choosing, and comply with reciprocal discovery obligations concerning the mental health evidence. The defendants opposed the motion, citing the court's lack of authority to impose discovery requirements outside those set forth in the Federal Rules of Criminal Procedure, as well as constitutional concerns regarding their privilege against self-incrimination.

Main Issue

May a defendant in a capital case be required to give notice of his intent to introduce mental health testimony bearing on sentencing, and be subjected to a court-ordered examination and reciprocal discovery obligations?

Court Holding

Yes, subject to certain procedural protections.

Court's Reasoning

The court first held that although the Federal Rules of Criminal Procedure do not specifically provide for notice, examination, or discovery in the penalty phase, the court could impose these requirements under its inherent judicial powers. The court also held that that 21 U.S.C. § 848, under which the defendants were charged, provides that the government "shall be permitted to rebut any information received at the [sentencing] hearing" as to mitigating factors. According to the court, in order to have a meaningful opportunity to rebut a defendant's mitigating evidence, the government needs to have advance notice, access to the defendant's expert reports, and its own expert to observe and evaluate the testimony of defense experts. As to the defendants' constitutional arguments, the court held that a defendant waives his right to remain silent by introducing psychiatric testimony—thus, the Fifth Amendment privilege against self-incrimination is not violated when the government is permitted to conduct its own psychiatric evaluation. However, the court also held that in order to adequately protect a defendant's Fifth Amendment rights, the release of expert reports to the government must be deferred until after there is a guilty verdict, and the defendant affirms that he will rely on mental health evidence in the penalty phase.

Quick Summary

In a capital murder case, the government moved for an order requiring defendants to provide pretrial notice of any intention to rely on mental health evidence as a mitigating factor in the penalty phase of trial, to submit to examination by the government's mental health expert, and to comply with reciprocal discovery obligations with respect to the mental health evidence. The court held that, although not explicitly required by the Federal Rules of Criminal Procedure, the government was entitled to advance notice and its own examination of defendants' mental health experts, in order to have a meaningful opportunity to rebut defendants' mitigating evidence. In order to protect defendants' Fifth Amendment rights, expert reports may not be released to the Government unless and until defendants are found guilty and affirm their intent to introduce mental health evidence at sentencing.

United States v. Brawner
471 F.2d 969 (D.C. Cir. 1972)
District of Columbia Circuit Court of Appeals

Case Facts

Archie Brawner, Jr. was convicted of second-degree murder. At his trial, expert witnesses testified that he was suffering from a psychiatric abnormality that included epilepsy, although exact diagnoses varied. The experts disagreed about to what extent (if any) his impairments contributed to his actions in the offense. While the defense expert opined that Mr. Brawner's mental condition was directly related to the alleged offense, the prosecution's expert opined that there was no causal relationship. Brawner appealed, claiming that the lower court erred by allowing such an opinion. The Court of Appeals reviewed to consider what *mental disease* or *defect* means and how to give the jury the information they need to decide the role, if any, that such disease or defect plays in the commission of an offense, without relying on the ultimate opinion of a mental health professional.

Main Issue

How should the test of insanity be revised to more accurately address the role of mental disease or defect in the commission of a crime, while not relying solely on the opinion of a mental health professional?

Court Holding

There should be a new test for insanity because the former test in *Durham v. U.S.* put too much emphasis on the testimony and opinions of experts, was unclear, and proved difficult to consistently apply. The American Law Institute (ALI), according to this court, offered a better framework for this test; whether the defendant lacked substantial capacity to either appreciate the criminality of the conduct or to conform their conduct to the requirements of the law (Model Penal Code, §4.01). Repeated criminal or antisocial conduct does not constitute a mental disease or defect. The court also differentiated insanity from diminished responsibility (e.g., negating specific intent).

Court's Reasoning

The court reasoned that there had been too much reliance on expert opinion without the primary focus being on educating the jury as to the mental state of the defendant at the time of the offense. Experts should explain the underlying reasons for their opinions to assist the trier of fact rather than giving an ultimate opinion. Another important point the court articulated was the benefit of adopting a uniform definition of insanity so that progress can be measured and applied from court to court without the confusion of differing jargon. Experts are not to invade the role of the jury by providing ultimate conclusions; rather, they are to educate about the mental health symptoms so the jury can arrive at the conclusion as it applies to the law.

Quick Summary

This case rejected the Durham rule, which had previously held that a defendant could be found not guilty by reason of insanity if their actions were the product of mental disease or defect. The court here adopted the American Law Institute definition of insanity.

United States v. Crews
781 F.2d 826 (1986)
No. 84-2211.
U.S. Court of Appeals, Tenth Circuit

Case Facts

While a voluntary patient in a hospital psychiatric unit, Crews watched a movie and subsequent discussion that depicted the nuclear annihilation of Lawrence, Kansas. The shows upset Crews, and he requested sedatives from a psychiatric nurse. He then told the nurse that if President Reagan went to that hospital, he would shoot the president. The nurse reported this statement to the hospital, which then contacted the Secret Service. Crews told the investigating Secret Service agent that he did not make that precise statement, but he admitted to an extreme dislike for the president, and he clarified that he told the nurse it "would be in the best interest of this nation if that red-necked, bigoted, war-mongering mother fucker were shot." Crews, who owned several guns, was indicted and found guilty of making a threat to kill President Reagan.

Crews, sentenced to four years in prison, appealed his conviction. Crews claimed: (1) the prosecution failed to satisfy its burden to prove he was sane at the time of the alleged threat; (2) his purported threat came within a psychotherapist-patient privilege; (3) the prosecution violated his First Amendment rights; (4) the district court erred in denying him a competency hearing; (5) the district court wrongly refused to appoint a psychiatrist to aid his attorney; (6) cross-examination of the psychiatrists who examined him to determine competency violated law; and (7) the court erred in not instructing the jury that he must intend to carry out his threat.

Main Issue

Multiple issues of relevance to mental health professionals and their involvement in criminal cases were raised in this case.

Court Holding

Of the seven primary points raised by Crews in his appeals, six were considered unfounded, while one was supported. Specifically, the district court erred in refusing to appoint a psychiatrist to help Crews in his defense. As result, Crews' conviction was vacated, and the district court was instructed to appoint a psychiatrist to aid Crews in his preparation for a new trial.

Court's Reasoning

1. A criminal defendant initially is presumed sane. Crews contended that the prosecution's statements and the testimony elicited by the prosecution was sufficient to place the burden of proving his sanity on the government. But opening statements do not constitute evidence; therefore, they cannot be used to overcome the presumption that Crews was sane. The only testimony the government introduced that could have placed Crews' sanity in question was that he was in a psychiatric hospital and was receiving antidepressant medications. The government's overall evidence indicated that Crews had been hospitalized for treatment of alcoholism, and it would have been unreasonable for the jury to determine that Crews was insane based on that evidence alone. Therefore, the burden did not switch to the government.
2. Crews asserted that his statement to the nurse was a privileged communication. However, the Federal Rules of Evidence do not explicitly recognize a psychotherapist-patient privilege. The Court of Appeals stated that it need not, and should not, decide in this case whether to adopt the psychotherapist-patient privilege. The court noted that even if it were to recognize such privilege, it would have to hold that Crews waived his right to the privilege; following this receipt of his *Miranda* warning, Crews openly discussed with the agent the comment that he made to the nurse. Thus, his disclosure of his version of the conversation waived privilege.
3. Crews contended that his statement was protected political speech under the First Amendment. However, the Court of Appeals found that Crews' statement was an innocuous threat more similar to instances of extortion than to protected political speech. The Court further noted that compelling government interest in protecting the president justifies imposition of criminal liability when it is reasonably clear that a person making such comments was not engaged in political advocacy. The court found that the First Amendment did not protect the statement.
4. Crews complained that the district court did not hold a competency hearing pursuant to his request. However, the Court of Appeals noted that a trial court need not conduct a competency hearing when there has been only minimal or no evidence of incompetence, as was the case with Crews.
5. Crews claimed that the district court erred in refusing to appoint a psychiatrist to help in his defense. Although four treating or court -appointed psychiatrists testified with respect to his mental condition, Crews was also entitled to the appointment of a psychiatrist that could both testify on his behalf and help his attorney prepare a defense. The court found that such assistance was wrongly withheld.
6. Crews claimed that the testimony of both the psychiatrist who conducted a competency examination and the psychiatrist who examined Crews to determine if he was sane at the time he made the threat was improper. However, neither doctor repeated any statements made to them by

Crews, which would have been inappropriate, but instead limited their reports to their impressions of his mental condition. Accordingly, the court determined that Crews' objections to the testimony of both psychiatrists were unfounded.

7. Crews' final contention relating to the trial of his case was that the court erred in instructing the jury that he could be convicted without proof of an intention to carry out the threat. However, his indictment was based on the statement he made to the nurse, not the statement he made to the Secret Service agent. In fact, the statement to the agent—that it would be in the best interest of the nation if the President were shot—was not a threat by Crews to kill the president. The Court of Appeals found no error in the refusal of the trial court to instruct the jury that Crews could be convicted only if he intended to carry out the threat.

Quick Summary

Among the multiple mental health issues that were adjudicated, it was determined that (a) the presumption of sanity remains until and unless some evidence of insanity is presented, at which time the prosecution assumes the burden of proving sanity; (b) testimony of a treating mental health professional is different from a forensic mental health professional appointed to assist with a defense; and (c) statements are not privileged once the accused/patient waives the privilege.

United States v. Duhon
104 F. Supp. 2d 663 (W.D. La. 2000)
United States District Court for the Western District of Louisiana

Case Facts

In 1997, Keith Duhon was charged with sexual exploitation of a child. Defense requested an evaluation of his competence to proceed to trial, and he was deemed incompetent and hospitalized for restoration. After eight weeks, he was deemed competent to proceed, but the procedure and opinion was questioned under *Daubert* due to the permanence of his disabilities (intellectual disability from birth). The doctor who examined Mr. Duhon indicated that although he was 20 years of age, he only read at the first-grade level, needed help with daily chores, and was not aware of basic current events and facts. His case-related knowledge was similarly compromised. Although hospitalization would not have been able to treat his disability, he was nonetheless hospitalized for restoration. After participating in the competency restoration groups, mental health evaluators deemed that he was able to learn and retain information and was competent to stand trial. He was also deemed not to be a risk of harm to self or others. In a subsequent competency hearing, the defense challenged the validity of the competency finding and argued that, unlike mental illness, "mental retardation" is static.

Main Issue

If competency to stand trial cannot be restored, what is to be done with the defendant and the charges? Is "rote" learning sufficient to establish competency?

Court Holding

The district court for Louisiana held that if the defendant has a "mental defect" that renders them non-restorable, and they do not meet criteria for danger to self-others, then hospitalization and ongoing attempts at restoration are inappropriate. Rote learning without a rational and factual understanding of the case is insufficient for competency.

Court's Reasoning

The defendant with a "mental disease" or intellectual disability cannot improve the way someone with a mental illness can. The fact that Mr. Duhon could learn some factual information and parrot it back in restoration classes is not tantamount to the skills required in *Dusky,* including the ability to make case-specific decisions. The person can be held only long enough to determine if restoration to competency can occur, because it is inappropriate to continue ongoing deprivation of liberties without purpose. If the person cannot be restored and they do not meet dangerousness criteria, they must be released, because holding them is without merit or legitimate likelihood of improvement. The court also noted that restoration to competency must be more than the ability to recite factual information; it must also include the ability to meaningfully think through legal decisions and effectively communicate those thoughts to counsel.

Quick Summary

A defendant cannot be held involuntarily for restoration to competency if it is determined that there is no reasonable likelihood that they will be meaningfully restored and if they do not meet the criteria for dangerousness. Mental disease (illness) is different from mental defect (intellectual disability) in terms of likelihood of restoration.

United States v. Greer
158 F.3d 228 (5th Cir. 1998)
Fifth Circuit Court of Appeals

Case Facts

Charles Greer was indicted on charges of kidnapping and possession of a stolen firearm. He was found incompetent to stand trial and sent for evaluation. The forensic psychologist who evaluated him found him not only to be competent to stand trial but also to be feigning psychosis. Mr. Greer's defense attorney requested another competency examination during trial preparations due to bizarre behavior observed. A psychiatrist offered the opinion that Mr. Greer was incompetent, and the prosecution "acquiesced." He was committed for restoration, during which time another forensic psychologist offered the opinion that Mr. Greer was not psychotic and was malingering. He was then found competent. During the trial, Mr. Greer acted out with odd behaviors, including removing his clothing and self-inflicting wounds. The judge reprimanded him for deliberately derailing the trial. He was convicted. At sentencing, the government asked for a sentence enhancement due malingering and wasting hospital and court time. Mr. Greer received a 210-month sentence (the maximum was 185 months). Greer appealed.

Main Issue

Should malingering be considered obstruction of justice and included as a potential sentence enhancer?

Court Holding

A court may sentence a defendant to additional punishment if they intentionally feign mental disorder to avoid prosecution/punishment. This additional punishment may be applied to individuals even if they have a substantiated mental health disorder if they additionally feign mental illness. The lower court did not err by enhancing Mr. Geer's sentence because malingering mental illness is obstructing justice.

Court's Reasoning

Feigning mental illness requires a deliberate and planful effort to interfere with the jurisprudence process. The court reasoned that even if someone has mental health problems, malingering is an additional willful attempt to manipulate and mislead the court, and those factors are permissible to consider at sentencing. The court analogized feigned mental illness to willfully disguising a handwriting sample, which had previously qualified for sentence enhancement by the Sentencing Guidelines Manual. Even if a defendant has a legitimate personality disorder that contributes to their behavior, they can still be found to have intentionally and voluntarily malingered mental illness and can be additionally punished for such behavior. The court did acknowledge the difficulty in distinguishing what is incompetence from extreme personality disorder as opposed to malingering.

Quick Summary

If there is sufficient basis to render an opinion that a defendant is willfully malingering, that may be taken into consideration regarding possible sentence enhancement. Mental health professionals must be careful when rendering an opinion on malingering due to the potential consequences.

United States v. Marble
940 F.2d 1543 (D.C. Cir. 1991)
District of Columbia Circuit Court of Appeals

Case Facts

Defendant Marble was convicted of bank robbery under federal law. The circumstances of the robbery indicated possible mental illness. Marble initially indicated he wanted to open an account, but gave two different names to the bank representative. He then scrawled a note on a piece of paper bag that said "This is a holdup," and collected money from six different tellers before walking out of the bank. He continued to walk down the street with an overflowing bag of money in each hand, oblivious to the fact that bills were spilling onto the ground. He was arrested with the money and an eight-inch steak knife wrapped in a paper towel. At trial, Marble's attorney urged him to plead not guilty by reason of insanity, but Marble resisted. His attorney also raised his competency to stand trial, and argued that the court should impose an insanity defense. Following a hearing with expert medical testimony, the court found Marble competent to stand trial. His lucidity varied according to the consistency with which he took his prescribed medication, and although he had not taken his medication in the months preceding the robbery, he was adequately medicated by the time of trial. Marble again declined to plead the insanity defense, asserting that he preferred a definite criminal sentence over an indefinite civil commitment. The court declined to impose the insanity defense against Marble's will, and appointed amicus counsel to appeal that decision to the Court of Appeals.

Main Issue

Did the trial court abuse its discretion by refusing to impose the insanity defense against the defendant's will, where he was found to be competent to stand trial?

Court Holding

No.

Court's Reasoning

In the D.C. Circuit, *Whalem v. U.S.* has been the guiding authority requiring a district court to raise the issue of insanity on its own motion. But *Whalem* is in tension with Supreme Court authority holding that a defendant who claims innocence may still make a strategic choice to acquiesce to a determinate criminal penalty (*North Carolina v. Alford*) and affirming a defendant's Sixth Amendment right to conduct his own defense (*Faretta v. California*). Moreover, the Insanity Defense Reform Act of 1984 (IDRA) made insanity an affirmative defense, indicating Congress's judgment that convicting the competent mentally ill is no longer "wrong" and providing standards to govern their confinement and treatment. Given the clear policy of the IDRA to hold most mentally ill offenders criminally responsible, and the Supreme Court's deference to a competent defendant's strategic decisions, the D.C. Circuit overruled *Whalen* and held that a district court must allow a competent defendant to accept responsibility for a crime committed when he may have been suffering from a mental illness.

Quick Summary

A competent defendant declined to assert an insanity defense for a crime committed when he was likely suffering from a mental illness. The D.C. Circuit Court of Appeals affirmed, holding that Congress's enactment of the Insanity Defense Reform Act indicated evolving policy in favor of holding most mentally ill offenders criminally responsible, and noting the Supreme Court's deference to a competent defendant's strategic decisions.

United States v. Scheffer
523 U.S. 303 (1998)
No. 96-1133
U.S. Supreme Court

Case Facts

In March 1992, Edward Scheffer, an airman stationed in California, volunteered to work as an informant on drug investigations for the Air Force Office of Special Investigations (OSI). He was advised that during the course of his undercover work, he would be required to submit to drug testing and polygraph examinations. In early April, Scheffer was required to submit to a urine test. Shortly after providing the urine sample, but before the results of the test were known, Scheffer agreed to take a polygraph test administered by an OSI examiner. In the opinion of the examiner, when Scheffer denied using drugs since joining the Air Force, the results did not indicate deception. On April 30, Scheffer failed to appear for work and could not be found on the base. He was absent without leave (AWOL) until May 13, when an Iowa state patrolman arrested him following a routine traffic stop and held him for return to the base. OSI agents later learned that Scheffer's urinalysis revealed the presence of methamphetamine. Scheffer was tried by general court-martial on charges of using methamphetamine, being AWOL, and, regarding an unrelated matter, generating 17 insufficient funds checks. He testified at trial on his own behalf, relying upon an "innocent ingestion" theory—denying that he had knowingly used drugs while working for OSI. Scheffer sought to introduce the polygraph evidence to support his testimony. The military judge denied the motion, relying on Military Rule of Evidence 707, which prohibits admission of polygraph evidence. Scheffer was convicted on all counts. The Air Force Court of Criminal Appeals affirmed, explaining that Rule 707 did not arbitrarily limit Scheffer's ability to present reliable evidence. The case went to the U.S. Supreme Court.

Main Issue

Does Military Rule of Evidence 707, which makes polygraph evidence inadmissible in court-martial proceedings, unconstitutionally abridge the right of accused members of the military to present a defense?

Court Holding

The U.S. Supreme Court held that the inadmissibility of polygraph evidence does not unconstitutionally abridge the rights of the accused to present a defense.

Court's Reasoning

Although state and federal governments have a legitimate interest in ensuring that reliable evidence is presented to the trier of fact in a criminal trial, such rule-makers have broad latitude under the constitution to establish rules excluding evidence from criminal trials. In fact, the exclusion of unreliable evidence is a principal objective of many evidentiary rules.

Rules excluding evidence do not abridge an accused's right to present a defense as long as the rules are not arbitrary or disproportionate to their purposes. There is no consensus that polygraph evidence is reliable; the scientific community remains divided about the reliability of polygraph techniques. A fundamental premise of the criminal trial system is that the jury, through their natural intelligence and practical knowledge of human beings, determines when someone is lying. Thus, polygraph evidence may diminish the jury's role in making credibility determinations.

Quick Summary

A defendant's right to present relevant evidence, including polygraph results, is not unlimited, but rather is subject to reasonable restrictions.

Vitek v. Jones
445 U.S. 480 (1980)
U.S. Supreme Court

Case Facts

Mr. Larry Jones was convicted of robbery and sentenced to prison in Nebraska. While incarcerated, he was transferred to a mental hospital for treatment pursuant to Nebraska statute authorizing the Director of Correctional Services to transfer a prisoner when a designated physician finds that a prisoner "suffers from a mental disease or defect" and "cannot be given proper treatment in that facility." He was eventually transferred back to the prison mental health unit but sought relief due to the possibility of further transfers to the hospital. The state argued that Jones was a danger to himself and others, but the lower court stated that he nonetheless had rights before such a transfer. The U.S. Supreme Court reviewed.

Main Issue

Does the Due Process Clause of the 14th Amendment entitle a prisoner to certain procedural protections, including notice, an adversary hearing, and appointment of counsel, before being transferred to a state mental hospital for treatment of a mental disease or defect?

Court Holding

Yes, a prisoner is entitled to written notice of transfer, an adversary hearing before an independent decision maker, written findings, effective and timely notice of such rights, and counsel, but counsel need not be a licensed attorney.

Court's Reasoning

The court determined that conviction allows a person to be incarcerated, taking away liberty, but does not allow the state to label the person mentally ill and commit them to a mental hospital, which can result in stigma and involuntary treatment for mental illness. While the state has an interest in segregating and treating mentally ill patients, the prisoner also has an interest in not being classified as mentally ill and subjected to involuntary treatment. A convicted felon is entitled to appropriate procedural protections, including: (1) written notice that a mental health transfer is being considered; (2) a hearing (following sufficient time to prepare after the notice is given) in which the individual may hear the evidence being used for transfer, be heard, and present documentary evidence; (3) the opportunity to present witnesses and cross-examine opposing witnesses; (4) an independent decision-maker; (5) a written statement of the findings; and (6) effective and timely notice of these rights.

Quick Summary

Prisoners have a liberty interest in not being labeled mentally ill and transferred to a psychiatric facility where they could be involuntarily treated. Therefore, they are entitled to appropriate procedural protections before being transferred to a psychiatric facility.

Don Wade v. United States
426 F.2d 64 (9th Cir. 1970)
U.S. Court of Appeals, Ninth Circuit

Case Facts

Don Wade robbed a bank. He used a gun. His mental health status led to a question of his mental state at the time of the offense. Wade argued that the M'Naghten test for insanity is inappropriate and questioned whether a trial court, when appointing a psychiatrist to examine the defendant pursuant, may properly order that the examination cover both competency to stand trial and criminal responsibility at the time of the alleged offense. Additionally, the question was raised regarding whether a court has the power to order the defendant to cooperate and provide information to the court-appointed psychiatrist, or else be "precluded at the time of trial from offering any evidence upon the defense of insanity."

This type of order requires the defendant to supply the court-appointed psychiatrist with information on the basis of which, in part, the psychiatrist can form an opinion of the defendant's mental state at the time of the offense. If the psychiatrist is subsequently permitted to testify for the prosecution during trial, the result may be that the defendant's own words are used against him. Therefore, coerced cooperation with a psychiatrist not chosen by the accused may violate the fifth amendment privilege.

Main Issues

1. Does the M'Naghten test of criminal responsibility remain appropriate?
2. Can a trial court, when appointing a psychiatrist to examine a defendant, order that the examination cover both competency to stand trial and criminal responsibility at the time of the alleged offense, and does a court have the power to order that the defendant cooperate with such examination?

Court Holding

1. The court rejected the M'Naghten test of criminal responsibility and adopted the American Law Institute test instead.
2. We have concluded, however, in light of our disposition of the case before us and the possibility that the question may not again arise, that we need not decide the constitutional issue on the present record.

The verdict was reversed, and the case was remanded.

Court's Reasoning

The Supreme Court approved the M'Naghten rule in 1897 in *Davis v. United States* and had not reexamined its position since that time, despite numerous conflicting decisions among the circuits. At that time, no other Circuit except the First continued to rely on what the court described as ancient M'Naghten rules, and that Circuit had not had the opportunity for reconsideration in the prior eight years.

The weakness and dangers of applying the traditional M'Naghten criteria as the determinant of insanity were very apparent to the court. The court noted that the M'Naghten rules fruitlessly attempt to relieve from punishment only those mentally diseased persons who have no cognitive capacity (i.e., those who are unable to know the nature and quality of their acts or that the acts were wrong). However, the court noted that that formulation does not comport with modern medical knowledge that an individual is a mentally complex being with varying degrees of awareness. That formulation also fails to address the problem presented in a case wherein an accused may have understood his actions but was incapable of controlling his behavior. Such a person has been allowed to remain a danger to himself and to society whenever, under M'Naghten, he is imprisoned without being afforded such treatment as may produce rehabilitation and is later released.

The court noted that the serious shortcomings of the M'Naghten rules were not overcome by the addition of the so-called "irresistible impulse" test, which had been applied in multiple jurisdictions. The irresistible impulse test, however, has been associated with major objections. Not only is there a debate among psychiatrists whether such impulses actually exist, but also, the test is too narrow in scope. The test's language refers to sudden, explosive actions, but more often the criminal acts of one who is unable to control their conduct follow excessive brooding and melancholy. Such considerations are a small sample of the many that had led, in the preceding years, to almost universal abandonment of the M'Naghten-irresistible impulse test by the Courts of Appeals.

An alternative to the M'Naghten test is the American Law Institute test, as set forth in its Model Penal Code § 4.01 (Final Draft, 1962). It reads:

(1) "A person is not responsible for criminal conduct if at the time of such conduct as a result of mental disease or defect he lacks substantial capacity either to appreciate the criminality [wrongfulness] of his conduct or to conform his conduct to the requirements of law."

(2) "As used in this Article, the terms, 'mental disease or defect' do not include an abnormality manifested only by repeated criminal or otherwise antisocial conduct."

The ALI test does not require total incapacity of either cognition or volition, and the ALI phraseology was considered more consistent with typical medical testimony than was that of the narrower tests.

The court noted that although it approved paragraph (1) of the ALI test, it was unable to support paragraph (2). The court noted that the drafters of the ALI test, in framing the second paragraph, seemed to have intended to exclude certain "psychopathic personalities," from those who might otherwise be found to suffer from a "mental disease or defect." For purposes of the insanity defense, "wrongfulness" means moral wrongfulness rather than criminal wrongfulness.

Quick Summary

The ALI test of criminal responsibility is preferred to the M'Naghten test.

Washington v Crawford
431 U.S. 36 (2004)
U.S. Supreme Court

Case Facts

Michael Crawford and his wife confronted a man who had allegedly attempted to rape the wife, and Mr. Crawford stabbed him. Mr. Crawford told the police that he acted in self-defense because he believed the victim had a weapon. Mrs. Crawford was separately interviewed by the police and stated that she did not see a weapon on the victim. At trial, the prosecutor wanted to admit her recorded statement to the police to show that Mr. Crawford had no reasonable basis for his belief that the victim had a weapon. The defense argued that if she testified, they would be unable to cross examine her without waiving spousal privilege, which would be a violation of the confrontation clause of the Sixth Amendment. The statement was admitted and relied upon heavily by the prosecution. Mr. Crawford was convicted. The appellate court overturned the conviction stating that the statement was inadmissible. The Washington Supreme Court reinstated the trial court's conviction stating that the statement was, in fact, admissible. U.S. Supreme Court granted certiorari.

Main Issue

Does presenting out-of-court evidence/statements without the opportunity for cross examination violate the Confrontation Clause of the Sixth Amendment?

Court Holding

Yes. The U.S. Supreme Court held that the use of Mrs. Crawford's out of court statements to police violated the defendant's Sixth Amendment right to confrontation because his wife elected not to testify and so was unavailable for confrontation in court.

Court's Reasoning

In a 9-0 opinion, The Court agreed with Mr. Crawford that the admission of videotaped evidence without the ability to cross examine a witness violated his

Sixth Amendment right to confrontation. The Court overruled the precedent set in *Ohio v. Roberts (1980),* which allowed for the admission of out-of-court statements that were "reliable" because, it reasoned, doing so deviated from the intent of the Framers of the Constitution who intended that out-of-court testimony is prohibited for use against defendants.

Quick Summary

This case overruled the prior precedent (*Ohio v. Roberts)*,which allowed for the admission of out-of-court statements if they were "reliable" and instead prohibited all out of court statements because of the violation of the defendant's Sixth Amendment right to confront witnesses in court.

Washington v. Harper
494 U.S. 210 (1990)
U.S. Supreme Court

Case Facts

In 1976, Mr. Walter Harper was sentenced to a Washington prison for robbery. He was paroled in 1980 but returned to prison after additional crimes. He was diagnosed with schizophrenia, bipolar disorder, and schizoaffective disorder and housed in the Special Offender Center (SOC) for inmates with mental illness. Eventually, he declined to take his medications, and the psychiatrist sought to forcibly medicate him against his will. The SOC had a policy regarding how they went about determining if involuntary medication was warranted, and, in Mr. Harper's case, they found him to be mentally ill and dangerous and issued an involuntary medication order for one year. He appealed, arguing that his rights were violated because the hospital process was not a judicial process. The Washington Supreme Court agreed and reversed and remanded because the "highly intrusive" nature of forcible medication with antipsychotics warranted more procedural protections and judicial oversight. The U.S. Supreme Court granted certiorari.

Main Issue

Is it permissible for a state to utilize a non-judicial process to determine whether antipsychotic medications can be administered involuntarily to an inmate?

Court Holding

Yes. The court held that Washington's process had enough procedural protections to ensure due process.

Court's Reasoning

The court reasoned that Washington's nonjudicial process had enough due process and procedural protections including:

- The presence of a mental disorder.
- A danger to self or others or a grave disability.
- Only a psychiatrist can approve the medications.
- The inmate is entitled to a hearing with a psychiatrist, a psychologist, and a superintendent (none can be part of the treatment team).

If the committee decides by a majority vote that the inmate is mentally ill and dangerous, the medications can be forcibly administered as long as the psychiatrist is in the majority. There are additional protections: a second psychiatrist must review and approve that the involuntary medications are in the best interest of the inmate; the inmate must be given 24 hours' notice before the hearing, and the diagnosis and reason for medication must be explained; the inmate can have a lay advisor who is aware of the issues and can help with the presentation of evidence and witnesses, and can appeal the decision; and, if medications are ordered, a review and report must be submitted every two weeks. The court reasoned that these decisions are better made by mental health professionals than by the court, as it "is not the business of judges." The procedures in place with this Washington policy balanced the rights of the inmate with the state's interests and therefore provided adequate due process. The lower court erred by not recognizing the reasonableness of the policy, given "legitimate penological interests," and the policy balanced the rights of the inmate with the safety of other inmates and the institution.

Quick Summary

There does not need to be a judicial process for involuntarily medicating an inmate if a state's policy provides enough due process protections, and the treatment is in the best interest of the inmate. The state has a legitimate interest in protecting not only the inmate but also the safety of the institution. The inmate does not need to be competent in order to progress through this process.

Washington v. United States
390 F.2d 444 (D.C. Cir. 1967)
District of Columbia Circuit Court of Appeals

Case Facts

Appellant, Mr. Thomas Washington, Jr., raised an insanity defense, but was still convicted of rape, robbery, and assault with a deadly weapon. He appealed to the D.C. Circuit Court, claiming that the lower court erred in its refusal to enter a not guilty by reason of insanity (NGRI) judgment.

Main Issue

1. What is the best way for expert testimony to inform the jury?
2. Did the lower court err in refusing to enter a judgment of acquittal by reason of insanity?

Court Holding

With regard to the first question, there should be rules for proper, helpful expert testimony that does not invade the province of the jury. With regard to the second question, the lower court did not err because the guilty verdict did not clearly violate the law or facts of the case as presented at trial.

Court's Reasoning

The court outlined the history of the insanity defense and said that the jury must be given wide latitude in examining a defendant's impairment, and their determination may only be overturned if a guilty verdict would clearly violate the law or facts. The court could not say that this was true in Washington's case, so the jury's verdict was not overturned. The court outlined defects in expert testimony during trial. Specifically, it asserted that the experts overused labels and jargon without adequate explanation of terms, and that there was a lack of sufficient data underlying the expert opinions. The court then expressed concern about the possibility that an expert might comment upon moral rather than medical issues. The court instructed that the expert should not provide conclusory statements without explanation of the basis for those statements and should comment only upon clinical issues, avoiding moral or legal issues that are the province of the jury. Specifically, the court held that the expert should do the following:

- Provide an opinion about whether the defendant had a mental disease or defect and, if so, how such a mental disease or defect relates to their behavior, but should not comment on whether the behavior was a "product" of that mental disease or defect.
- Discuss only matters within their area of expertise.
- Use simple language.
- Explain not only their final opinion, but the bases for the opinion(s).
- Discuss any limitations to their opinion and testimony.

Quick Summary

This case provided guidance to experts for effective testimony.

Whalem v. United States
346 F.2d 812 (D.C. Cir. 1965)
District of Columbia Circuit Court of Appeals

Case Facts

Mr. Thomas Whalem was civilly committed at age 13 to a psychiatric hospital in 1956 after he committed "an act of homicide" on an 80-year-old woman he claimed tried to arouse him sexually. He was deemed to have "psychosis with mental deficiency." While on leave from the hospital in 1962, he committed additional offenses and was again committed for evaluation. He was diagnosed with Schizophrenia, but two experts opined that he was competent to proceed with his trial, and he was transferred to a correctional setting. At trial, and without a formal competency hearing, no issue regarding Mr. Whalem's sanity was raised by defense, and the defendant was convicted of attempted rape and robbery. On appeal, Mr. Whalem argued that the judge erred by not imposing the sanity defense upon him over his objections and by failing to conduct a formal hearing on competency despite both parties agreeing with the opinions of hospital evaluators.

Main Issue

Is it ever acceptable for a court to impose a sanity defense over a defendant's objection?

Court Holding

The D.C. Circuit Court held that while there was no failure in this case because of a lack of evidence to support lack of criminal responsibility, there would be cases in which it was acceptable and even necessary to impose a sanity defense over a defendant's objections. The court also held that it is within the discretion of the trial judge to determine if a hearing on competency is warranted based on the facts.

Court's Reasoning

The appellate court explained that, "in the pursuit of justice," the trial judge has a duty to refuse "to allow the conviction of an obviously mentally irresponsible defendant." The court did not specify in which cases this duty would be imposed and acceptable and instead indicated that it would be a case-by-case determination. Regarding the issue of failing to hold a formal competency hearing, the court explained that competency was never an issue in this case, neither in the 1956 case nor the 1962 one. Both the defense and prosecution agreed with the hospital mental health evaluators' opinions that the defendant was competent. The trial judge did not abuse his discretion by not holding a hearing on competency, given the totality of the circumstances in this case.

Quick Summary

The Whalem Rule, as it became known, came from this case in which the U.S. Court of Appeals held that a trial judge can impose a sanity defense over the objection of a competent defendant.

Wiggins v. Smith
539 U.S. 510 (2003)
U.S. Supreme Court

Case Facts

Defendant Wiggins was convicted at a bench trial of first-degree murder, for killing a 77-year-old woman. Maryland sought the death penalty, and Wiggins elected to be sentenced by a jury. His attorneys moved to bifurcate sentencing, in hopes of first proving that Wiggins had not killed the victim by his own hand and then, if necessary, presenting a mitigation case. The court denied the bifurcation motion, and counsel elected to focus on relitigating Wiggins' involvement in the murder. Counsel presented scant mitigation evidence, offering no evidence of Wiggins' life history or family background. The jury sentenced Wiggins to death. Wiggins sought habeas relief, claiming ineffective assistance of counsel. According to Wiggins, counsel had failed to properly investigate his family and social history, which contained evidence of a lifetime of physical abuse, sexual abuse, and neglect. Counsel claimed that they did investigate, but made a strategic decision to concentrate on trying to convince the jury that Wiggins was not directly responsible for the crime. The district court granted Wiggins' petition for habeas relief, holding that counsel's performance was deficient. The Fourth Circuit reversed, and the Supreme Court granted review.

Main Issue

Did counsel's decision not to fully investigate the defendant's life history for mitigating evidence fall short of prevailing professional standards and prejudice defendant?

Court Holding

Yes.

Court's Reasoning

Under the standard for ineffective assistance of counsel set in *Strickland v. Washington*, 466 U.S. 668 (1984), a defendant must show that counsel's performance fell below an objective standard of reasonableness. With regard to strategic choices, *Strickland* held that choices made after thorough investigation of law and relevant facts are virtually unchallengeable, but strategic choices made after less than complete investigation are reasonable only to the extent that reasonable professional judgments support the limitations on investigation. Following *Strickland*, the court focused on whether counsel's investigation into Wiggins' background was reasonable. It held that counsel's conduct fell short of both the professional standards in Maryland capital cases at the time of trial, and the American Bar Association's standards for capital defense work. Wiggins' presentencing report and reports from the Department of Social Services revealed that his mother abused alcohol and left Wiggins and his siblings alone for days without food; that he was shuttled from foster home to foster home; that he had frequent, lengthy absences from school; and that he had displayed emotional difficulties. According to the Court, a reasonable investigation into these facts would have uncovered the physical and sexual abuse later chronicled in the expert report supporting Wiggins' habeas petition. Moreover, the court found that counsel had not actually focused solely on its strategy of relitigating Wiggins' involvement in the crime, but had presented "half-hearted" mitigating evidence. Accordingly, counsel's failure to thoroughly investigate and present mitigating evidence of Wiggins' life history was due to inattention, and not to a true strategic choice to pursue another avenue of relief. Under *Strickland*, counsel's performance was ineffective. The court reversed the Fourth Circuit and remanded for further proceedings.

Quick Summary

The Supreme Court ruled in favor of a defendant on his claim for ineffective assistance of counsel, after his attorneys failed to fully investigate and present mitigating evidence of his life history during his death penalty sentencing proceedings.

Wilson v. United States
391 F.2d 460 (D.C. Cir. 1968)
District of Columbia Circuit Court of Appeals

Case Facts

Robert Wilson was accused of assault with a pistol and robbery. He fled the scene, got into a car accident, and suffered a brain injury resulting in a three-week coma. He was amnesic for the incident. He was evaluated and found to be of sound mental health, but incompetent to stand trial due to amnesia and was held for 14 months for restoration. He was found not to be suffering from a mental disease or defect but was deemed by the evaluator to be unable to assist in his defense because he could not recall the alleged acts. The expert, however, opined that Mr. Wilson was able to have a rational understanding of the charges and did not have a mental illness so the court found the defendant competent to stand trial regardless, and he was tried and convicted.

Main Issue

Does amnesia for the crime preclude a defendant from being competent to stand trial?

Court Holding

The court of appeals identified six factors for the judge to consider when amnesia is at issue:

1. The extent to which amnesia affected the defendant's ability to consult with counsel.
2. The extent to which the amnesia affected the ability to testify on their own behalf.
3. The extent to which the evidence could be extrinsically reconstructed in view of the defendant's amnesia.
4. The extent to which the Government assisted the defense in that reconstruction.
5. The strength of the prosecution's case, whether the Government's case is such as to negate all reasonable hypotheses of innocence. If there is any substantial possibility that the accused could, but for amnesia, establish an alibi or other defense, it should be presumed that s/he would have been able to do so.
6. Any other facts and circumstances which would indicate whether the defendant had a fair trial.

Remanded for more extensive post-trial findings of whether the appellant's memory loss did in fact deprive him of a fair trial and effective assistance of counsel.

Court's Reasoning

Amnesia for the crime per se does not make a defendant incompetent to stand trial. The question hinges upon whether the defendant has the ability to reconstruct events from extrinsic sources. Courts must also look at the case post-trial to determine whether the defendant was actually able to meet the *Dusky* standard during the trial (i.e., present ability to consult with the lawyer with a reasonable degree of rational understanding, and whether they had a rational as well as factual understanding of the proceedings against them).

Quick Summary

When amnesia for the crime is at issue, judges must not only make a pretrial finding regarding a defendant's competency to stand trial, but must also make a finding just before sentencing to determine the extent to which the defendant's amnesia affected their competency under the *Dusky* standard.

Windom v. State
886 So.2d 915 (Fla. 2004)
Florida Supreme Court

Case Facts

Defendant Windom was convicted of three counts of first-degree murder and one count of attempted first-degree murder, and sentenced to death, after he killed three people and seriously wounded a fourth in an afternoon shooting spree. On appeal, Windom claimed, among other things, that his trial counsel had been ineffective for failing to present an insanity defense during the guilt phase of the trial, and for failing to investigate and present mitigating evidence during the penalty phase of the trial. With regard to both claims, the post-conviction court heard evidence that four mental health professionals had evaluated Windom and come to disparate conclusions: Of Windom's three experts, which included a neurologist, psychologist, and psychiatrist, two determined that Windom was psychotic at the time of the crime. But the experts did not agree as to whether Windom was insane at the time of the offense, or whether he suffered from brain damage. The experts also could not reach a specific psychiatric diagnosis. The state's single expert was a neuropsychologist, who concluded that Windom was not insane at the time of the shootings and did not have brain damage. Although Windom's counsel elected not to present an insanity defense in part based on this conflicting information, he was more concerned with the risk that an insanity defense would open the door to harmful evidence the state intended to present in order to rebut Windom's claim of insanity. Specifically, the state had evidence that Windom ran a large-scale drug operation and had recently learned that some or all of the victims were police informants. Accordingly, rather than present an insanity defense, Windom's counsel presented the shootings as a "senseless act" and emphasized the inherent bizarreness of the acts in order to suggest to the jury that Windom must have been in an altered mental state when he committed the crimes.

Main Issue

Was defendant's trial counsel ineffective for failing to present an insanity defense and mitigation evidence pertaining to the defendant's mental health?

Court Holding

No.

Court's Reasoning

Trial counsel is not ineffective when they make a reasonable strategic decision to not present an insanity defense or mitigation testimony regarding mental health, when doing so could open the door to other damaging testimony.

Here, the evidence as to Windom's mental health was in conflict, and counsel made a reasonable strategic decision to forego an insanity defense and mitigation testimony, where it would have opened the door to damaging evidence about Windom's activities as a drug dealer and his possible motive to shoot the victims because they were police informants.

Quick Summary

A defendant who was sentenced to death for multiple murders sought post-conviction relief for ineffective assistance of counsel, because his trial attorney elected not to present an insanity defense or mitigation testimony regarding the defendant's mental health. The court held that because the expert evidence on the defendant's mental health was equivocal, and because presenting that evidence would have opened the door to damaging evidence from the State, trial counsel had made a reasonable strategic decision, and was not ineffective.

Notes

1 The court also directed the parties to address the question of whether it had jurisdiction to review the Louisiana Supreme Court's decision, which the court determined it did.
2 In dicta, the court also stated that there may be cases where the defendant's evidence of insanity will be so clear and overpowering that reasonable minds cannot differ as to the issue of sanity. In those cases, a trial court can rule on the issue as a matter of law.
3 The consolidated cases are *State v. Rotherham*, *State v. Lopez*, *State v. Epperson*, *State v. Martinez (Ortega)*, and *State v. Lucas*.
4 This standard for insanity, upon which the Third Circuit relies, is set forth in *U.S v. Currens*, 290 F.2d 751 (3d Cir. 1961).

Index

Note: Page numbers in *Italic* refer to figures; and in **Bold** refer to tables; page numbers followed by 'n' refer to notes.

E

N